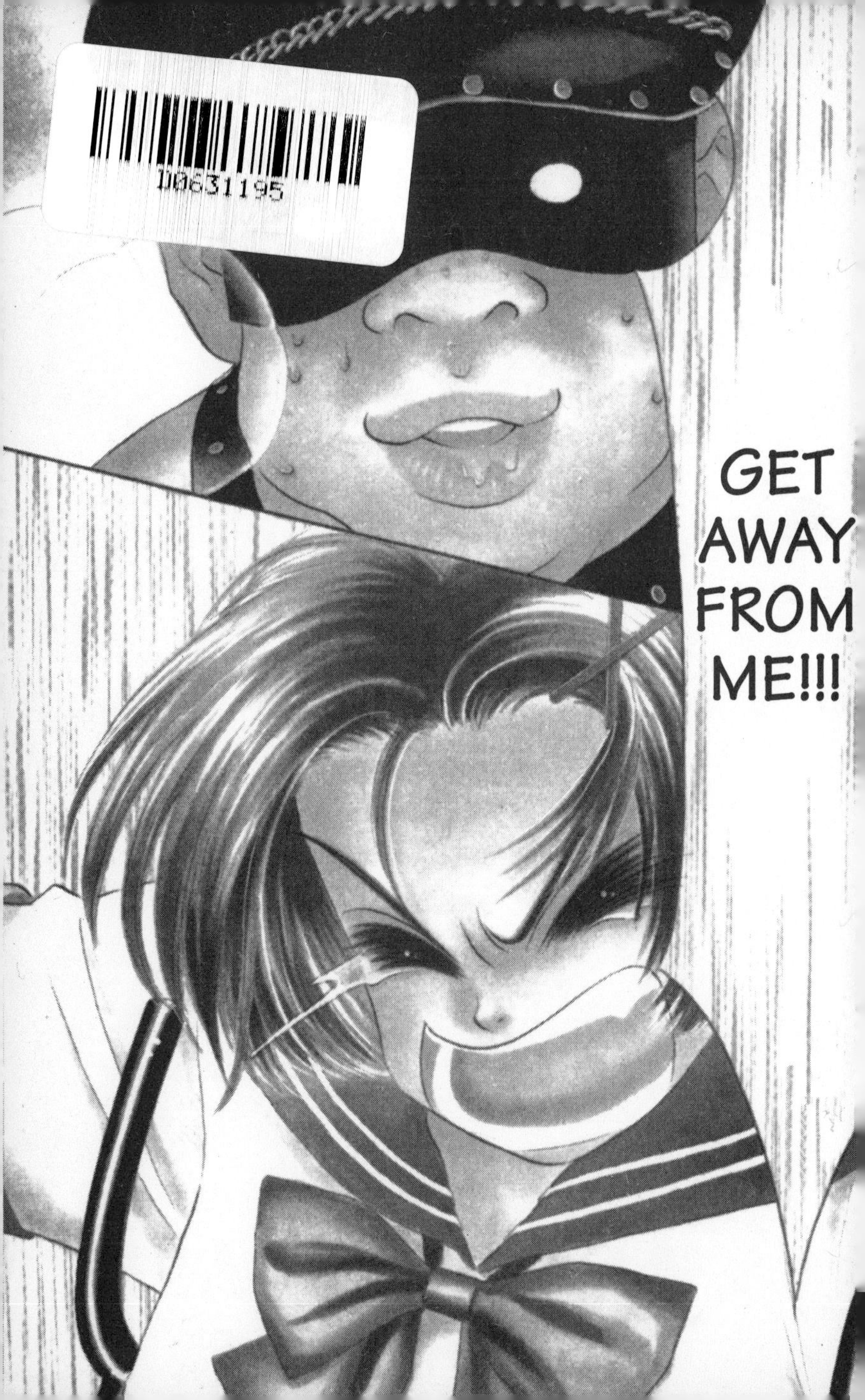
GET AWAY FROM ME!!!

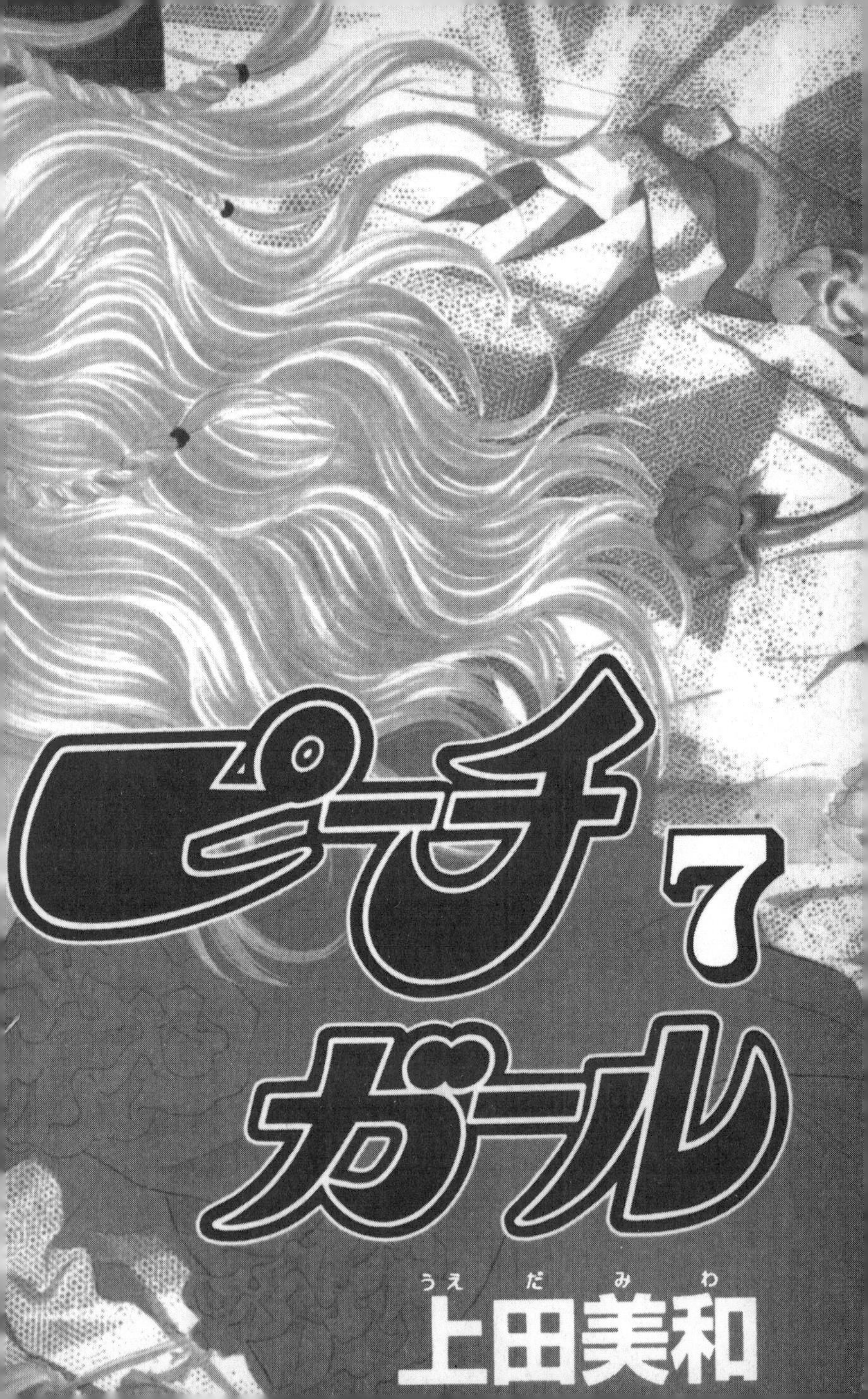
ピーチガール
7
うえだみわ
上田美和

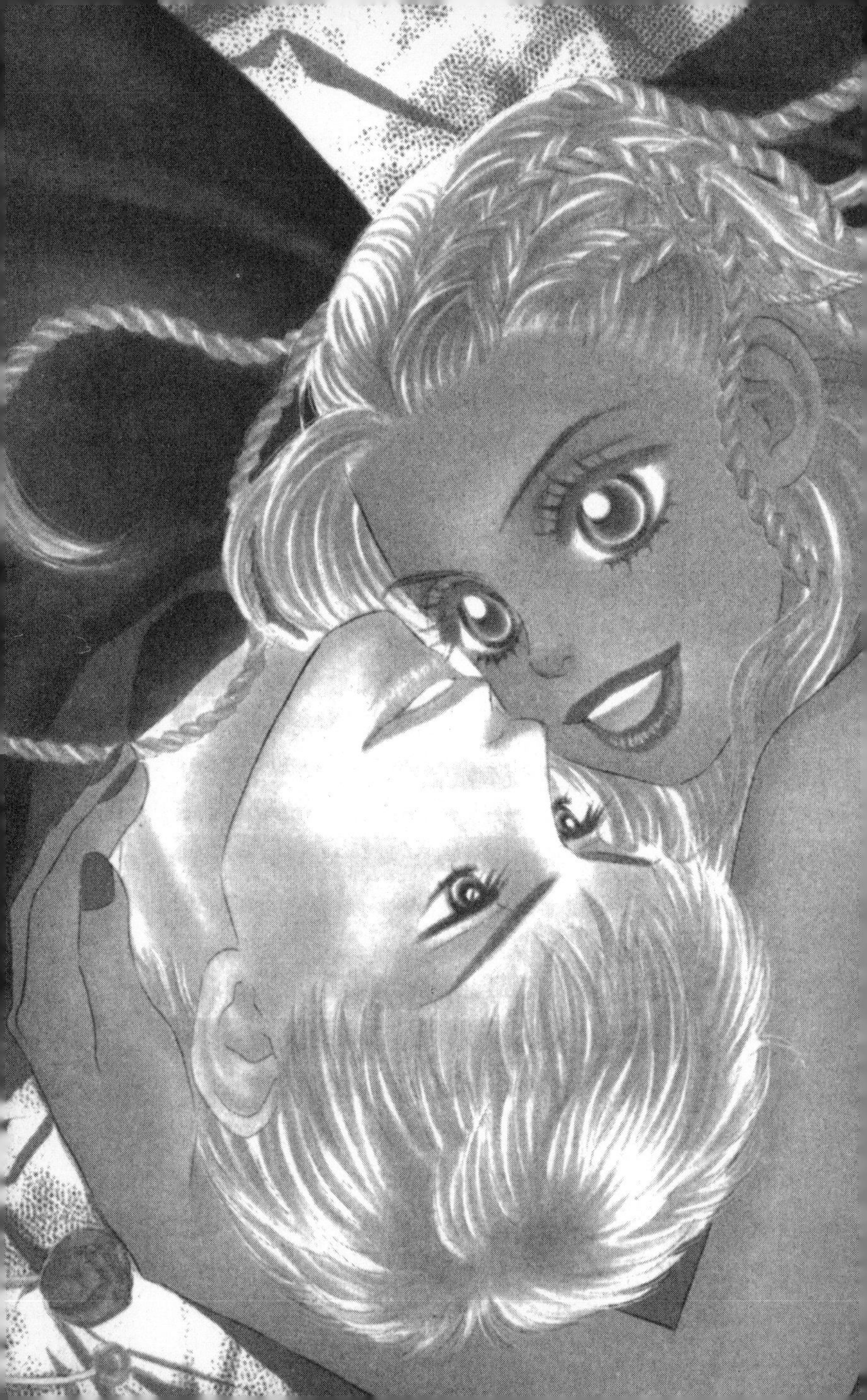

Peach Girl Vol. 7
Created by Miwa Ueda

Translation - Dan Papia
English Adaptation - Jodi Bryson
Copy Editor - Peter Ahlstrom
Retouch and Lettering - James Lee
Production Artist - Anthony Daulo
Cover Artist - Anna Kernbaum

Editor - Lillian Diaz-Przybyl
Digital Imaging Manager - Chris Buford
Production Managers - Jennifer Miller and Mutsumi Miyazaki
Managing Editor - Lindsey Johnston
VP of Production - Ron Klamert
Publisher and E.I.C. - Mike Kiley
President and C.O.O. - John Parker
C.E.O. - Stuart Levy

A  Manga

TOKYOPOP Inc.
5900 Wilshire Blvd. Suite 2000
Los Angeles, CA 90036

E-mail: info@TOKYOPOP.com
Come visit us online at www.TOKYOPOP.com

ISBN: 1-59532-177-2

First TOKYOPOP printing: January 2006
10 9 8 7 6 5 4 3 2 1
Printed in Canada

Peach Girl

by Miwa Ueda (7)

TOKYOPOP.

HAMBURG // LONDON // LOS ANGELES // TOKYO

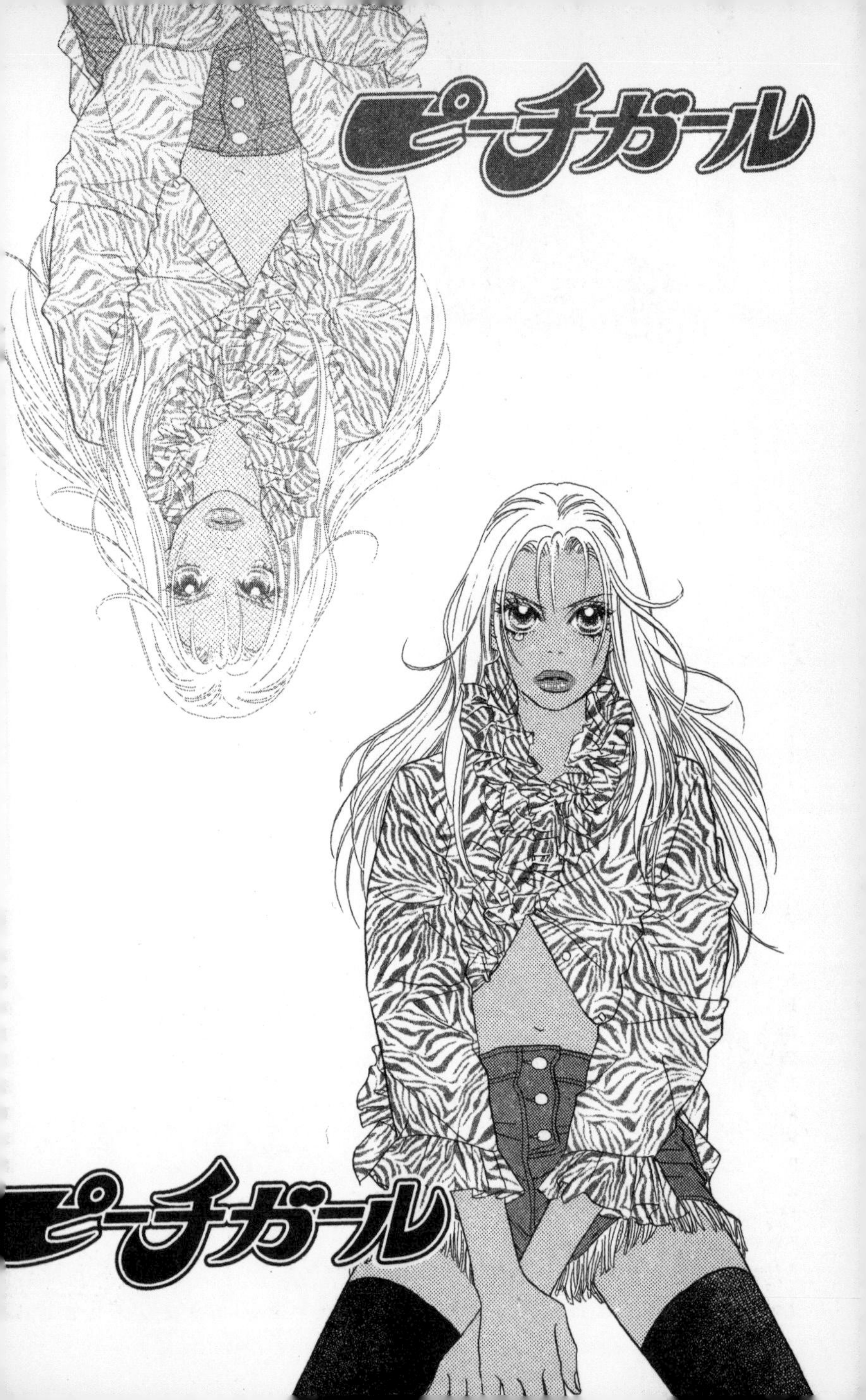
ピーチガール
ピーチガール

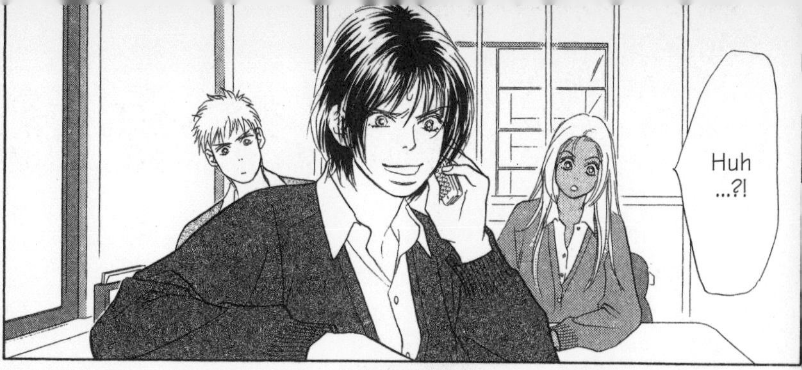
Huh ...?!

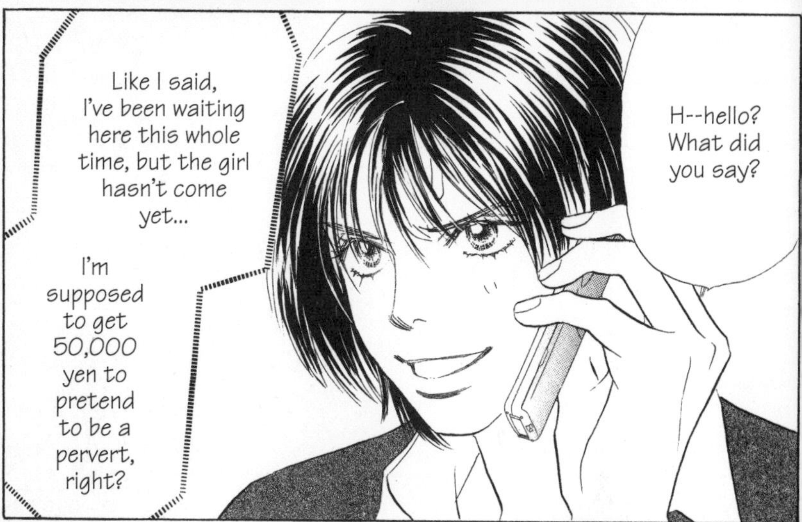
H--hello? What did you say?
Like I said, I've been waiting here this whole time, but the girl hasn't come yet...
I'm supposed to get 50,000 yen to pretend to be a pervert, right?

MOMO vs SAE:
Death match: the whole story!

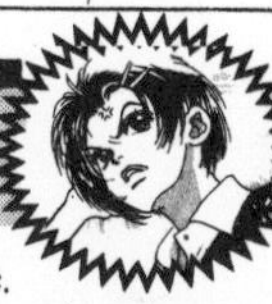

Momo and Toji were happily in love. But trouble starts when Sae, who always wants what Momo has, plots to steal Toji away. Sae plans to drug Momo's drink and while she's knocked out and helpless, have her devoted boy-toy, Goro "The Gigolo," take her virginity. Momo is devastated, but Toji's love helps to ease her pain. Then Kiley discovers Sae's part in the plot! Toji and Kiley try to help Momo to teach Sae a lesson by drugging her up and getting an actor to play a pervert and put a little scare into her. But Kiley screws up, and Sae falls into the clutches of a real pervert. Now Momo has to decide if she wants to save the evil Sae...

Everything you need to know.

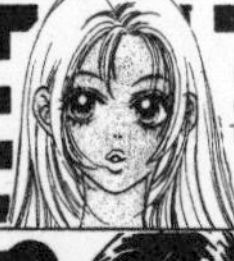

MOMO ADACHI: Currently dating Toji. Has she lost her virginity to GORO?

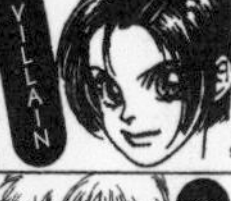

VILLAIN

SAE KASHIWAGI: Momo's relentlessly jealous enemy. Loser in Round 1. Vows to steal Toji anyway.

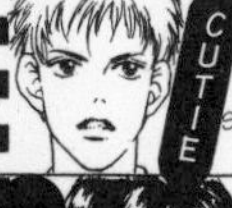

CUTIE

TOJI TOJIKAMORI: Momo's boyfriend. He once kissed Sae, but he's in love with Momo now.

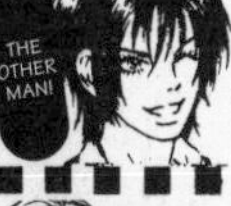

THE OTHER MAN!

KILEY OKAYASU: He knows Momo better than anyone. When it's time to take Sae down, Kiley's the man!

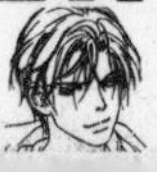

GORO: The male supermodel who declared his love to Sae. Did he really deflower Momo?

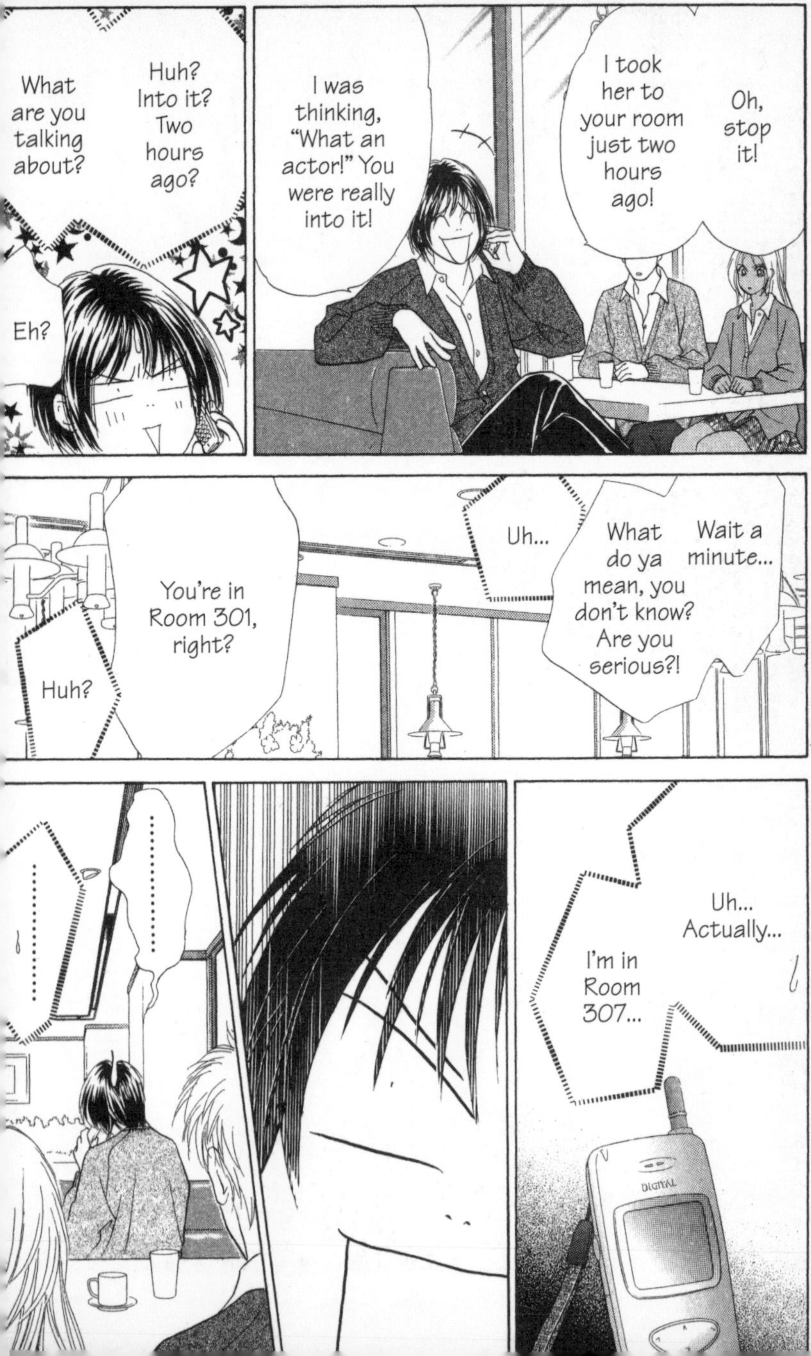
Oh, stop it!
I took her to your room just two hours ago!
I was thinking, "What an actor!" You were really into it!
Huh? Into it? Two hours ago?
What are you talking about?
Eh?
Wait a minute...
What do ya mean, you don't know? Are you serious?!
Uh...
You're in Room 301, right?
Huh?
Uh... Actually...
I'm in Room 307...
DIGITAL
....
....

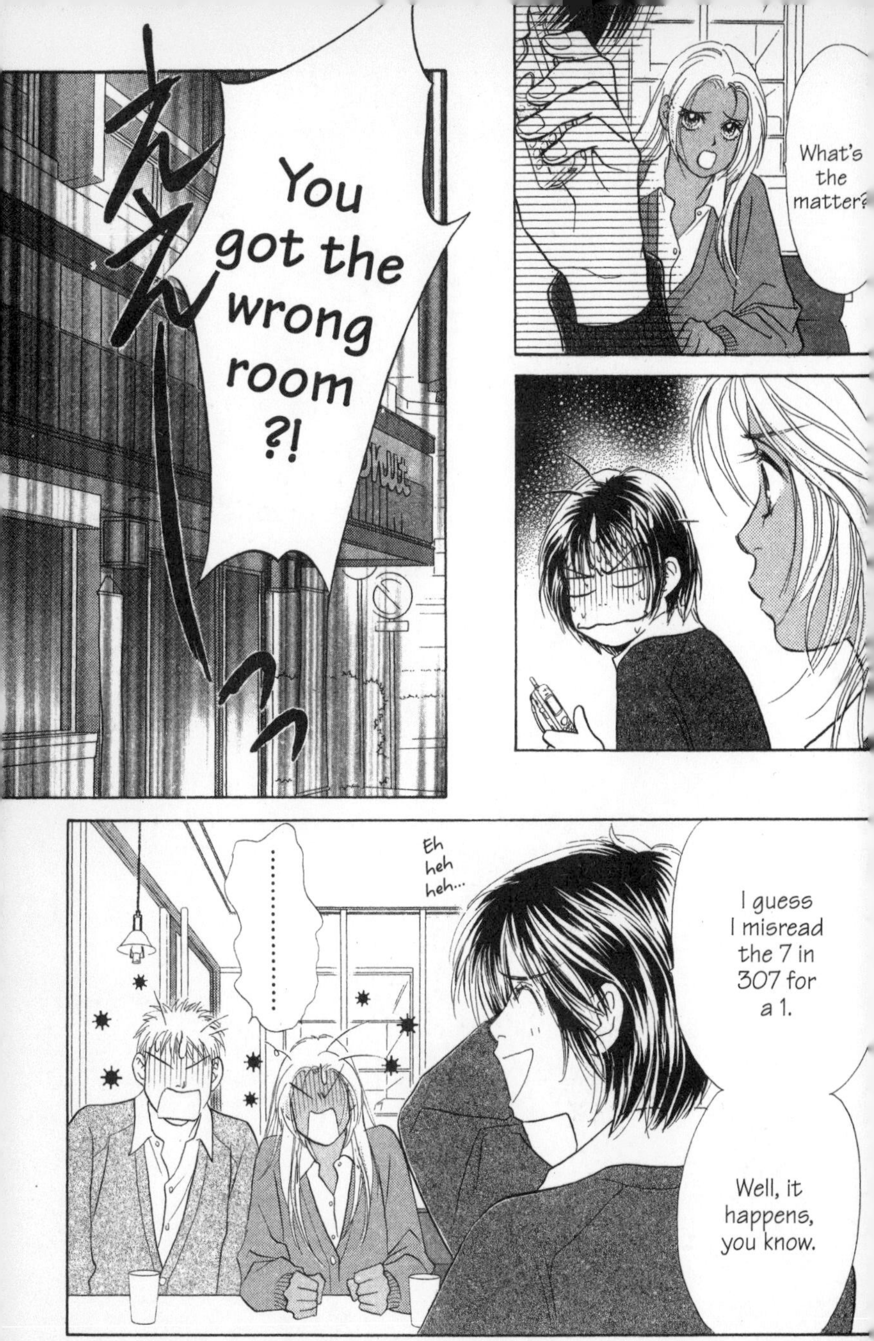
What's the matter?
You got the wrong room ?!
I guess I misread the 7 in 307 for a 1.
Well, it happens, you know.
Eh heh heh...
....

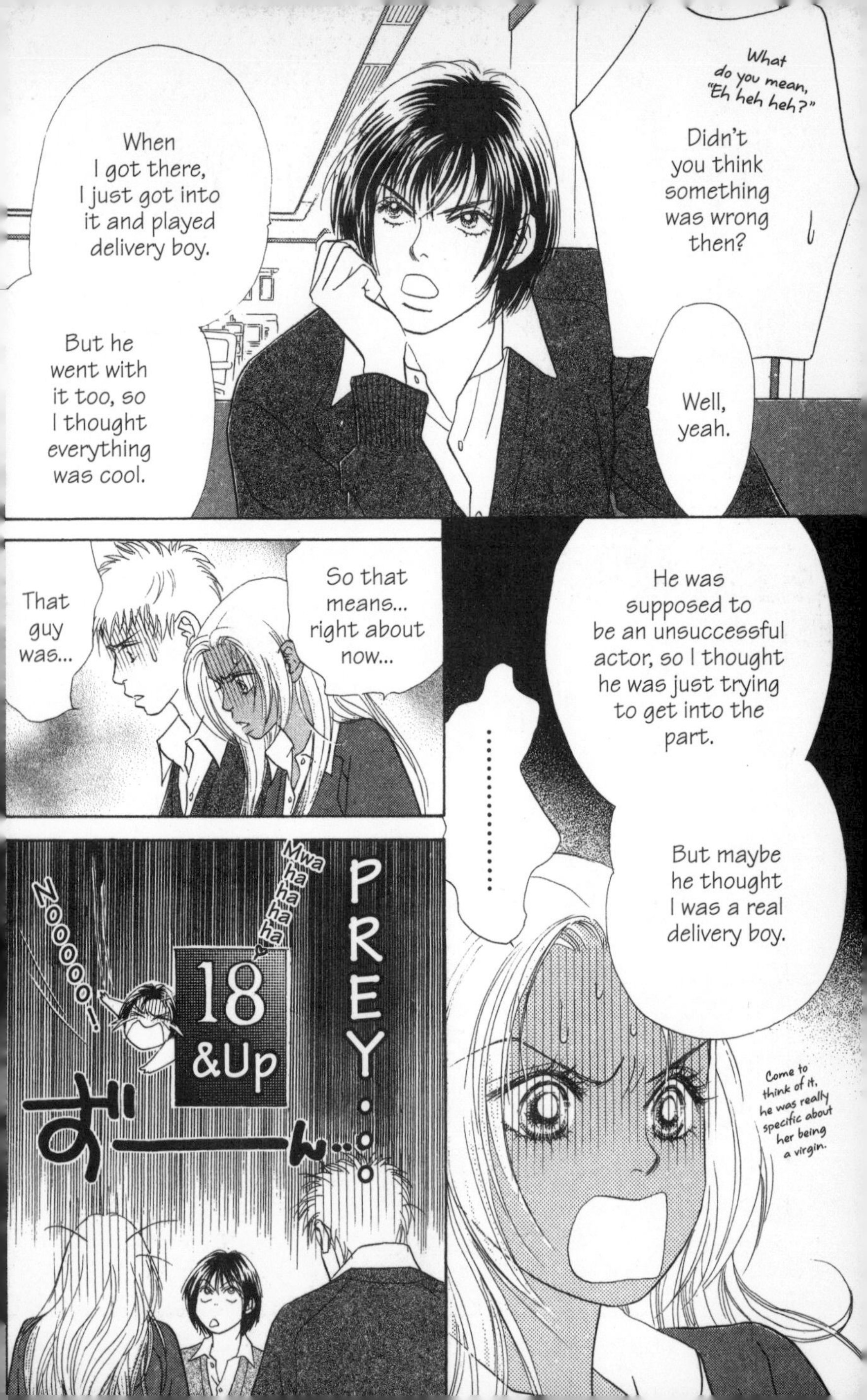
What do you mean, "Eh heh heh?"
Didn't you think something was wrong then?
Well, yeah.
When I got there, I just got into it and played delivery boy.
But he went with it too, so I thought everything was cool.
He was supposed to be an unsuccessful actor, so I thought he was just trying to get into the part.
But maybe he thought I was a real delivery boy.
....
Come to think of it, he was really specific about her being a virgin.
So that means... right about now...
That guy was...
PREY...
Mwa ha ha ha ha
Zoooooo!
18 &Up
ずーーん...

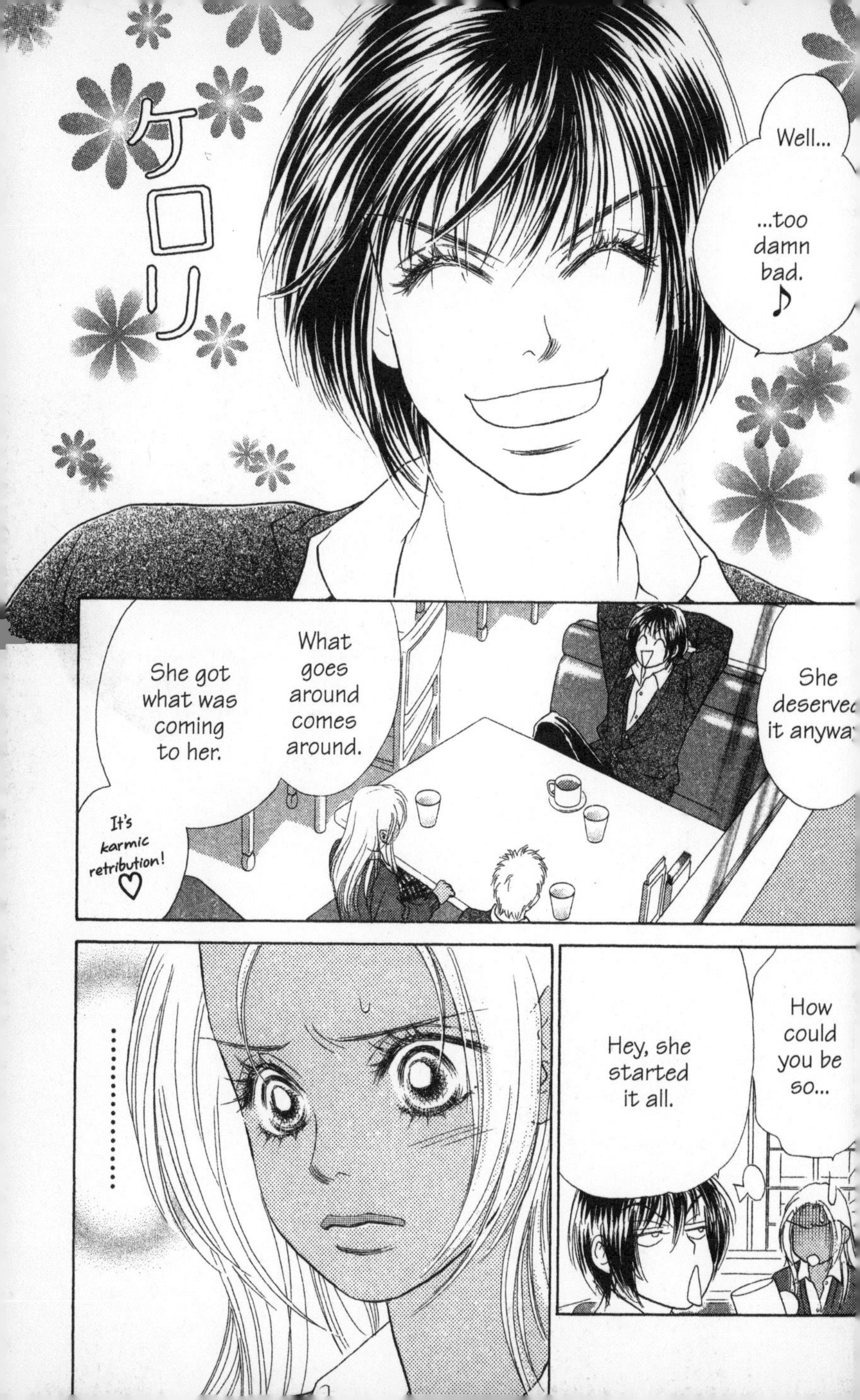
Well...
...too damn bad. ♪
ケロリ
She deserve it anywa
What goes around comes around.
She got what was coming to her.
It's karmic retribution! ♡
How could you be so...
Hey, she started it all.
....

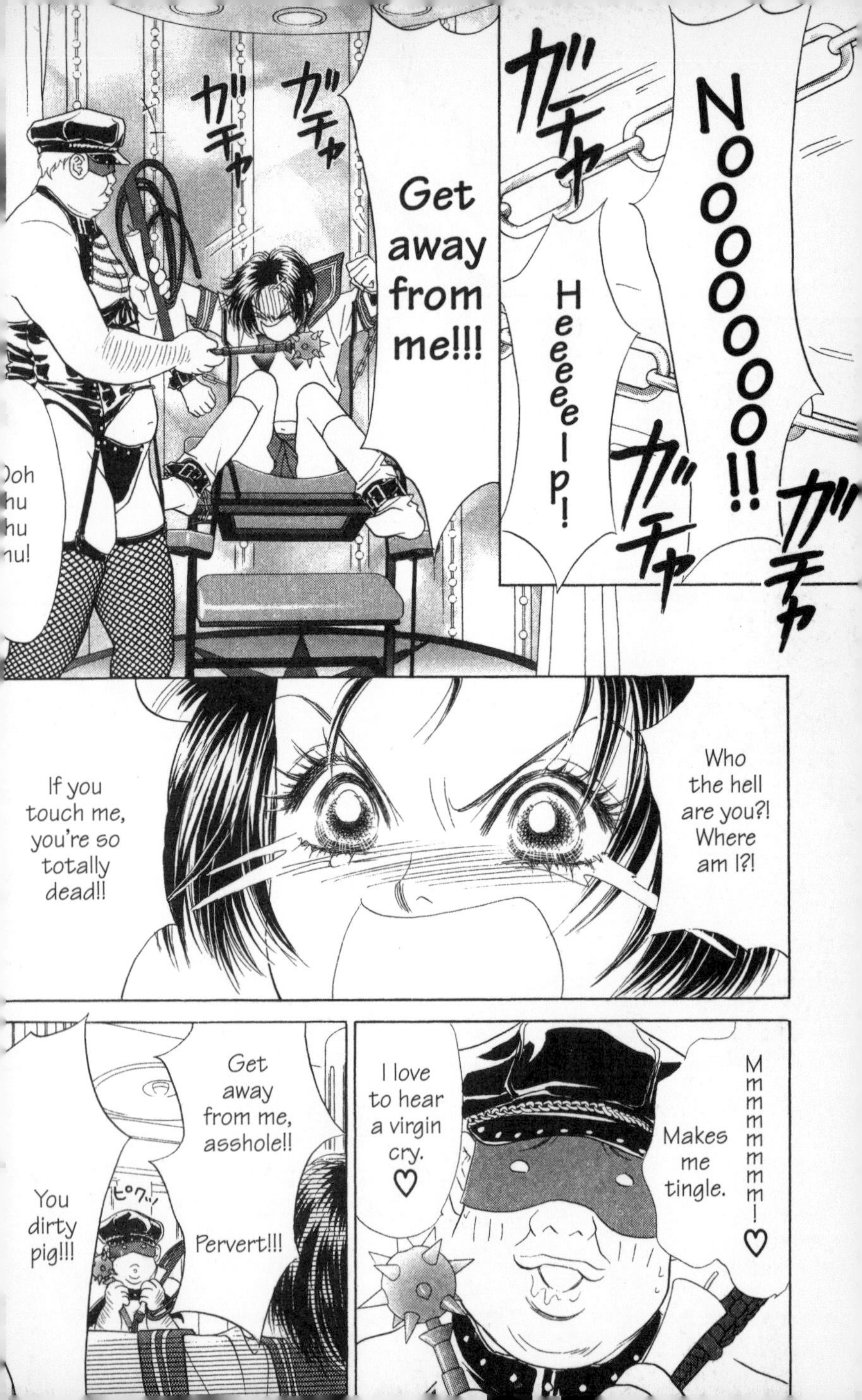
ガチャ
NOOOOOOO!!
Heeeelp!
ガチャ
ガチャ
ガチャ
ガチャ
Get away from me!!!
oh hu hu u!
Who the hell are you?! Where am I?!
If you touch me, you're so totally dead!!
Mmmmmmm!♡
Makes me tingle.
I love to hear a virgin cry. ♡
Get away from me, asshole!!
Pervert!!!
ピクッ
You dirty pig!!!

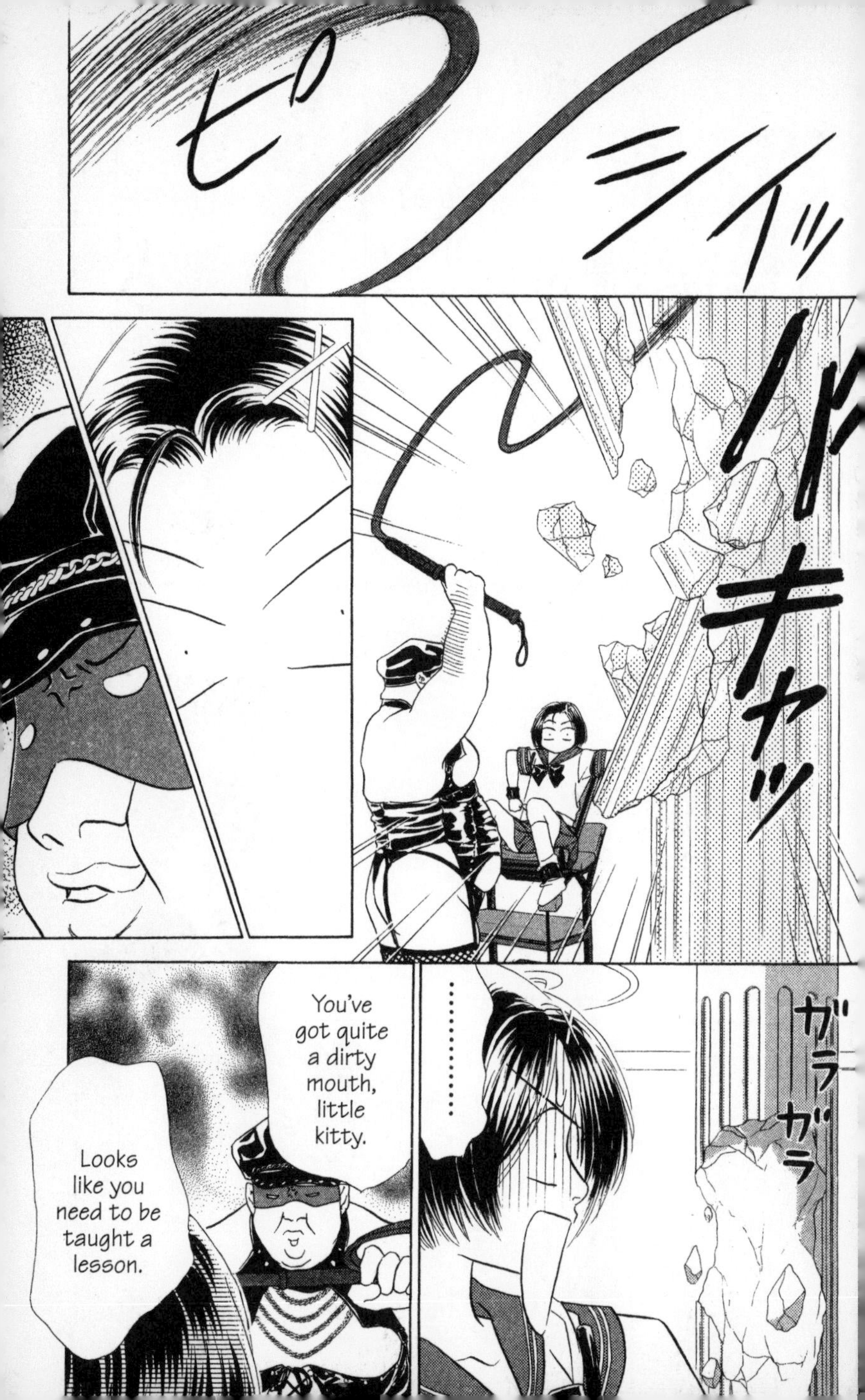
ピシィッ
ドキャッ
ガラガラ
......
You've got quite a dirty mouth, little kitty.
Looks like you need to be taught a lesson.

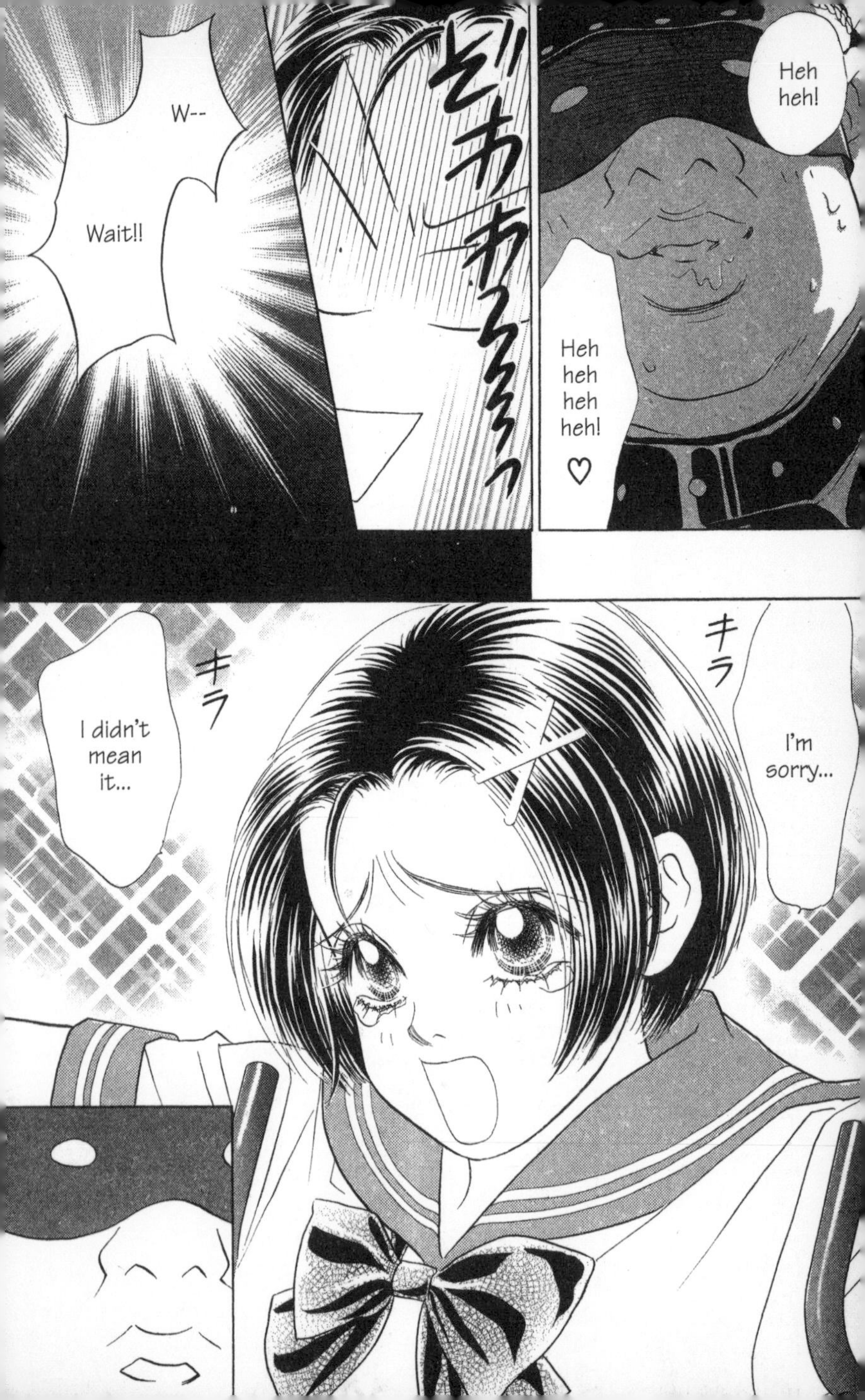
Heh heh!
Heh heh heh heh! ♡
W--
Wait!!
I'm sorry...
キラ
キラ
I didn't mean it...

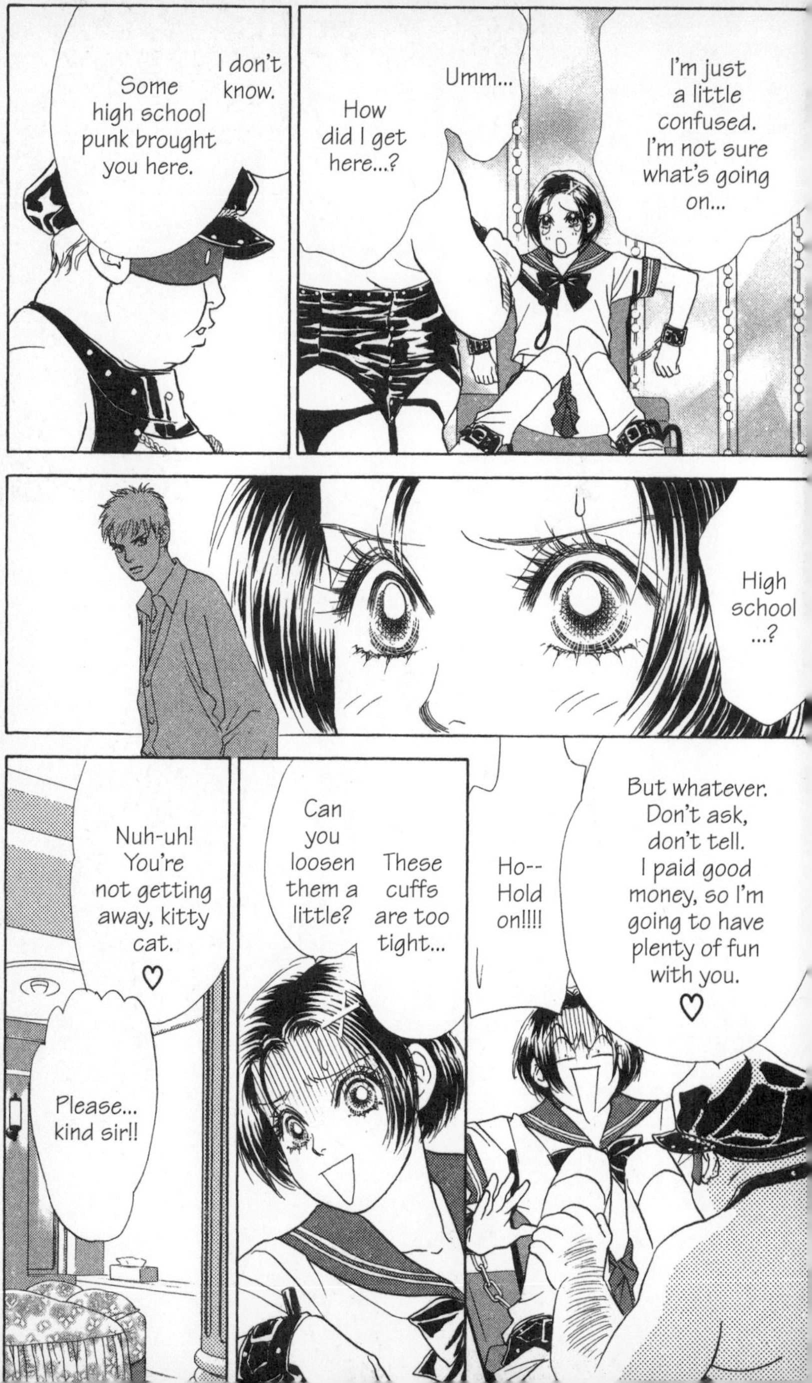
I'm just a little confused. I'm not sure what's going on...
Umm...
How did I get here...?
I don't know.
Some high school punk brought you here.
High school ...?
But whatever. Don't ask, don't tell. I paid good money, so I'm going to have plenty of fun with you. ♡
Ho-- Hold on!!!!
These cuffs are too tight...
Can you loosen them a little?
Nuh-uh! You're not getting away, kitty cat. ♡
Please... kind sir!!

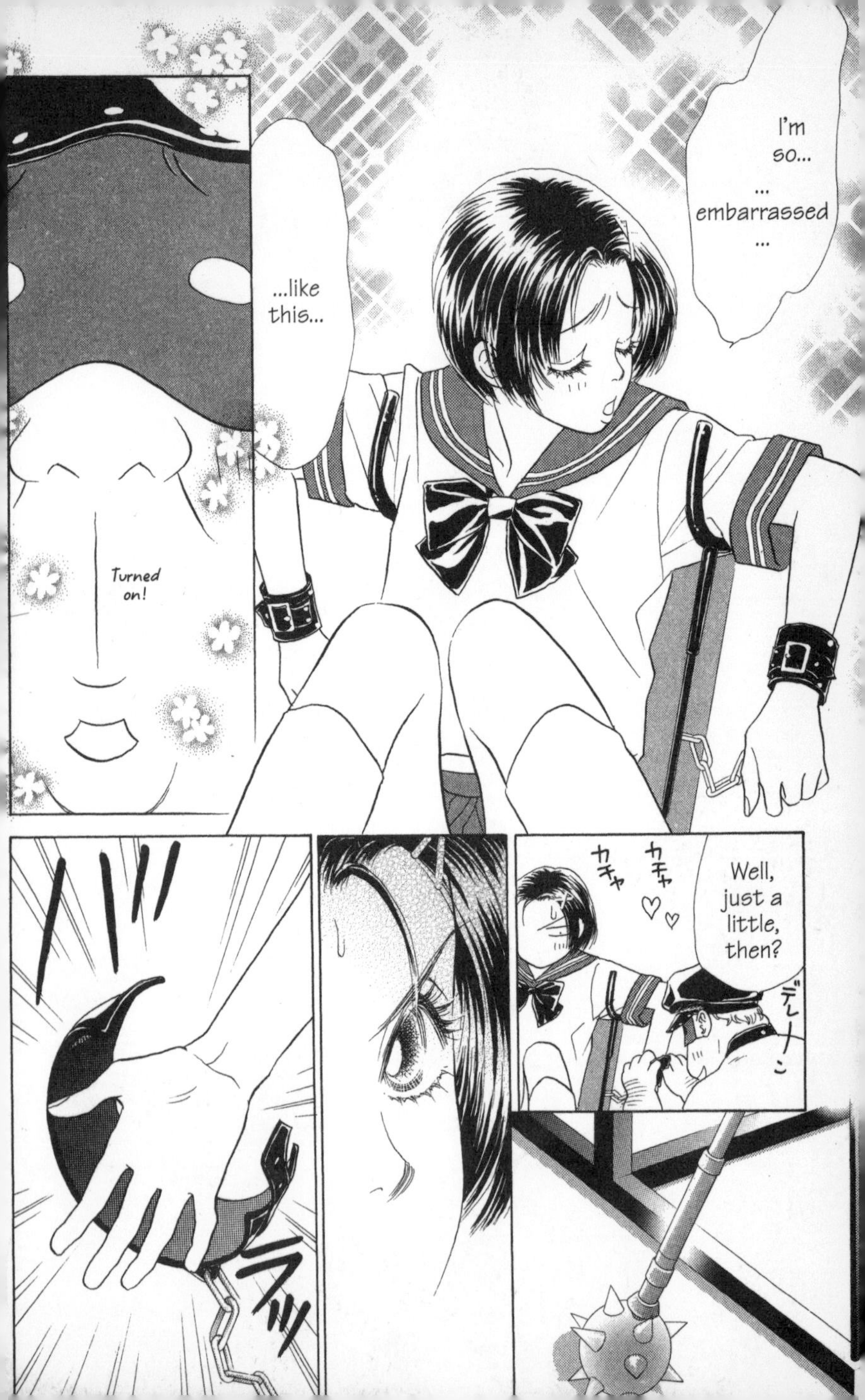
I'm so... ... embarrassed ...
...like this...
Turned on!
カチャ
カチャ
Well, just a little, then?

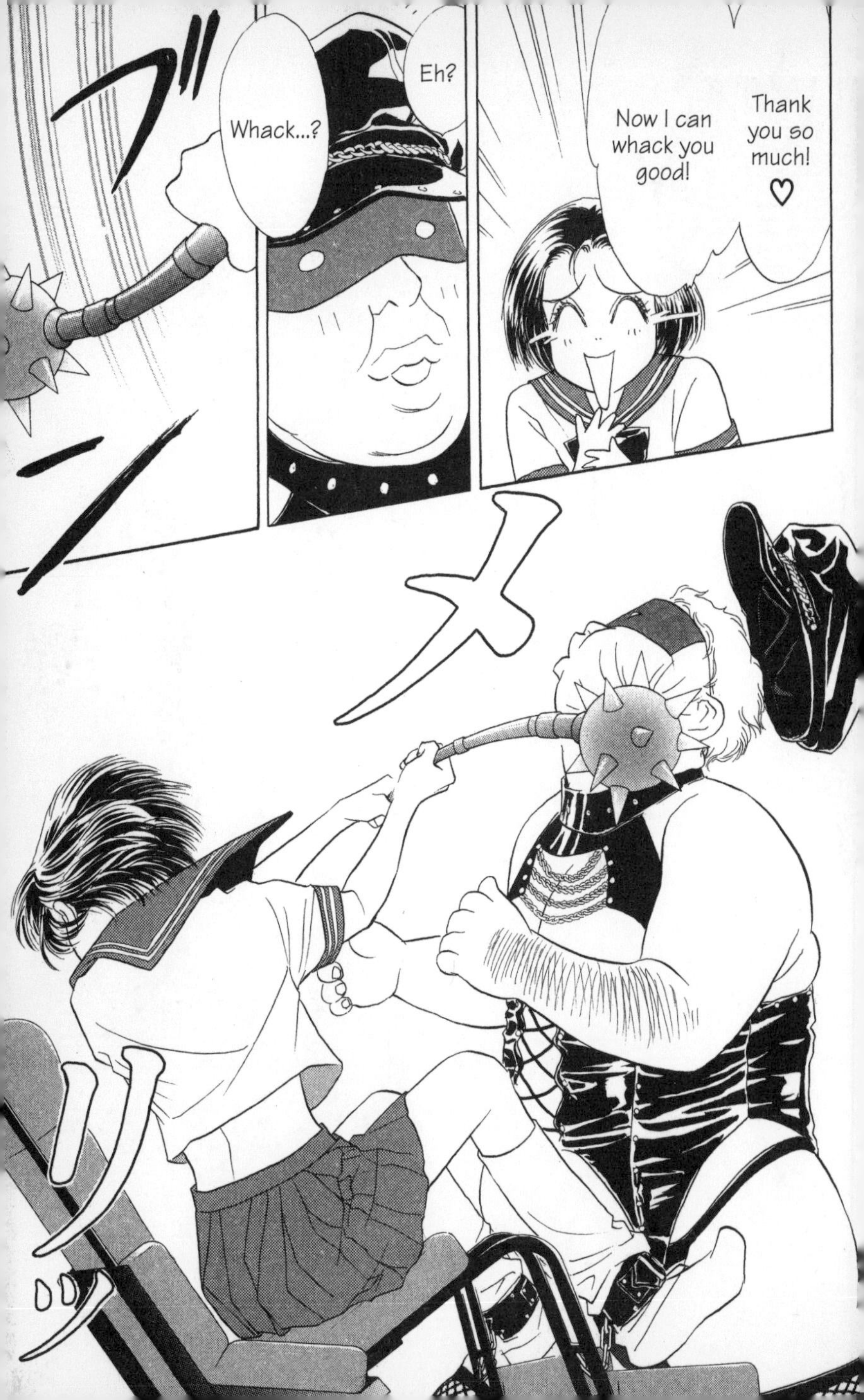
Thank you so much! ♡
Now I can whack you good!
Eh?
Whack...?
ブ
メ

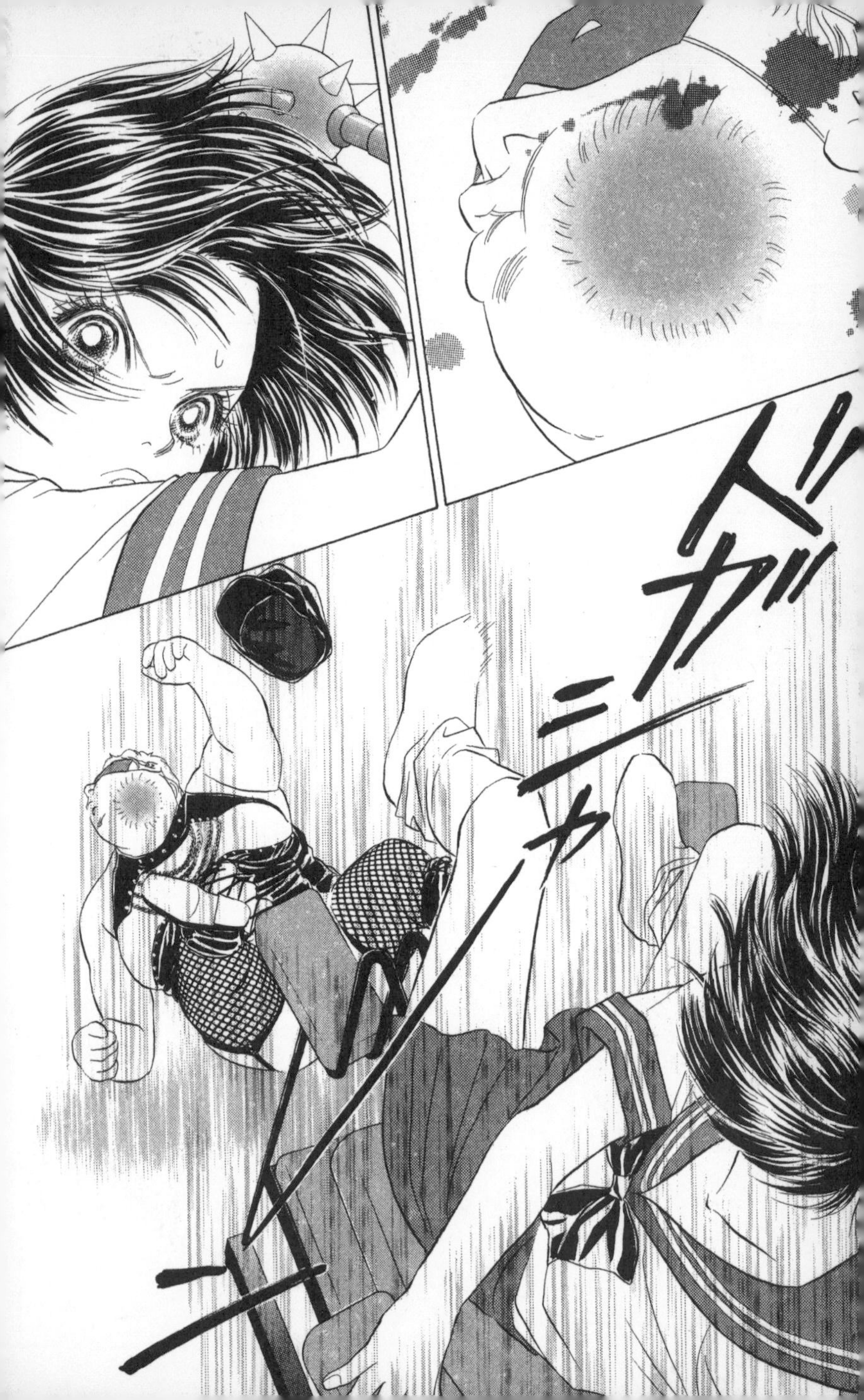
ドガシャーン

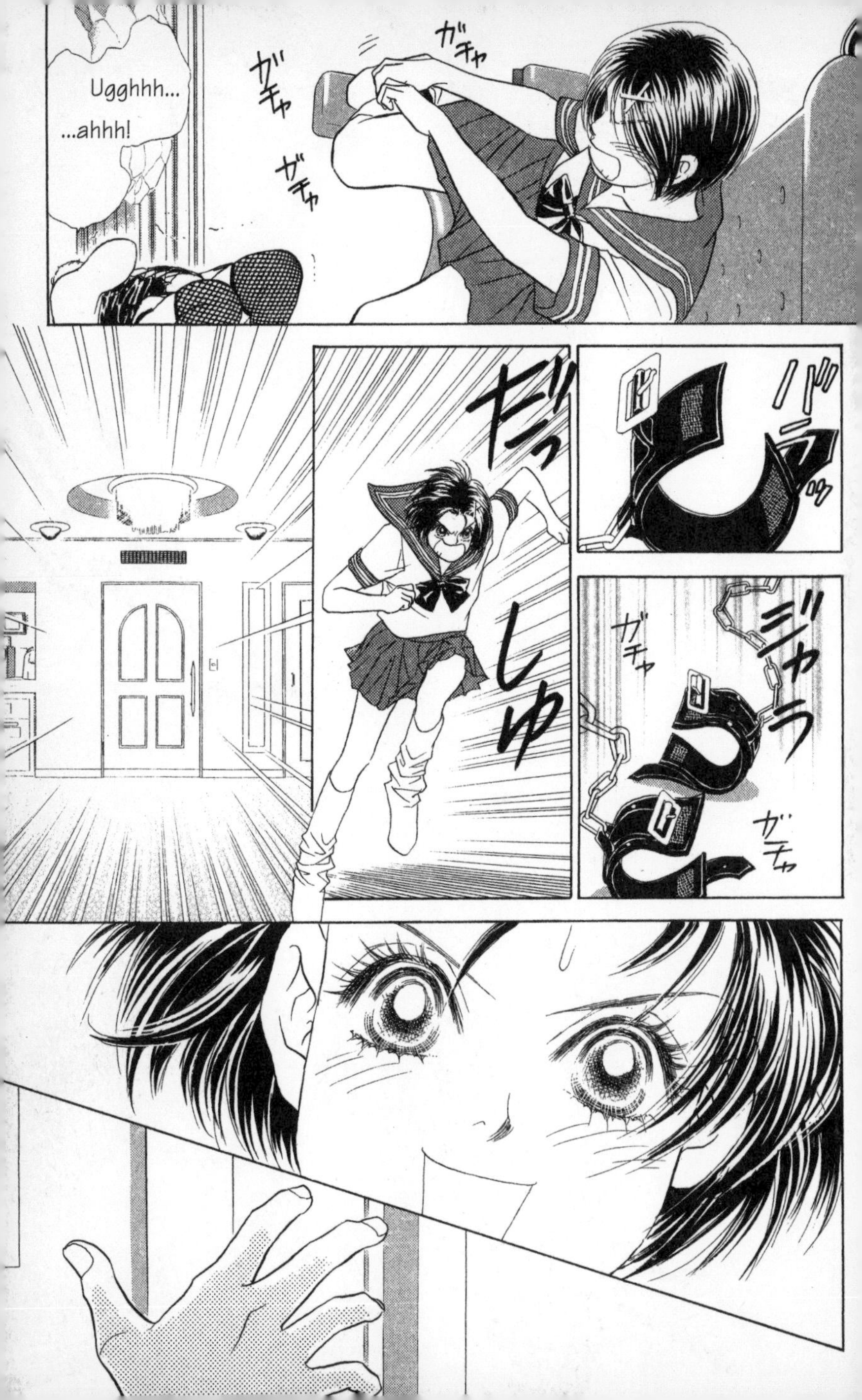
ガチャ
ガチャ
ガチャ
Ugghhh...
...ahhh!
バラッ
ジャラ
ガチャ
ガチャ
ダッ
しゅ

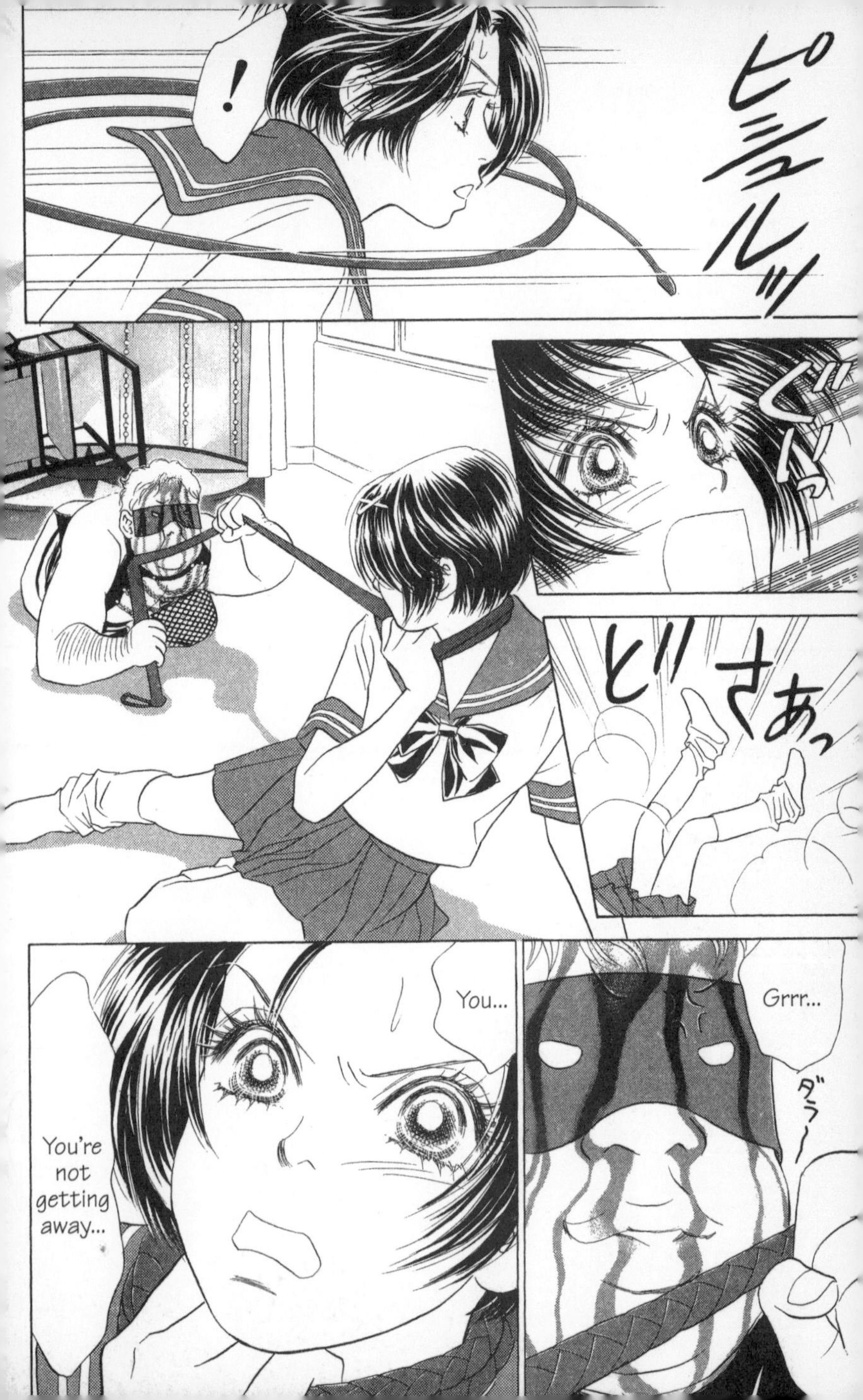
!
ピシュルッ
ぐいっ
どさあっ
Grrr...
ダラ～
You...
You're not getting away...

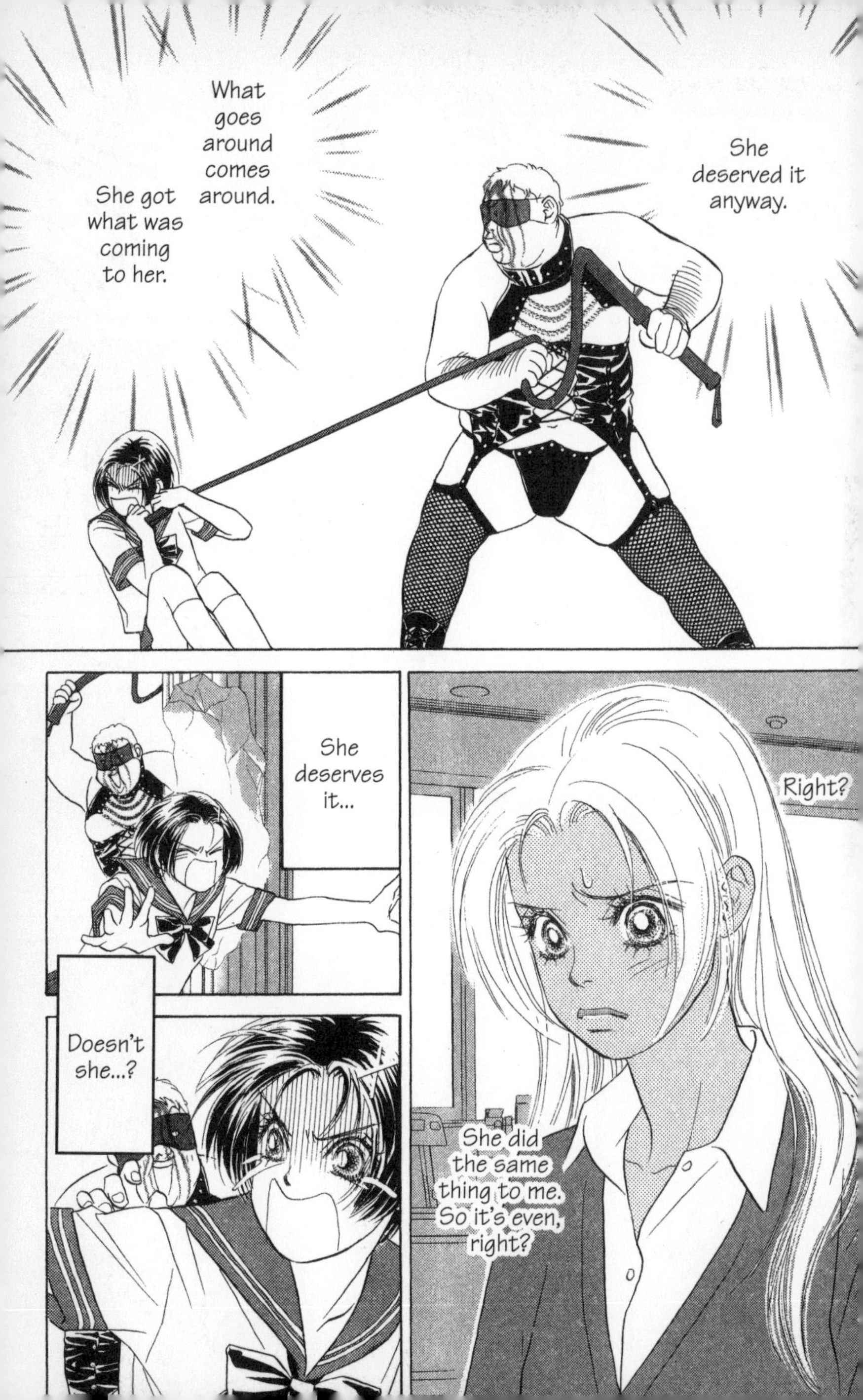
She deserved it anyway.
What goes around comes around.
She got what was coming to her.
Right?
She did the same thing to me. So it's even, right?
She deserves it...
Doesn't she...?

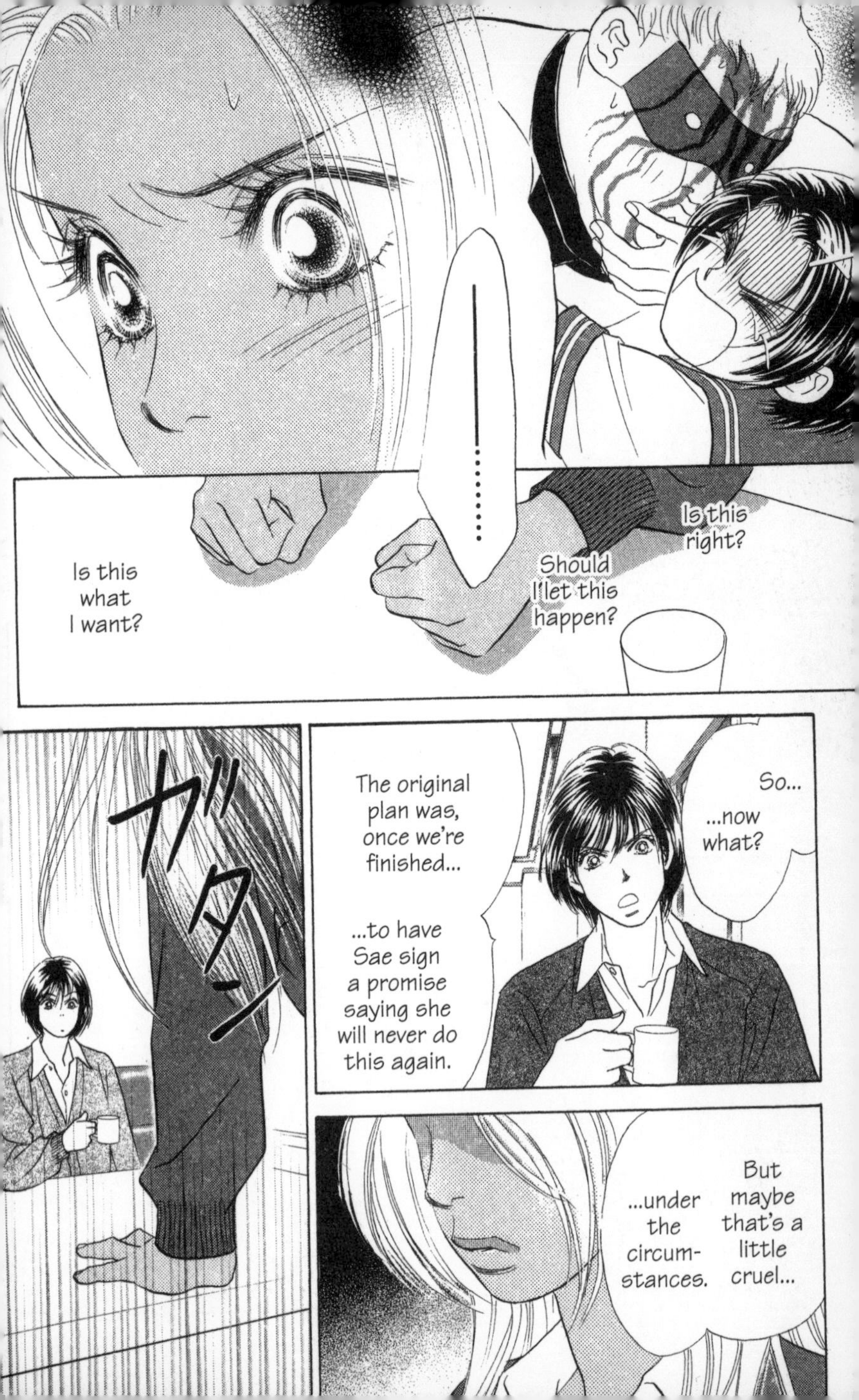
——......
Is this right?
Should I let this happen?
Is this what I want?
So...
...now what?
The original plan was, once we're finished...
...to have Sae sign a promise saying she will never do this again.
But maybe that's a little cruel...
...under the circumstances.
ガタン

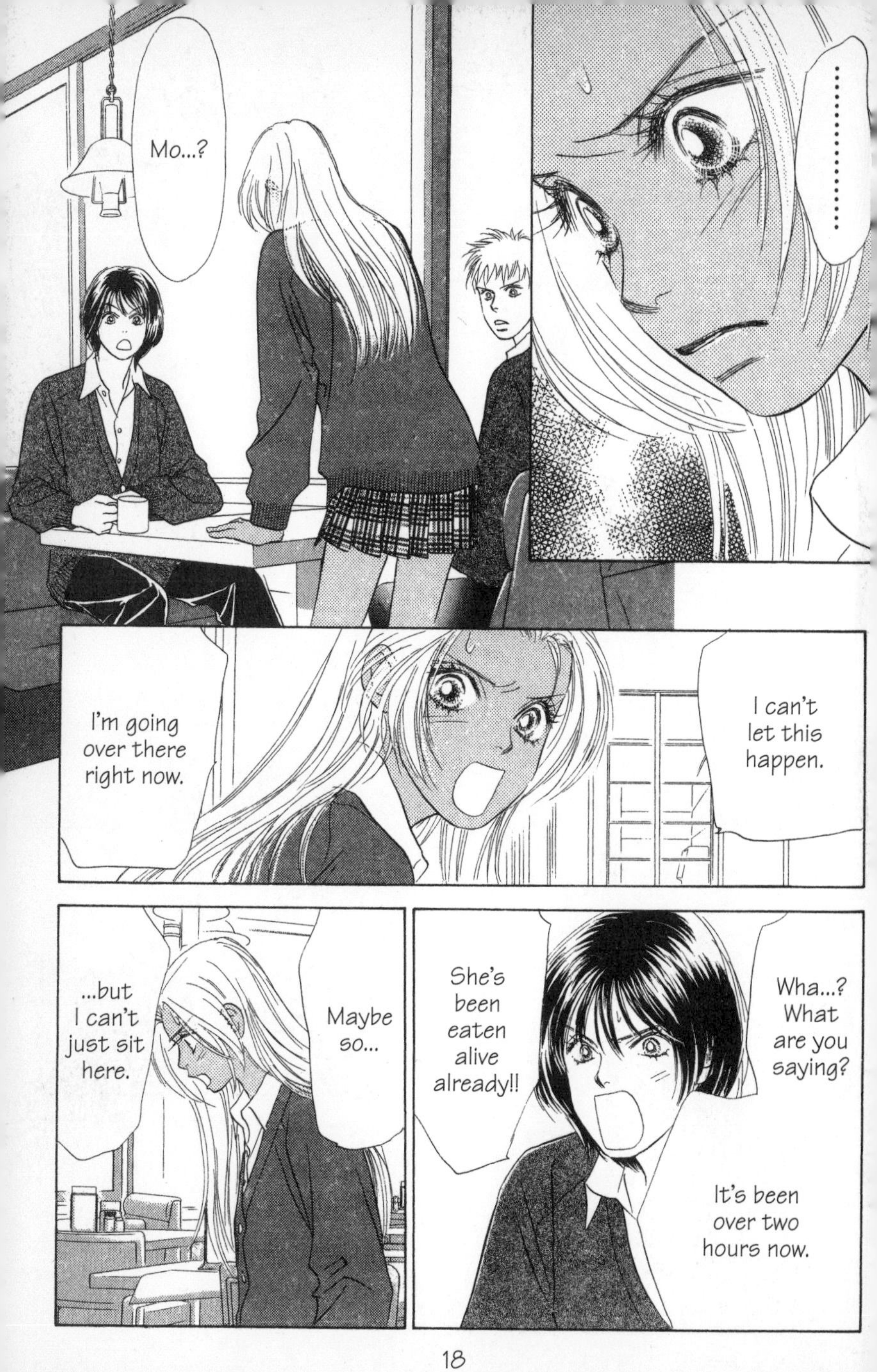
……
Mo...?
I can't let this happen.
I'm going over there right now.
Wha...? What are you saying?
She's been eaten alive already!!
It's been over two hours now.
Maybe so...
...but I can't just sit here.

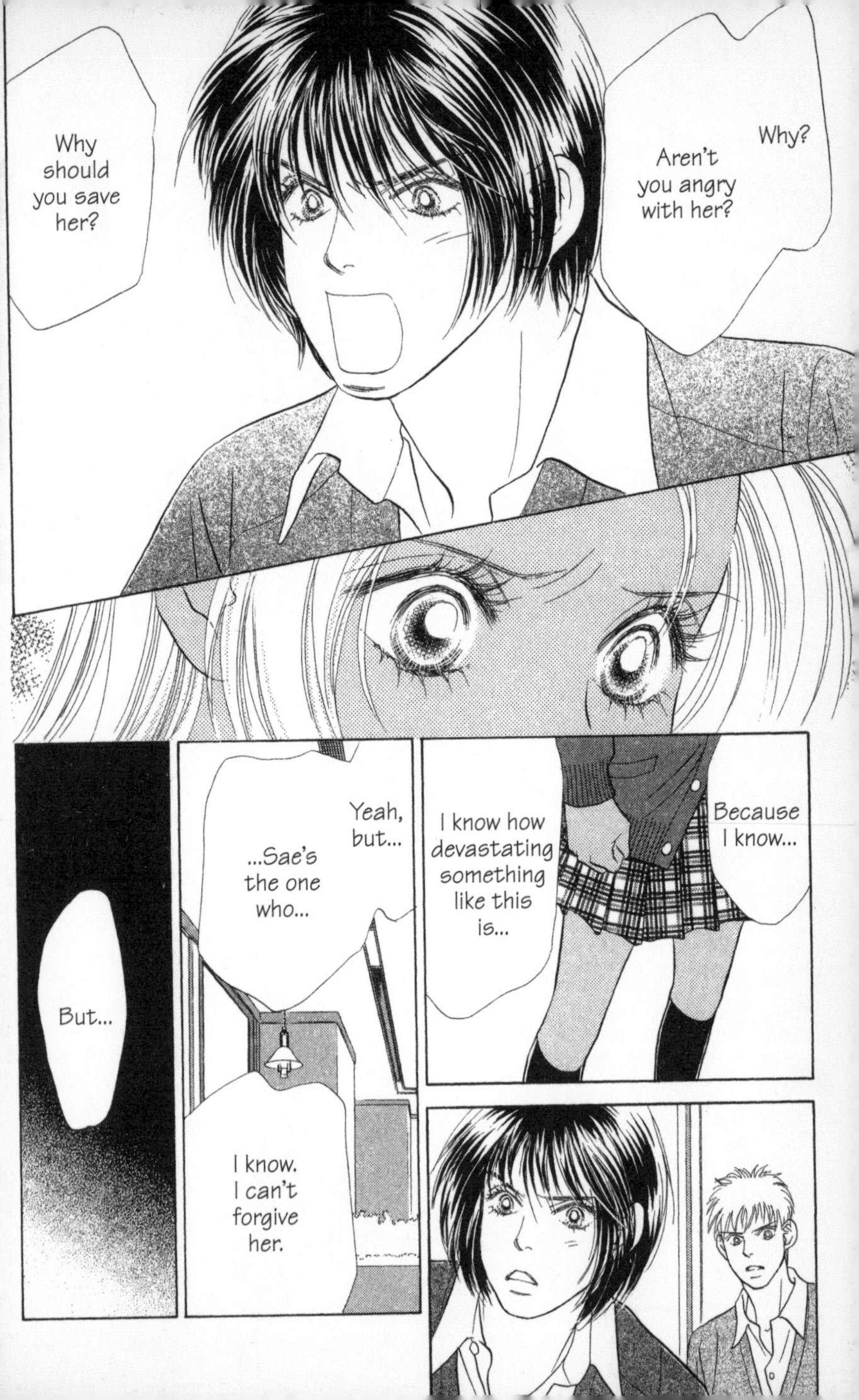
Why?
Aren't you angry with her?
Why should you save her?
Because I know...
I know how devastating something like this is...
Yeah, but...
...Sae's the one who...
I know. I can't forgive her.
But...

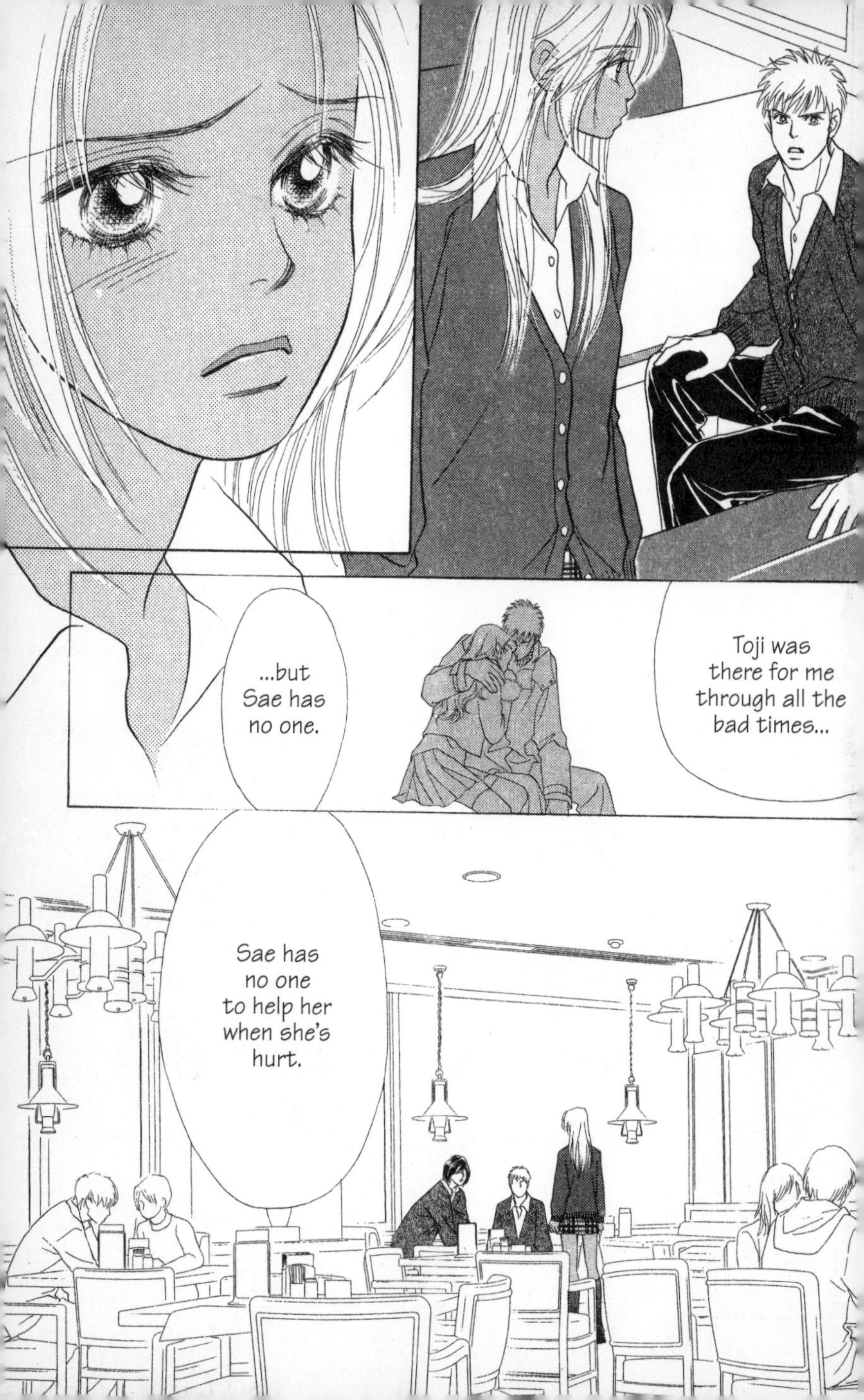
Toji was there for me through all the bad times...
...but Sae has no one.
Sae has no one to help her when she's hurt.

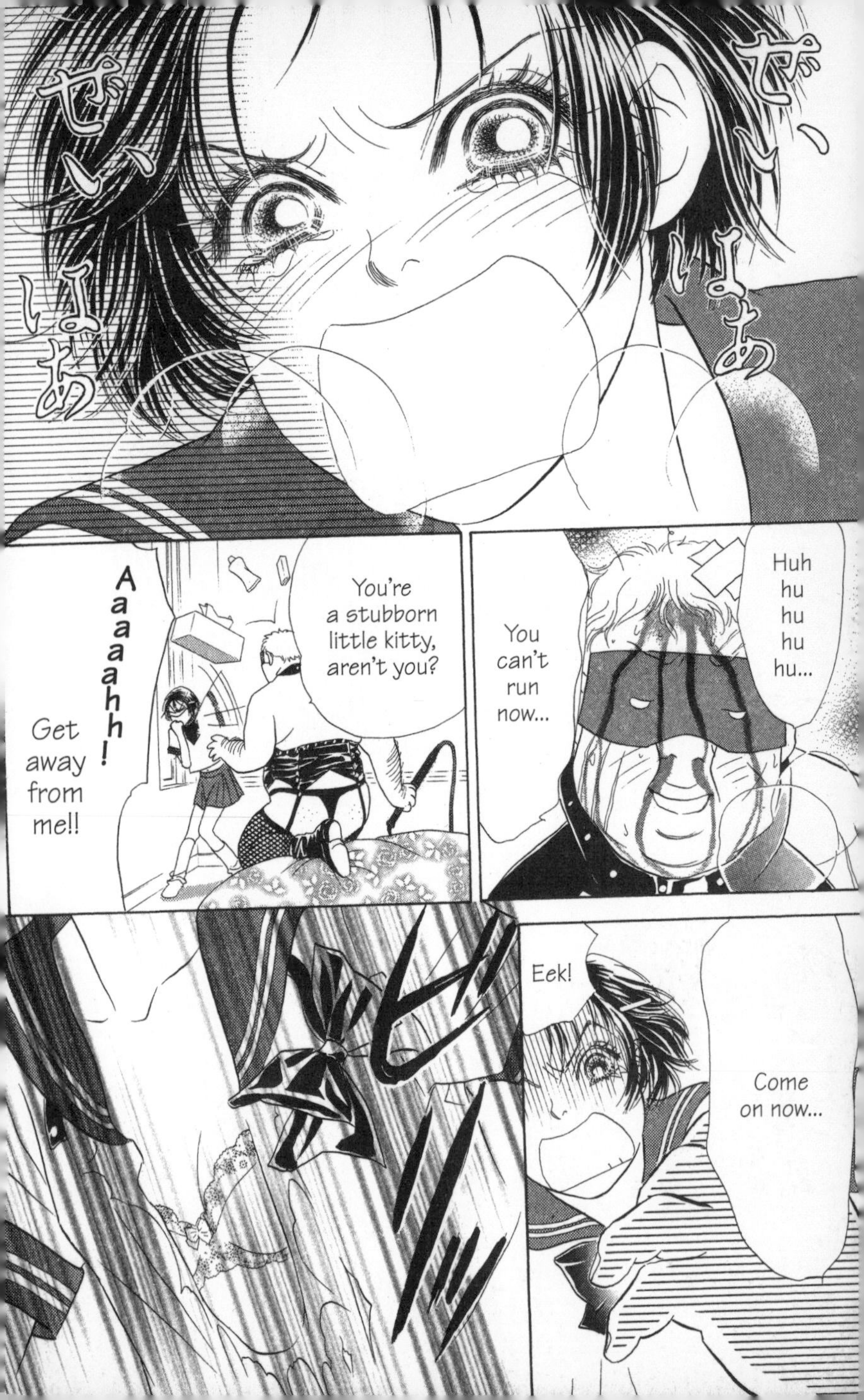
ぜいはあ
ぜいはあ
Huh hu hu hu hu...
You can't run now...
You're a stubborn little kitty, aren't you?
Aaaaaahh!
Get away from me!!
Come on now...
Eek!

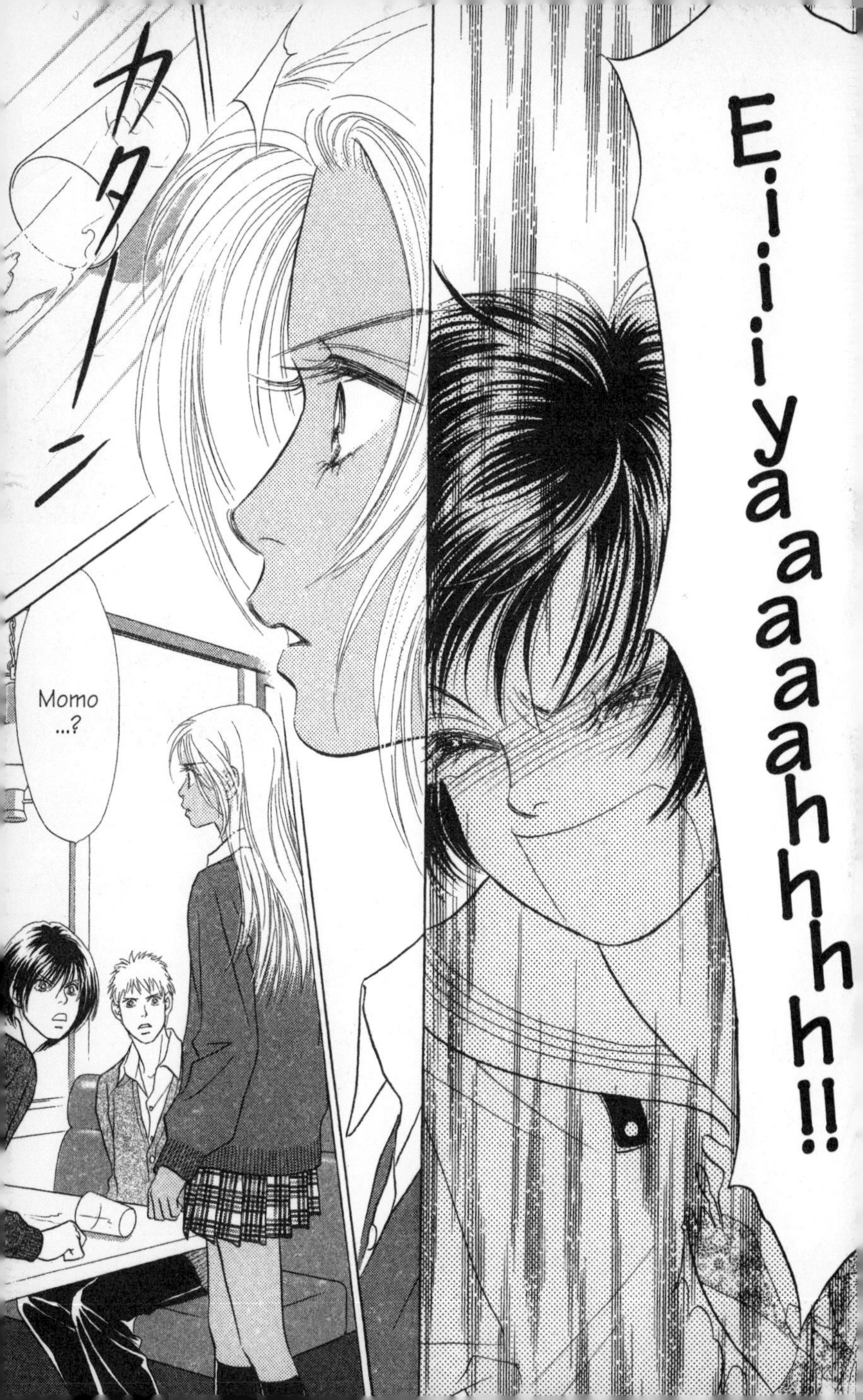
Eiiiyaaaaahhhh!!
カターン
Momo ...?

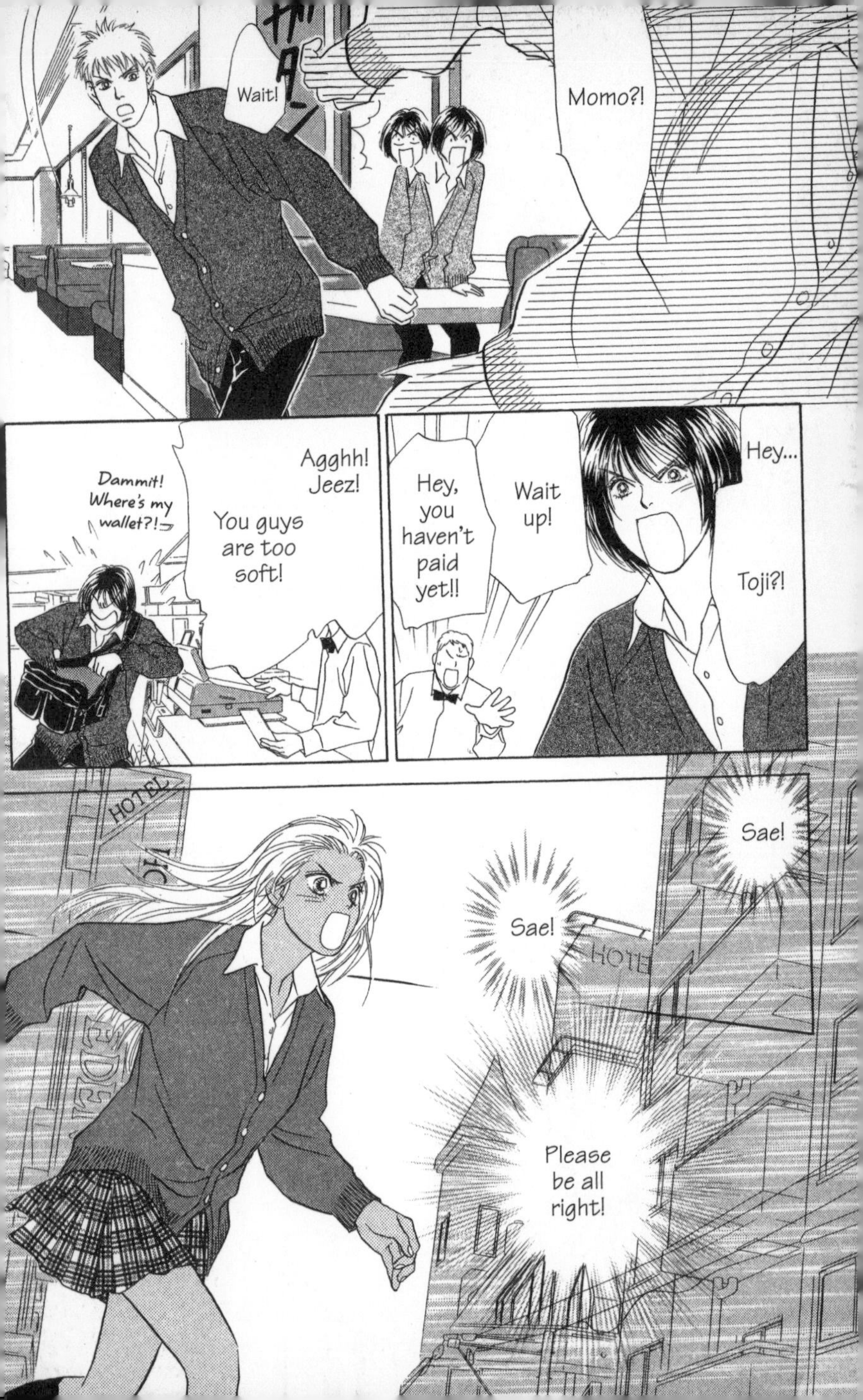
Momo?!
Wait!
Hey...
Toji?!
Wait up!
Hey, you haven't paid yet!!
Agghh! Jeez!
You guys are too soft!
Dammit! Where's my wallet?!
Sae!
Sae!
Please be all right!

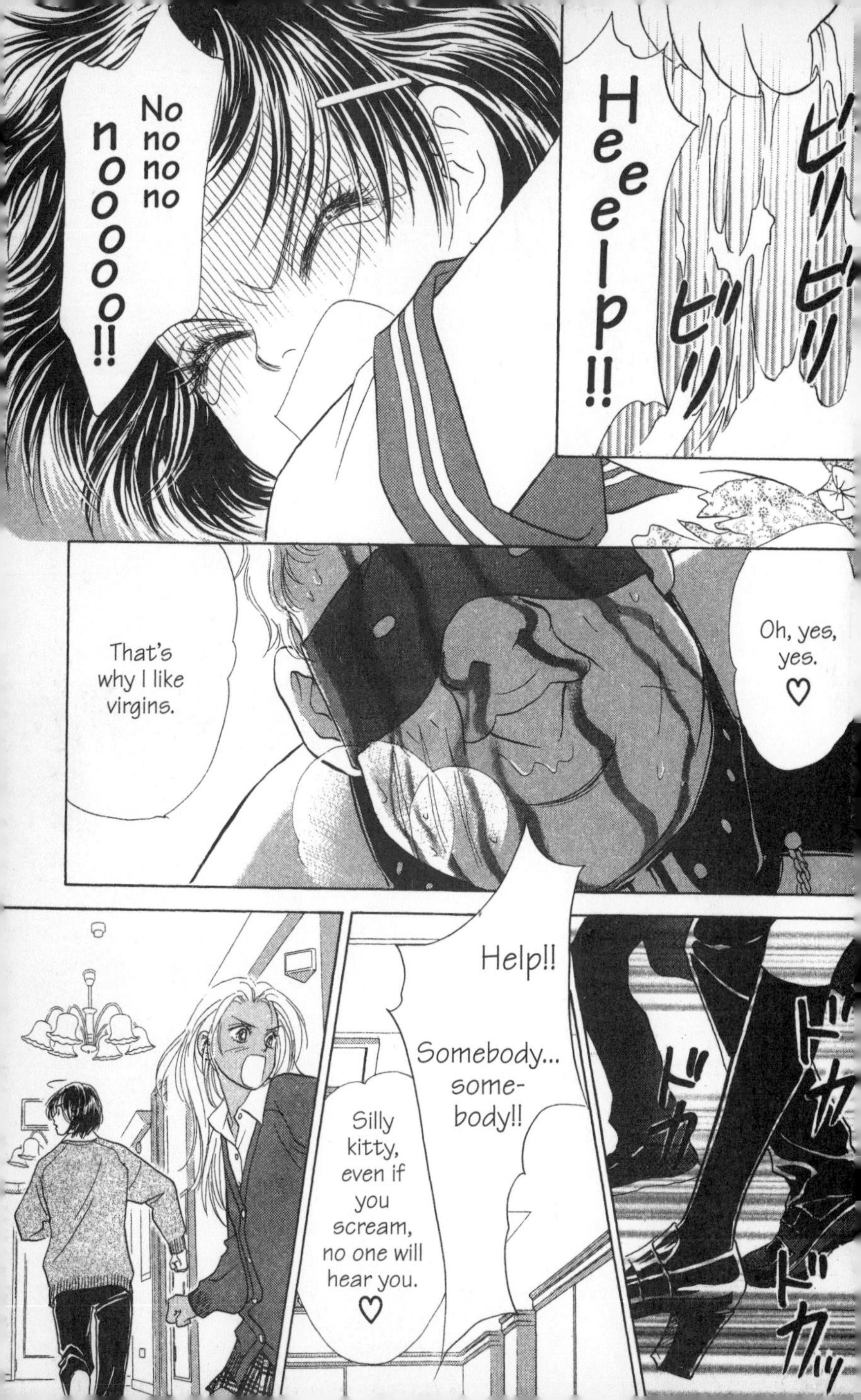
ビリビリ
ビリッ
Heeelp!!
No no no no nooooooo!!
Oh, yes, yes. ♡
That's why I like virgins.
Help!!
Somebody... some-body!!
ドカドカ
ドカドカッ
Silly kitty, even if you scream, no one will hear you. ♡

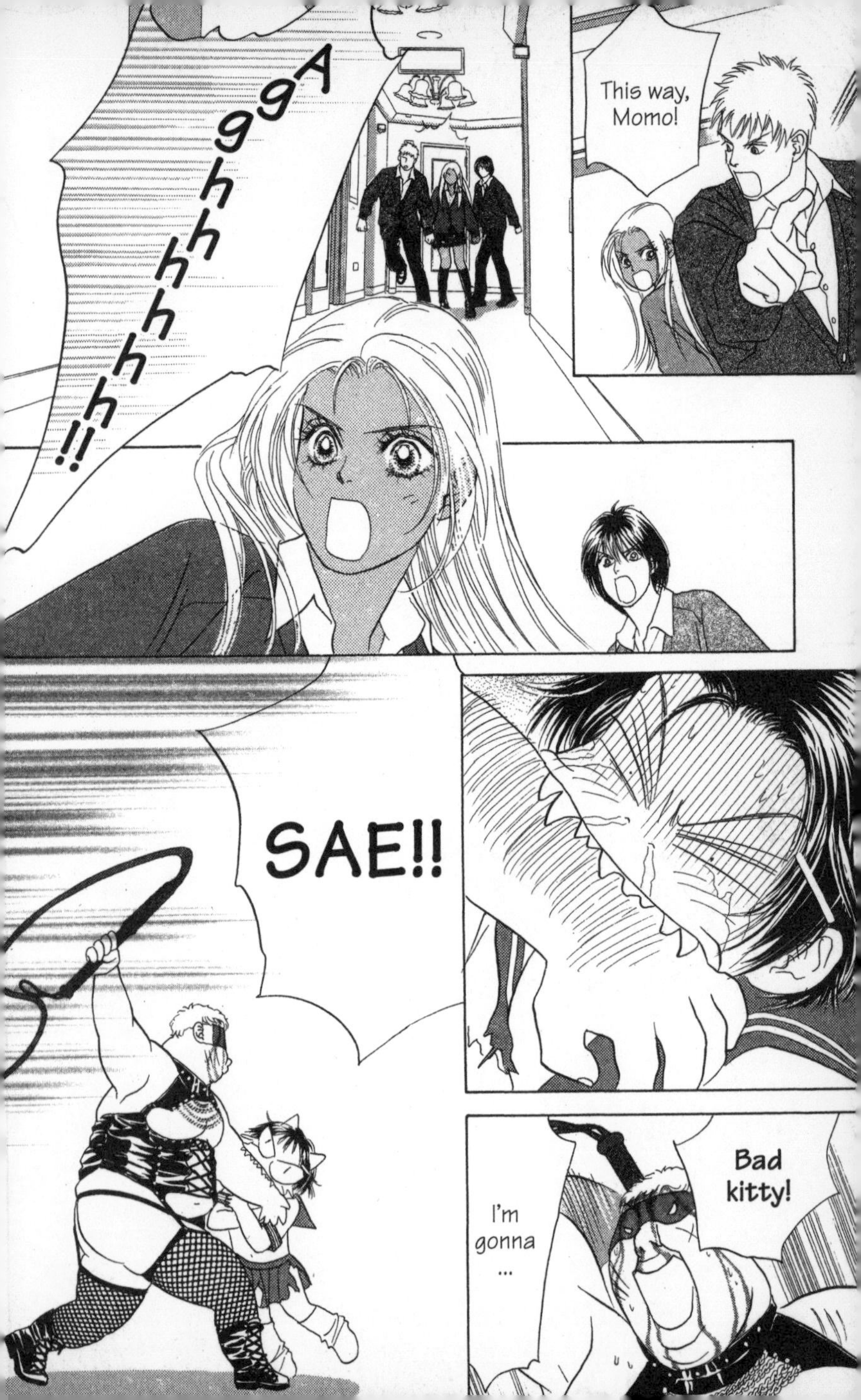
This way, Momo!
Agghhhhhh!!
SAE!!
Bad kitty!
I'm gonna ...

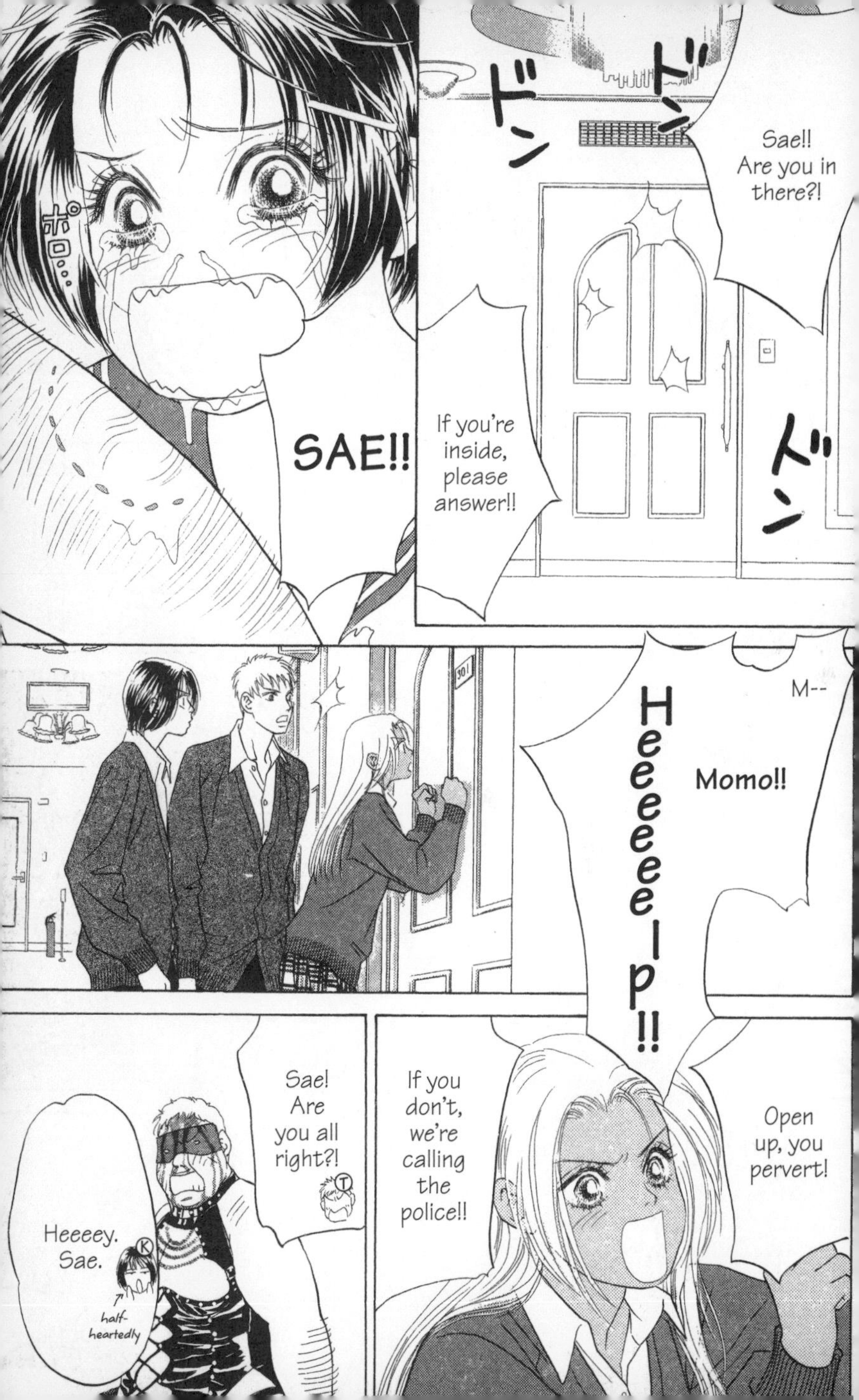
ドン
ドン
Sae!! Are you in there?!
If you're inside, please answer!!
ドン
SAE!!
ポロ…
M--
Momo!!
Heeeeeelp!!
301
Open up, you pervert!
If you don't, we're calling the police!!
Sae! Are you all right?!
T
Heeeey. Sae.
K
half-heartedly

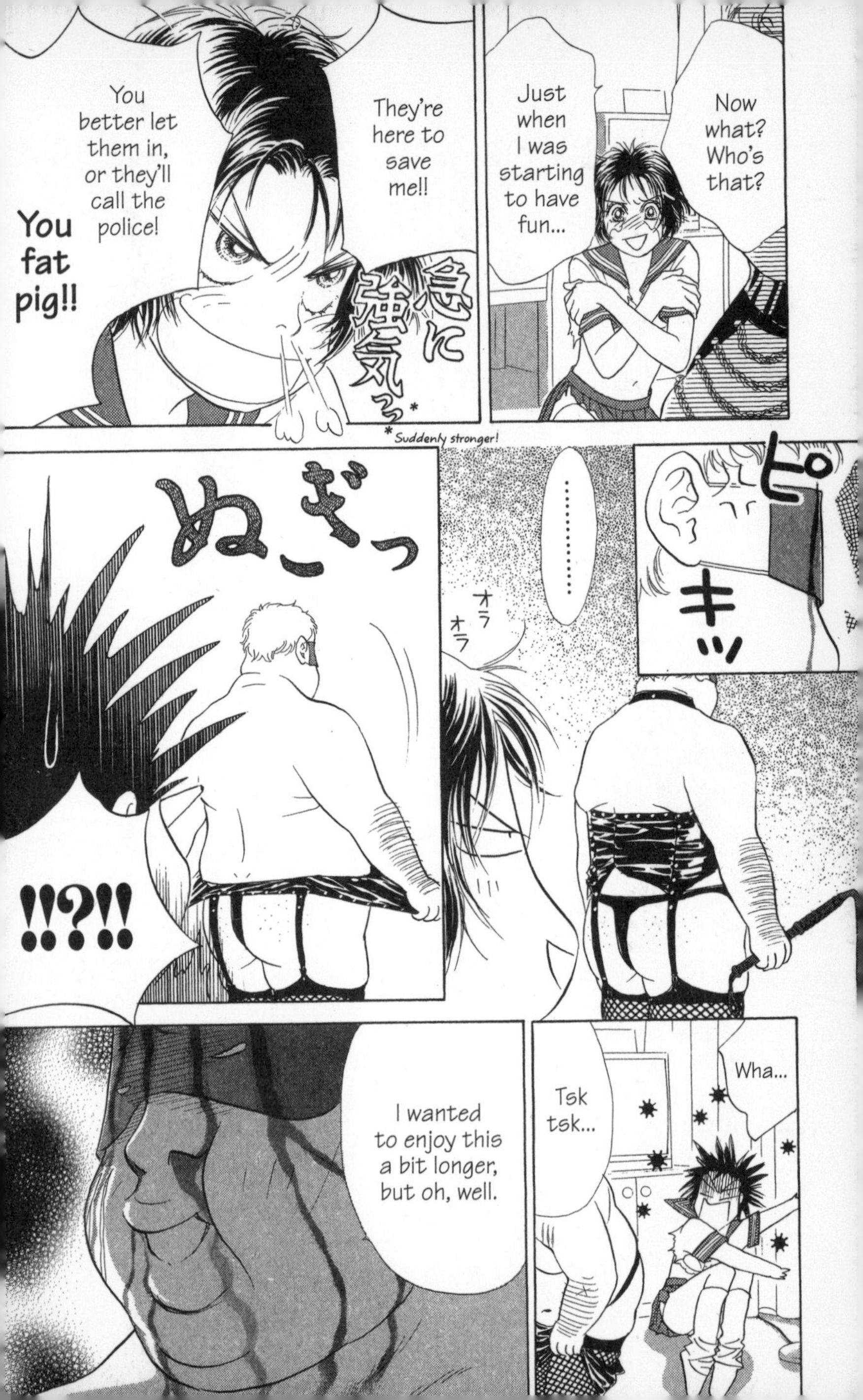
Now what? Who's that?
Just when I was starting to have fun...
They're here to save me!!
You better let them in, or they'll call the police!
You fat pig!!
急に強気っ*
*Suddenly stronger!
ピ
キッ
......
オラ
オラ
ぬぎっ
!!?!!
Wha...
Tsk tsk...
I wanted to enjoy this a bit longer, but oh, well.

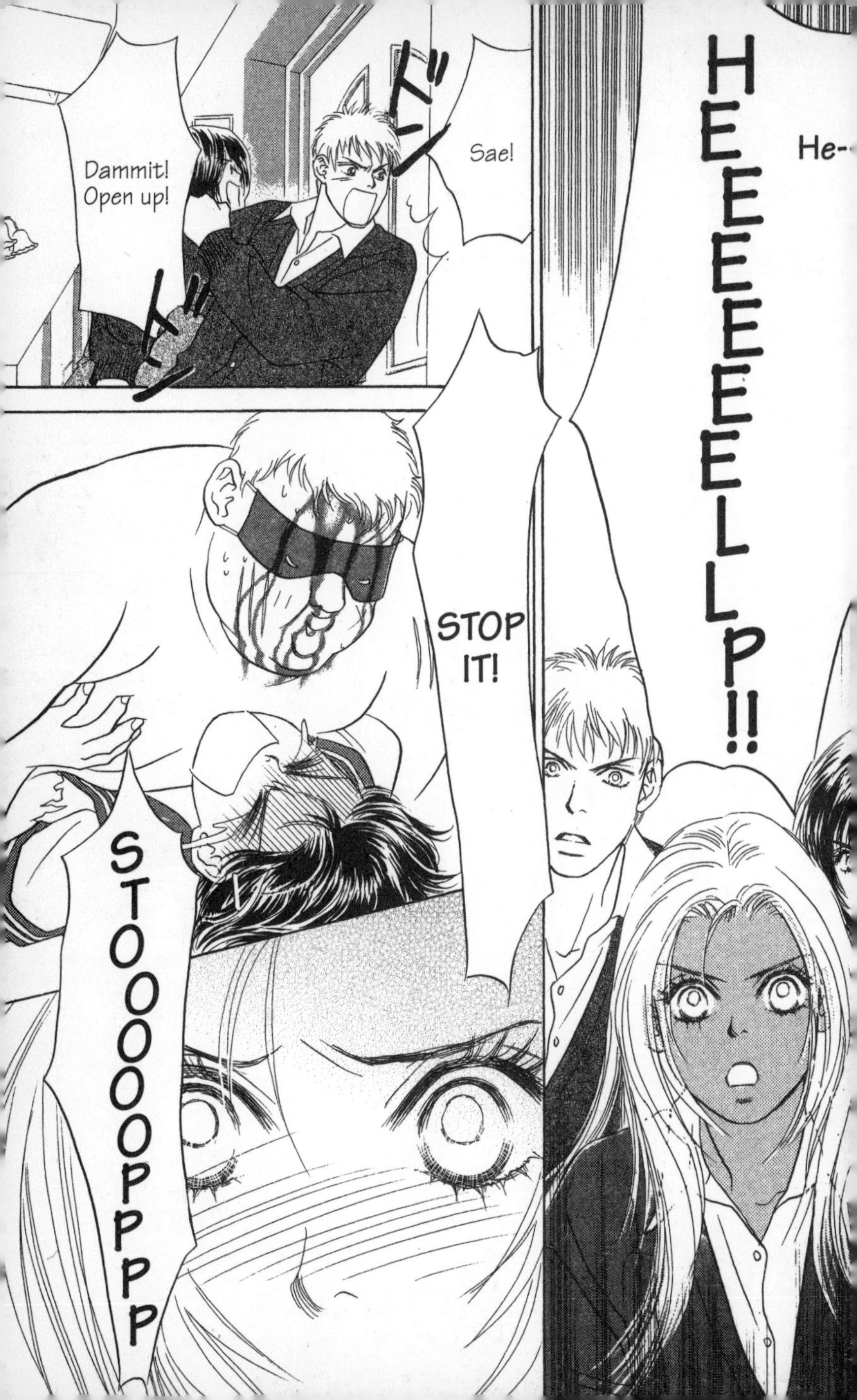
He--
HEEEEEELLP!!
Sae!
Dammit! Open up!
STOP IT!
STOOOOPPPP

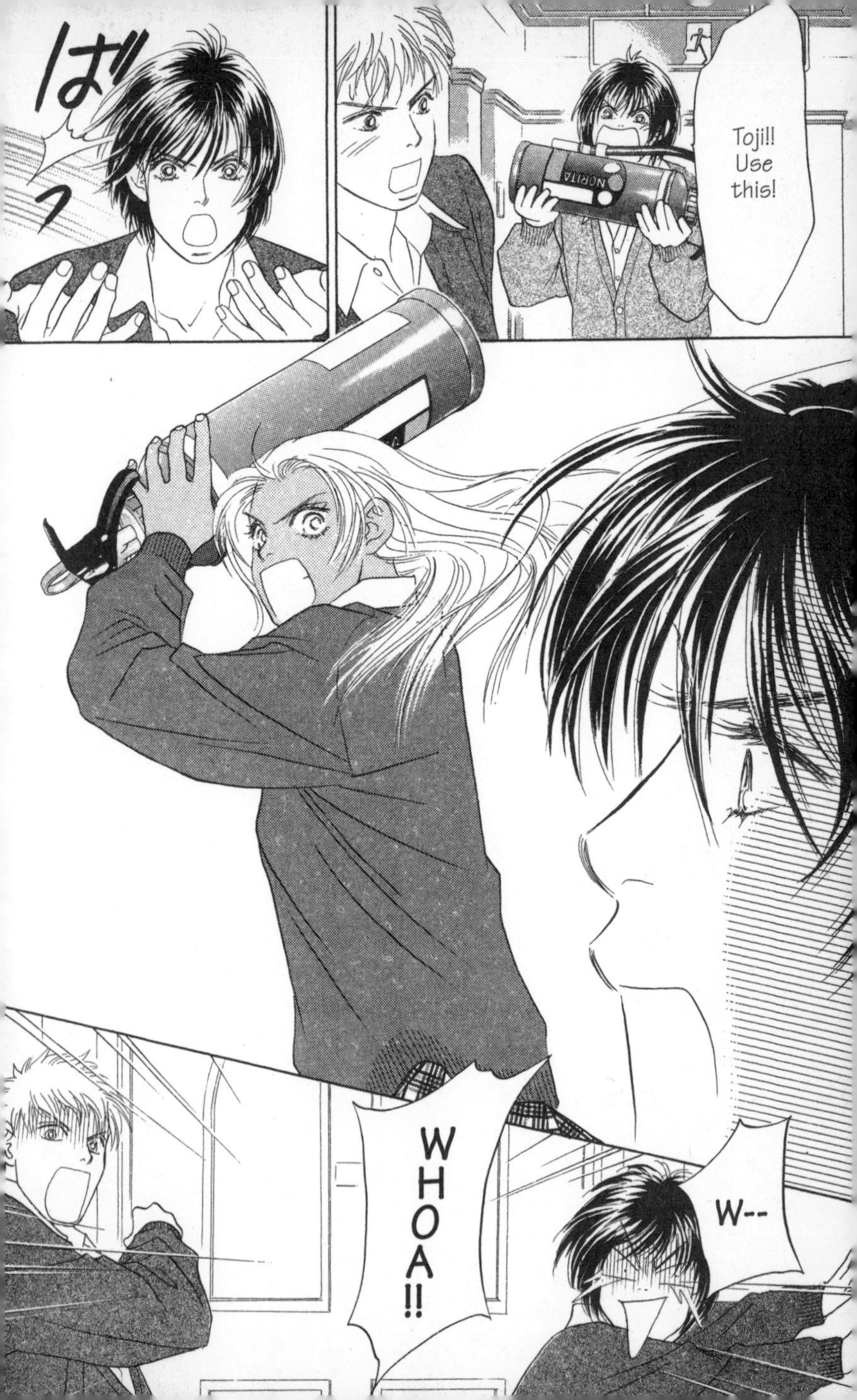
Toji!! Use this!
ばっ
W--
WHOA!!

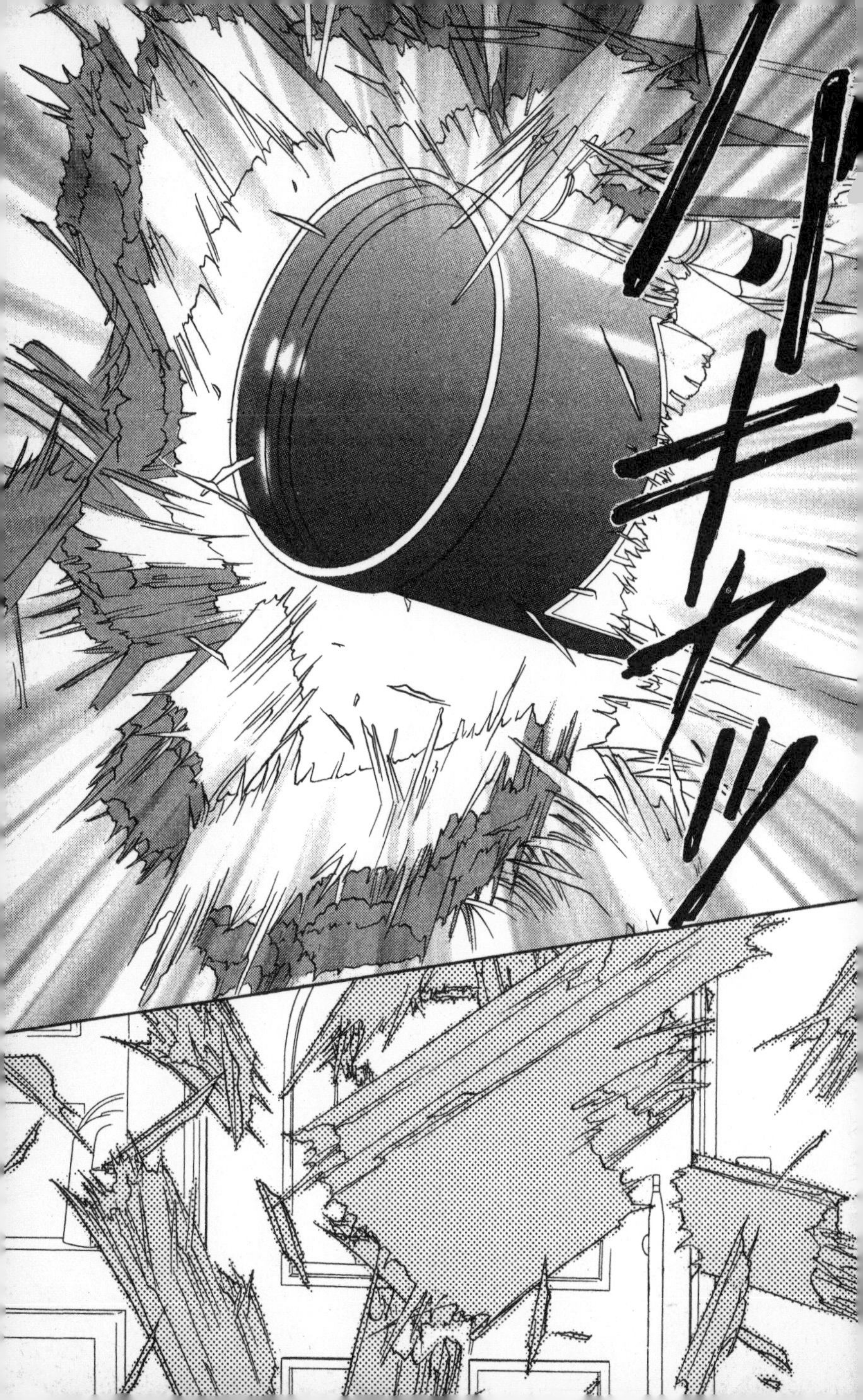
バキャッ

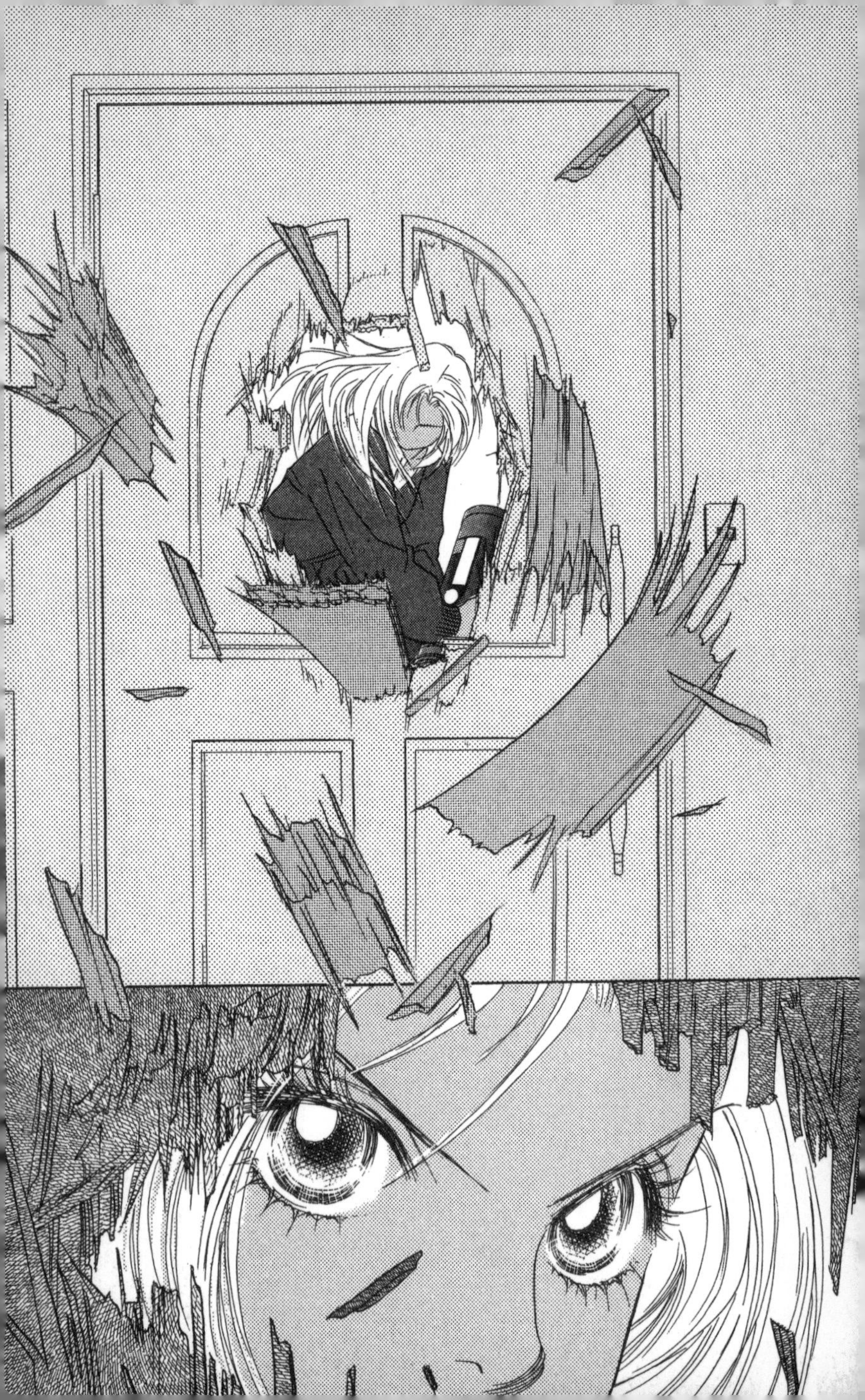

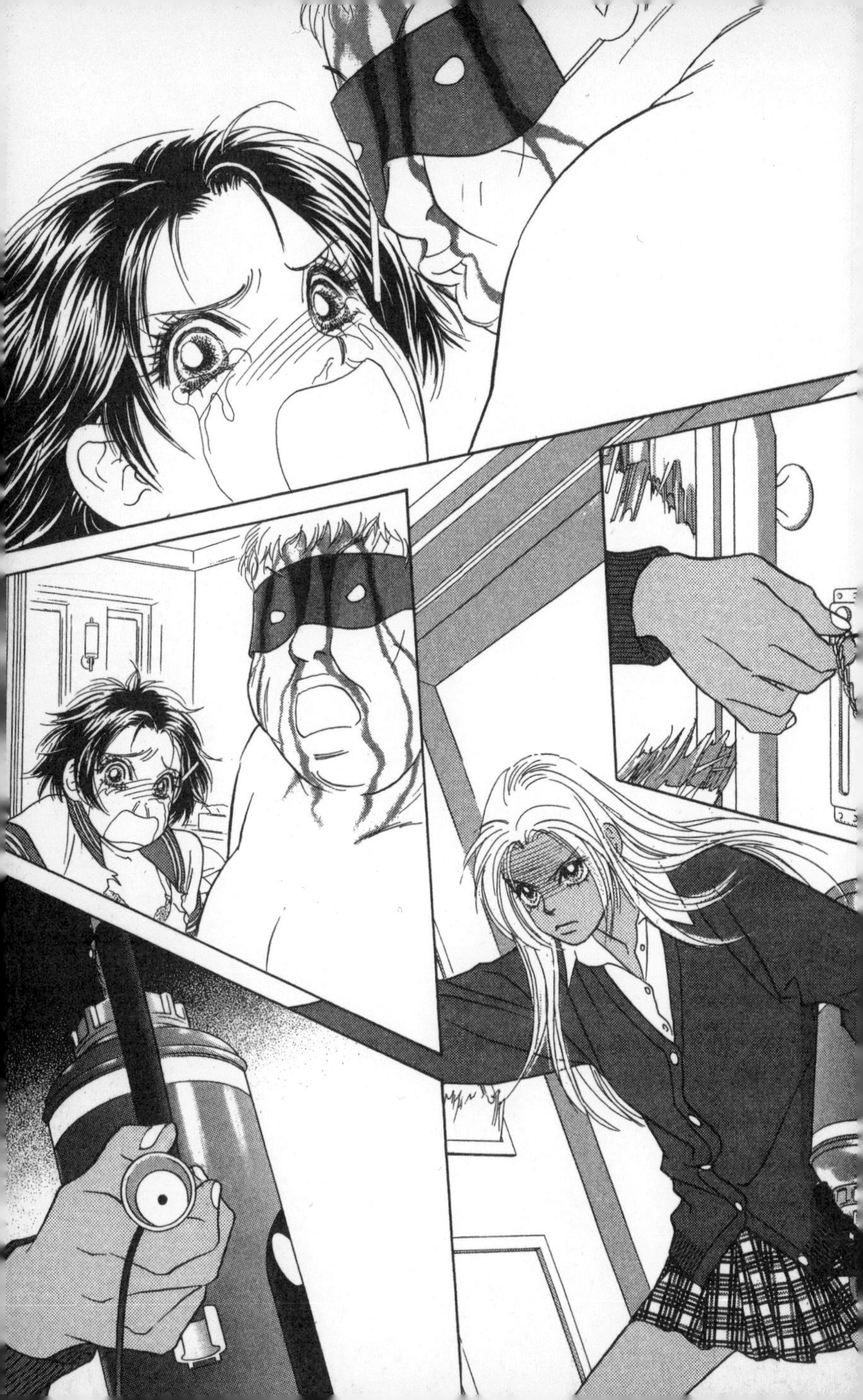

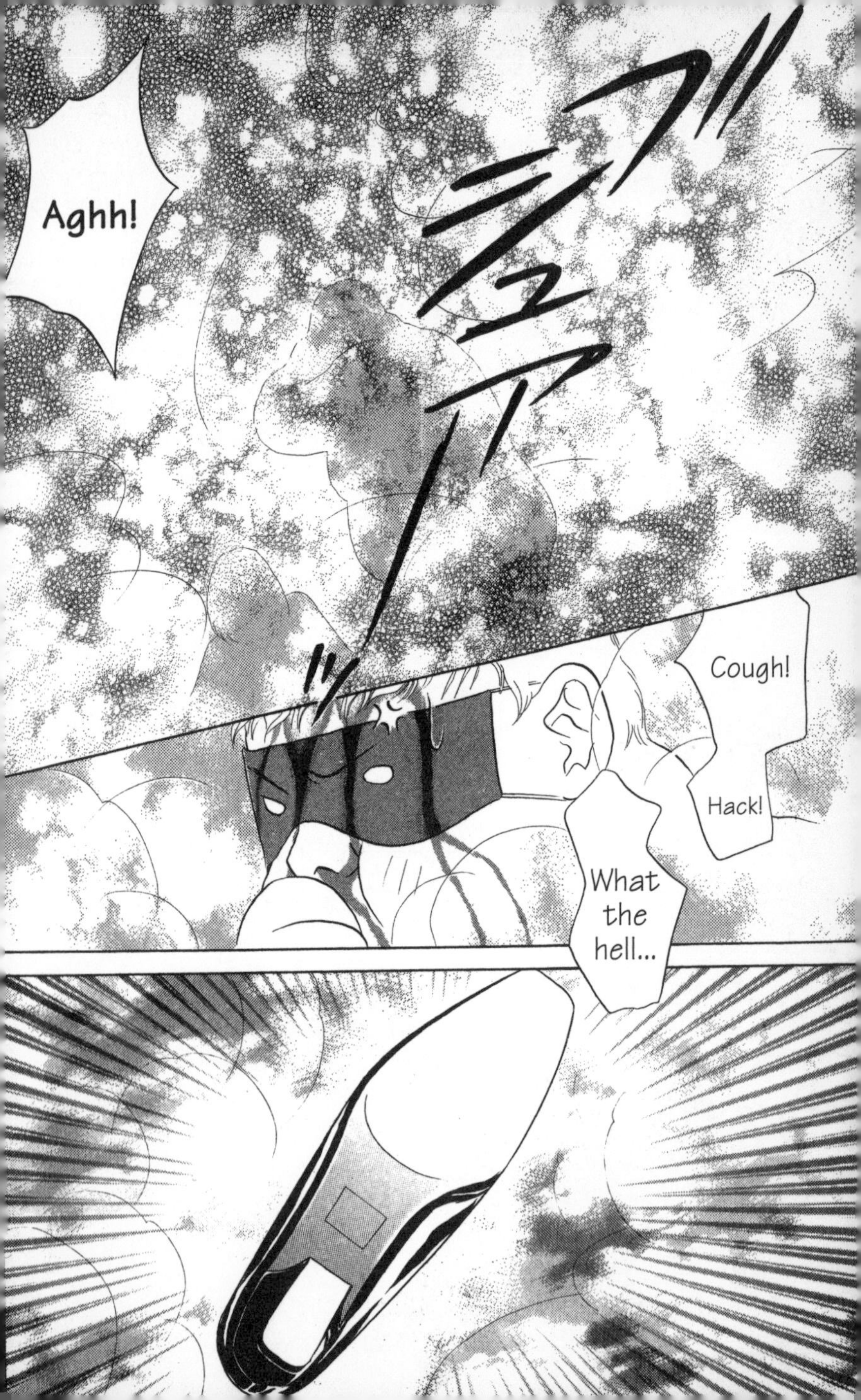
ブシュアーッ
Aghh!
Cough!
Hack!
What the hell...

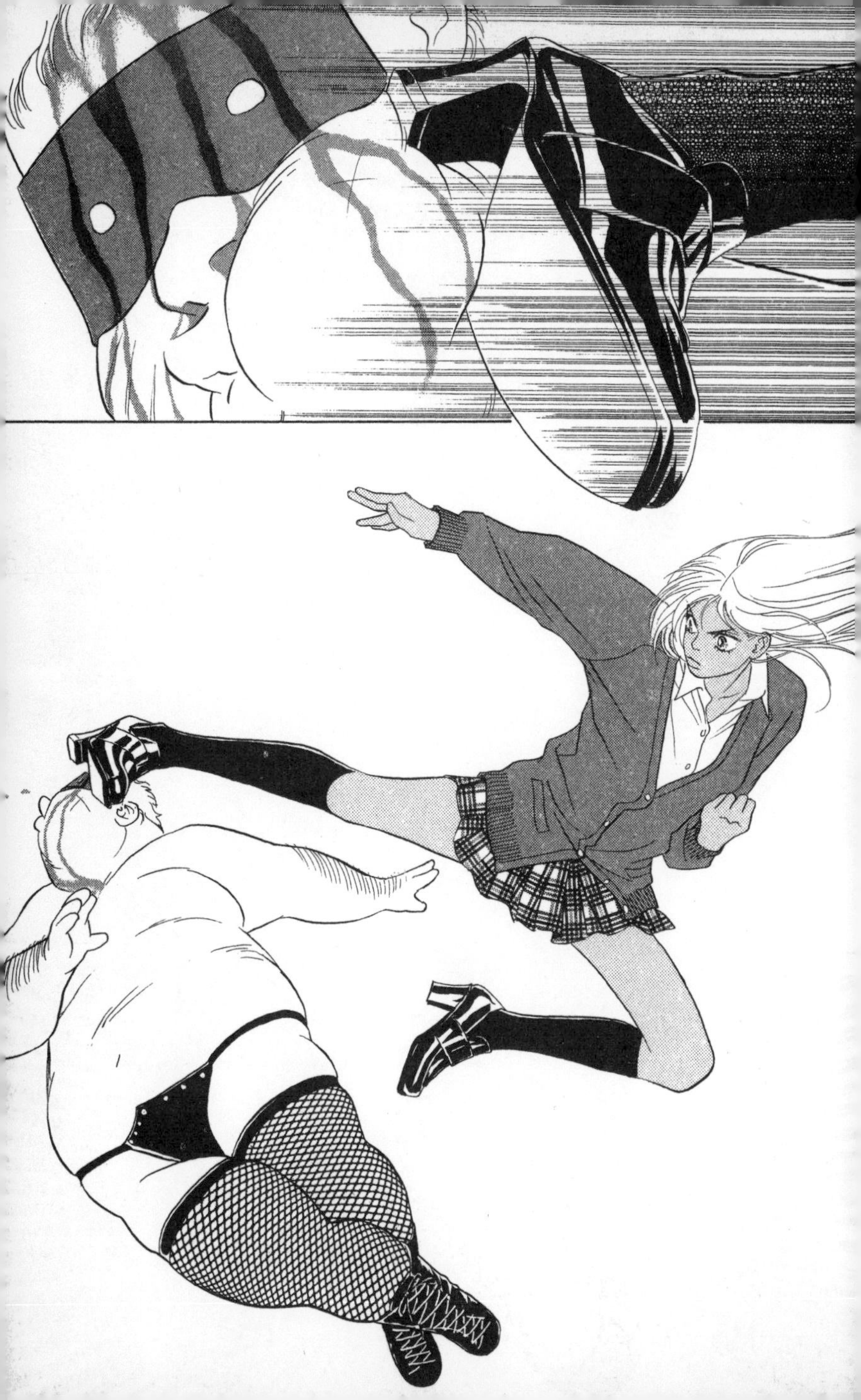

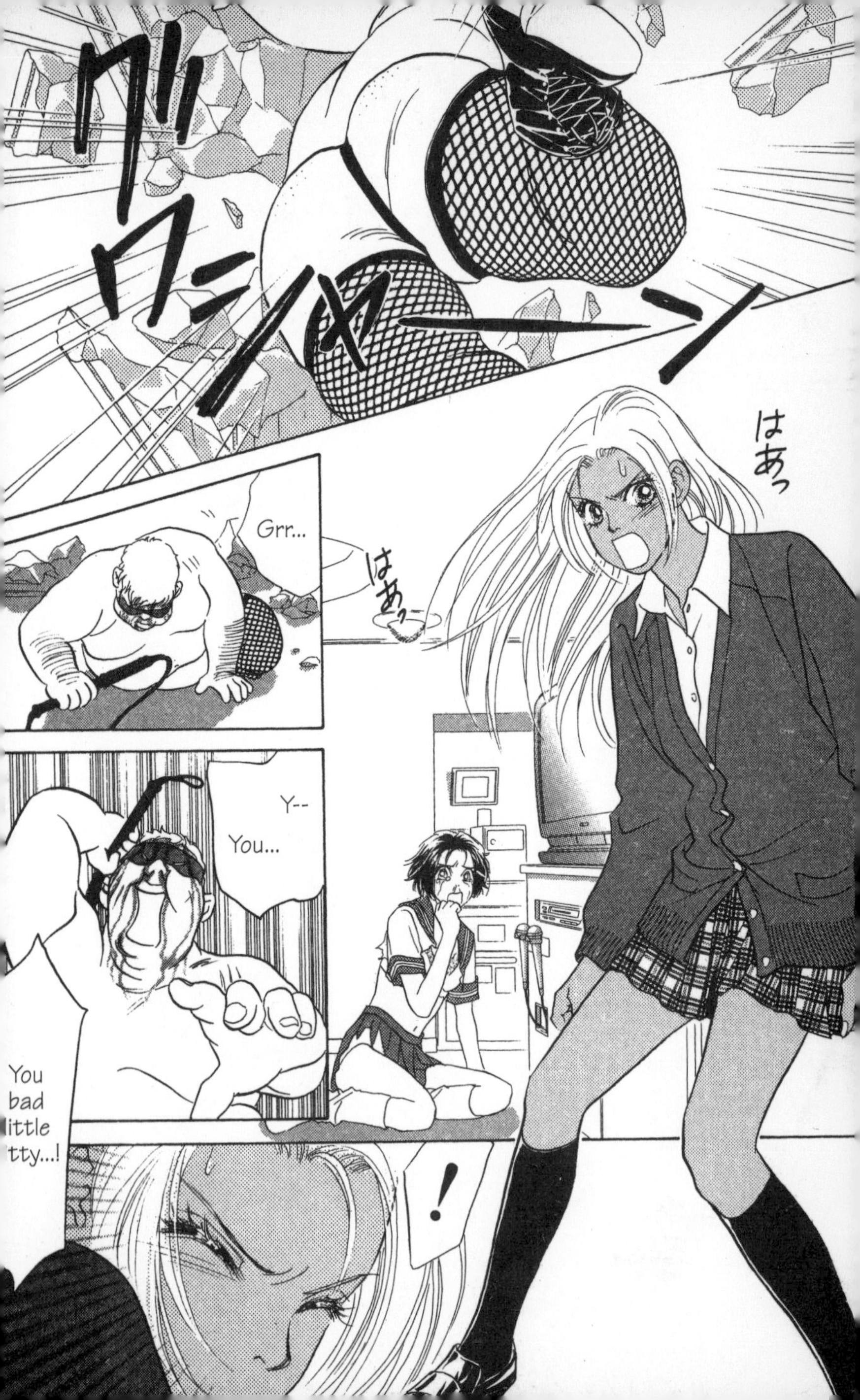

グワシャーン
はあっ
はあっ
Grr...
Y--
You...
You bad little tty...!
!

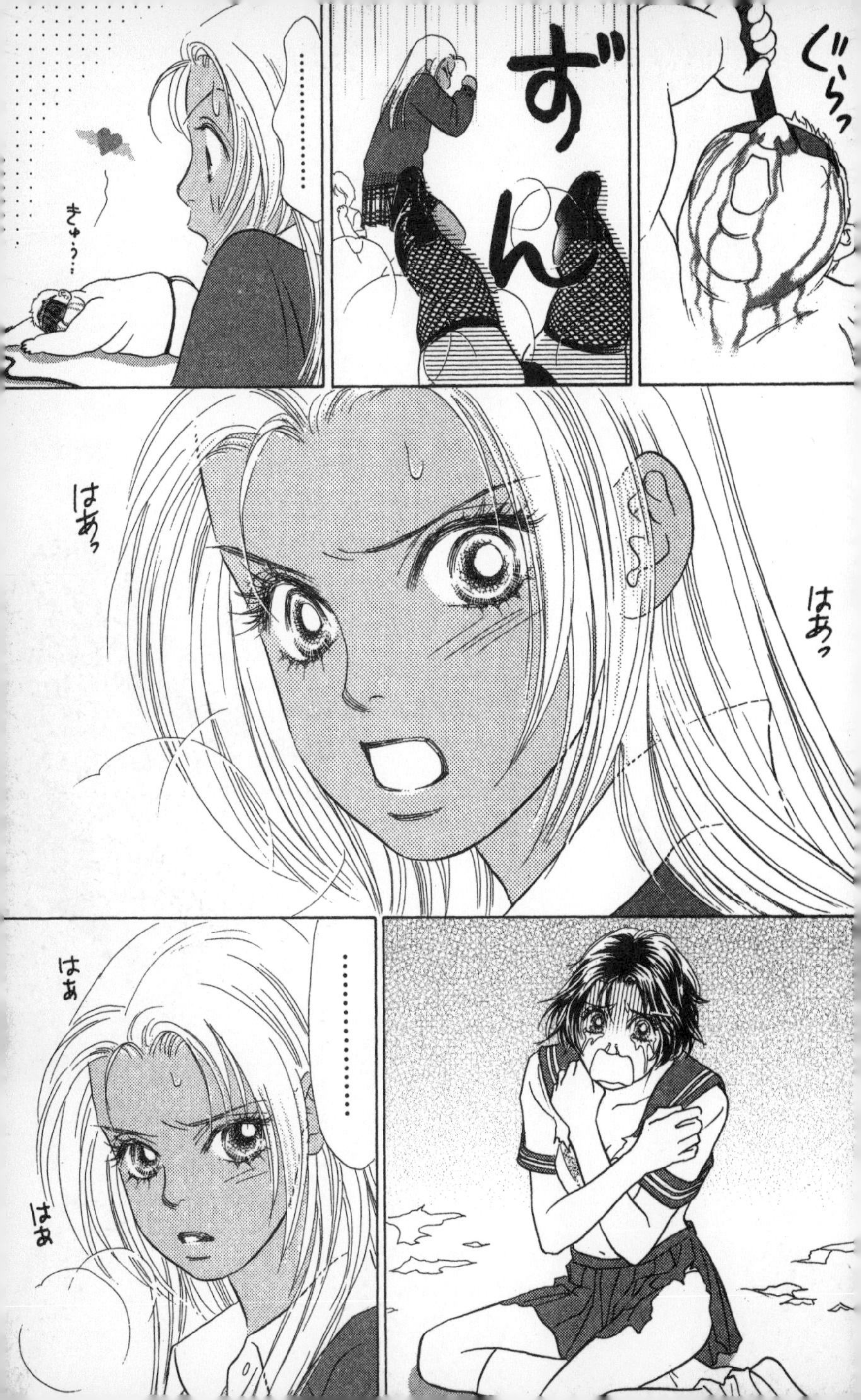
ぐらっ
ずん
……
きゅう…
はあっ
はあっ
……
はあ
はあ

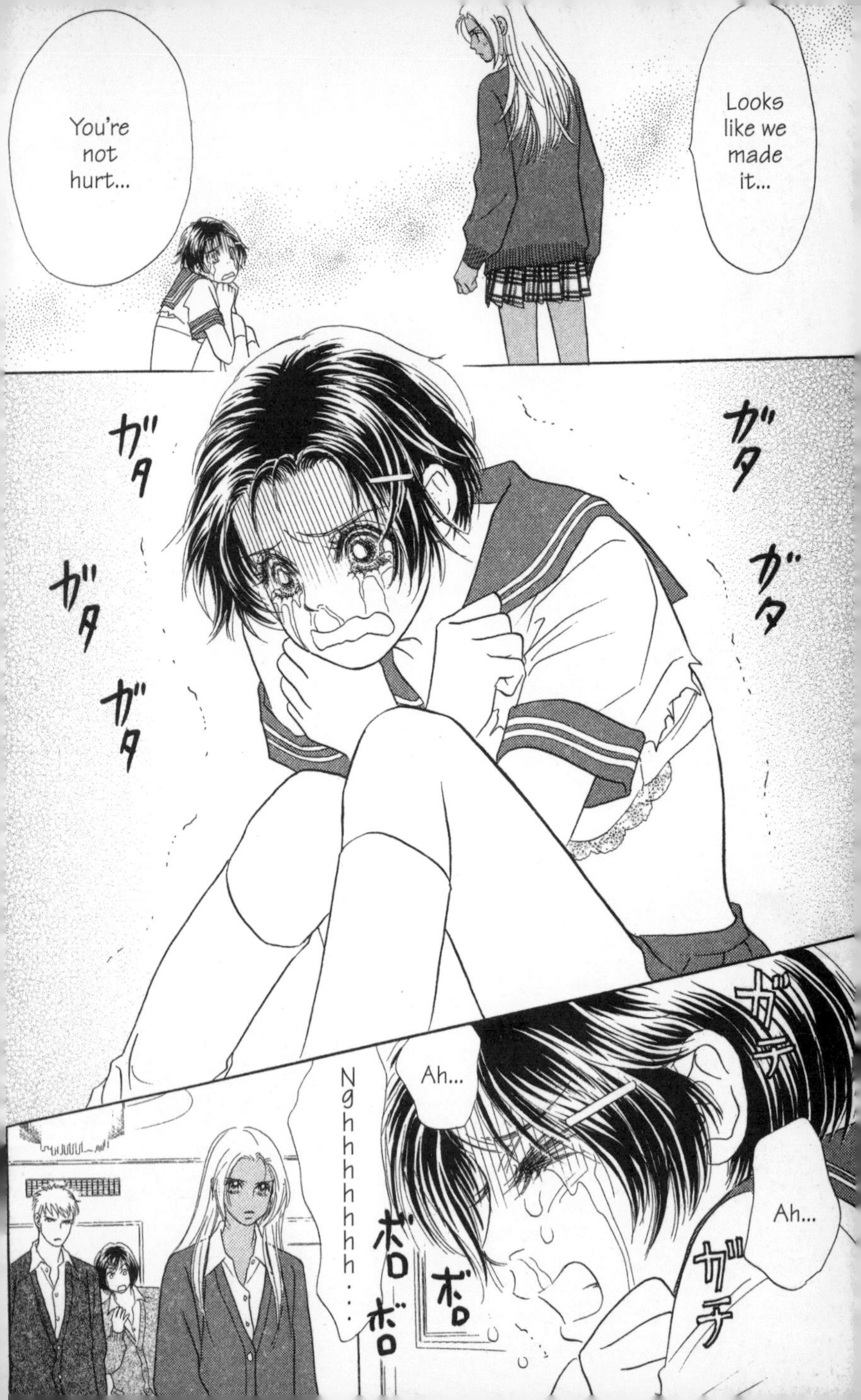
Looks like we made it...
You're not hurt...
ガタ ガタ
ガタ ガタ
ガチ
Ah...
Ah...
ガチ
ボロ ボロ
Nghhhhhhh...

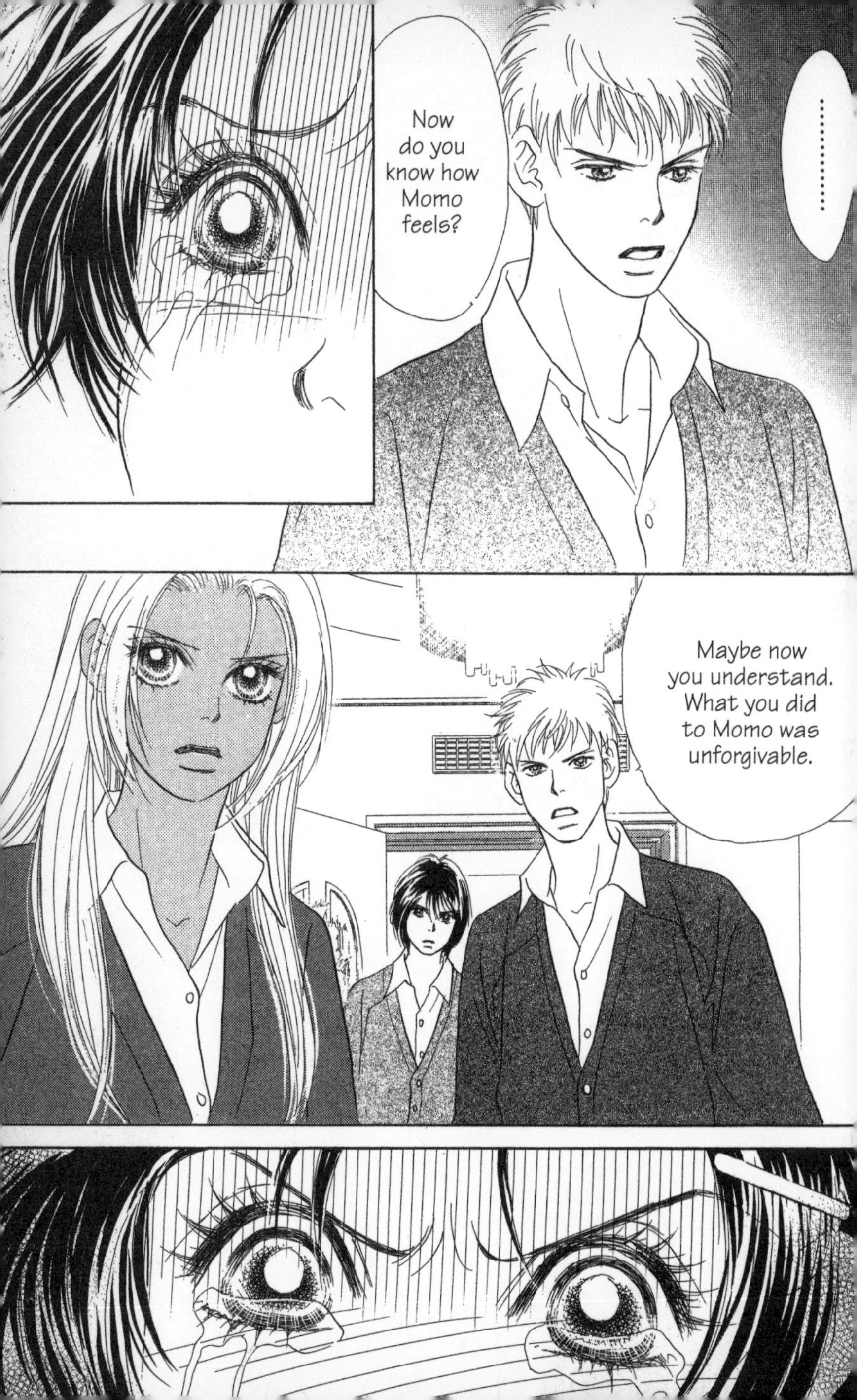
......
Now do you know how Momo feels?
Maybe now you understand. What you did to Momo was unforgivable.

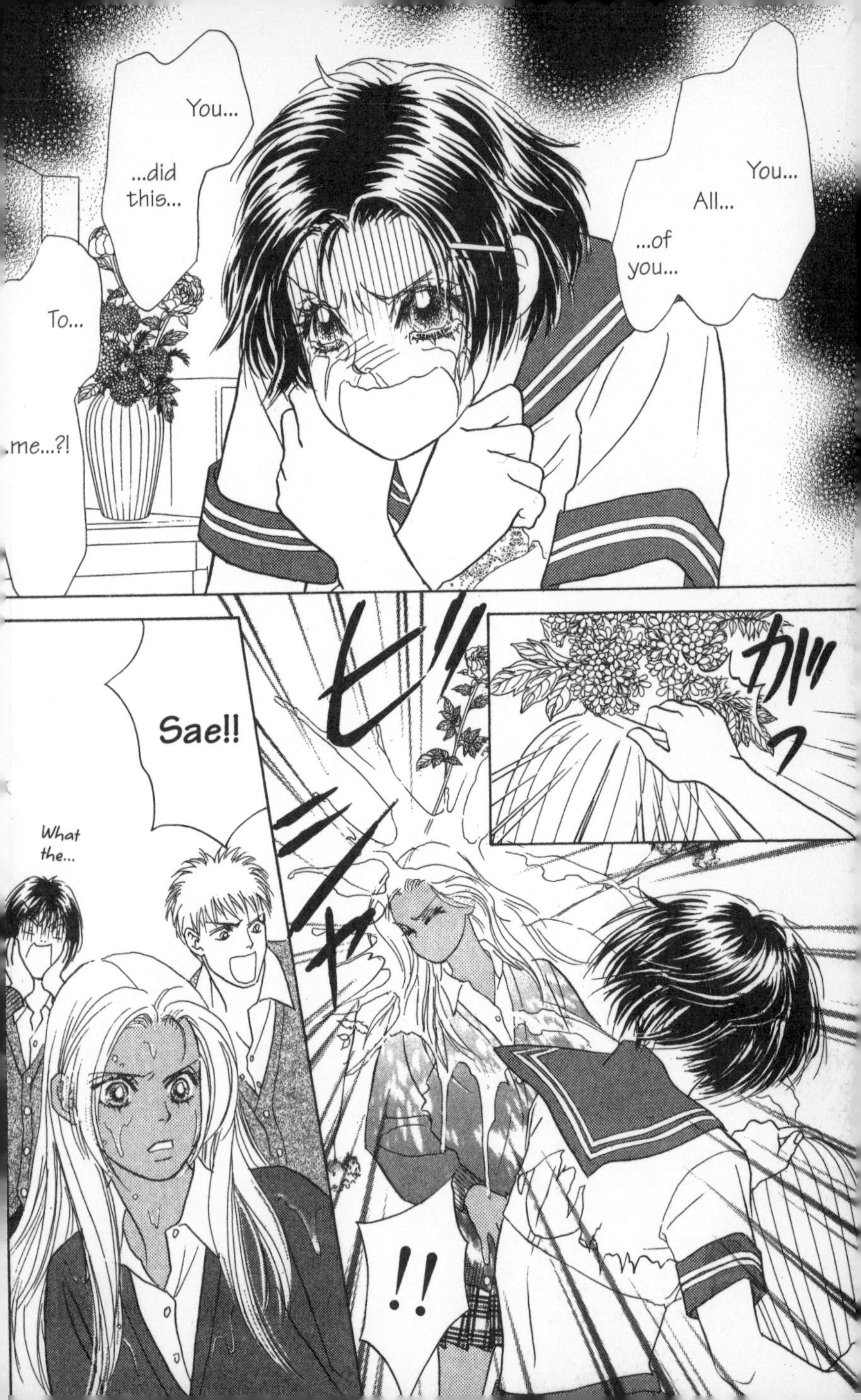
You...
All...
...of you...
You...
...did this...
To...
...me...?!
ガッ
ビシャ
!!
Sae!!
What the...

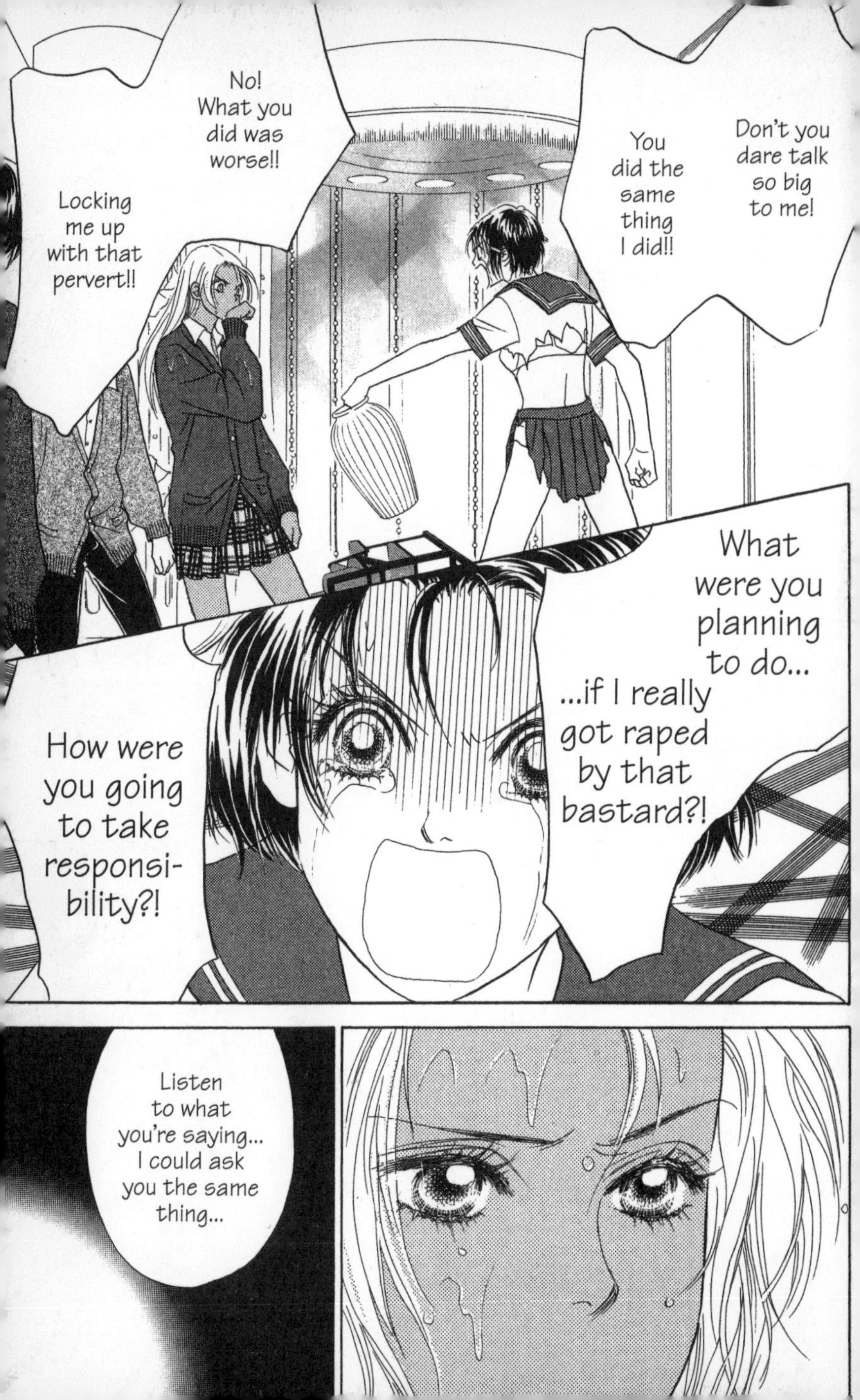

Don't you dare talk so big to me!
You did the same thing I did!!
No! What you did was worse!!
Locking me up with that pervert!!
What were you planning to do...
...if I really got raped by that bastard?!
How were you going to take responsi-bility?!
Listen to what you're saying... I could ask you the same thing...

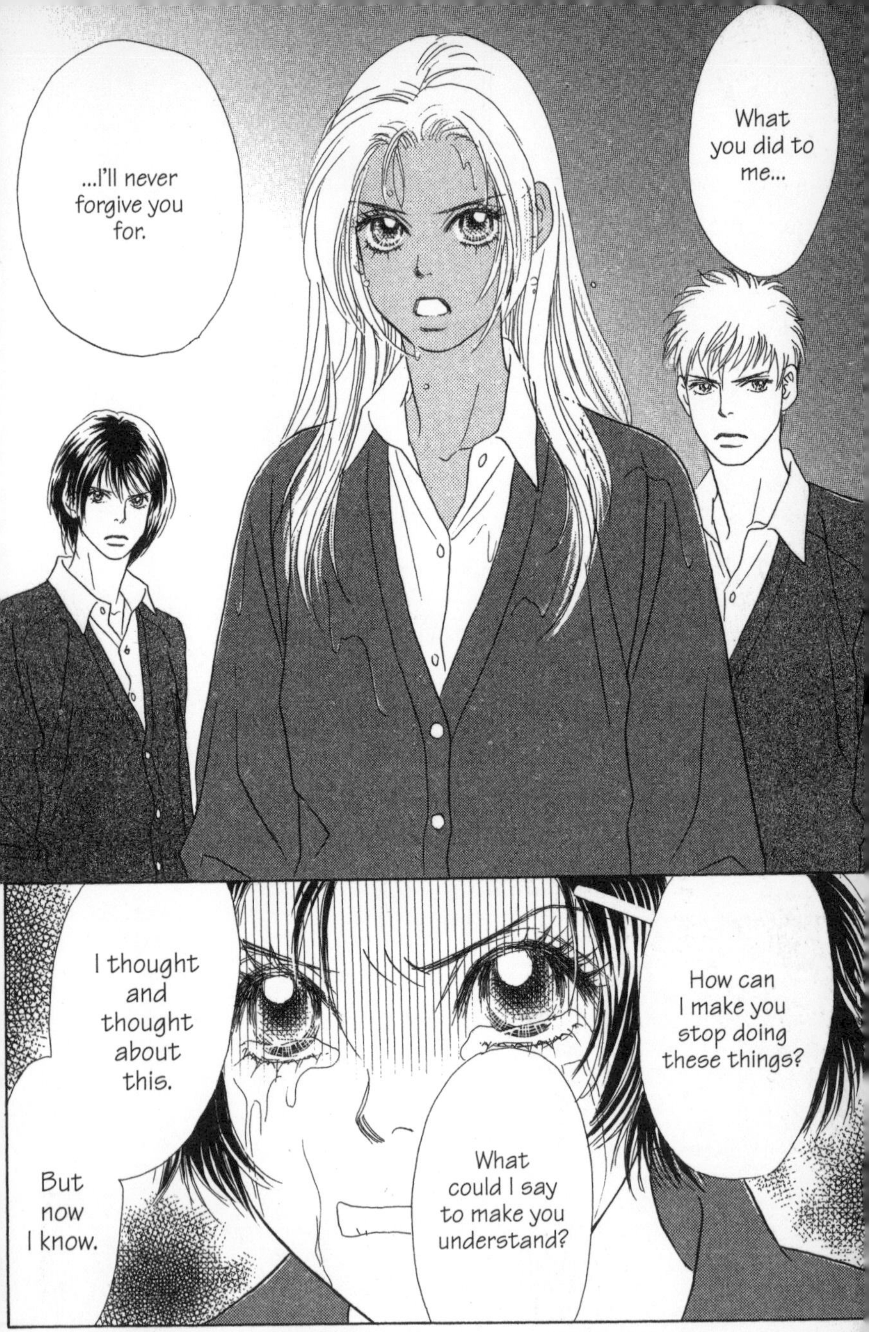
What you did to me...
...I'll never forgive you for.
How can I make you stop doing these things?
I thought and thought about this.
What could I say to make you understand?
But now I know.

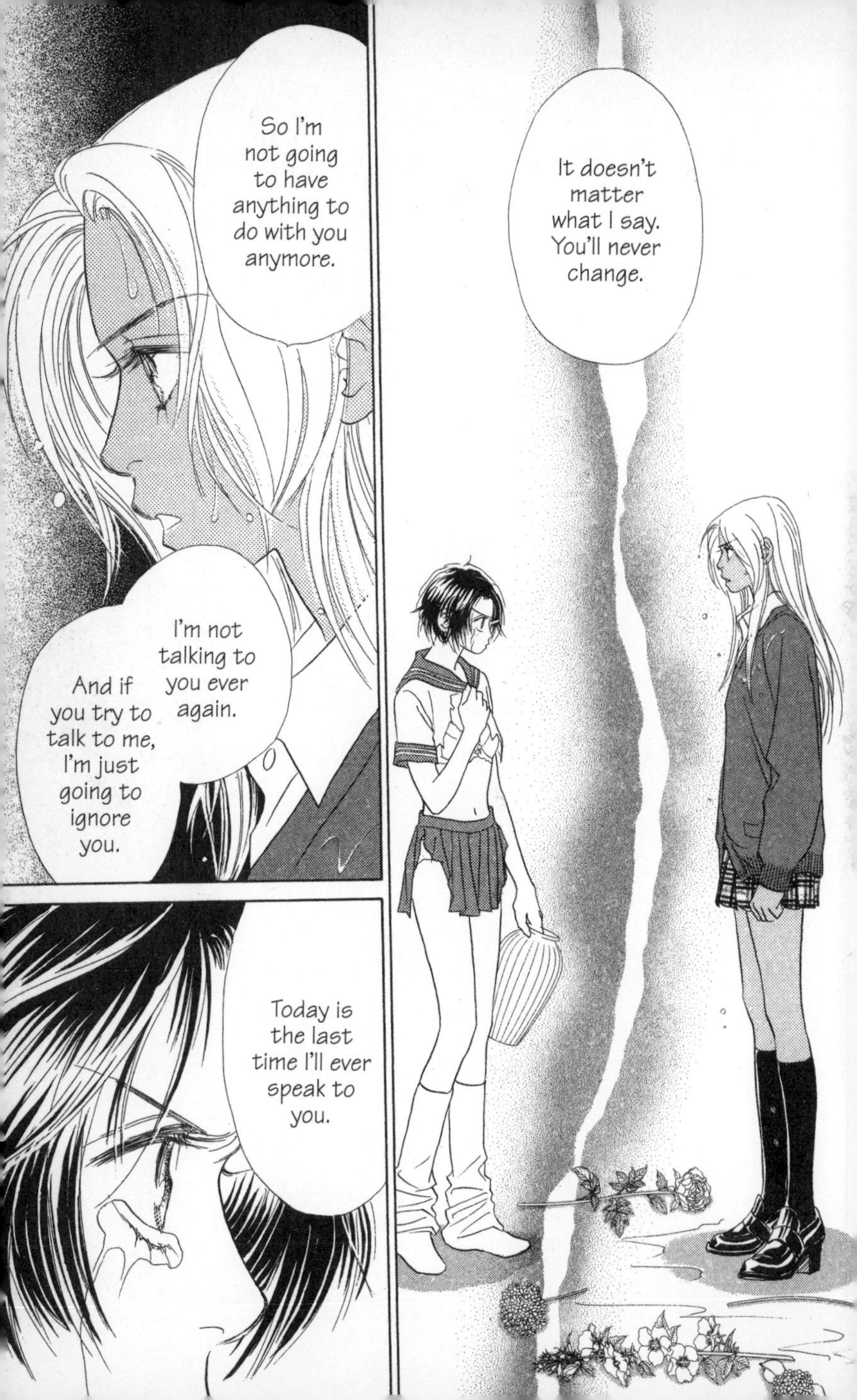
It doesn't matter what I say. You'll never change.
So I'm not going to have anything to do with you anymore.
I'm not talking to you ever again.
And if you try to talk to me, I'm just going to ignore you.
Today is the last time I'll ever speak to you.

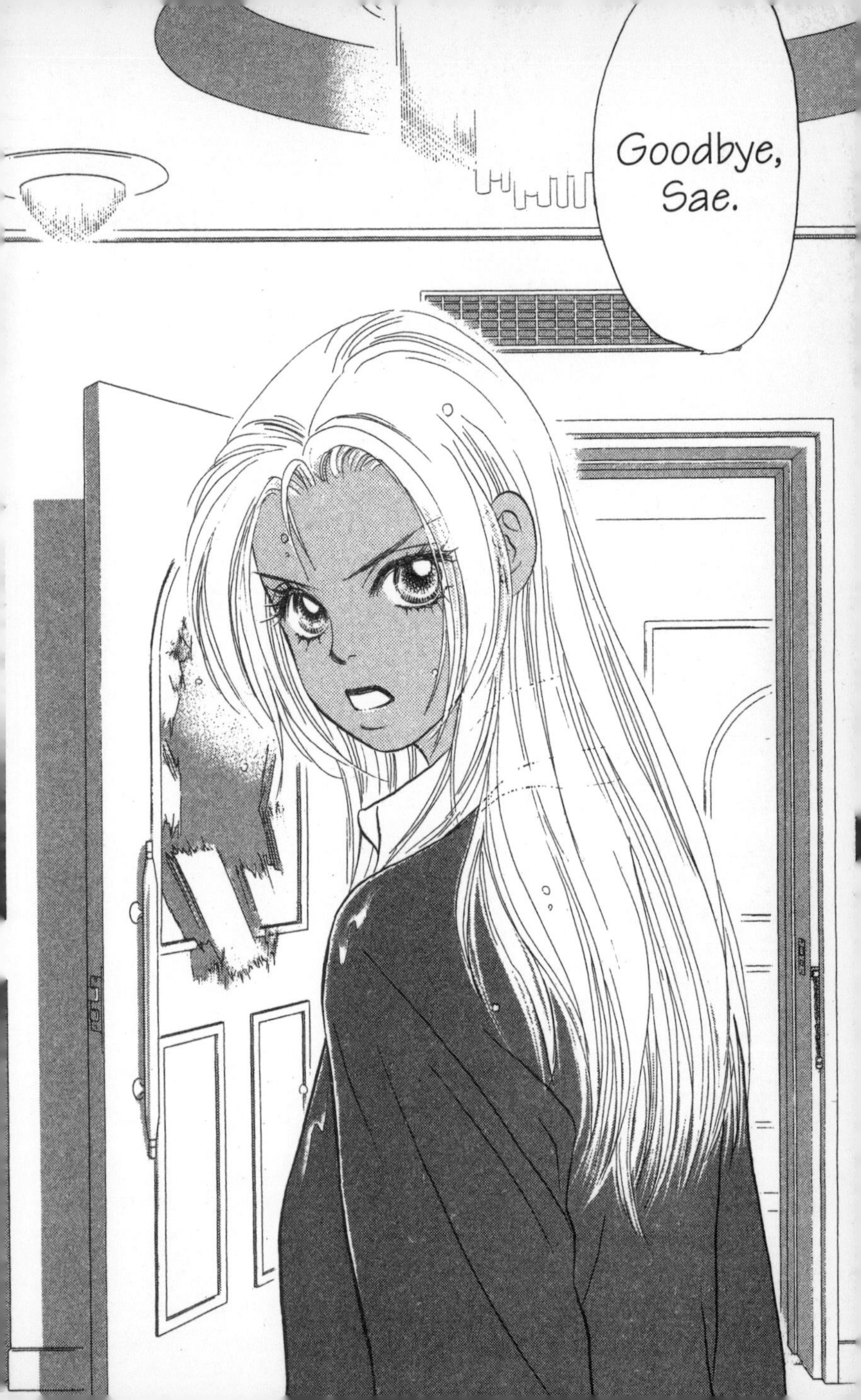
Goodbye, Sae.

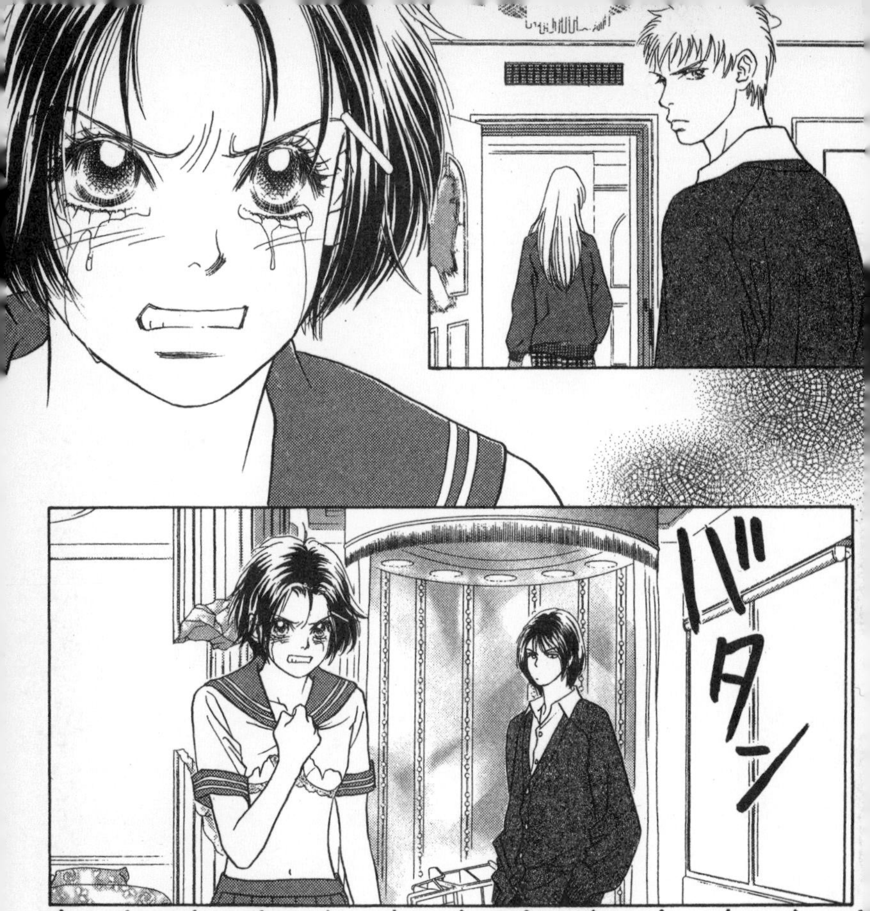
バタン

PEACH CLUB

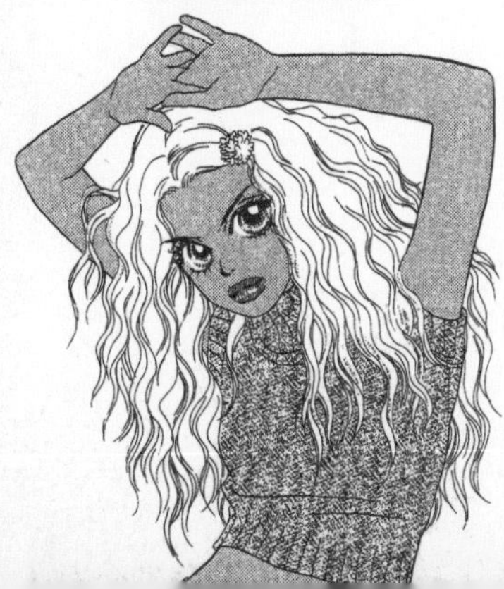

Hello, everyone! Welcome to *Peach Girl* Book 7. So, let's start with comments from my male readers. Actually, when I put out the invitation, I was worried that no boys would write, but they came. What a relief! (giggle)

Most of the letters were from readers who said that they asked their boyfriends (and family) for their opinions. Actually, I only got about ten letters from boys. Oh well. Anyway, check out the juicy details you'll find in these bonus pages and in the Peach Club pages at the end of this book!

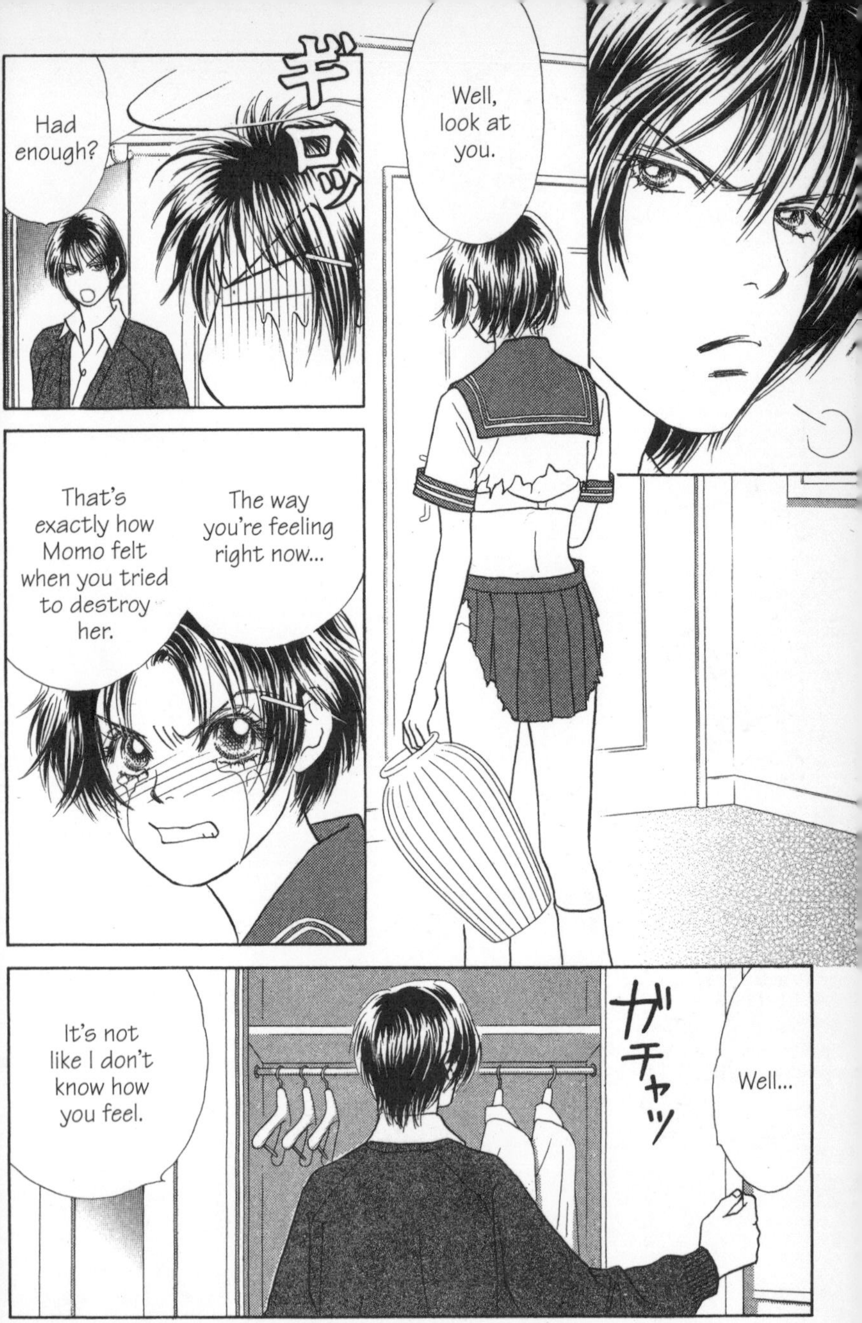

Well, look at you.
ギロッ
Had enough?
The way you're feeling right now...
That's exactly how Momo felt when you tried to destroy her.
Well...
ガチャッ
It's not like I don't know how you feel.

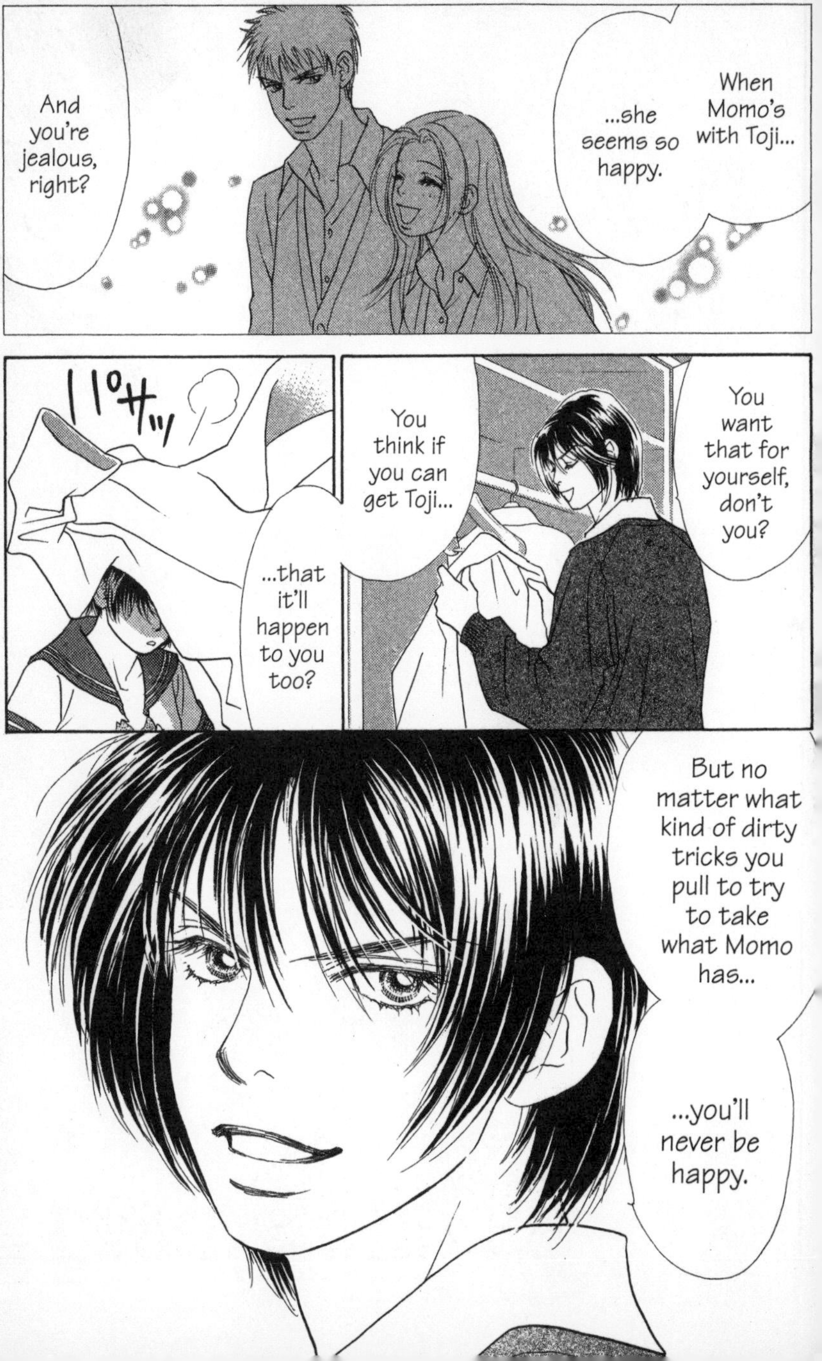

When Momo's with Toji...
...she seems so happy.
And you're jealous, right?
You want that for yourself, don't you?
You think if you can get Toji...
...that it'll happen to you too?
パサッ
But no matter what kind of dirty tricks you pull to try to take what Momo has...
...you'll never be happy.

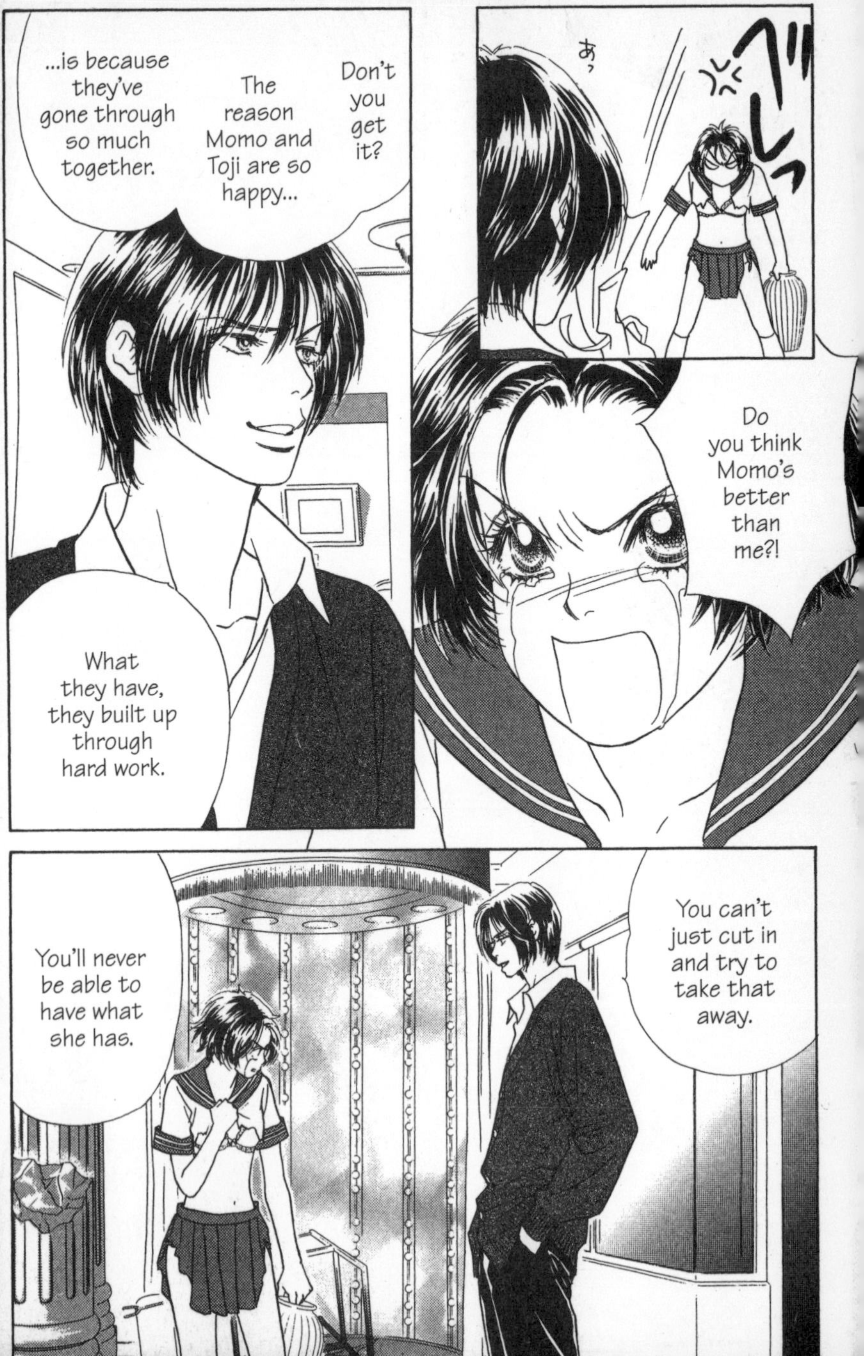
あっ
ベリッ
Do you think Momo's better than me?!
Don't you get it?
The reason Momo and Toji are so happy...
...is because they've gone through so much together.
What they have, they built up through hard work.
You can't just cut in and try to take that away.
You'll never be able to have what she has.

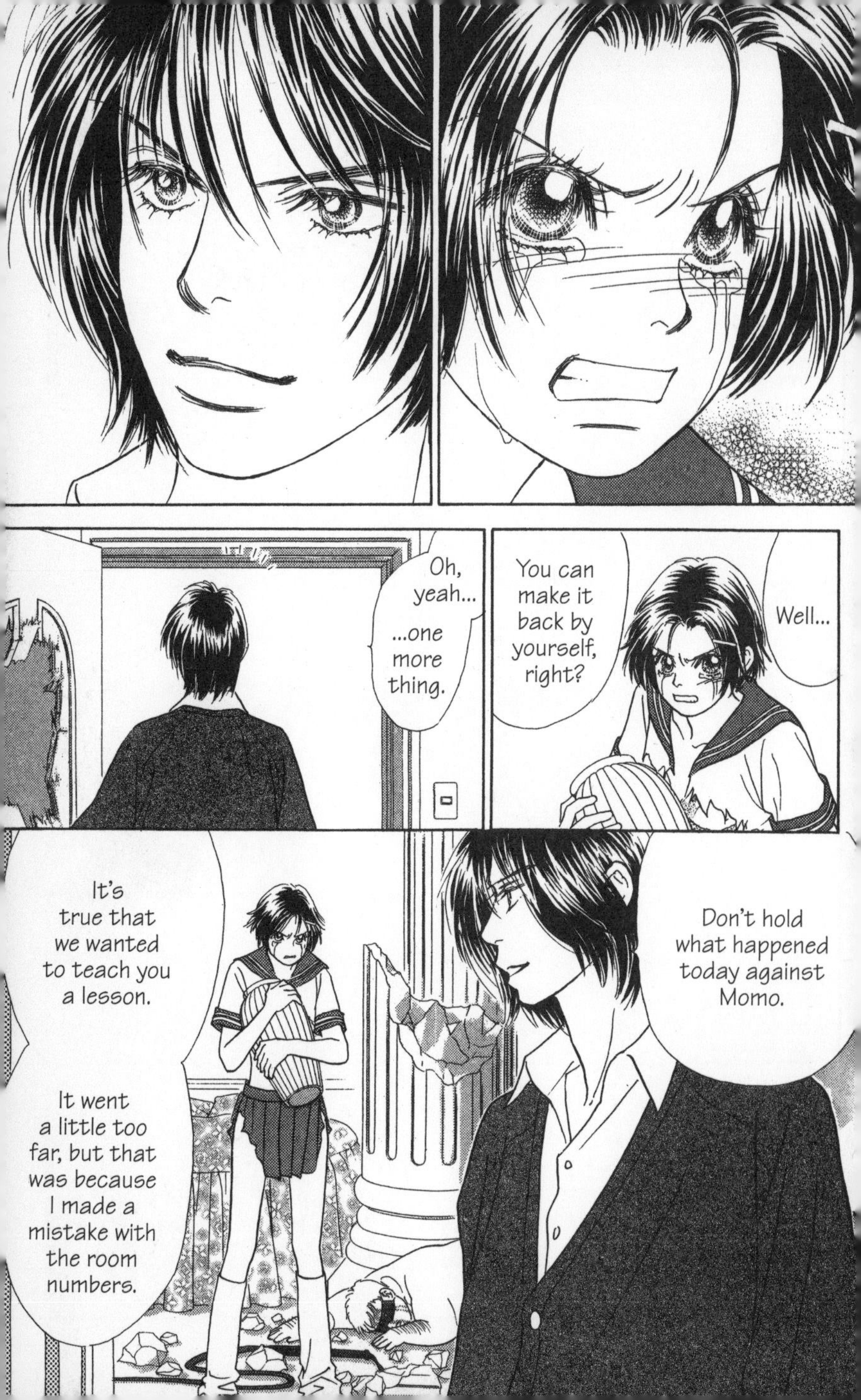
Well...
You can make it back by yourself, right?
Oh, yeah...
...one more thing.
Don't hold what happened today against Momo.
It's true that we wanted to teach you a lesson.
It went a little too far, but that was because I made a mistake with the room numbers.

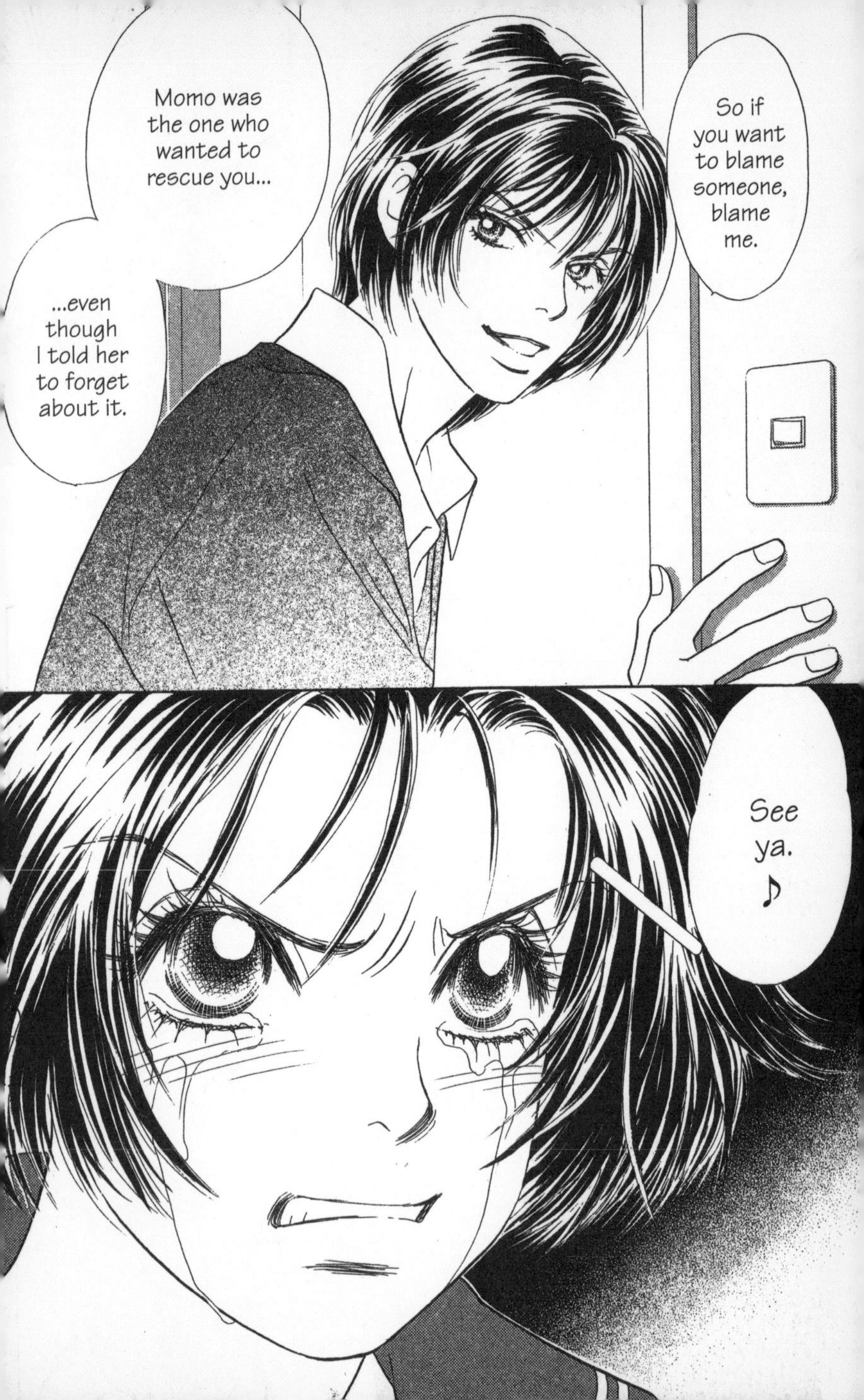
Momo was the one who wanted to rescue you...
...even though I told her to forget about it.
So if you want to blame someone, blame me.
See ya. ♪

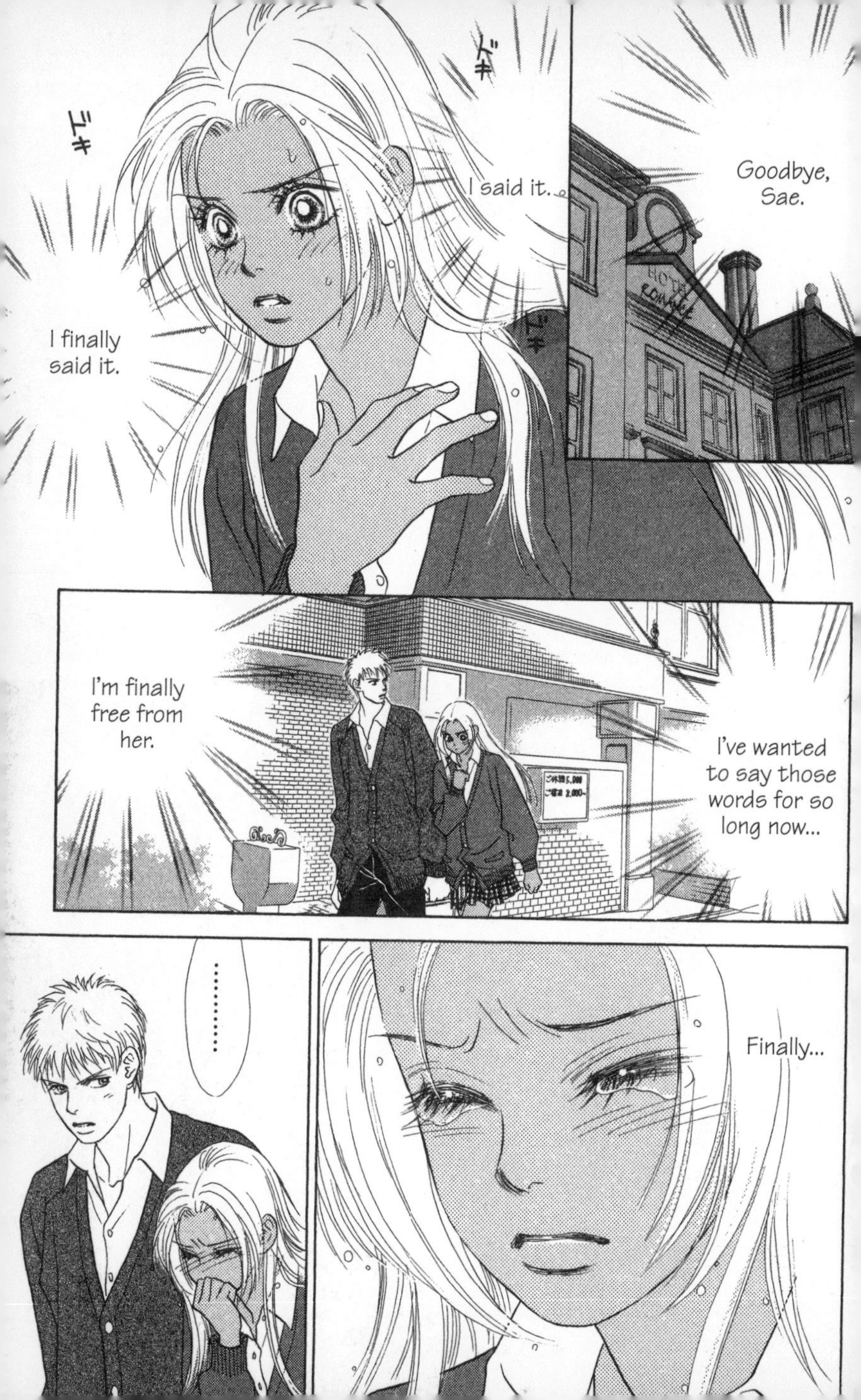
Goodbye, Sae.
ドキ
ドキ
I said it.
I finally said it.
ドキ
I've wanted to say those words for so long now...
I'm finally free from her.
Finally...
....

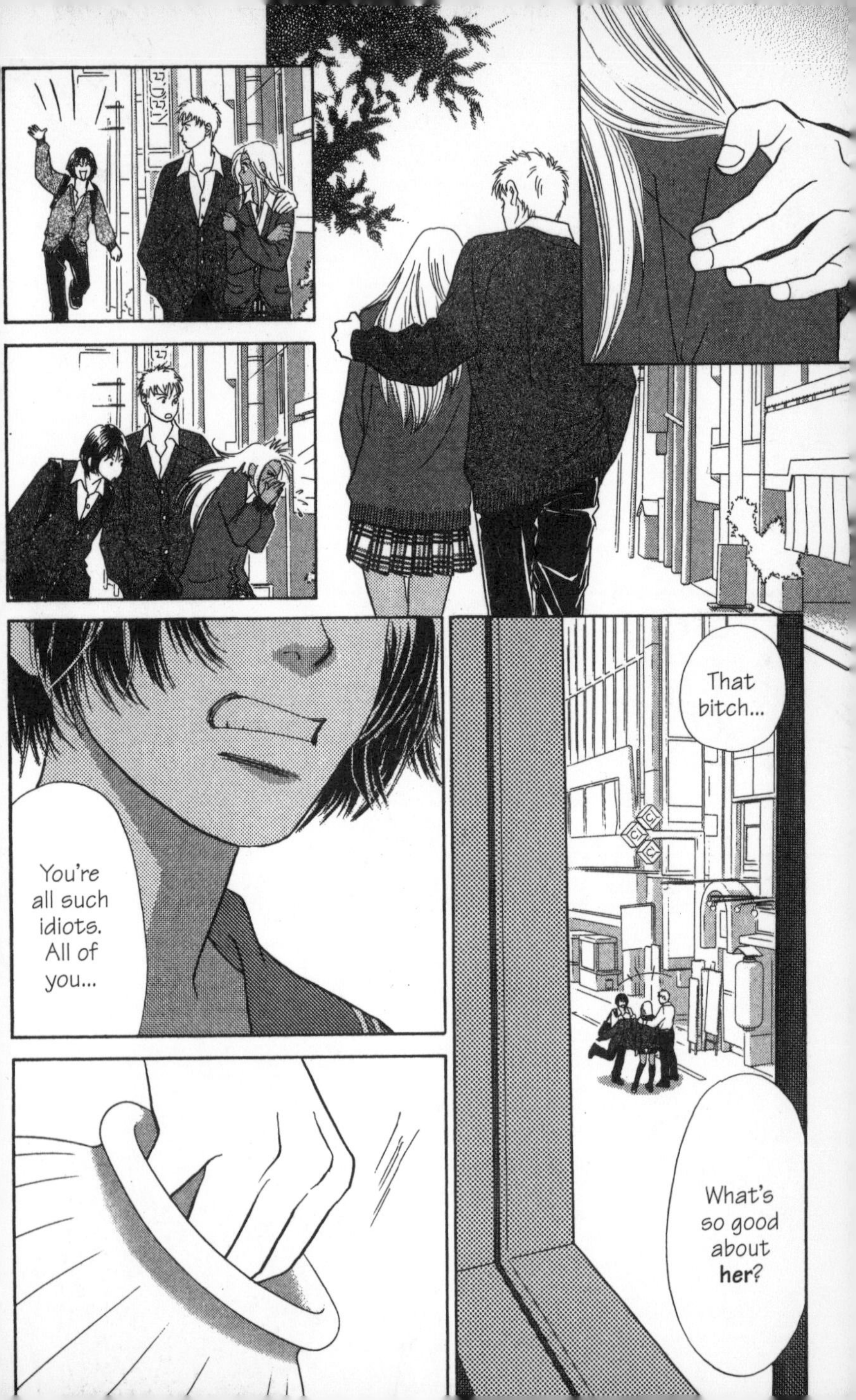
That bitch...
What's so good about **her**?
You're all such idiots. All of you...

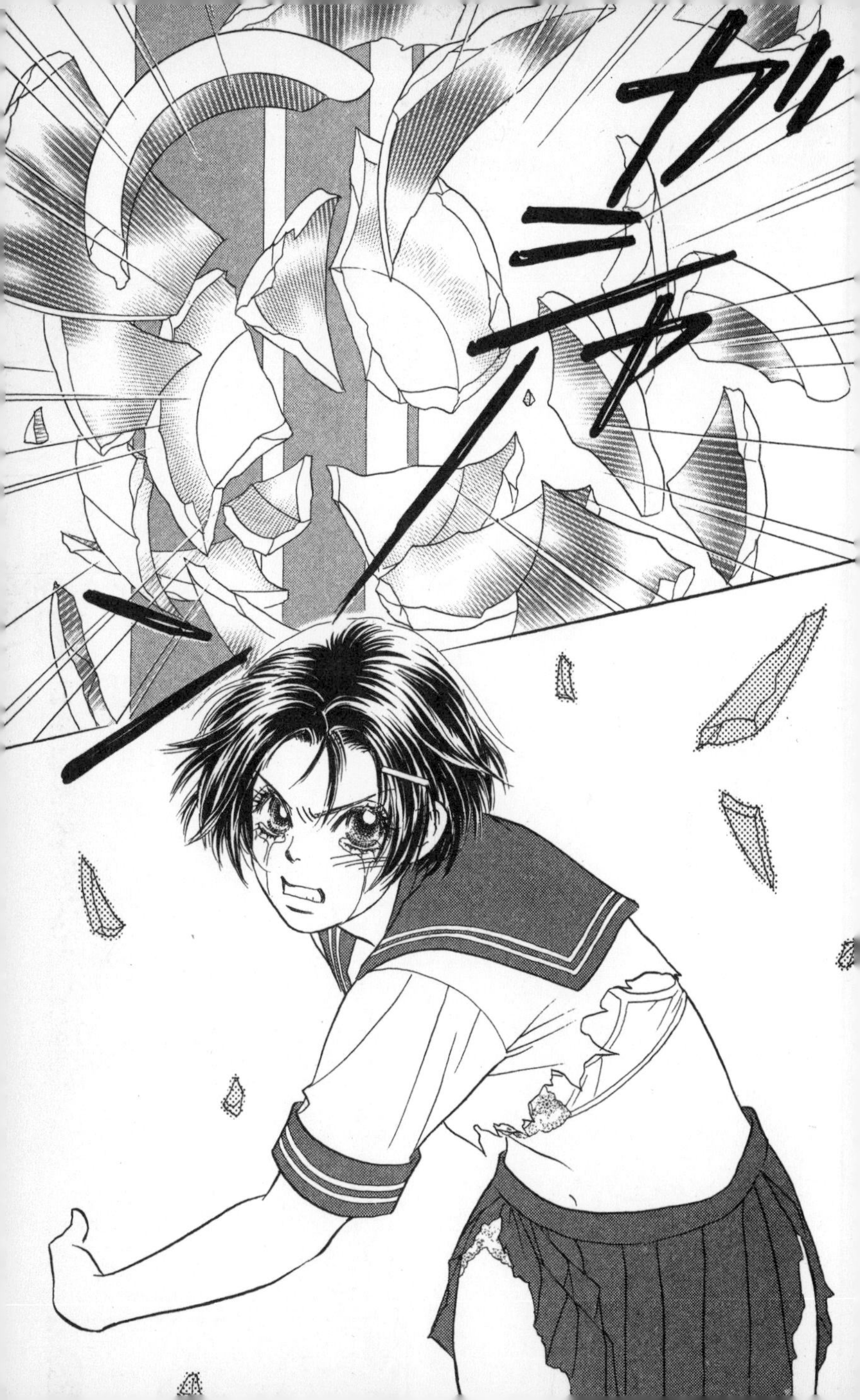
ガシャーン

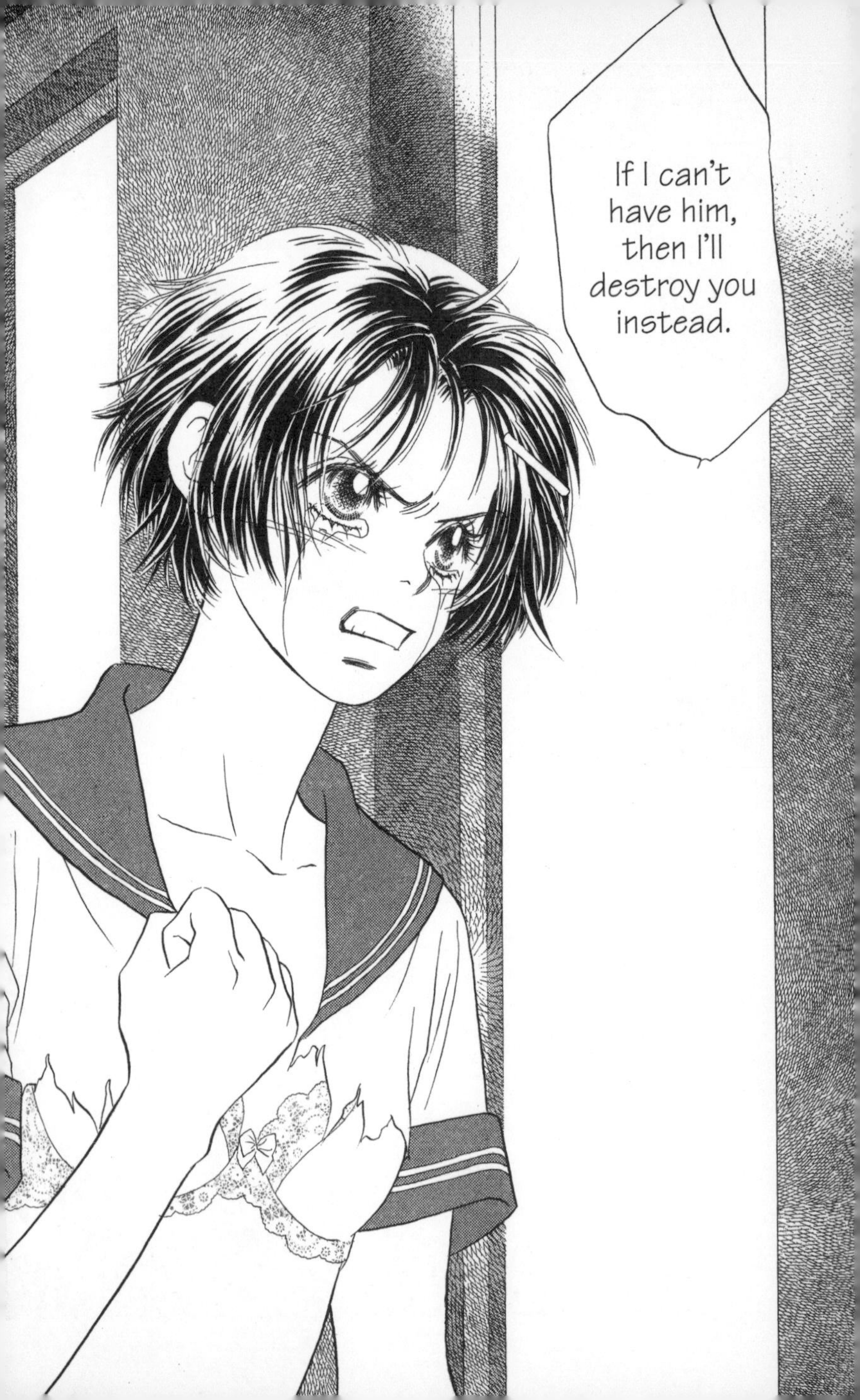
If I can't have him, then I'll destroy you instead.

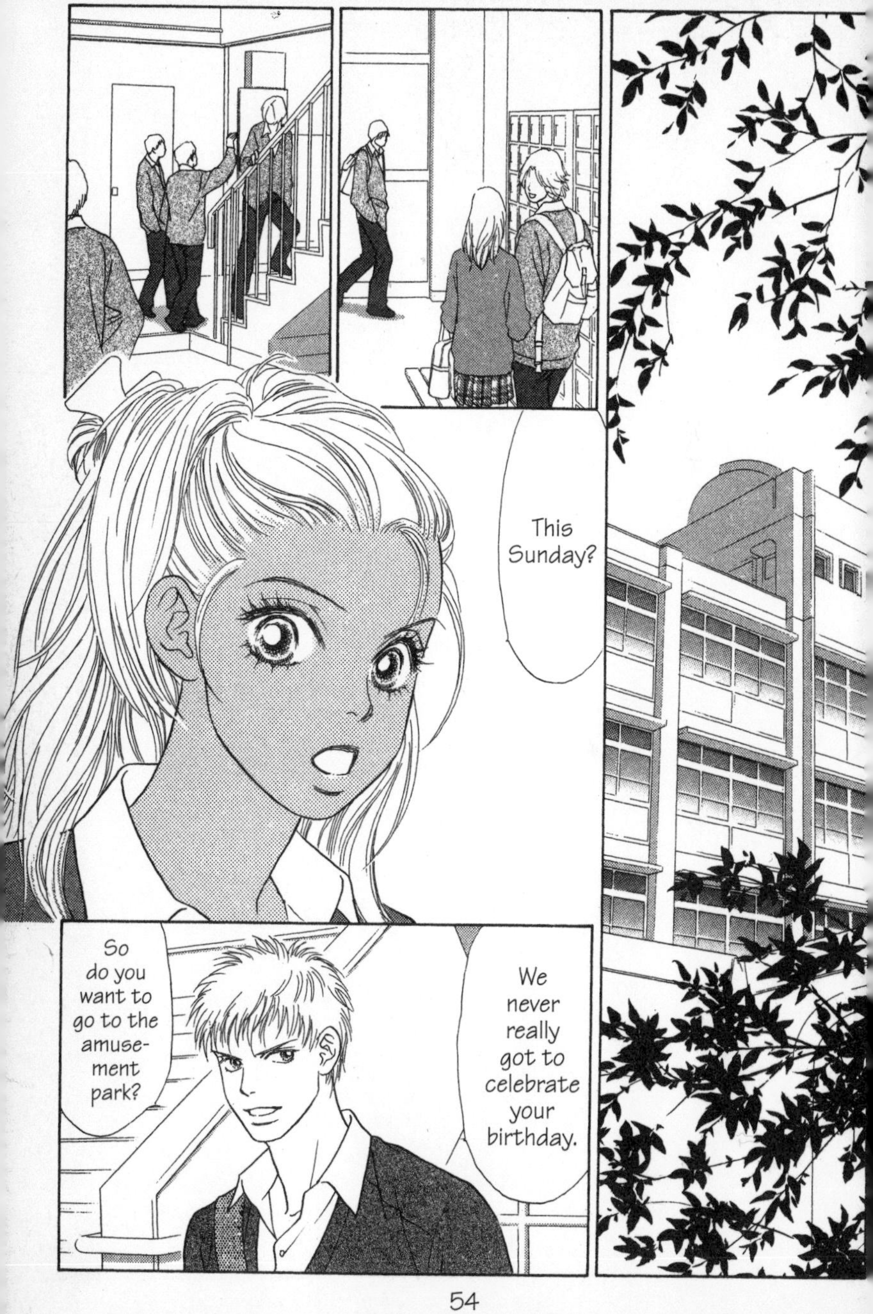

This Sunday?
We never really got to celebrate your birthday.
So do you want to go to the amusement park?

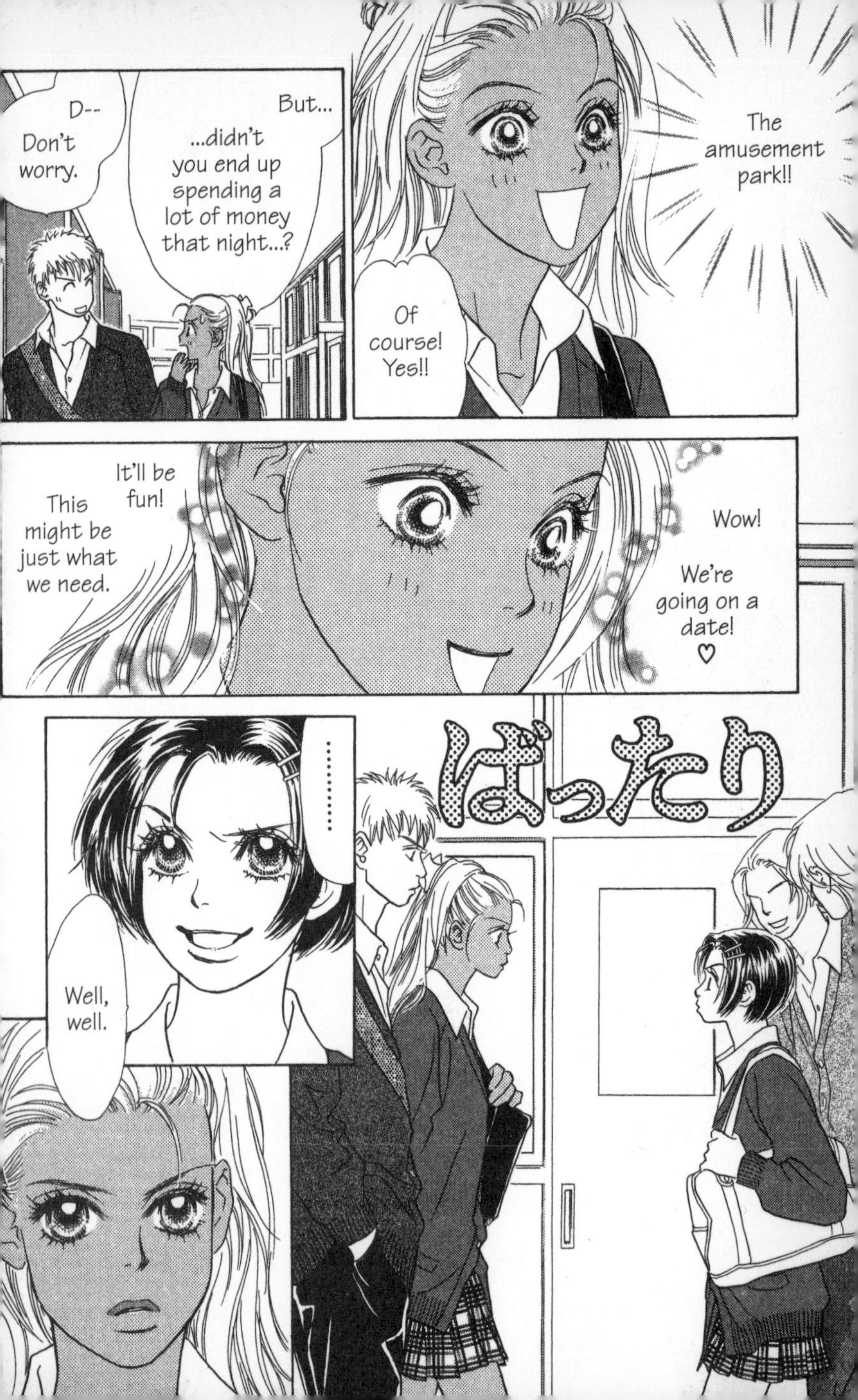
The amusement park!!
Of course! Yes!!
But...
...didn't you end up spending a lot of money that night...?
D-- Don't worry.
Wow!
We're going on a date! ♡
It'll be fun!
This might be just what we need.
ぱったり
......
Well, well.

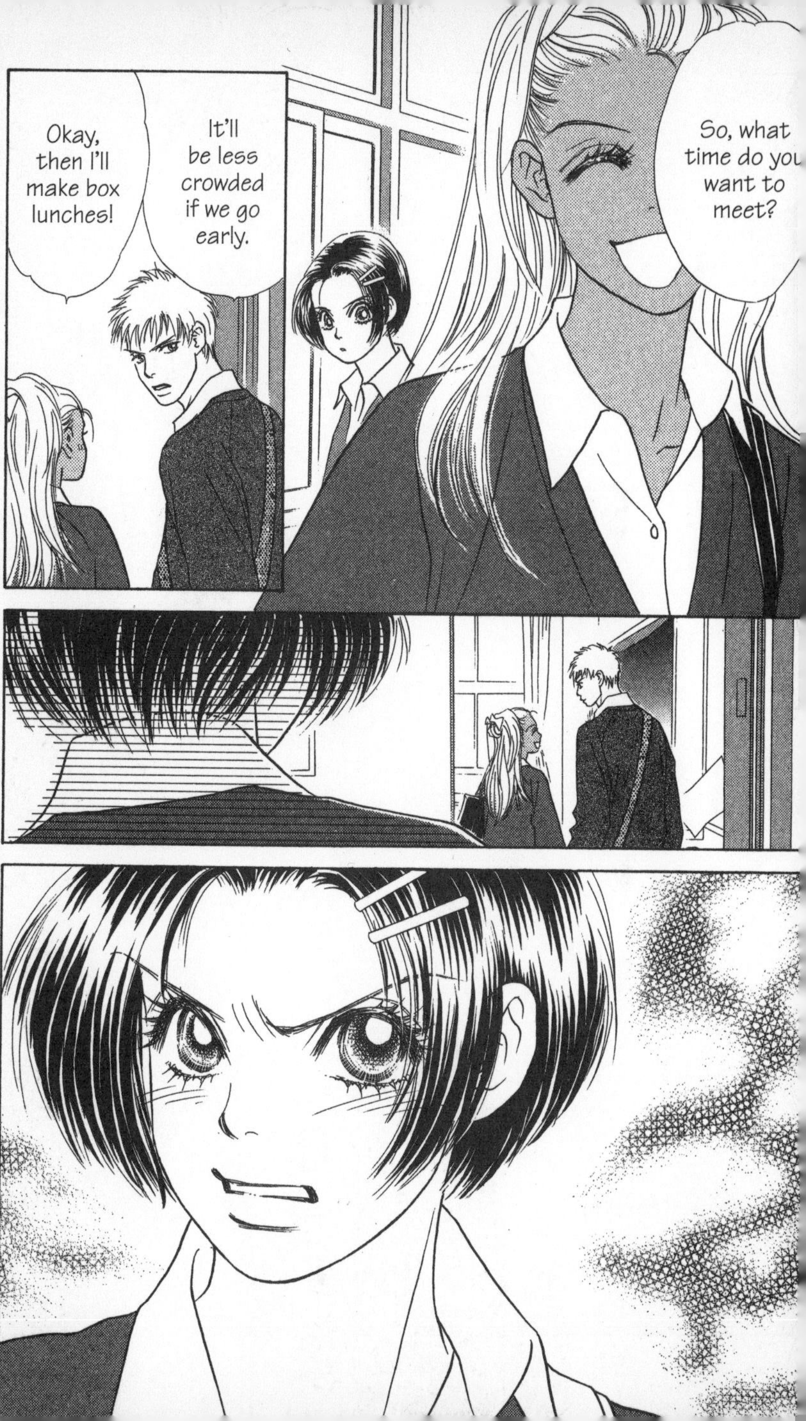
So, what time do you want to meet?
It'll be less crowded if we go early.
Okay, then I'll make box lunches!

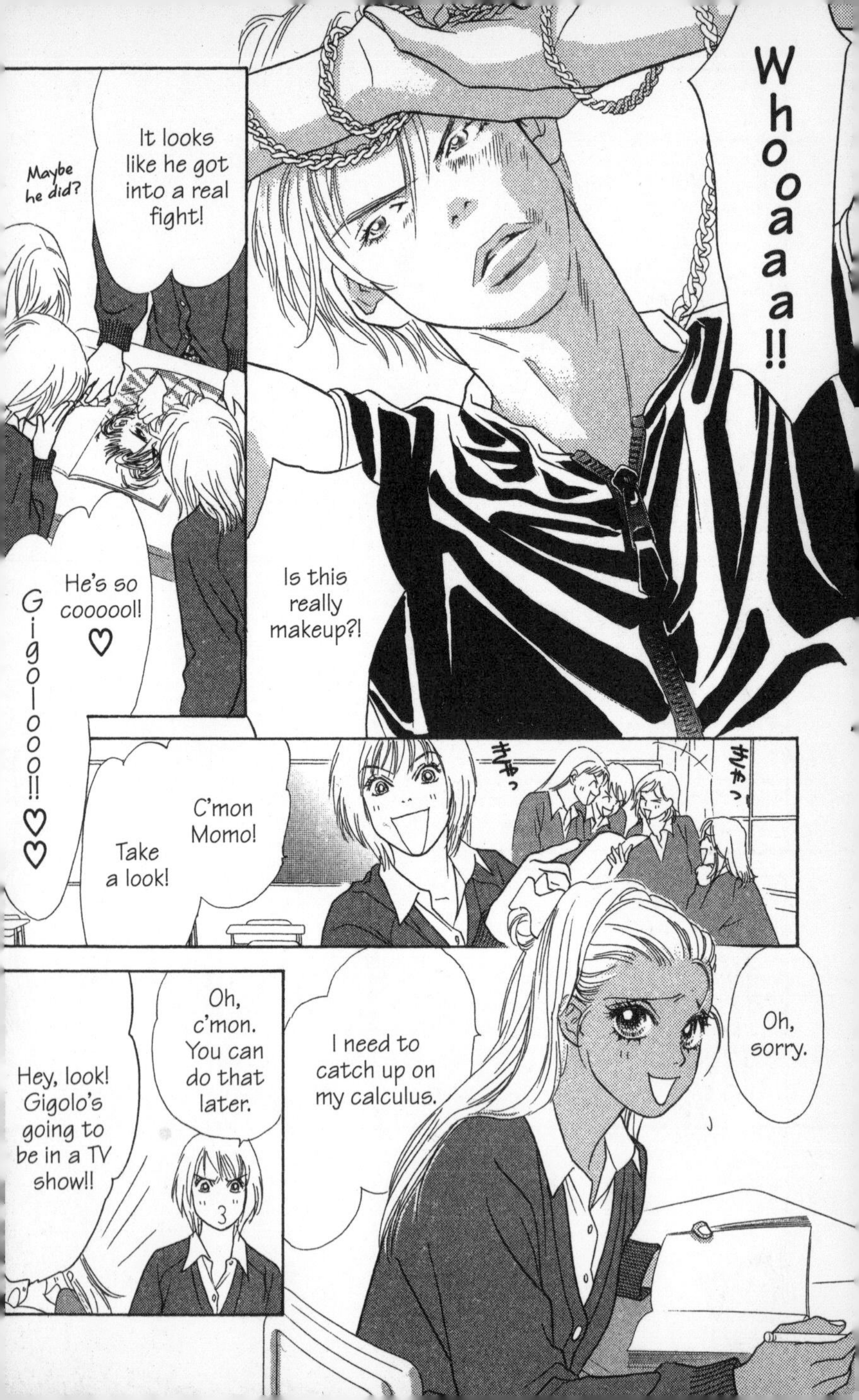
Whooaaa!!
Is this really makeup?!
It looks like he got into a real fight!
Maybe he did?
He's so coooool! ♡
Gigolooo!! ♡♡
きゃっ
きゃっ
C'mon Momo!
Take a look!
Oh, sorry.
I need to catch up on my calculus.
Oh, c'mon. You can do that later.
Hey, look! Gigolo's going to be in a TV show!!

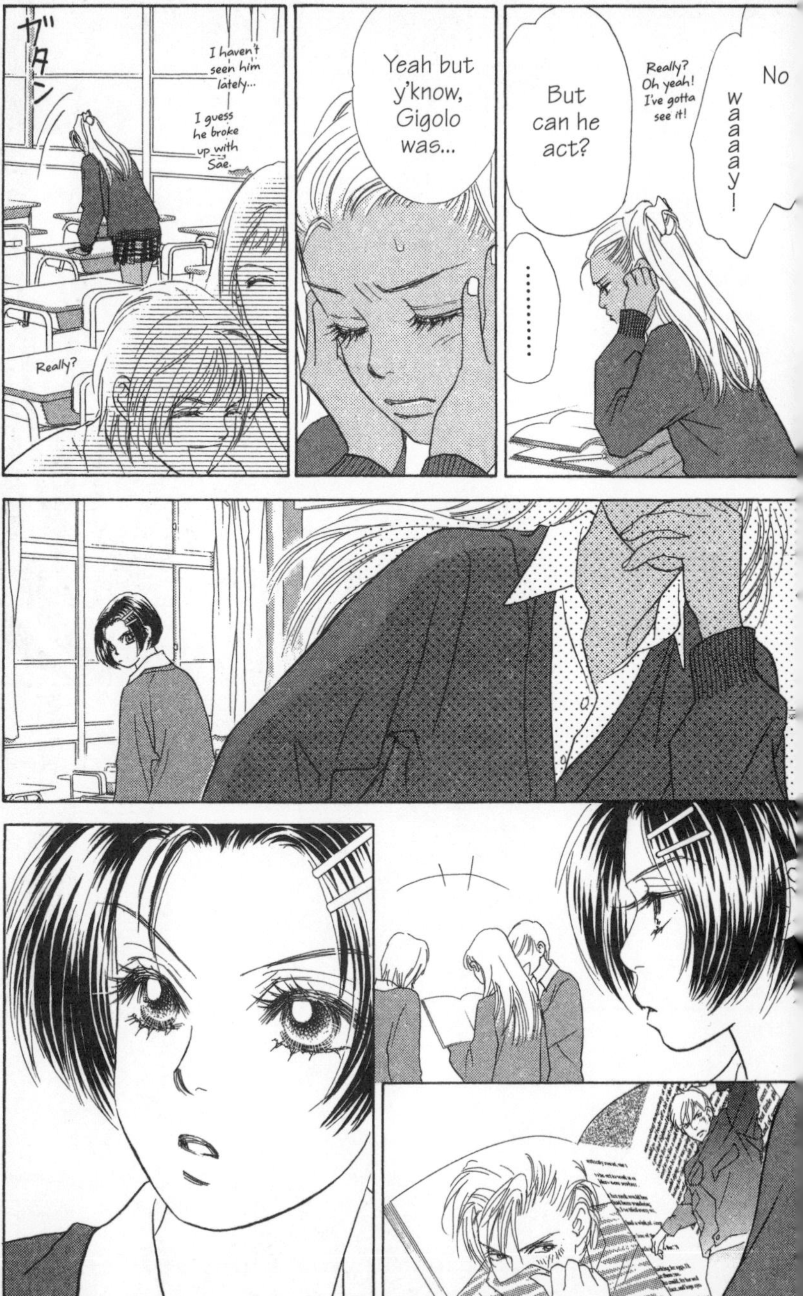
No waaaaay!
Really? Oh yeah! I've gotta see it!
But can he act?
......
Yeah but y'know, Gigolo was...
ガタン
I haven't seen him lately...
I guess he broke up with Sae.
Really?

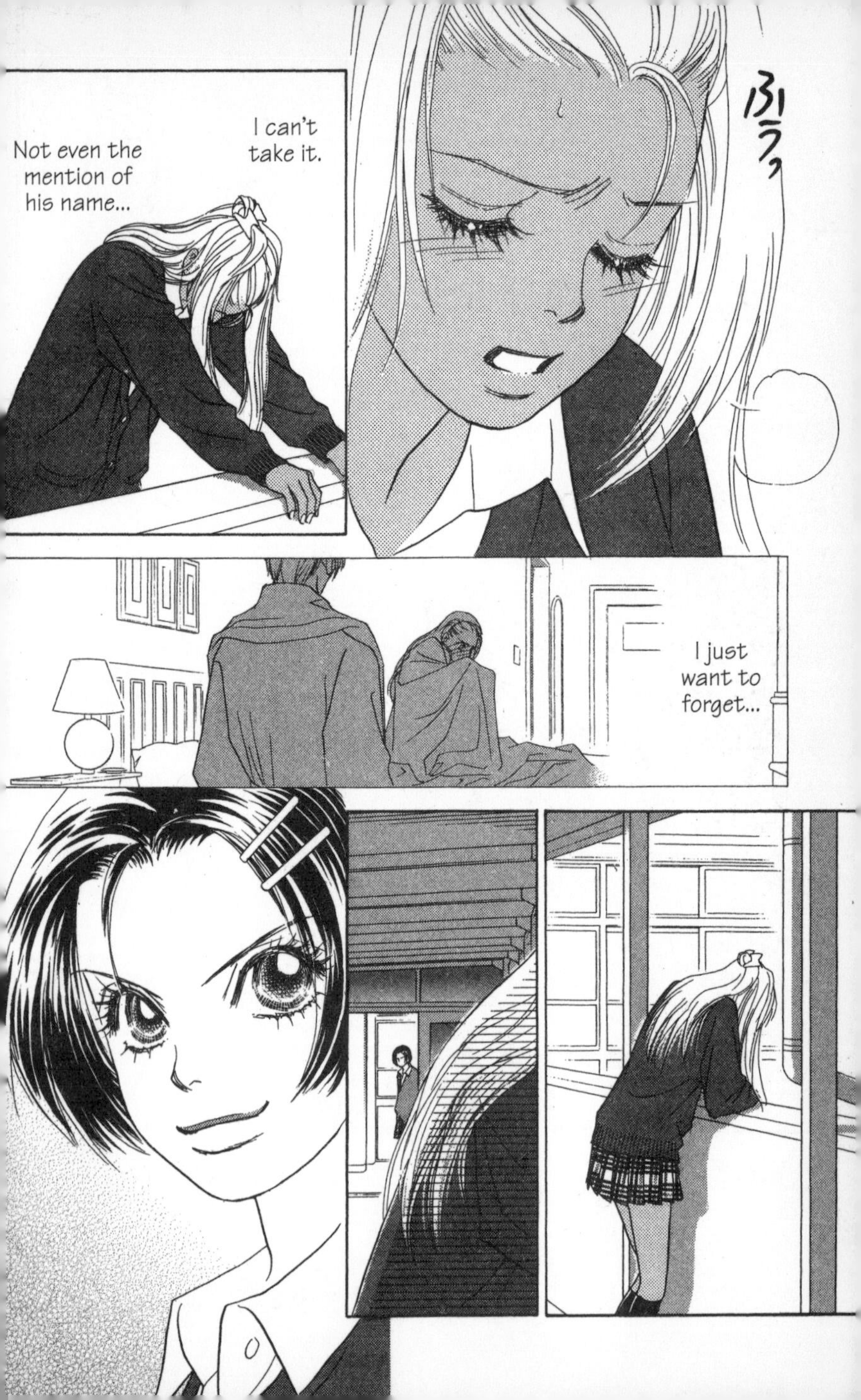
ふらっ
I can't take it.
Not even the mention of his name...
I just want to forget...

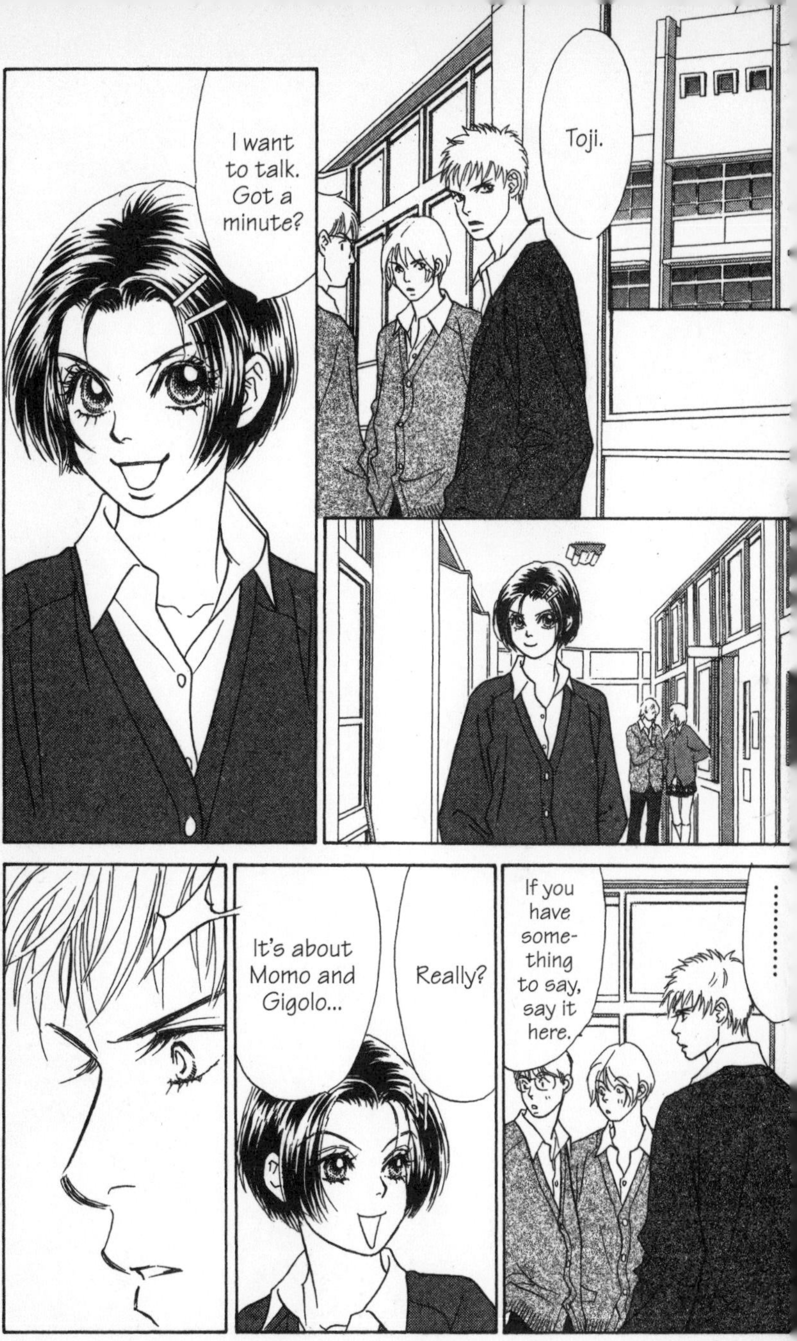
Toji.
I want to talk. Got a minute?
......
If you have some-thing to say, say it here.
Really?
It's about Momo and Gigolo...

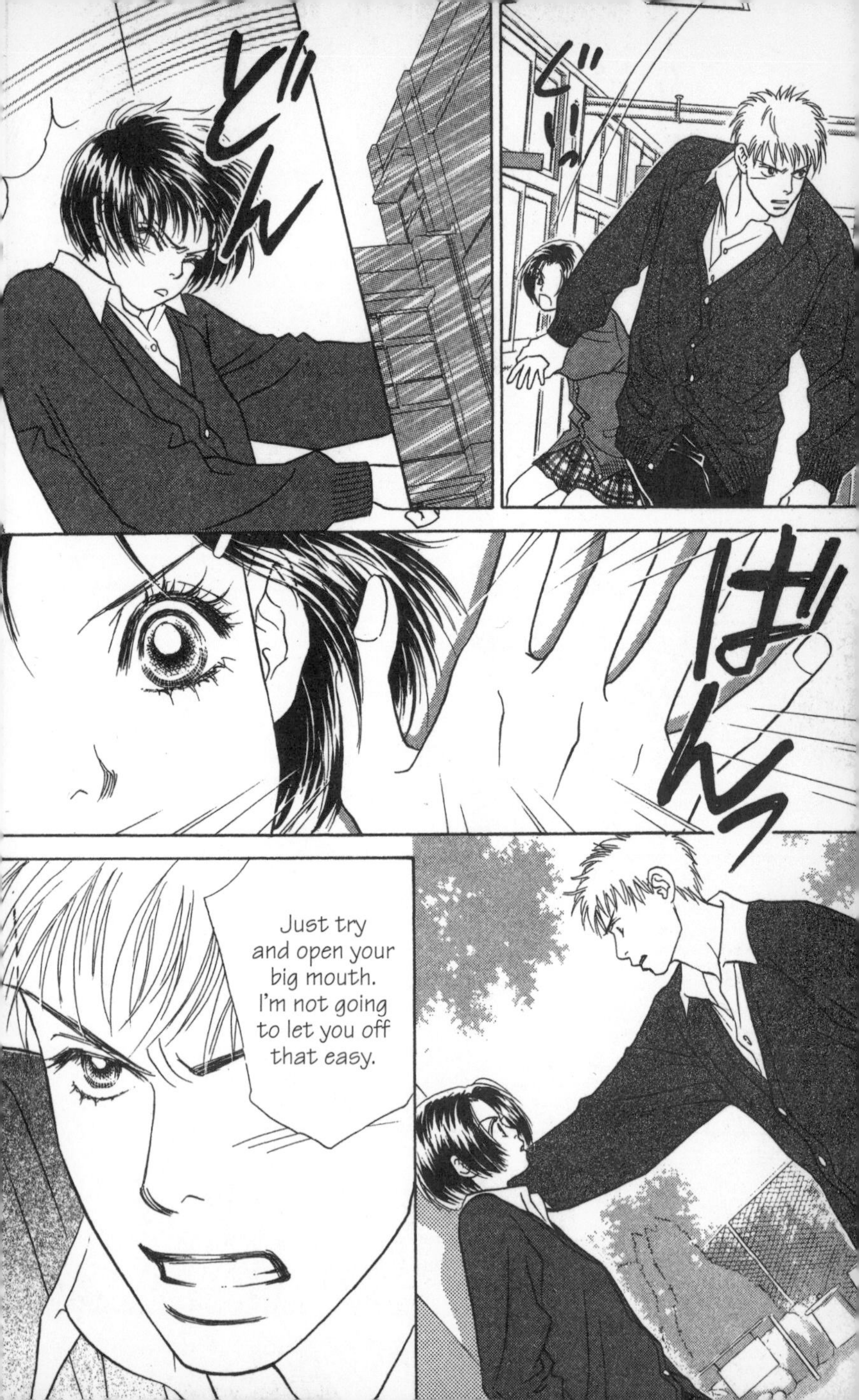
ぐいっ
どん
ばんっ
Just try and open your big mouth. I'm not going to let you off that easy.

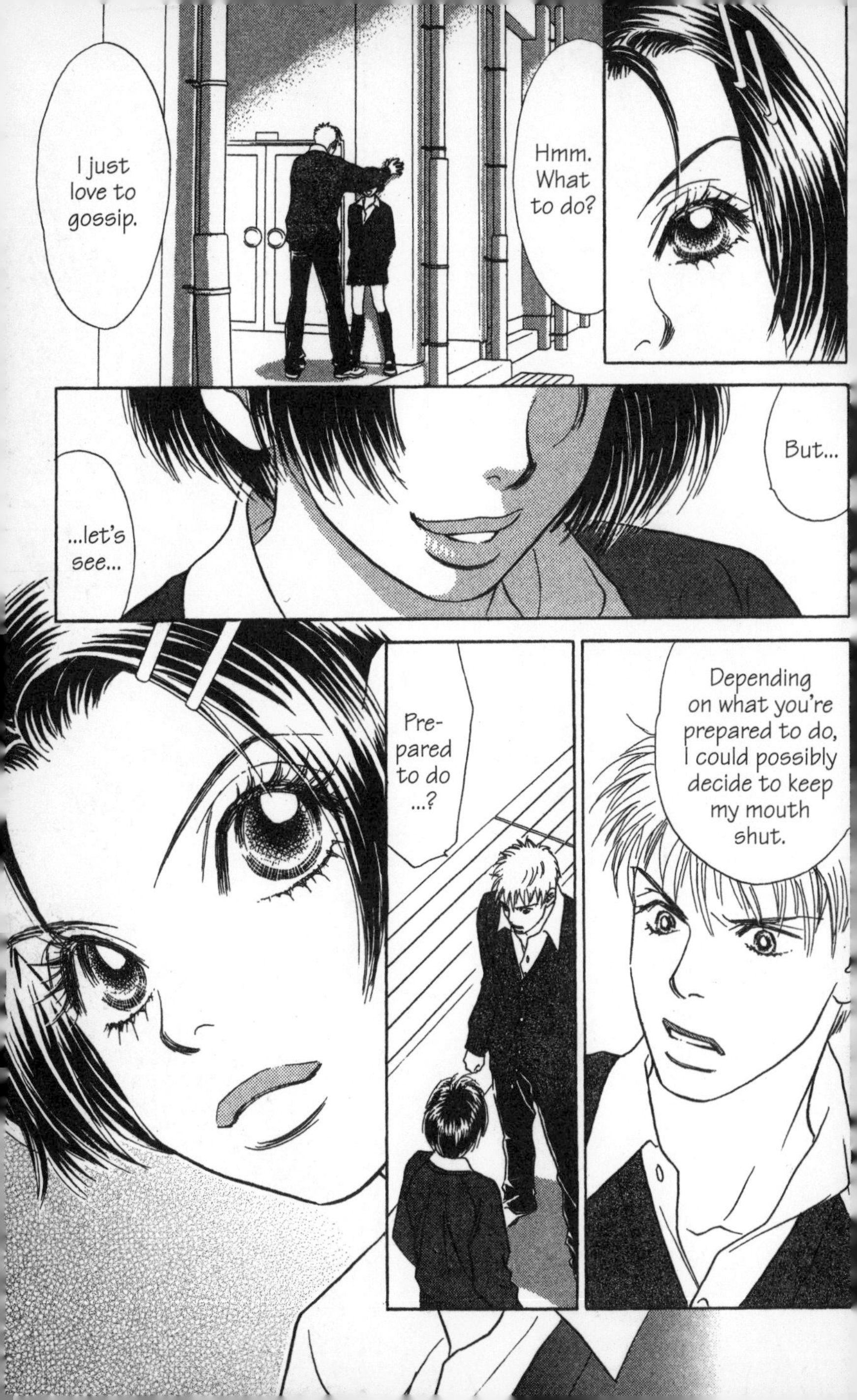
Hmm. What to do?
I just love to gossip.
But...
...let's see...
Depending on what you're prepared to do, I could possibly decide to keep my mouth shut.
Pre-pared to do ...?

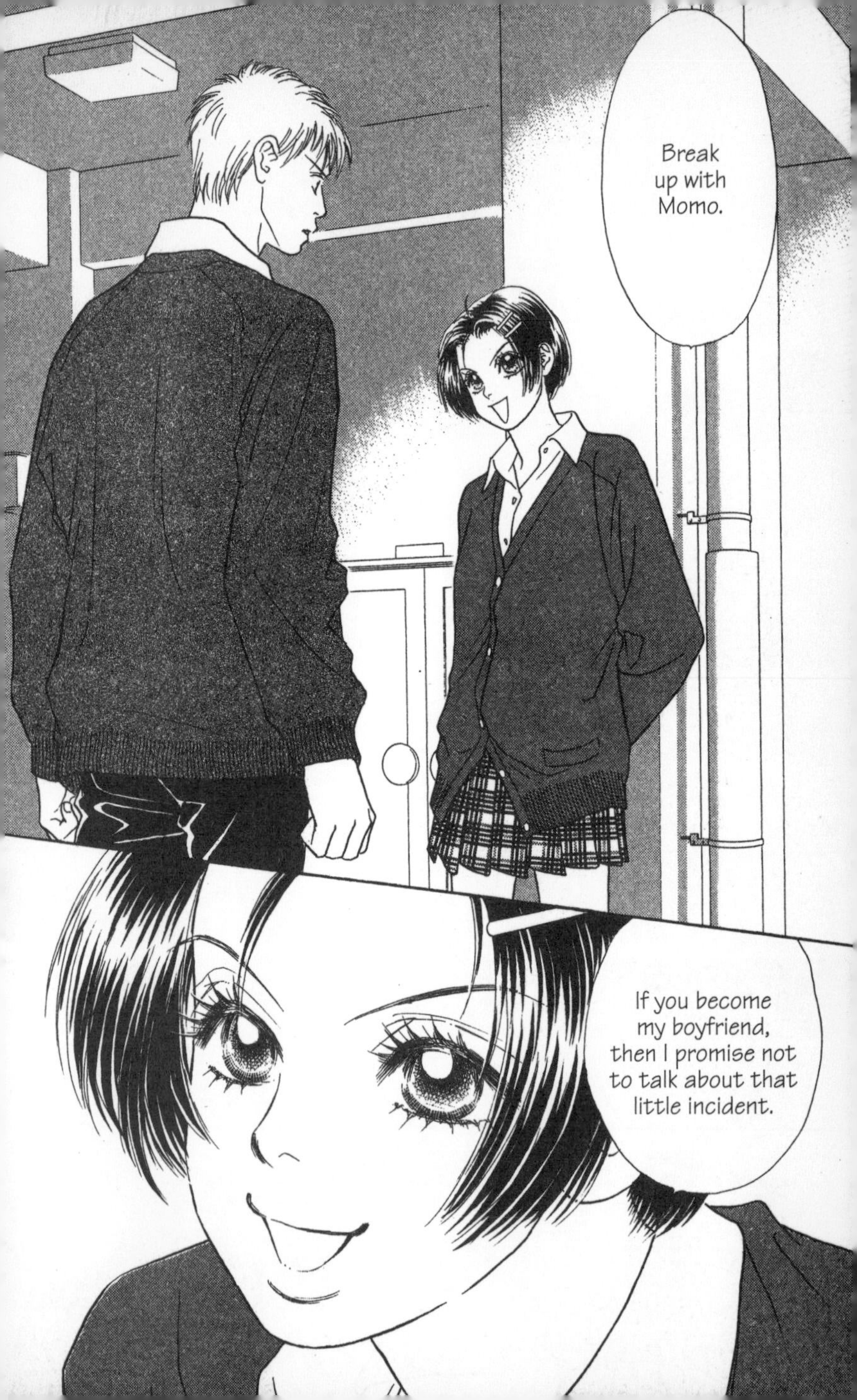
Break up with Momo.
If you become my boyfriend, then I promise not to talk about that little incident.

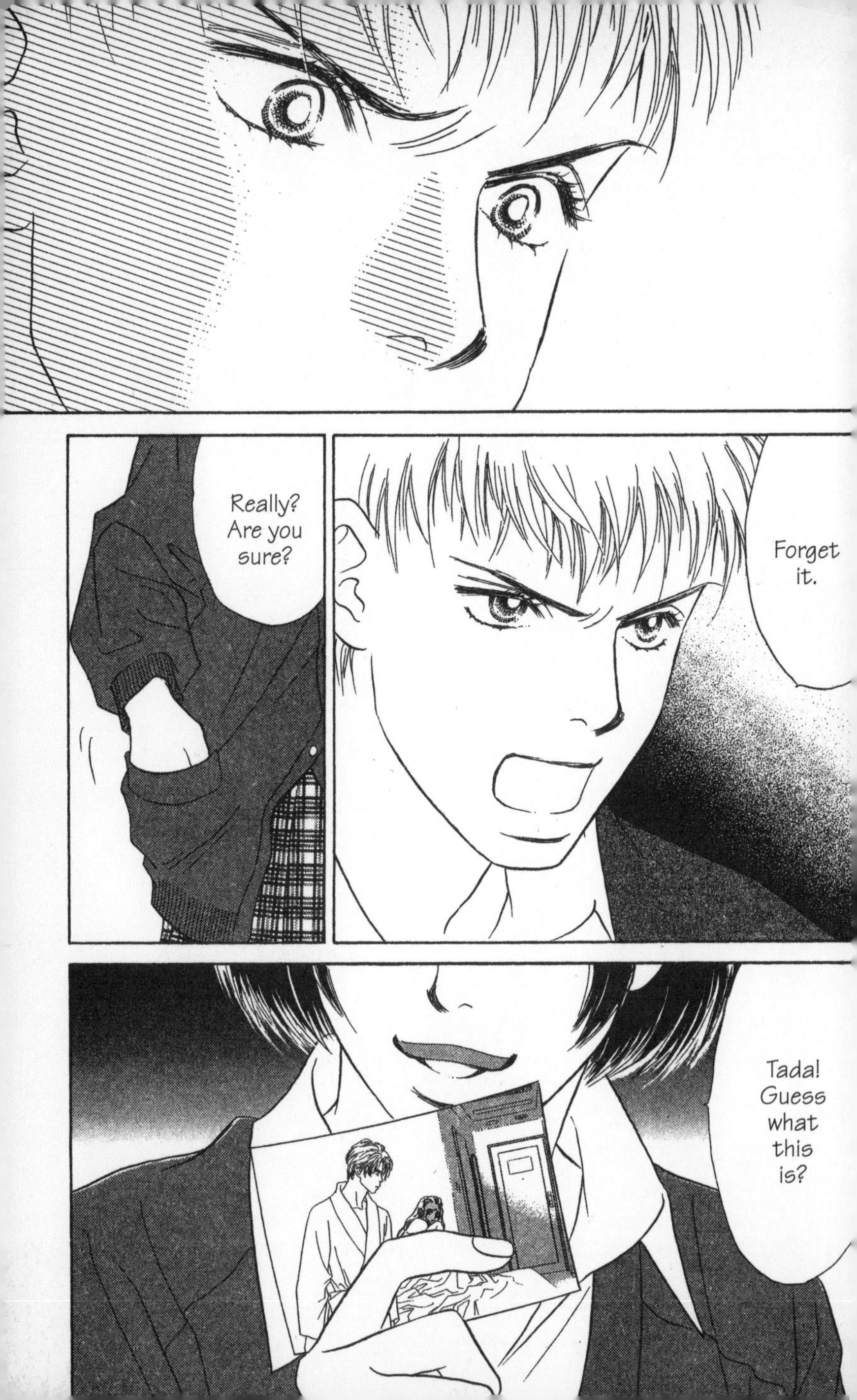
Forget it.
Really? Are you sure?
Tada! Guess what this is?

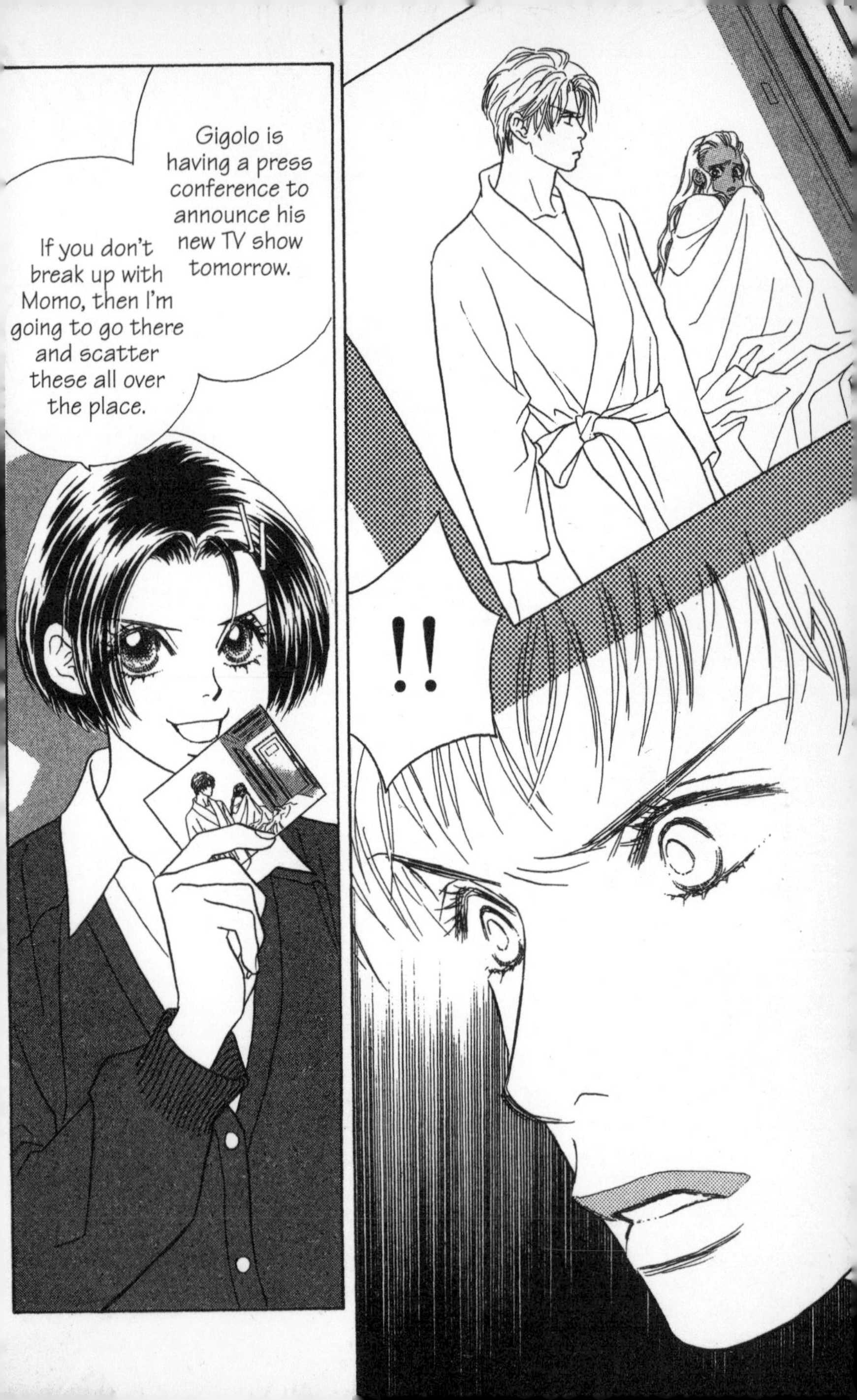
!!
Gigolo is having a press conference to announce his new TV show tomorrow.
If you don't break up with Momo, then I'm going to go there and scatter these all over the place.

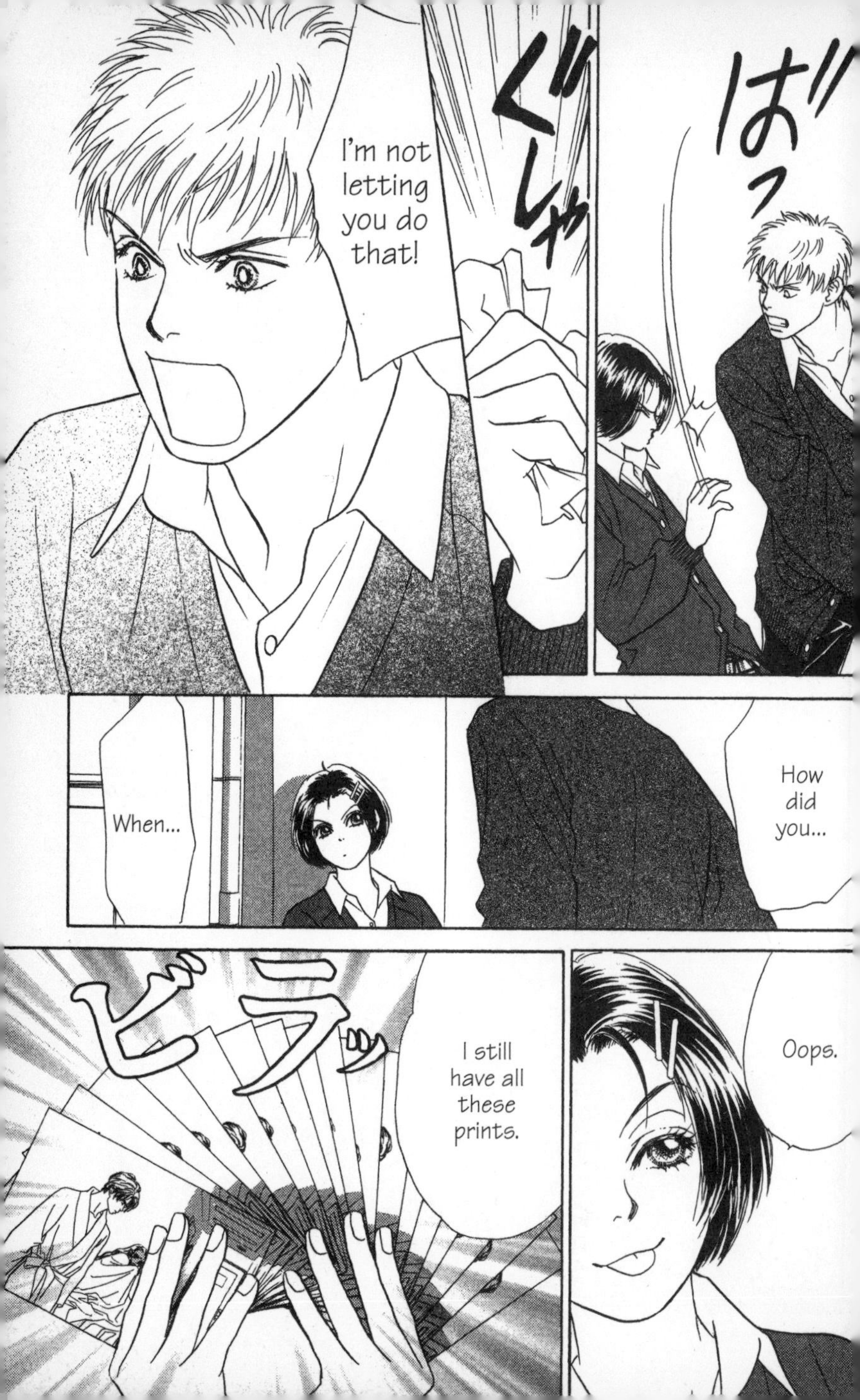
ばっ
ぐしゃ
I'm not letting you do that!
How did you...
When...
Oops.
I still have all these prints.
ビラッ

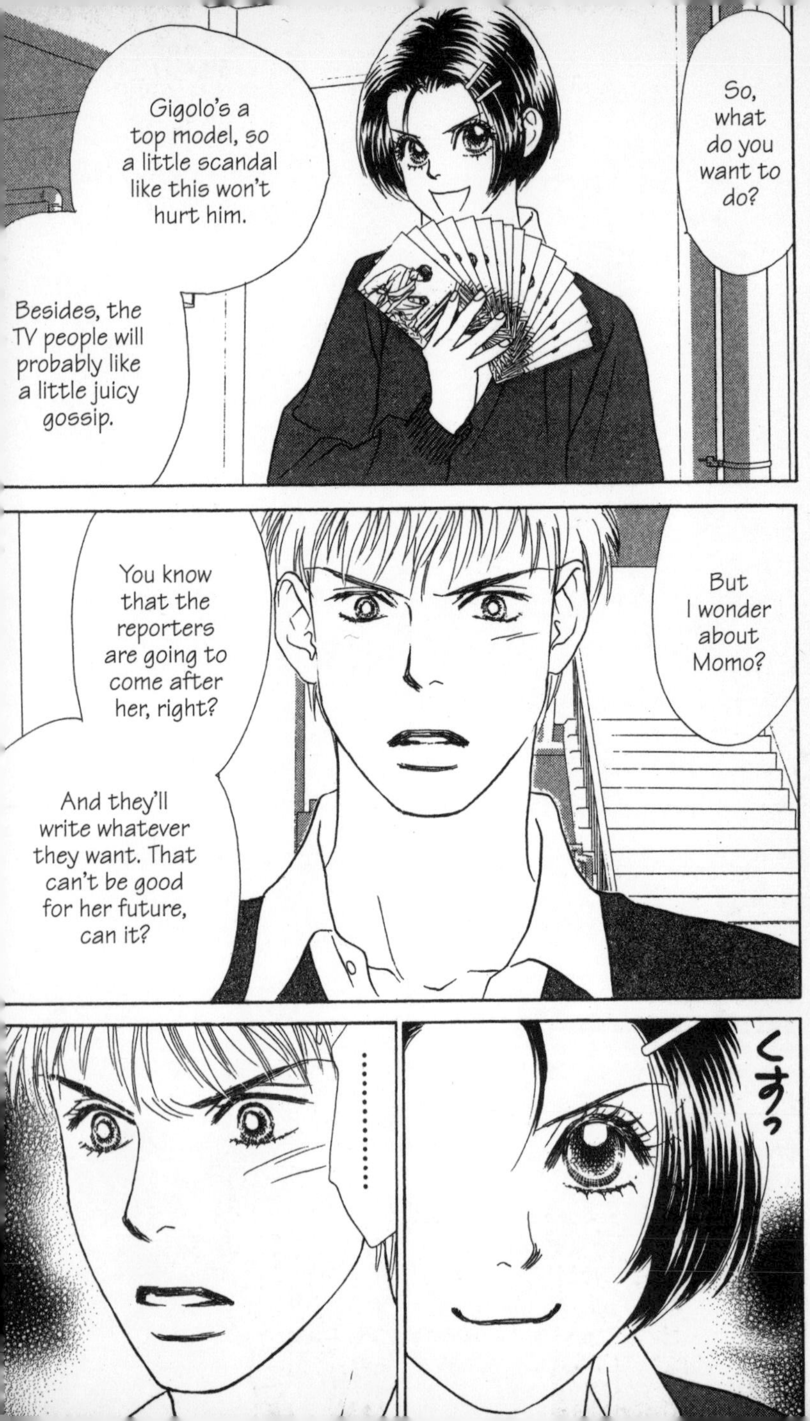
So, what do you want to do?
Gigolo's a top model, so a little scandal like this won't hurt him.
Besides, the TV people will probably like a little juicy gossip.
But I wonder about Momo?
You know that the reporters are going to come after her, right?
And they'll write whatever they want. That can't be good for her future, can it?
くすっ
....

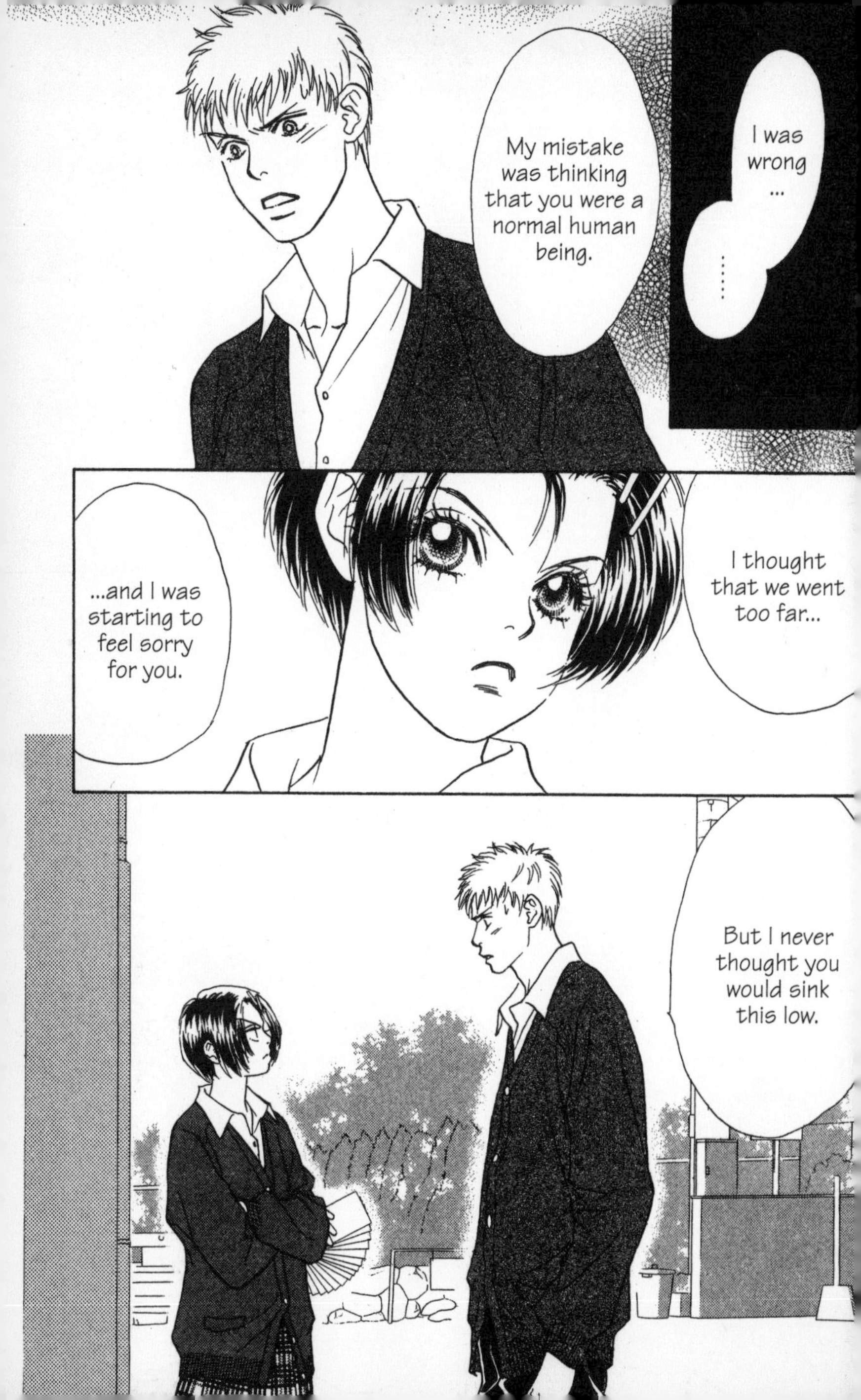
I was wrong ...
......
My mistake was thinking that you were a normal human being.
I thought that we went too far...
...and I was starting to feel sorry for you.
But I never thought you would sink this low.

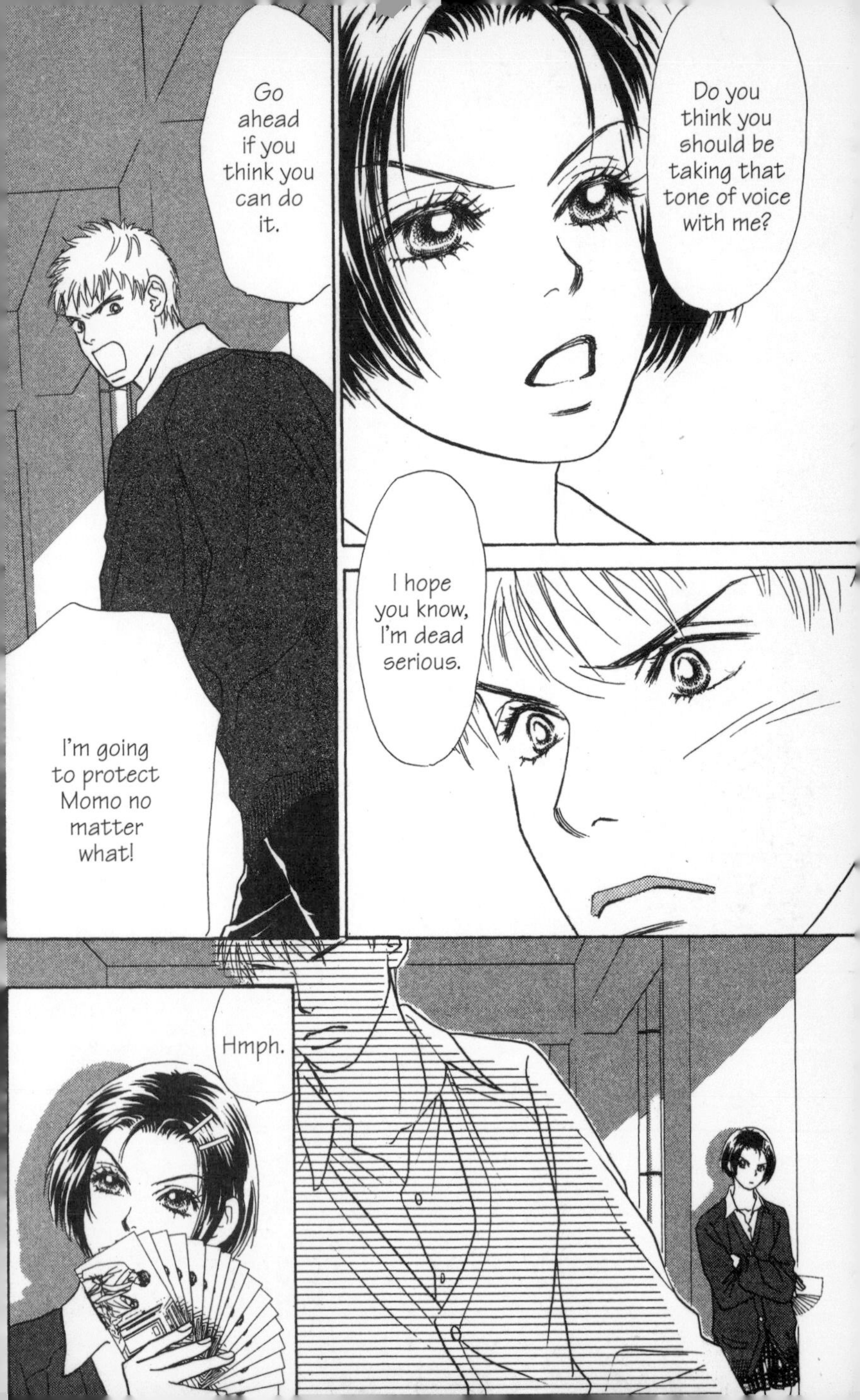
Do you think you should be taking that tone of voice with me?
I hope you know, I'm dead serious.
Go ahead if you think you can do it.
I'm going to protect Momo no matter what!
Hmph.

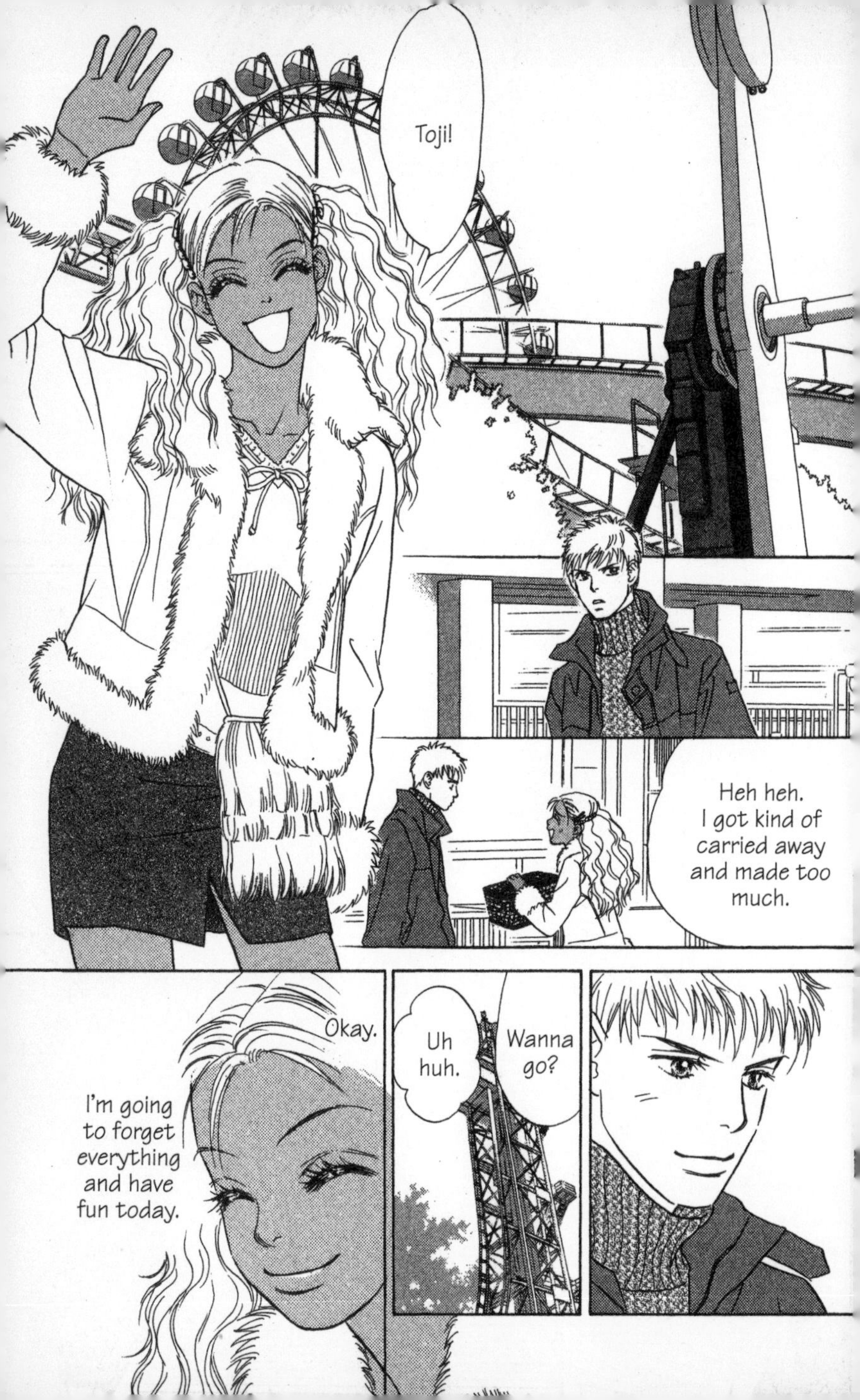
Toji!
Heh heh. I got kind of carried away and made too much.
Wanna go?
Uh huh.
Okay.
I'm going to forget everything and have fun today.

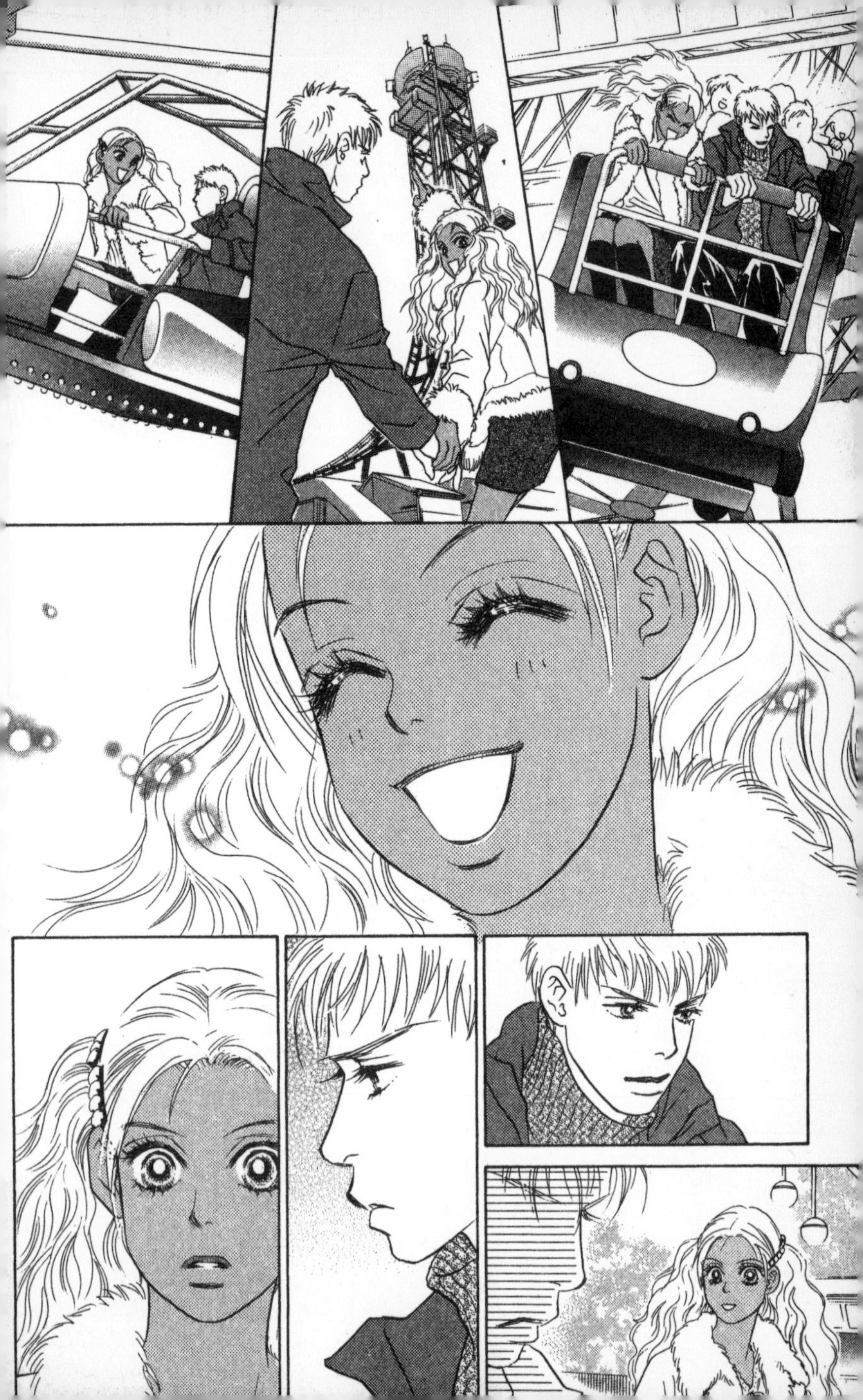

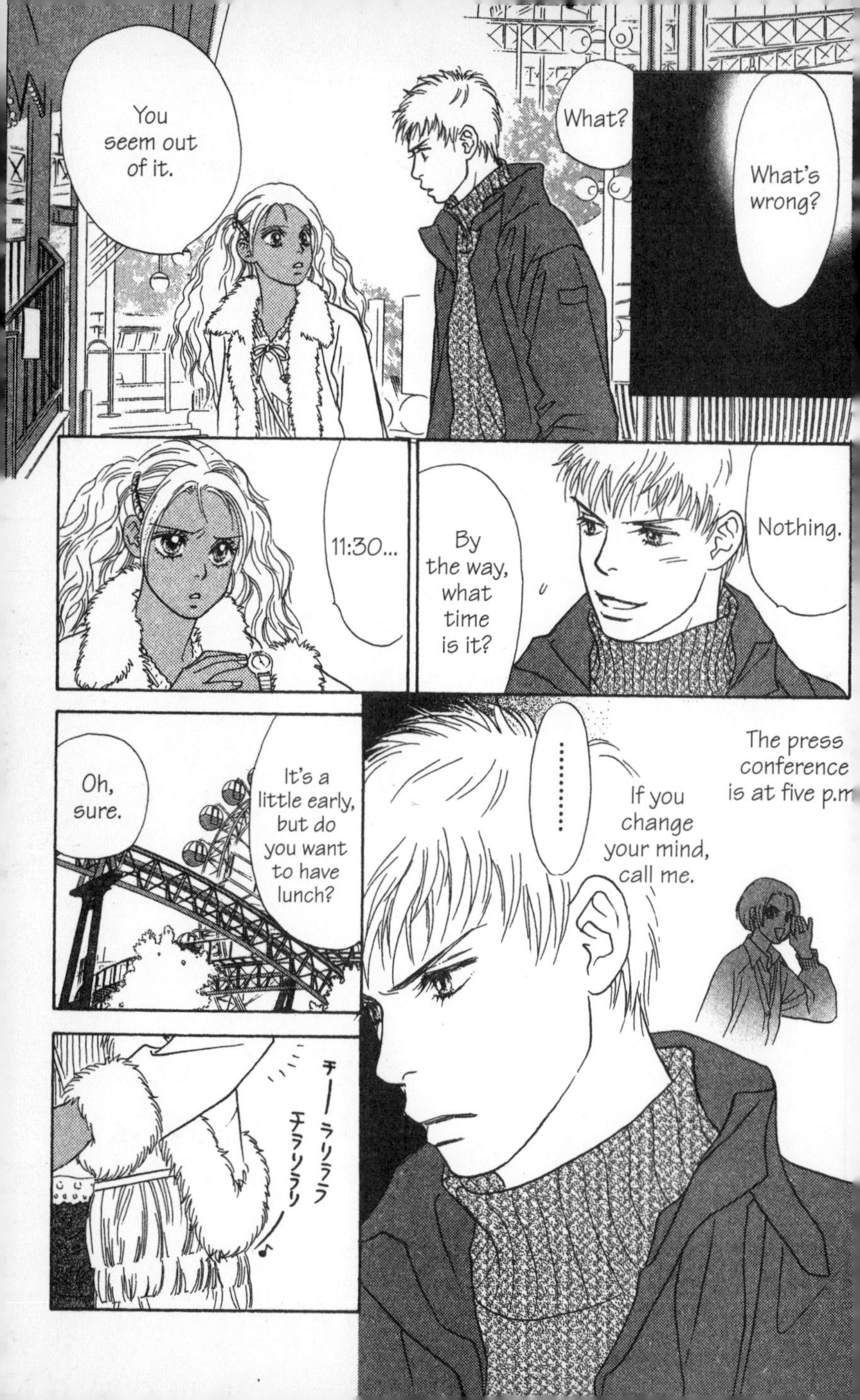
What's wrong?
What?
You seem out of it.
Nothing.
By the way, what time is it?
11:30...
The press conference is at five p.m
If you change your mind, call me.
....
It's a little early, but do you want to have lunch?
Oh, sure.
チーラリララ
チラリラリ

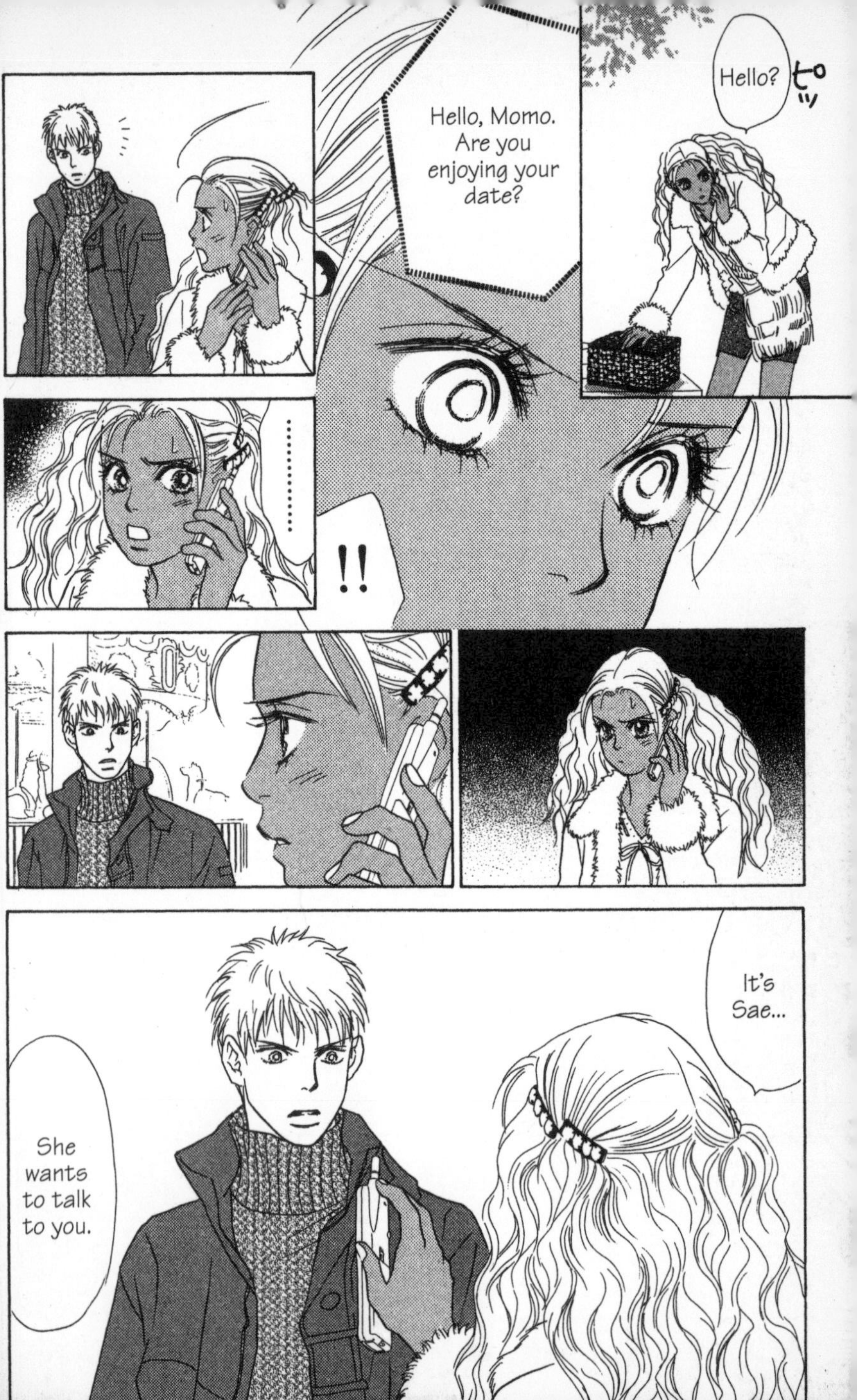
Hello?
ピッ
Hello, Momo. Are you enjoying your date?
!!
......
It's Sae...
She wants to talk to you.

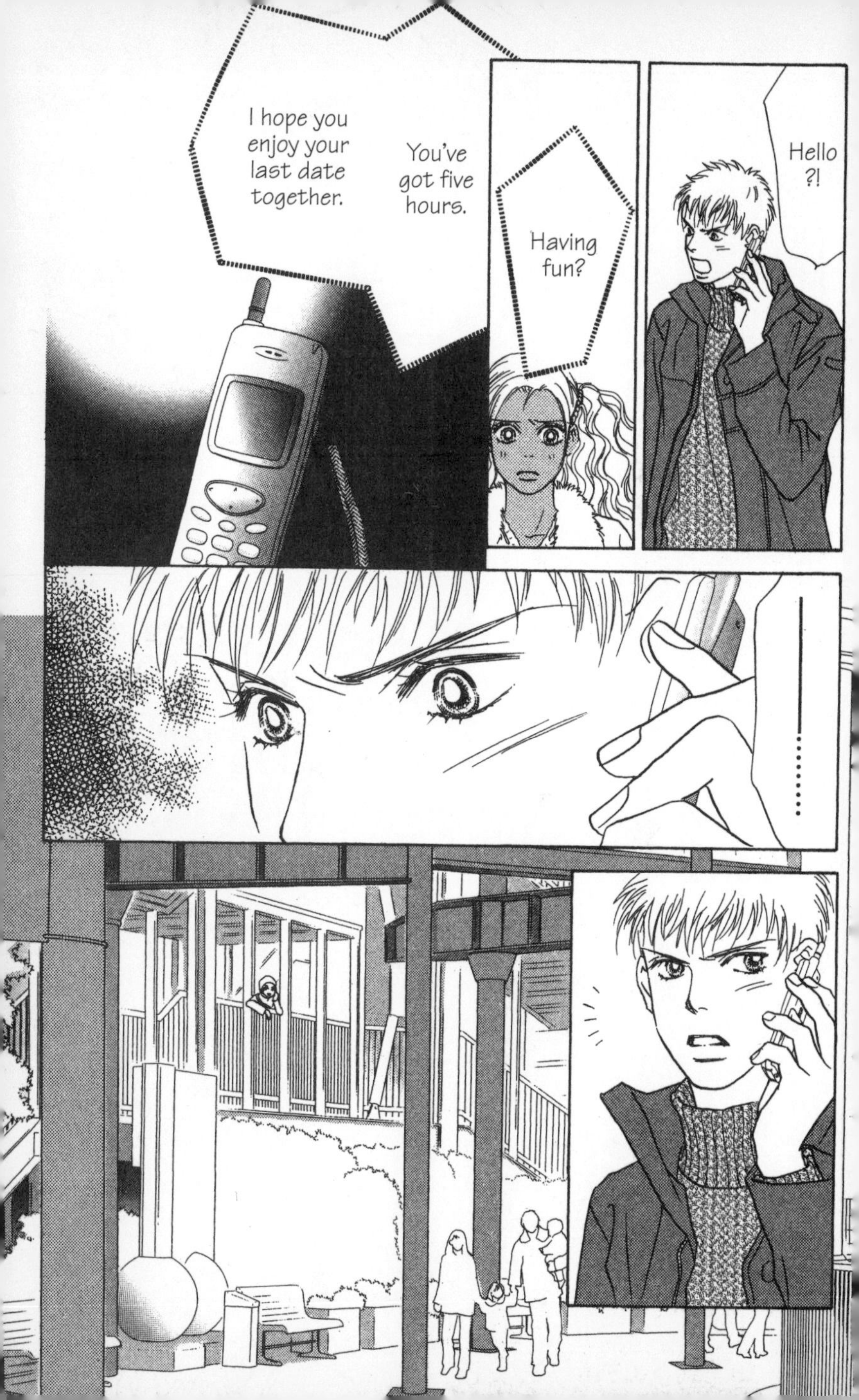
Hello ?!
Having fun?
You've got five hours.
I hope you enjoy your last date together.
......

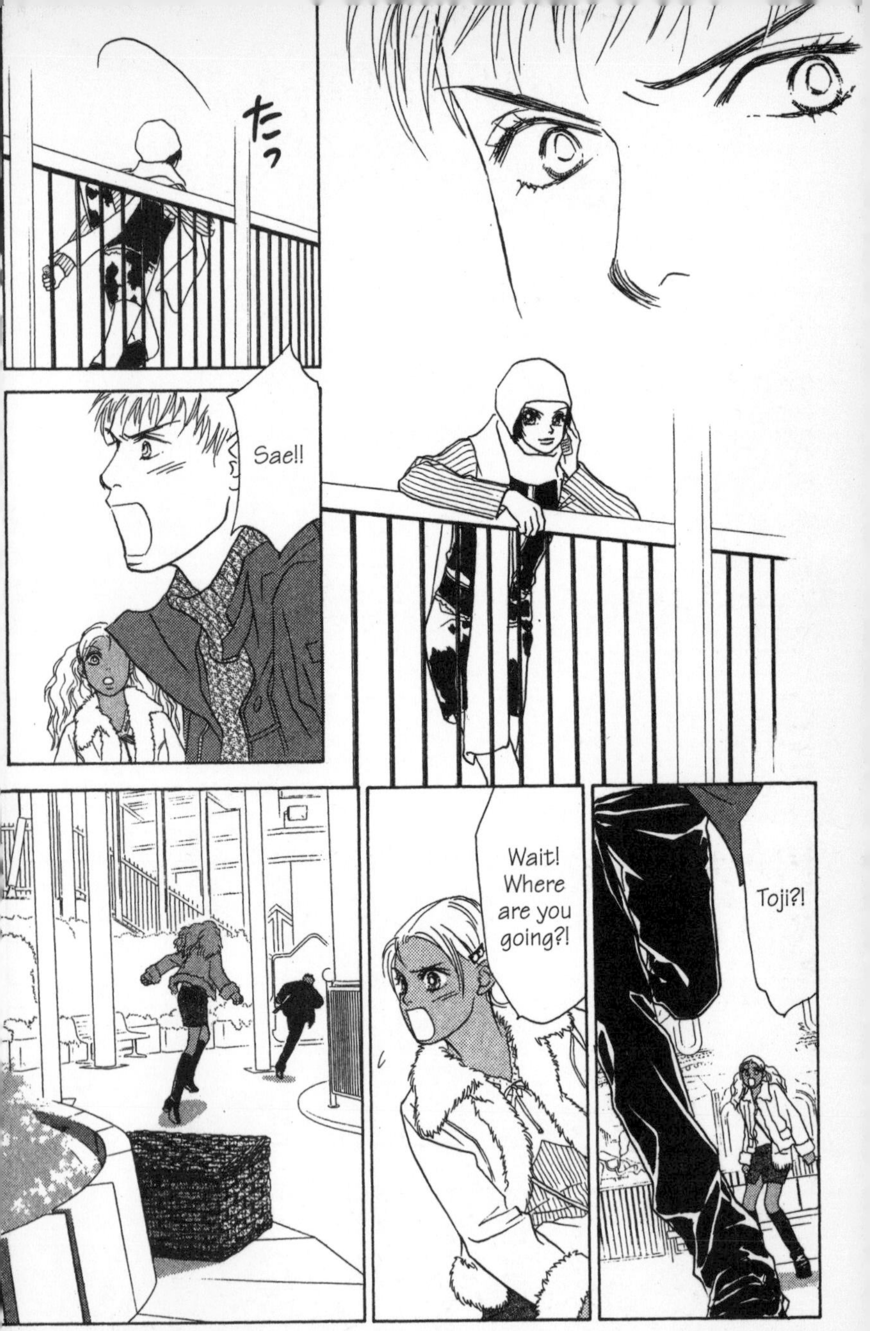
たっ
Sae!!
Toji?!
Wait! Where are you going?!

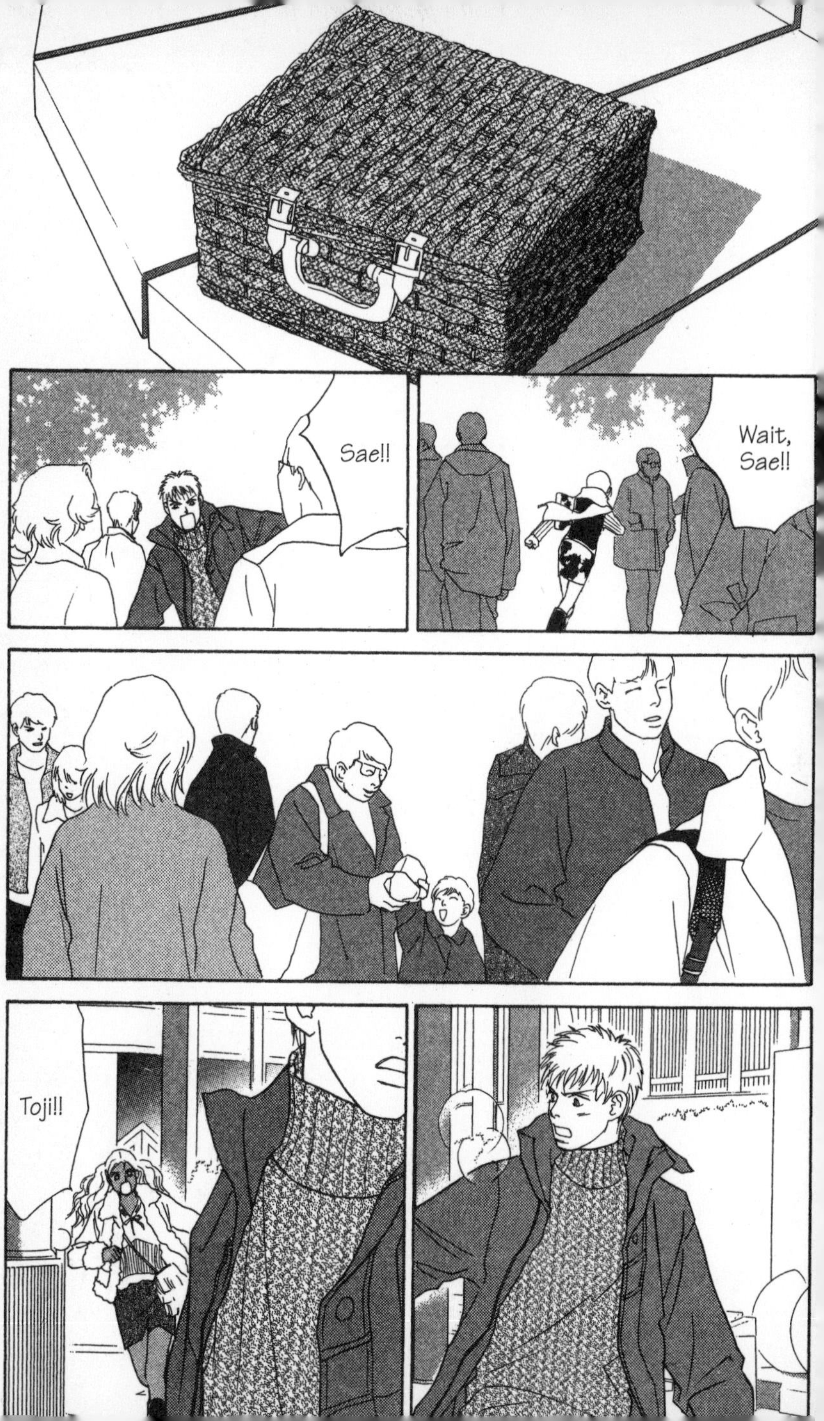
Wait, Sae!!
Sae!!
Toji!!

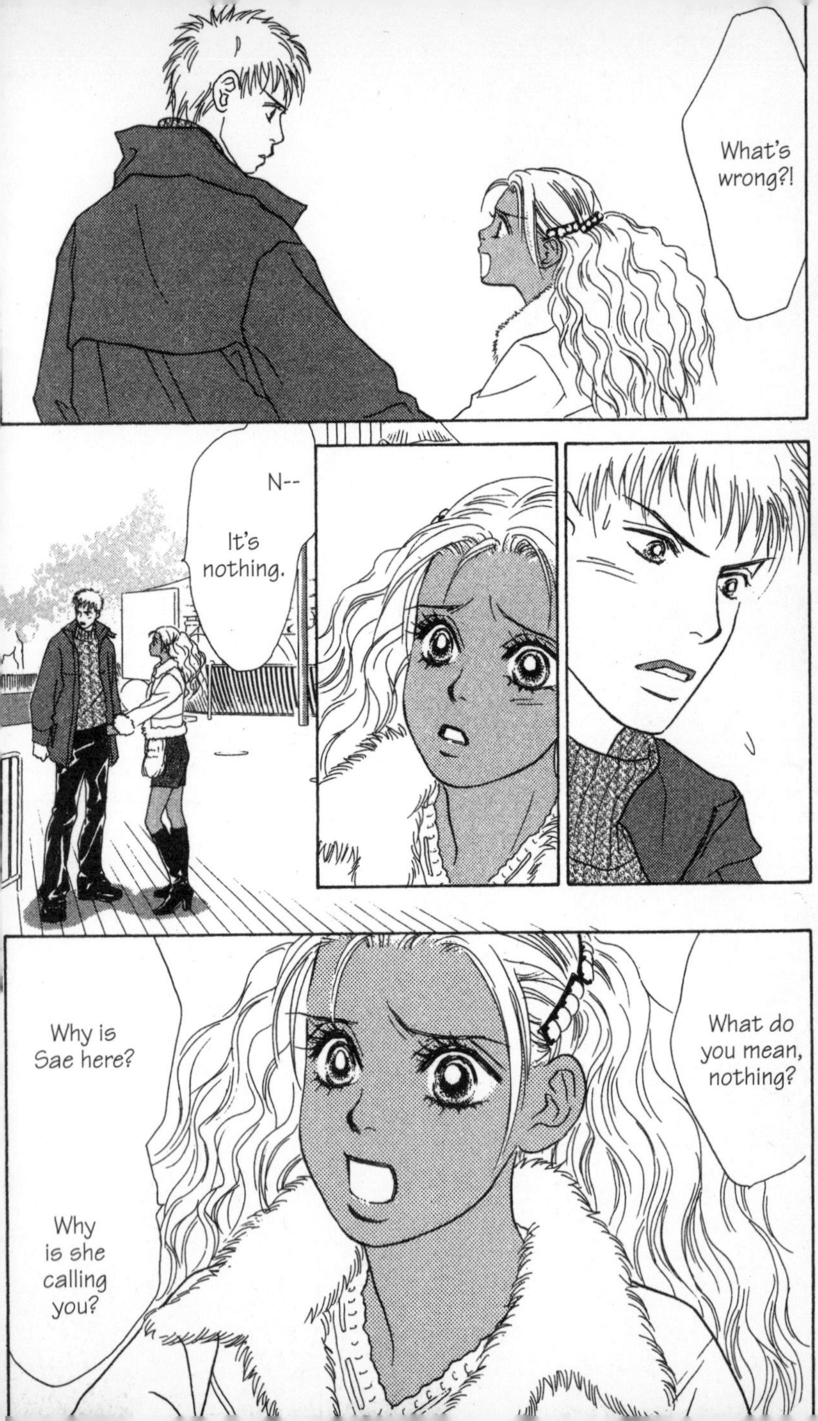
What's wrong?!
N-- It's nothing.
What do you mean, nothing?
Why is Sae here?
Why is she calling you?

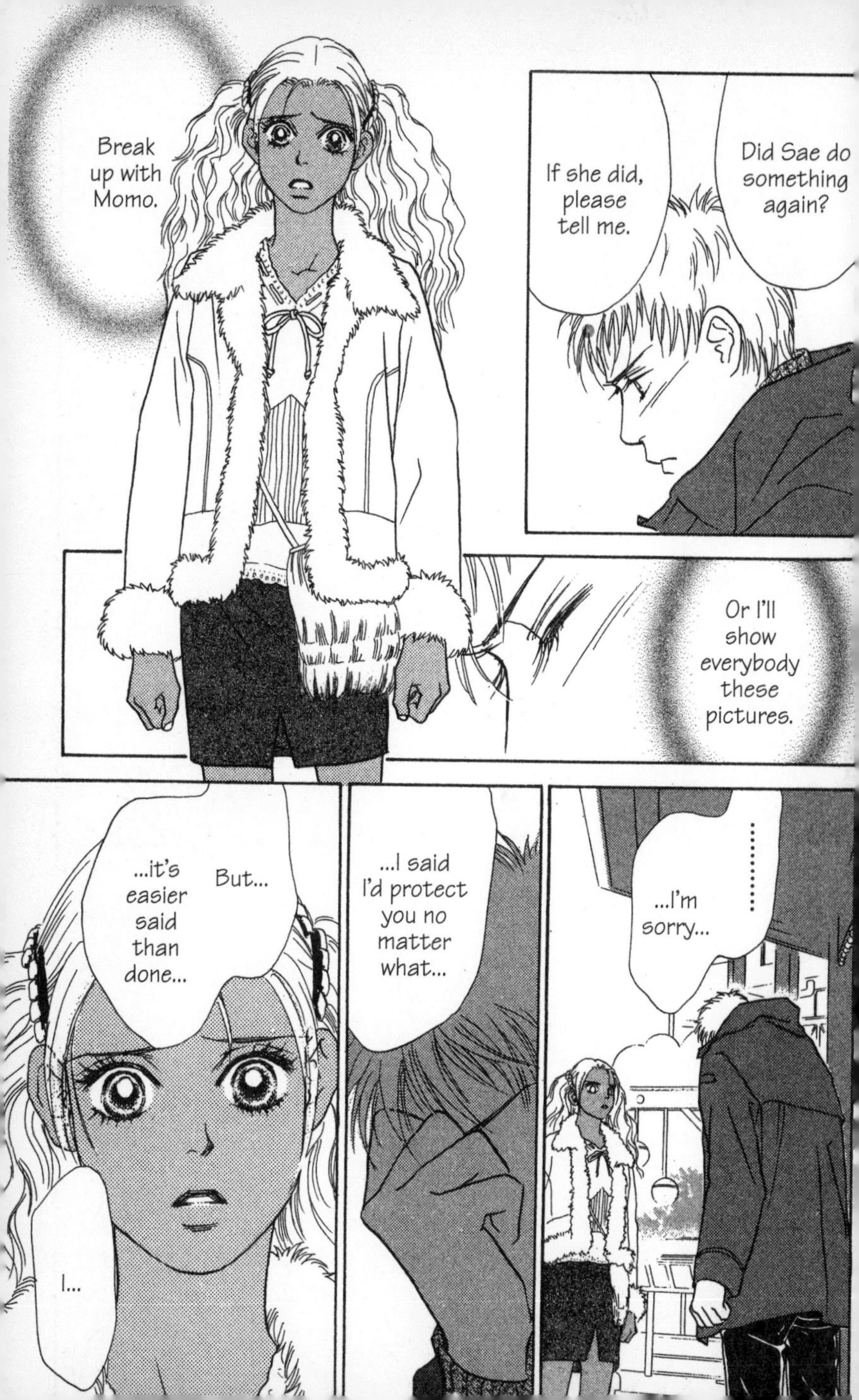
Did Sae do something again?
If she did, please tell me.
Break up with Momo.
Or I'll show everybody these pictures.
......
...I'm sorry...
...I said I'd protect you no matter what...
But...
...it's easier said than done...
I...

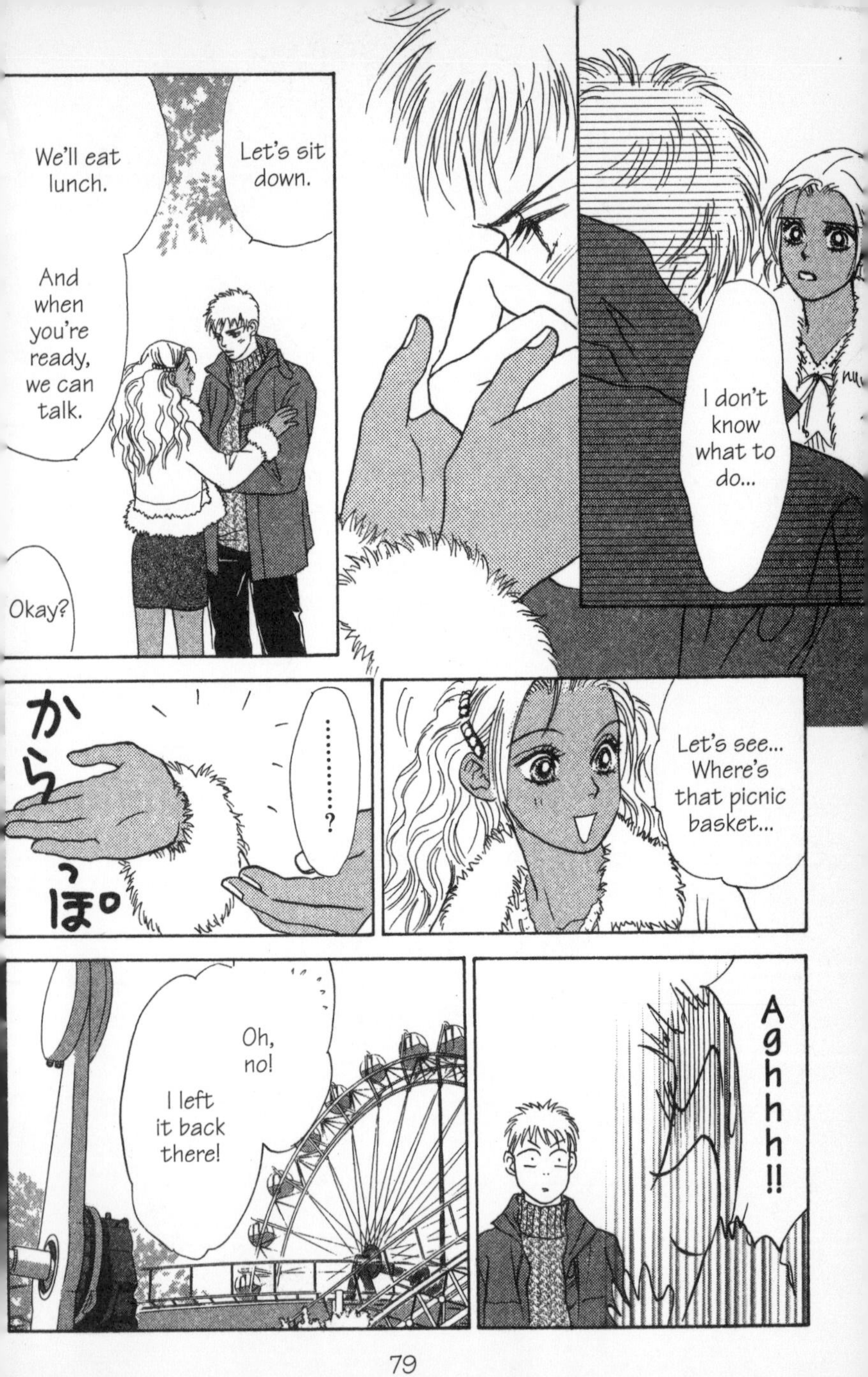

I don't know what to do...
Let's sit down.
We'll eat lunch.
And when you're ready, we can talk.
Okay?
Let's see... Where's that picnic basket...
......?
からっぽ
Aghhh!!
Oh, no!
I left it back there!

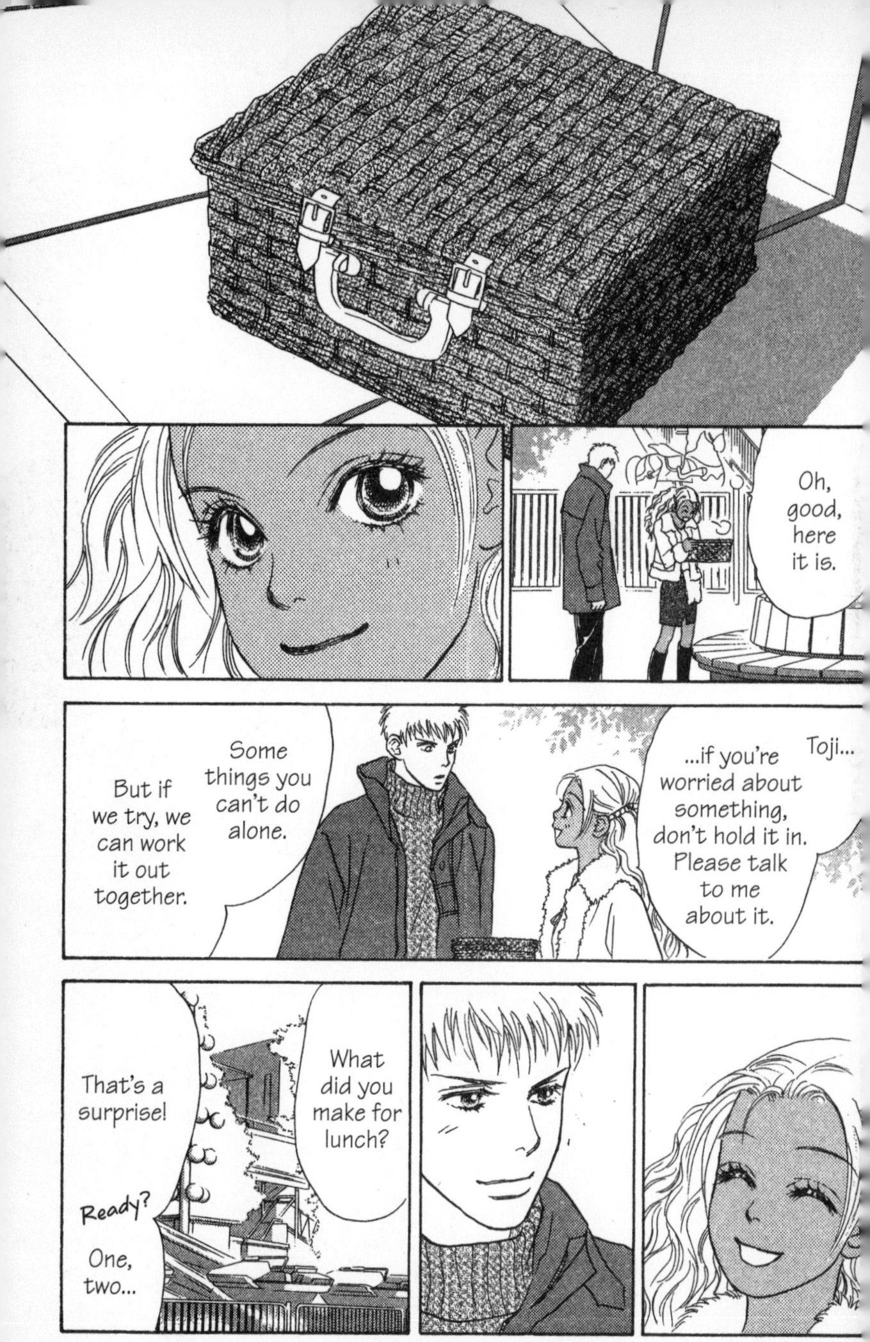
Oh, good, here it is.
Toji...
...if you're worried about something, don't hold it in. Please talk to me about it.
Some things you can't do alone.
But if we try, we can work it out together.
What did you make for lunch?
That's a surprise!
Ready?
One, two...

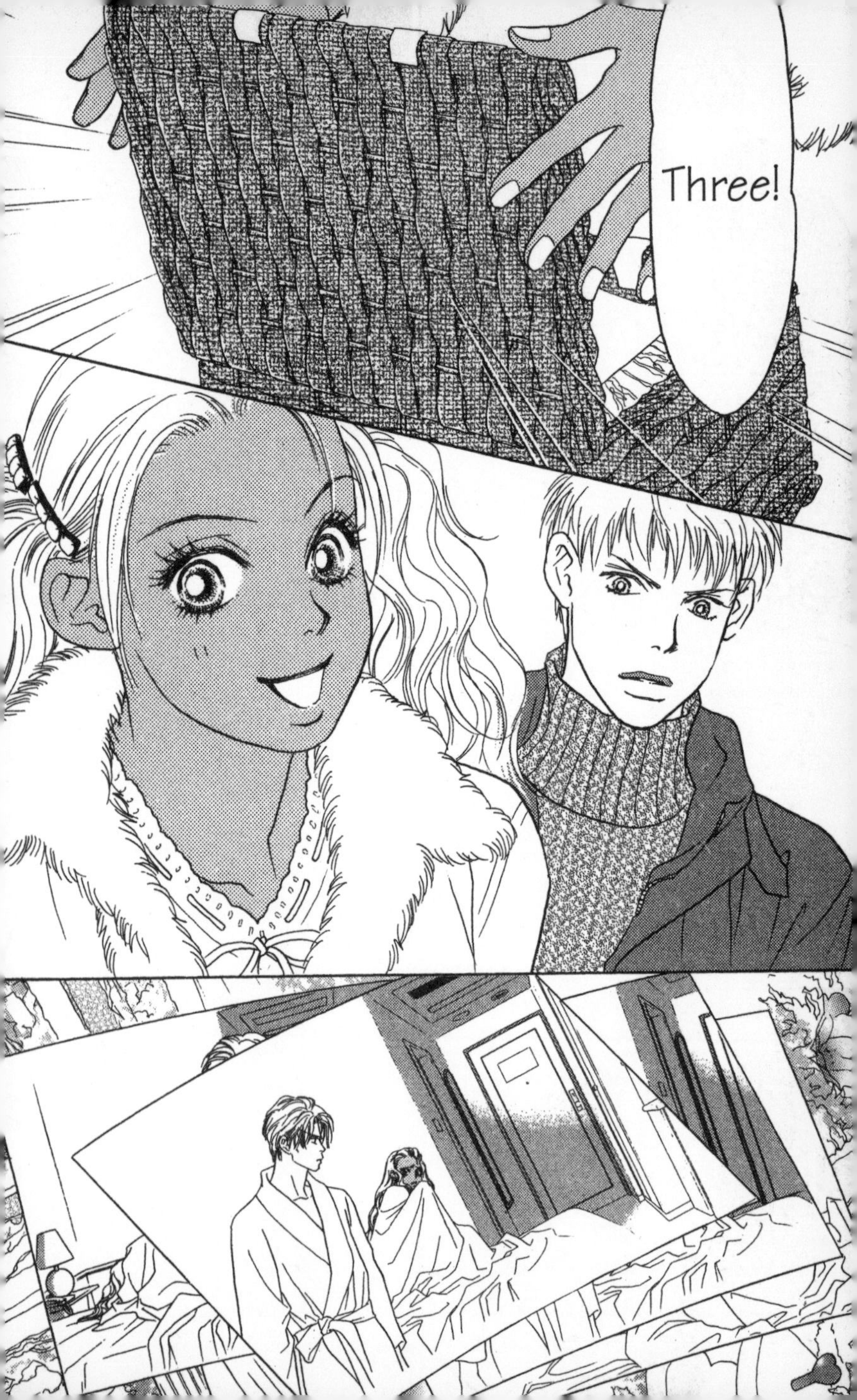
Three!

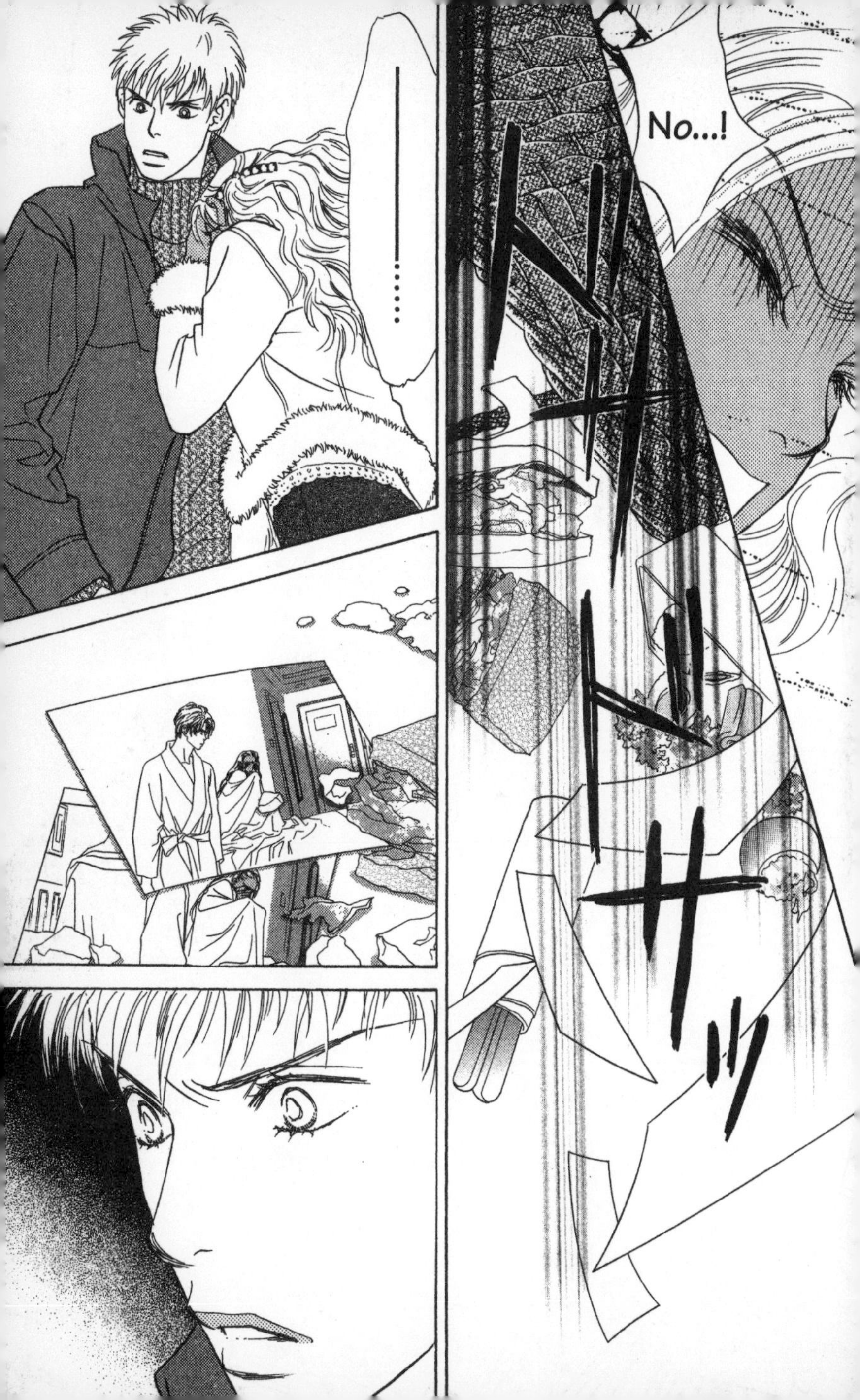
No...!
......

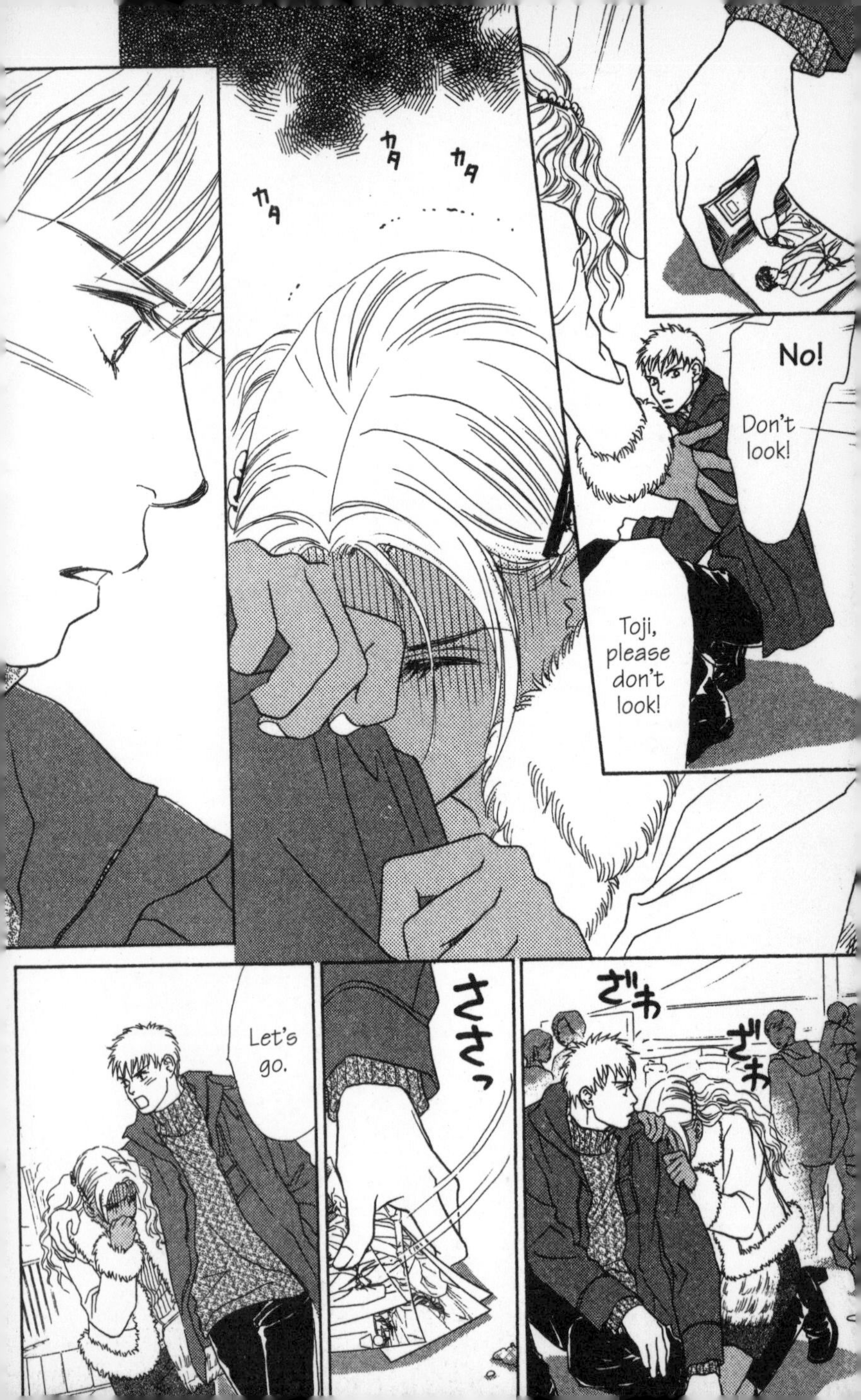
No!
Don't look!
Toji, please don't look!
カタ
カタ
カタ
ざわ
ざわ
ささっ
Let's go.

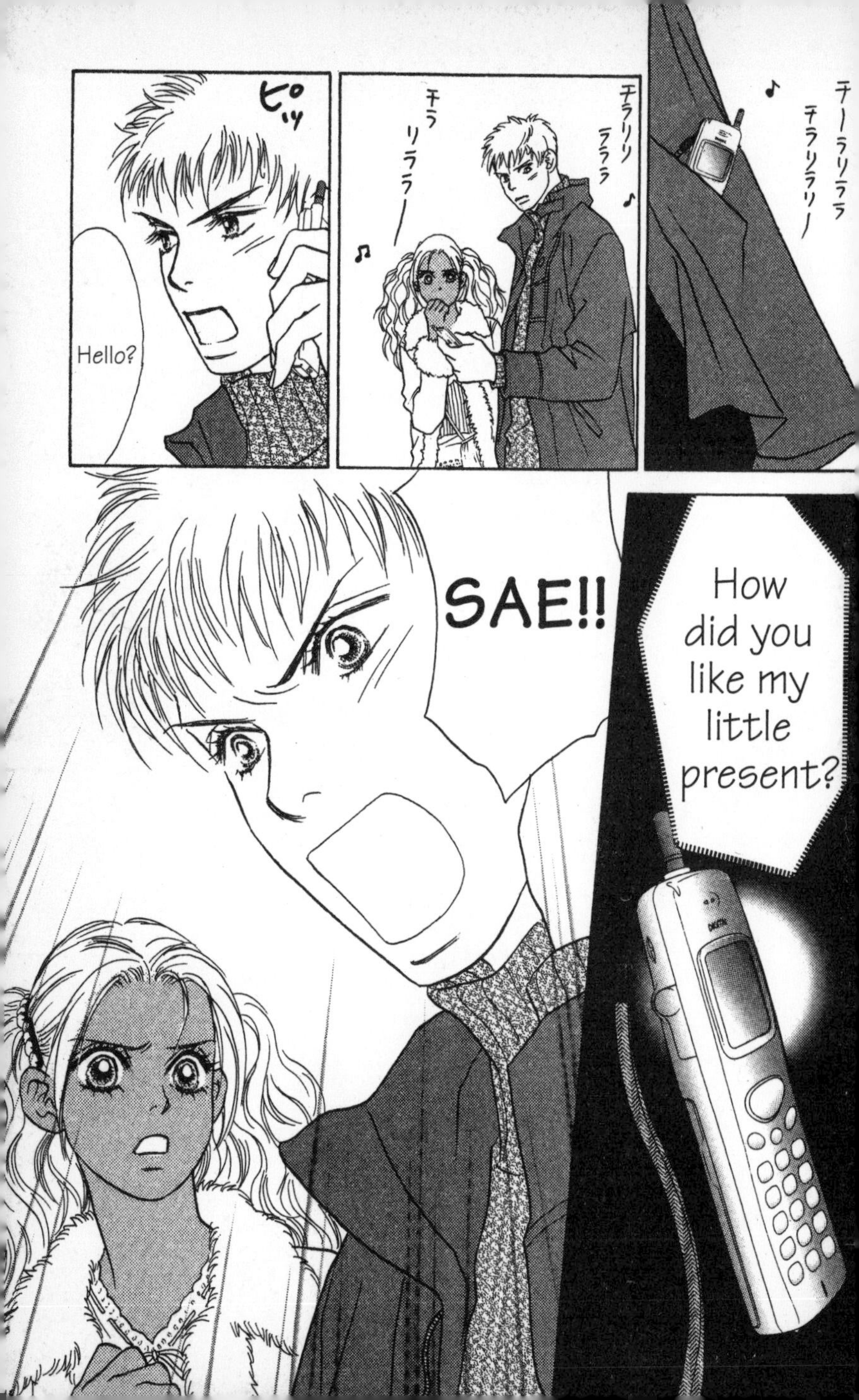
チーラリララ
チラリラリ
チラリリ
ラララ
チラ
リララー
ピッ
Hello?
How did you like my little present?
SAE!!

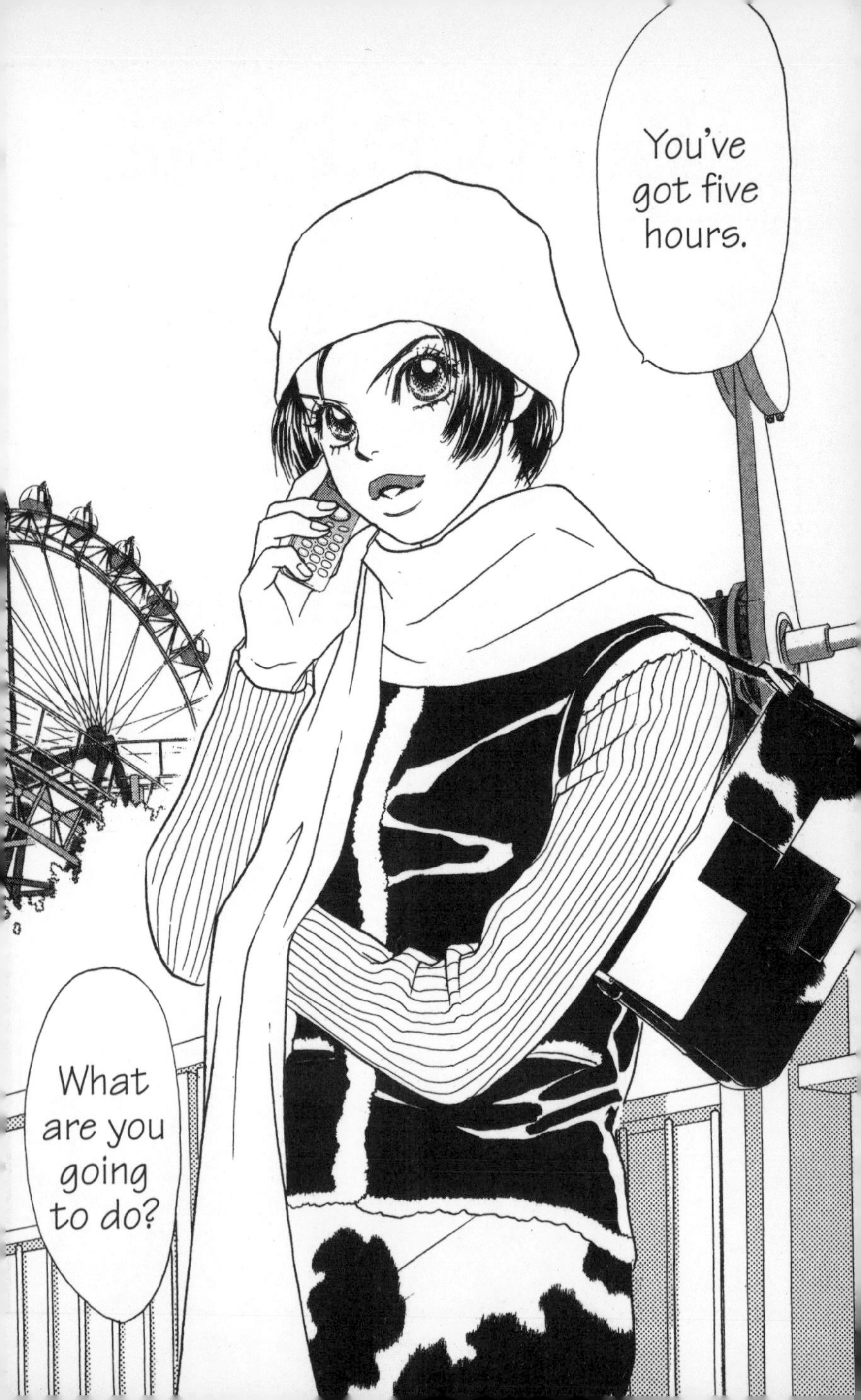
You've got five hours.
What are you going to do?

BONUS PAGE

"Boys don't seem to be interested in whether popular girls are, in reality, disliked."

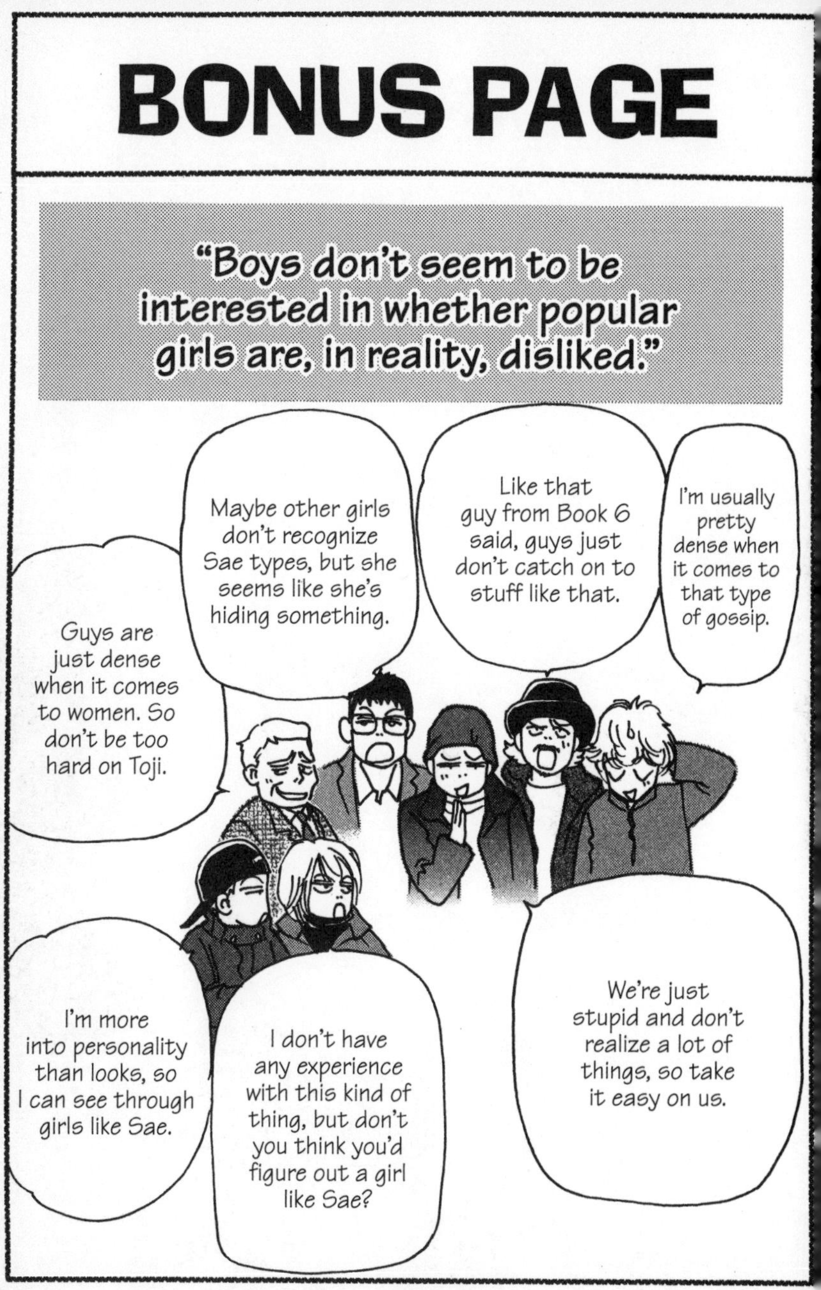
I'm usually pretty dense when it comes to that type of gossip.
Like that guy from Book 6 said, guys just don't catch on to stuff like that.
Maybe other girls don't recognize Sae types, but she seems like she's hiding something.
Guys are just dense when it comes to women. So don't be too hard on Toji.
We're just stupid and don't realize a lot of things, so take it easy on us.
I don't have any experience with this kind of thing, but don't you think you'd figure out a girl like Sae?
I'm more into personality than looks, so I can see through girls like Sae.

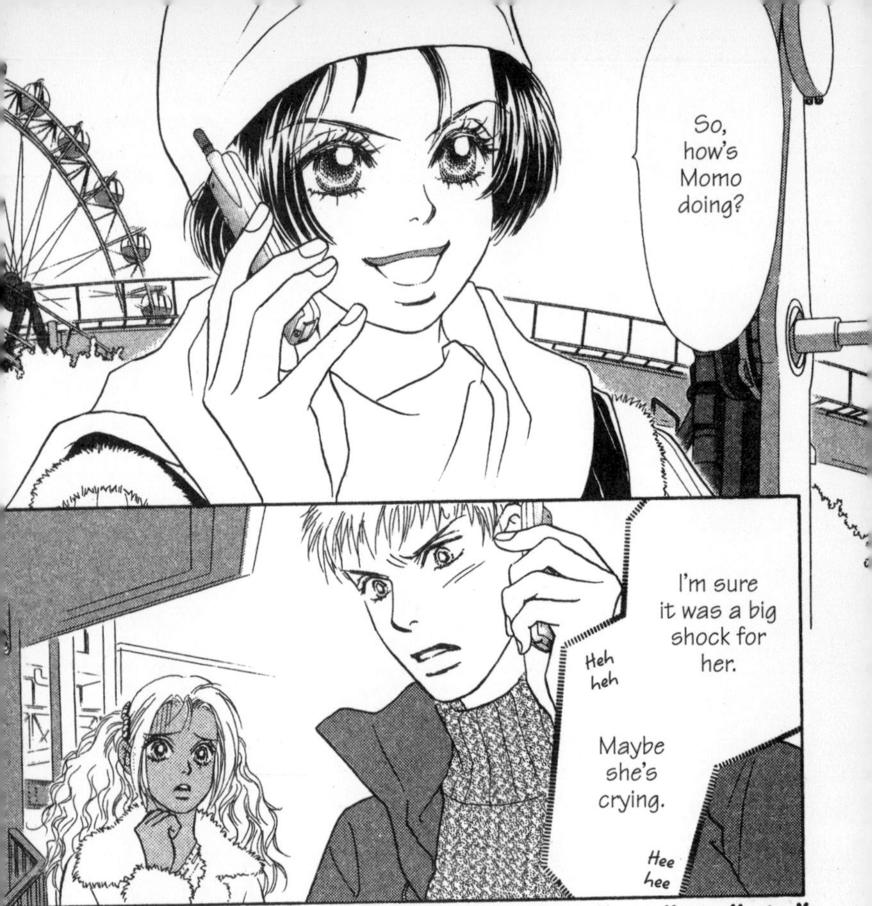
So, how's Momo doing?
I'm sure it was a big shock for her.
Heh heh
Maybe she's crying.
Hee hee

PEACH CLUB The Boys Vote: Sae or Momo?

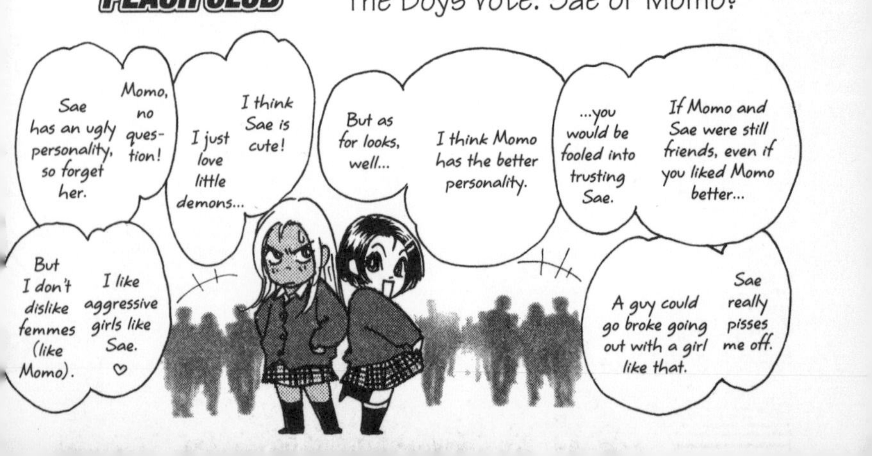
If Momo and Sae were still friends, even if you liked Momo better...
...you would be fooled into trusting Sae.
I think Momo has the better personality.
But as for looks, well...
I think Sae is cute!
I just love little demons...
Momo, no question!
Sae has an ugly personality, so forget her.
Sae really pisses me off.
A guy could go broke going out with a girl like that.
I like aggressive girls like Sae. ♡
But I don't dislike femmes (like Momo).

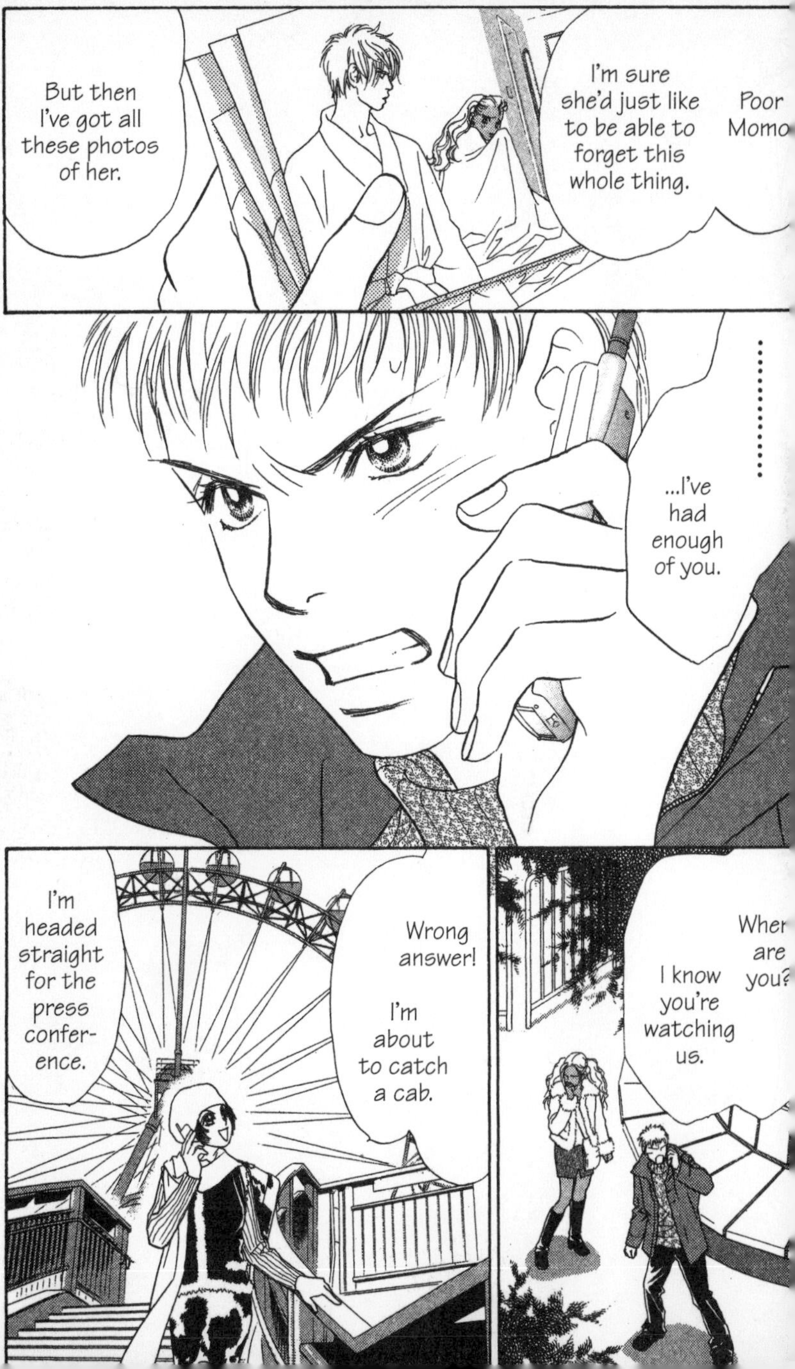
Poor Momo
I'm sure she'd just like to be able to forget this whole thing.
But then I've got all these photos of her.
....
...I've had enough of you.
Wher are you?
I know you're watching us.
Wrong answer! I'm about to catch a cab.
I'm headed straight for the press conference.

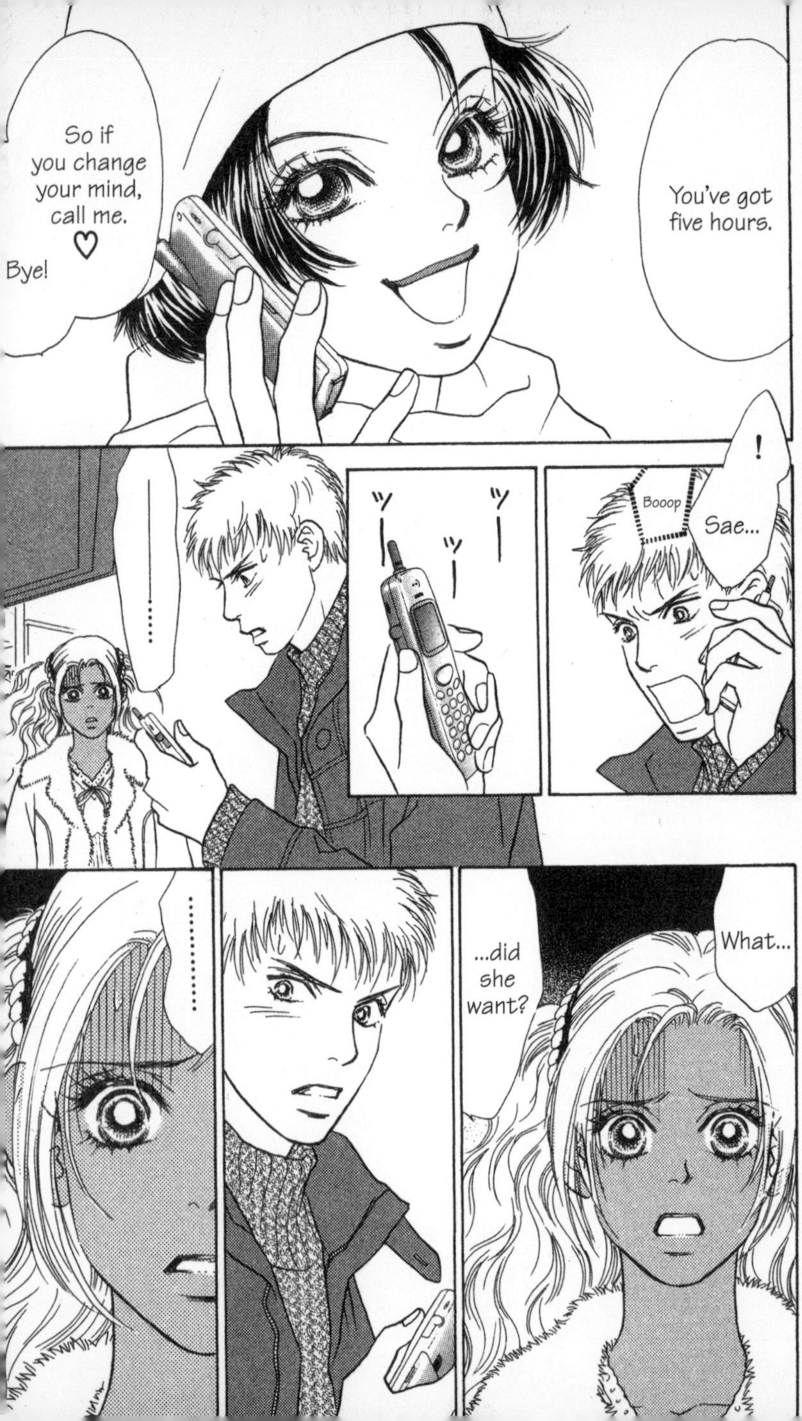

You've got five hours.
So if you change your mind, call me. ♡
Bye!
!
Booop
Sae...
ツー
ツー
ツー
......
What...
...did she want?
....

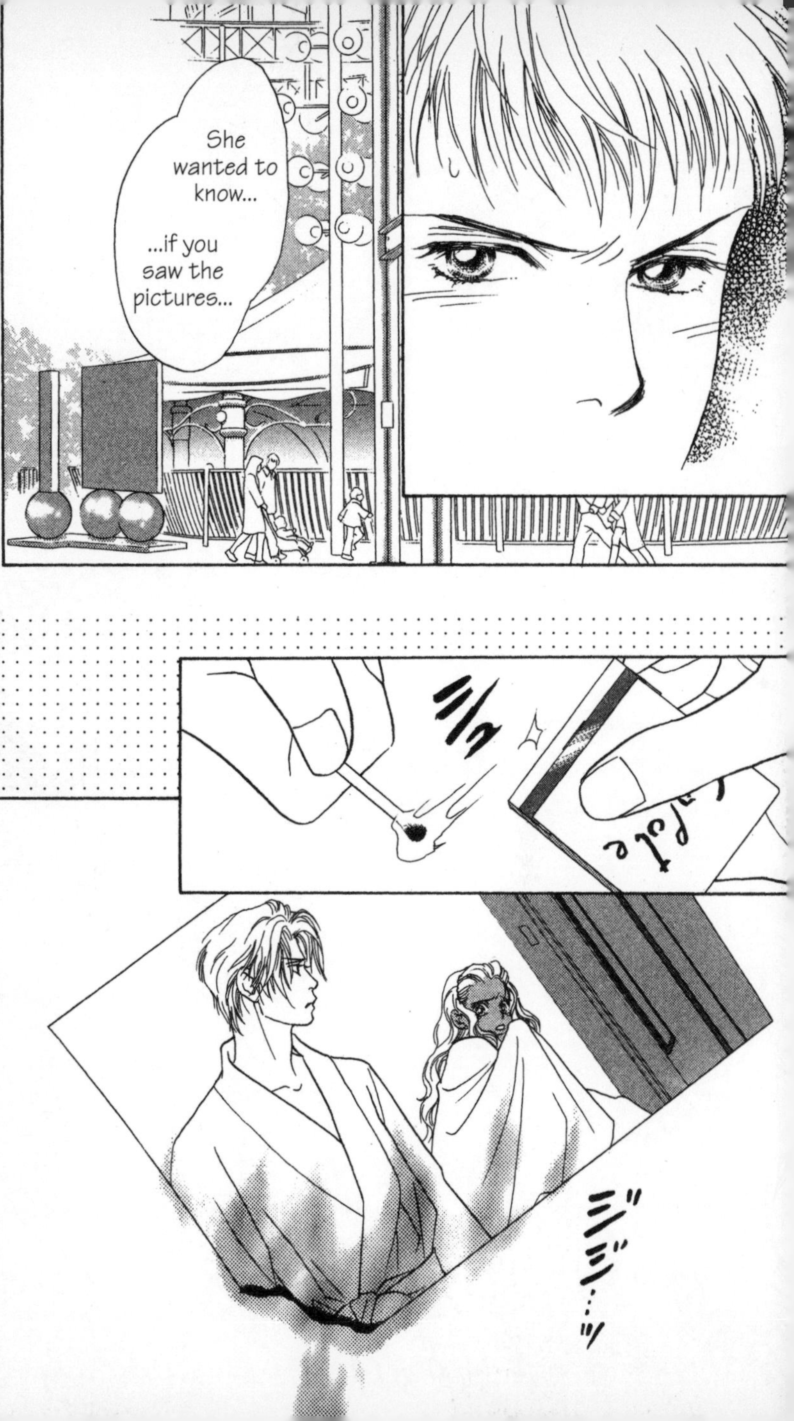
She wanted to know...
...if you saw the pictures...
ジジジ…ッ

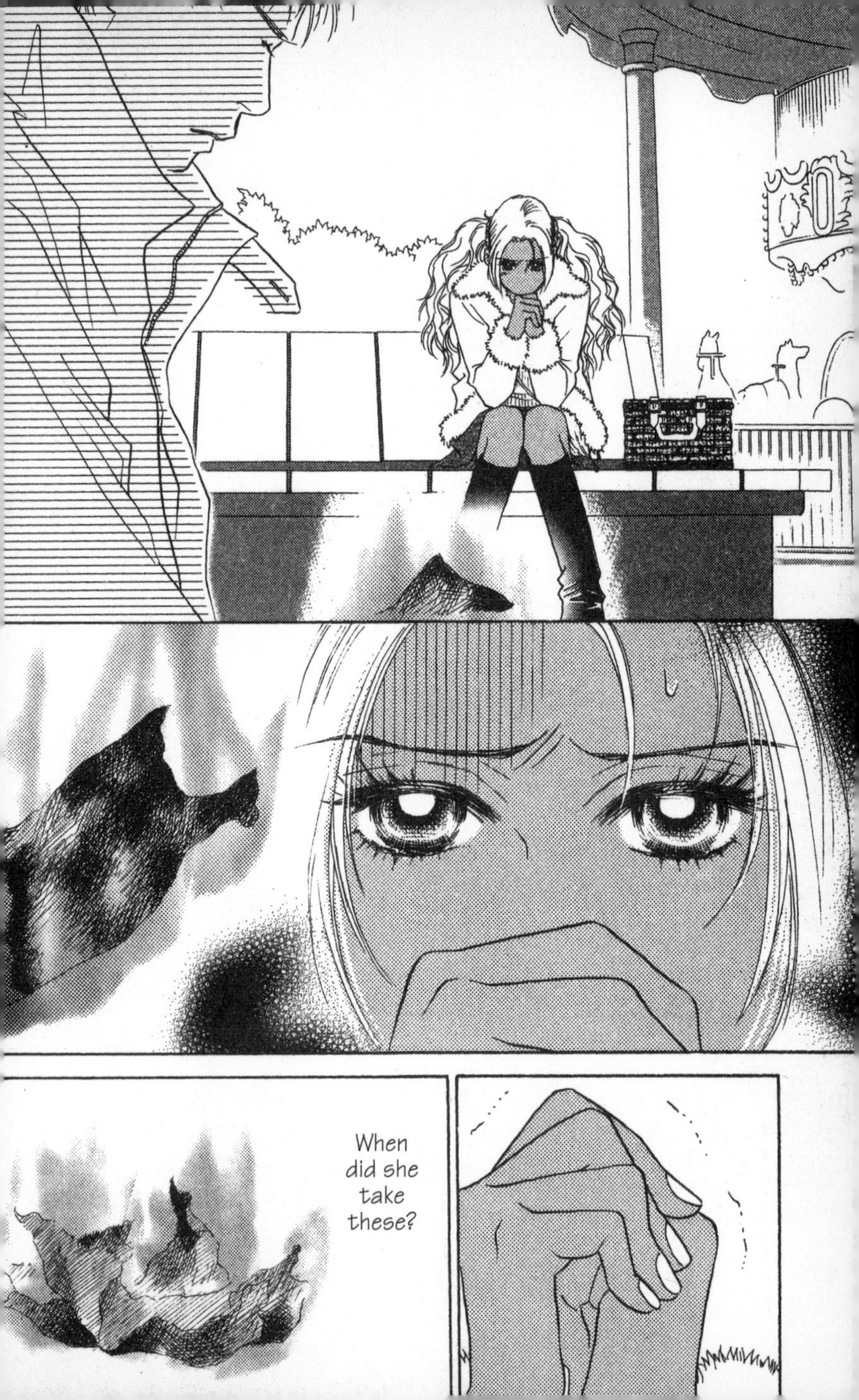
When did she take these?

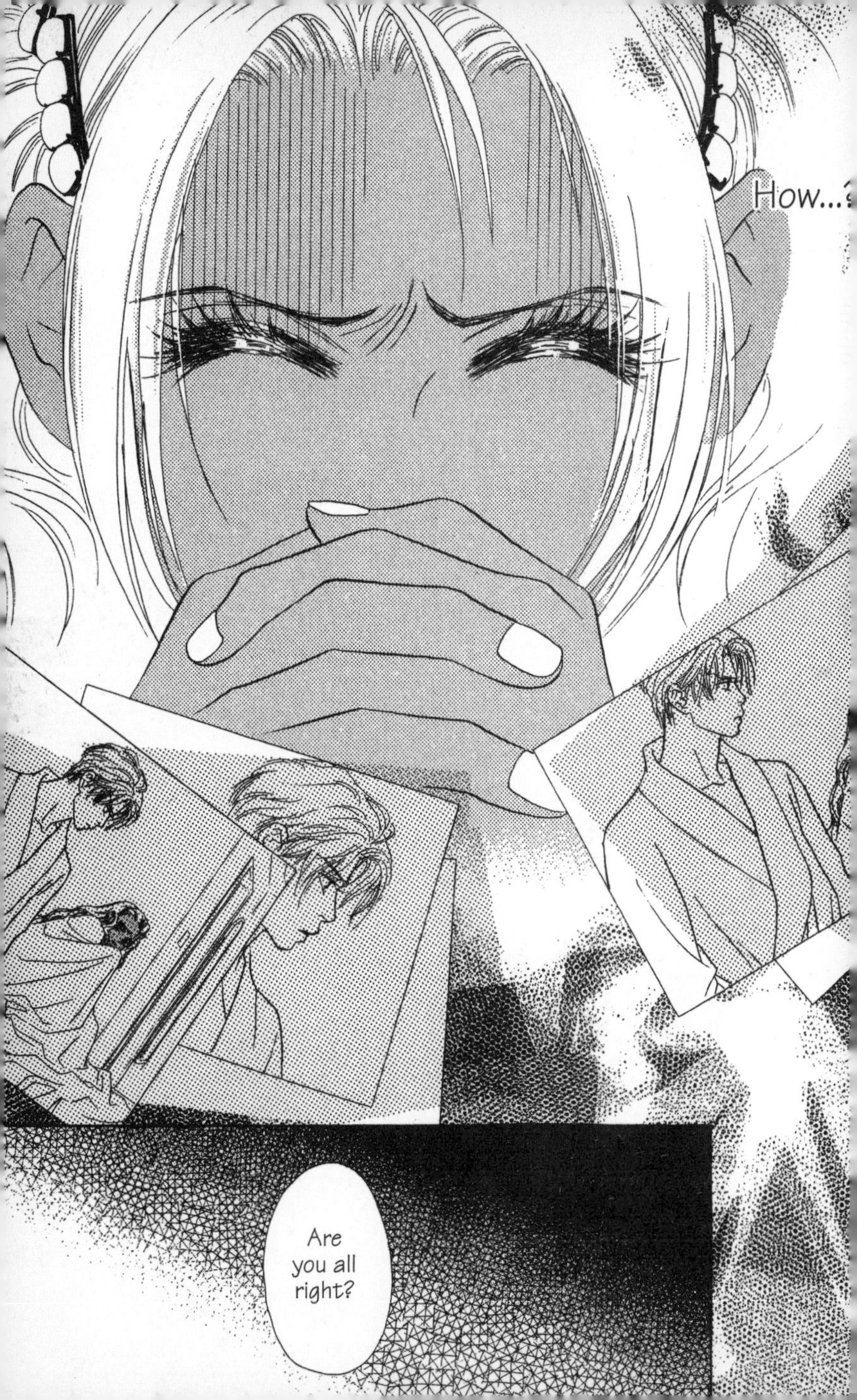
How...?
Are you all right?

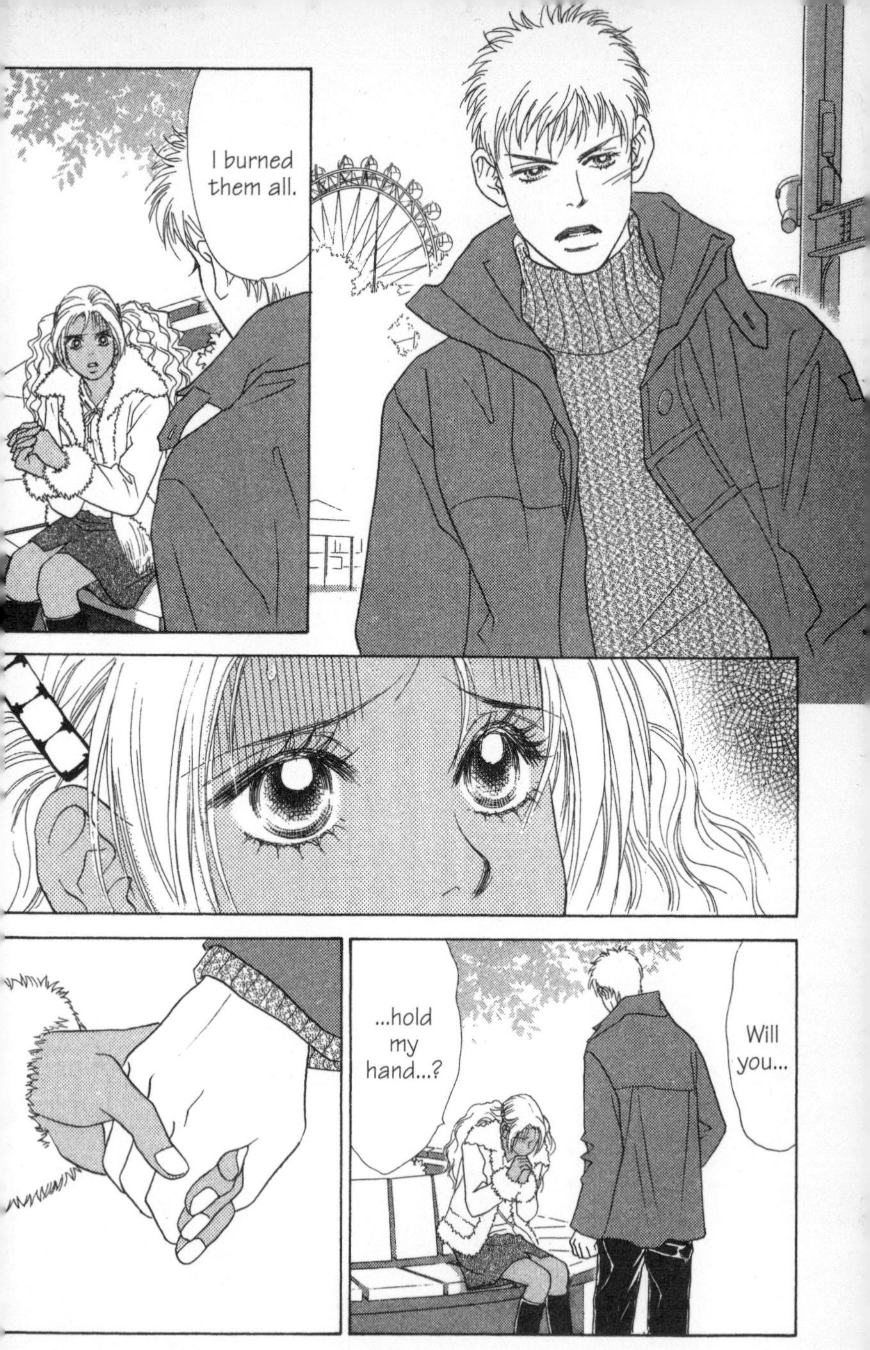
I burned them all.
Will you...
...hold my hand...?

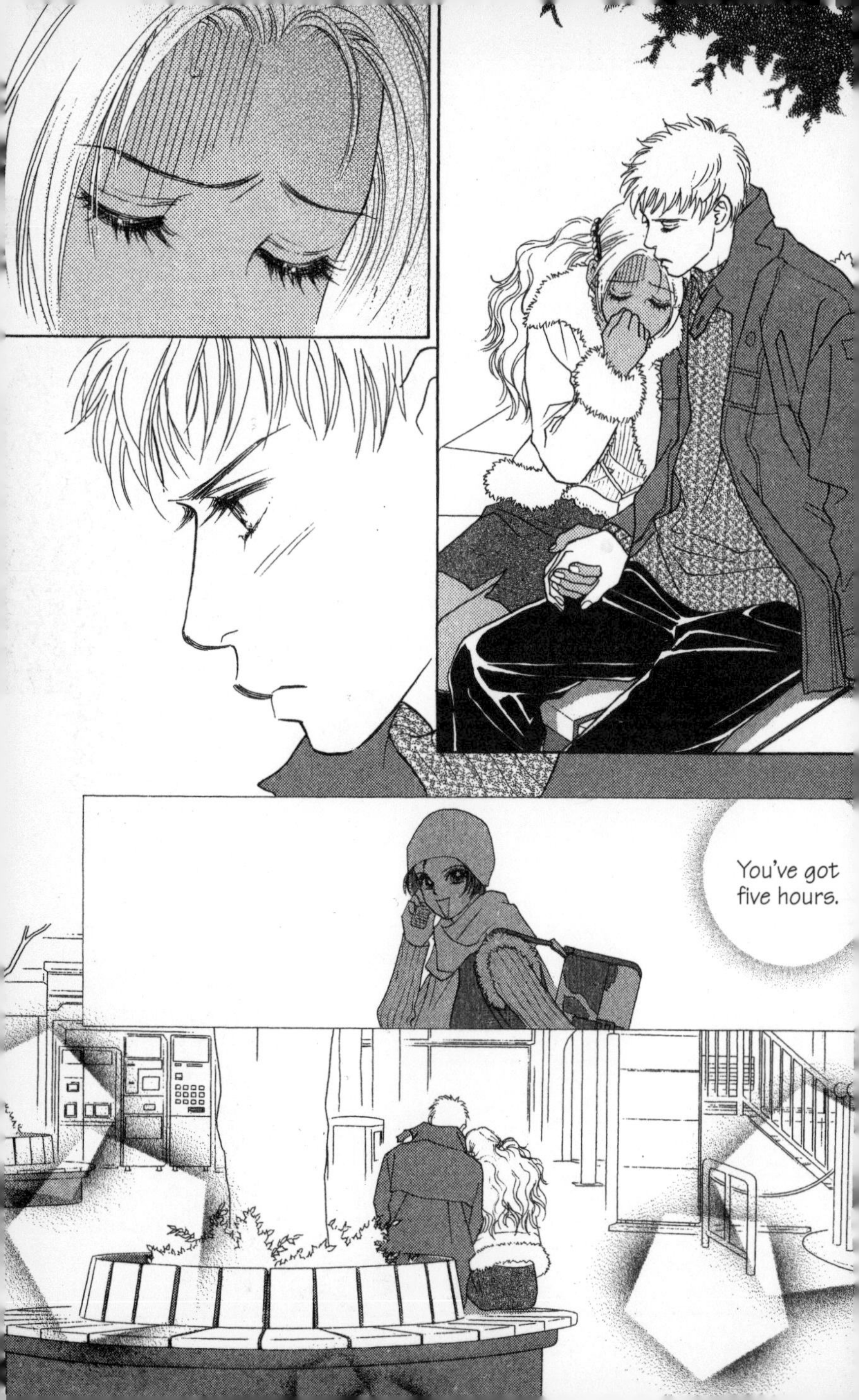
You've got five hours.

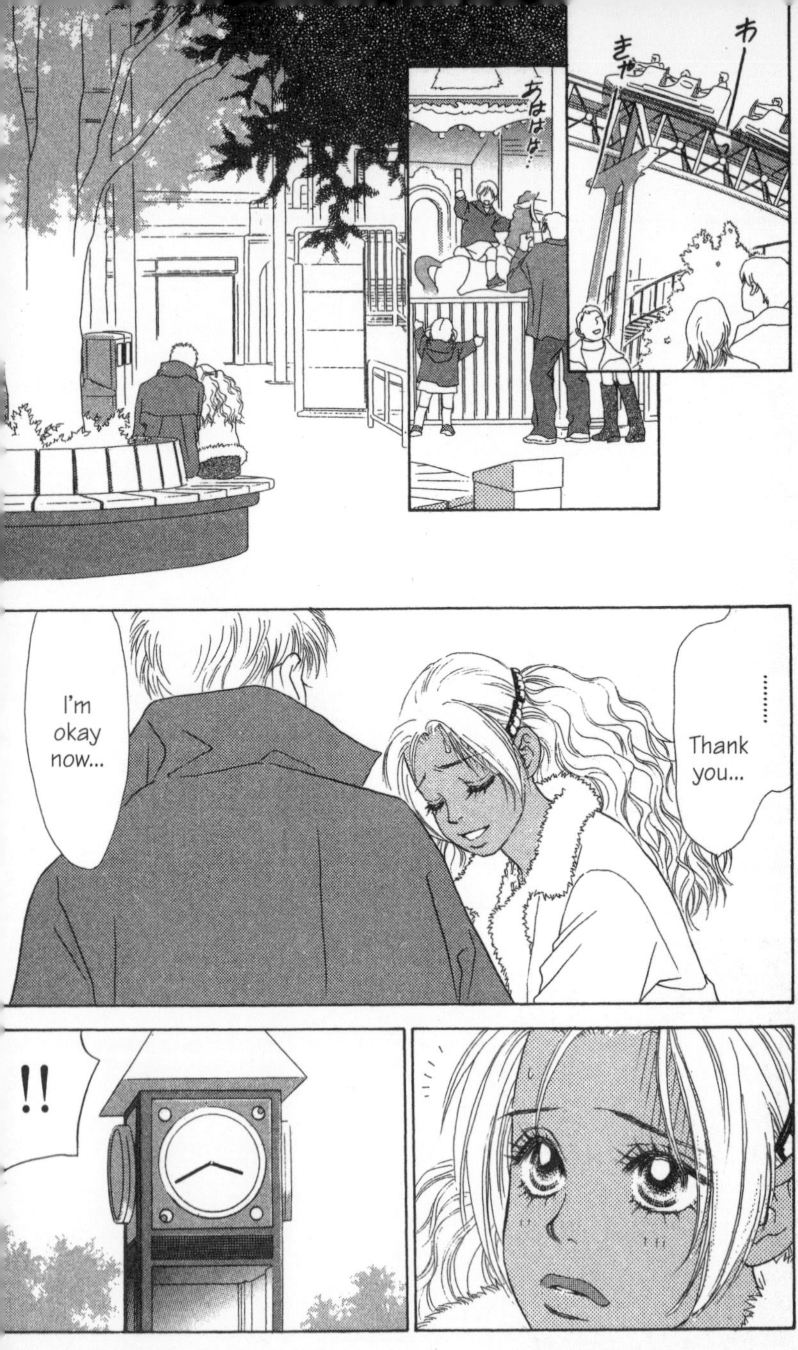
わー
きゃ
あははは…
……
Thank you...
I'm okay now...
!!

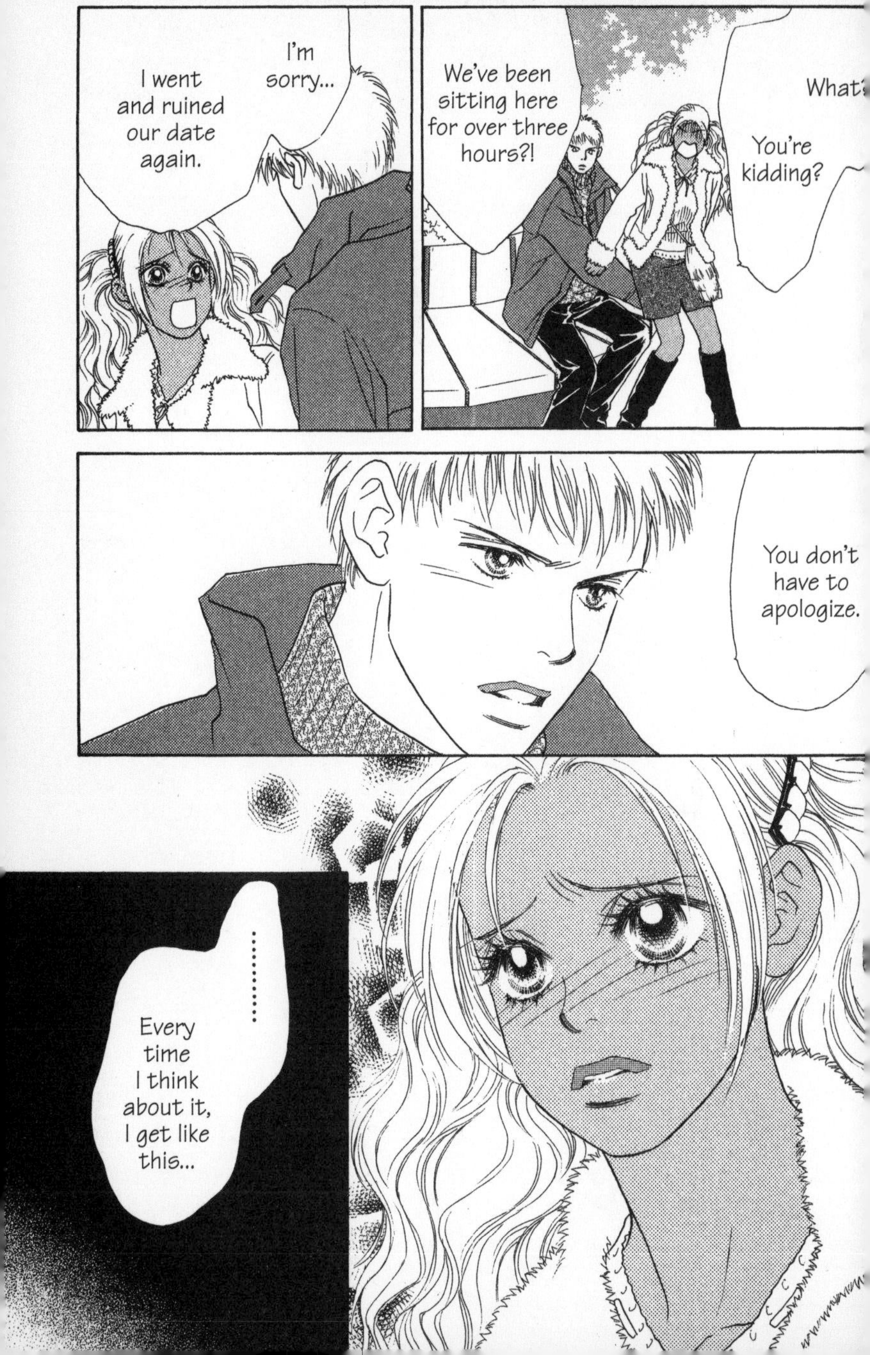

What?
You're kidding?
We've been sitting here for over three hours?!
I'm sorry...
I went and ruined our date again.
You don't have to apologize.
......
Every time I think about it, I get like this...

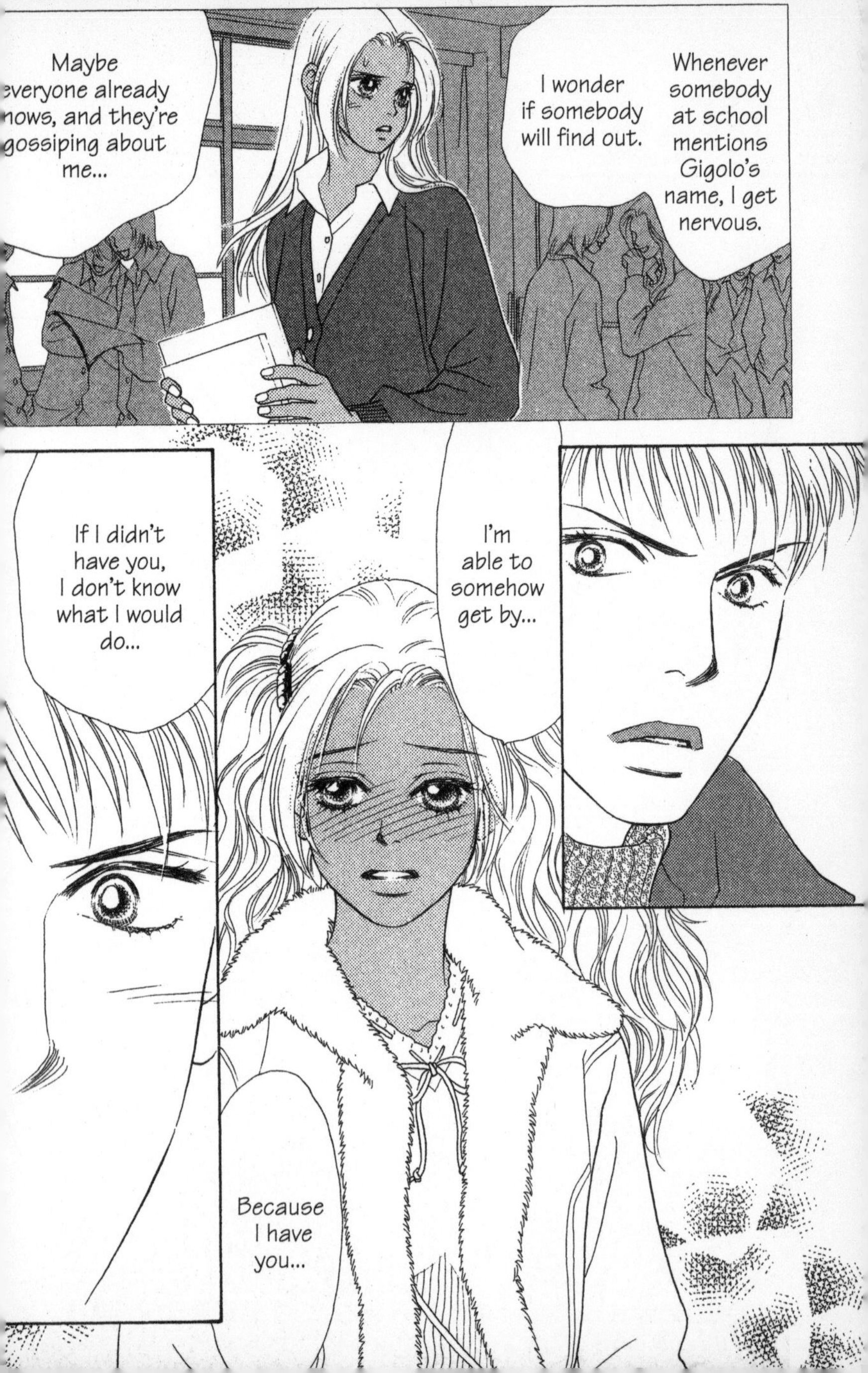
Whenever somebody at school mentions Gigolo's name, I get nervous.
I wonder if somebody will find out.
Maybe everyone already nows, and they're gossiping about me...
I'm able to somehow get by...
If I didn't have you, I don't know what I would do...
Because I have you...

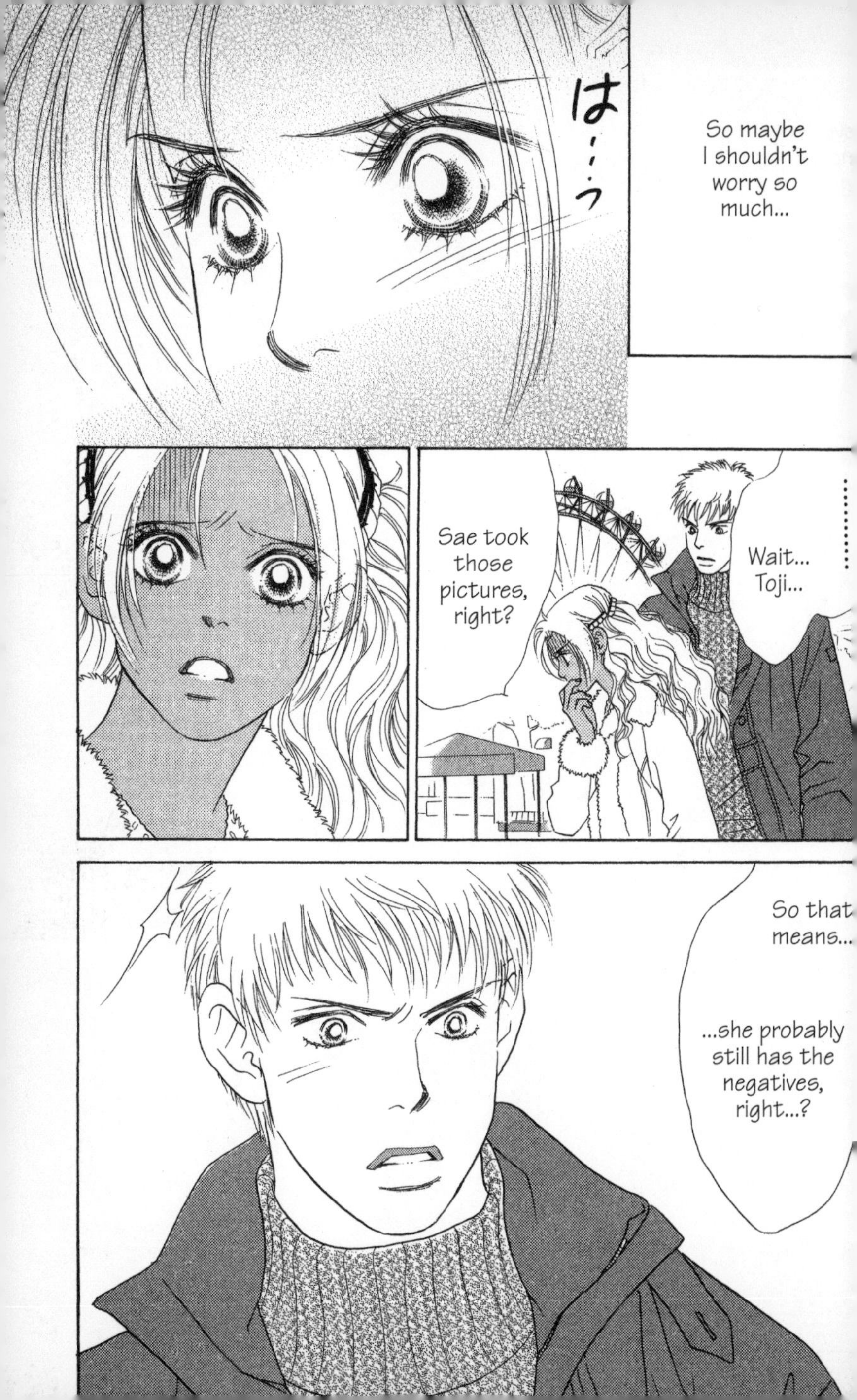
So maybe I shouldn't worry so much...
はっ
Wait... Toji...
Sae took those pictures, right?
So that means...
...she probably still has the negatives, right...?

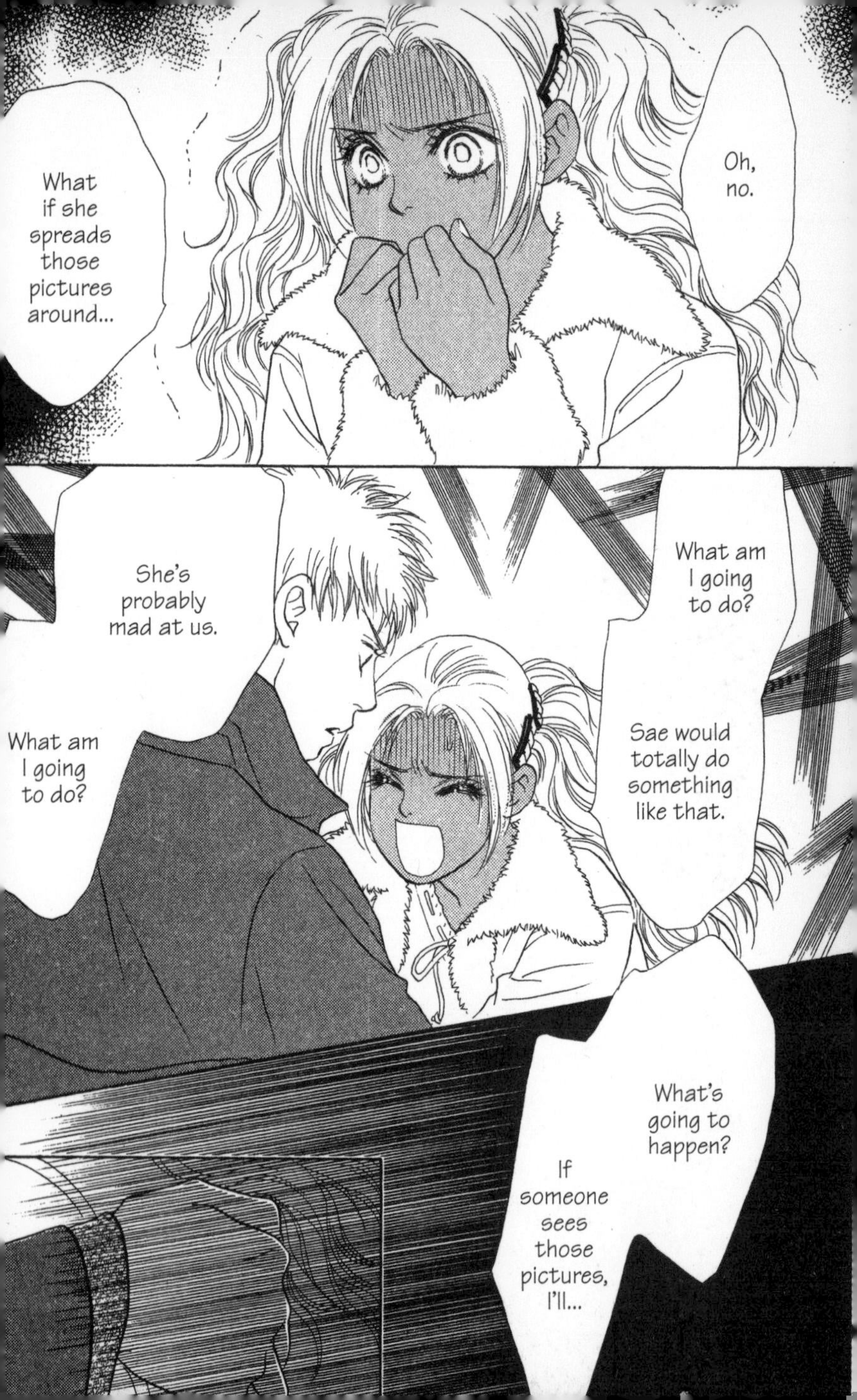

Oh, no.
What if she spreads those pictures around...
What am I going to do?
Sae would totally do something like that.
She's probably mad at us.
What am I going to do?
What's going to happen?
If someone sees those pictures, I'll...

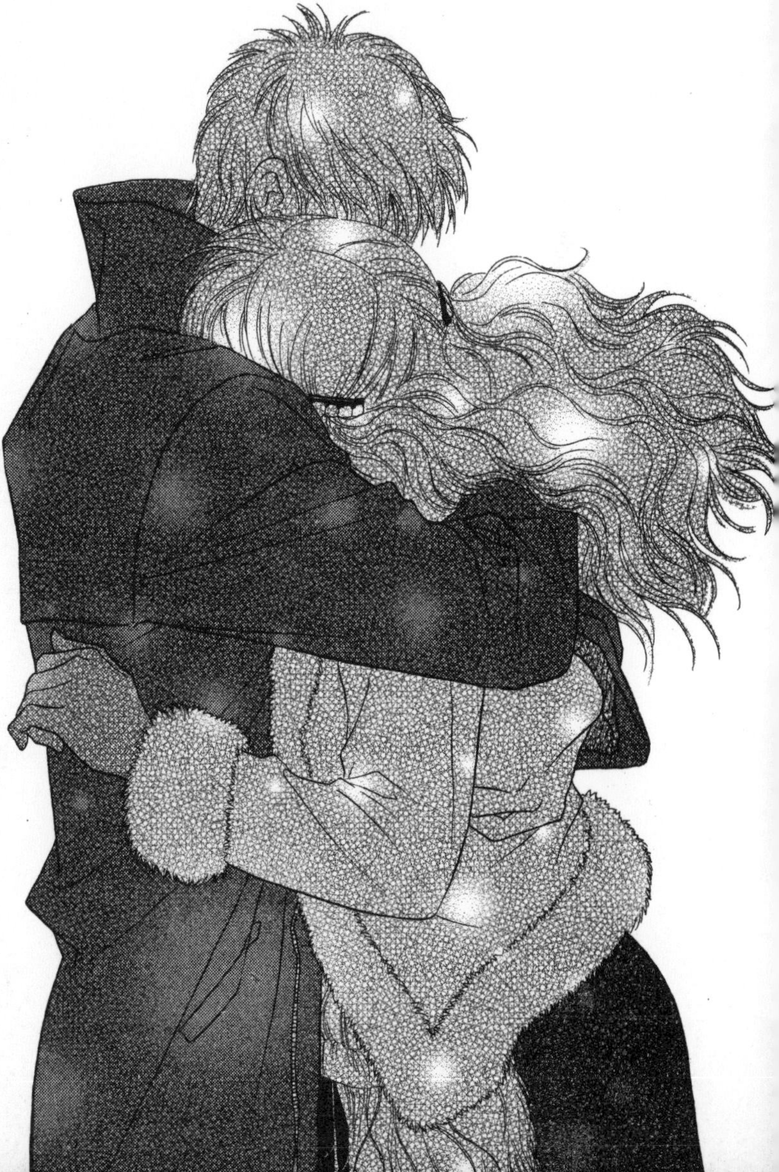

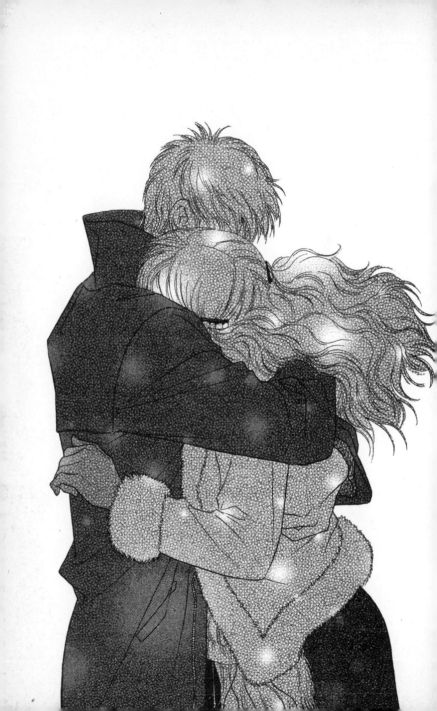

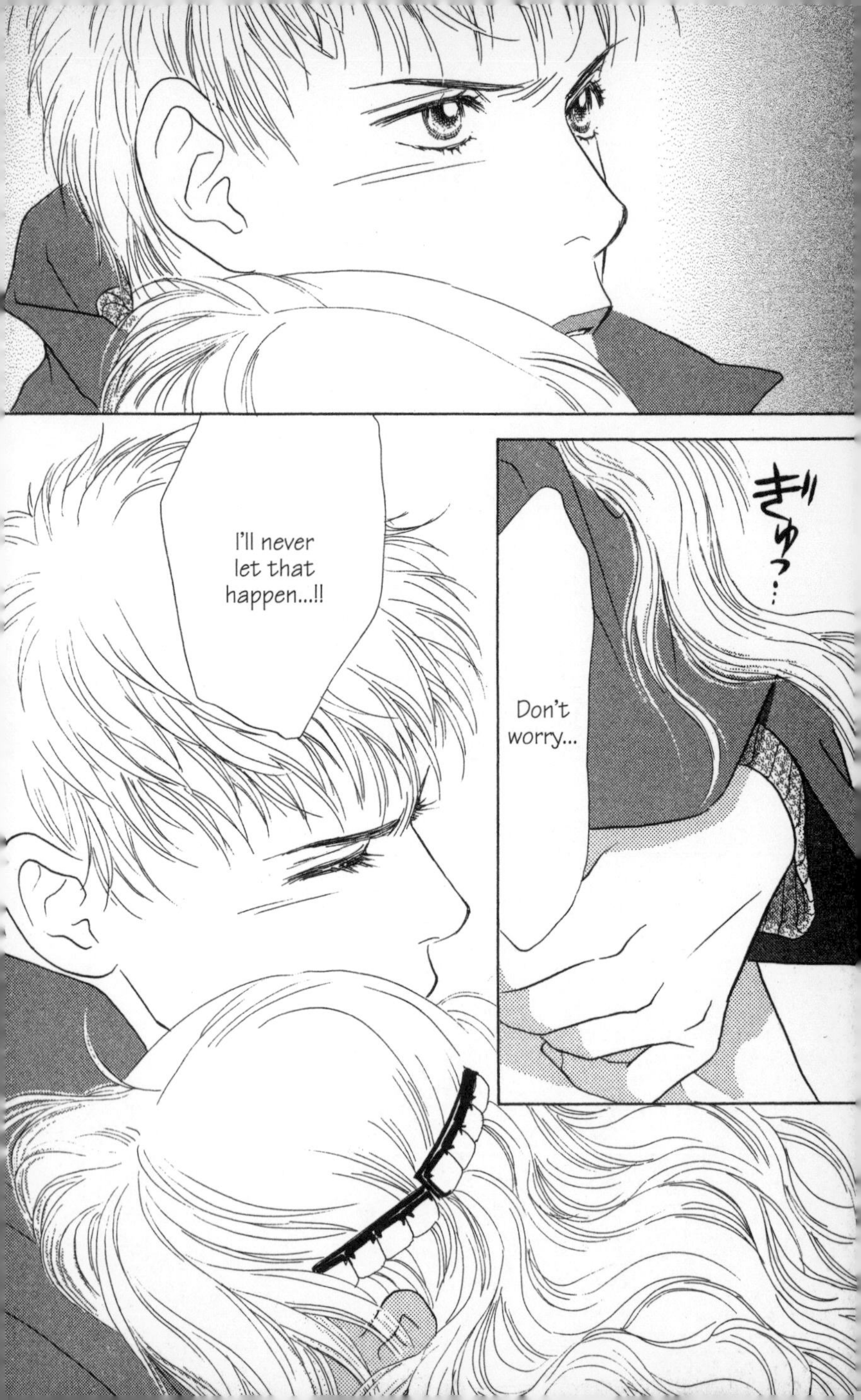
ぎゅっ…
Don't worry...
I'll never let that happen...!!

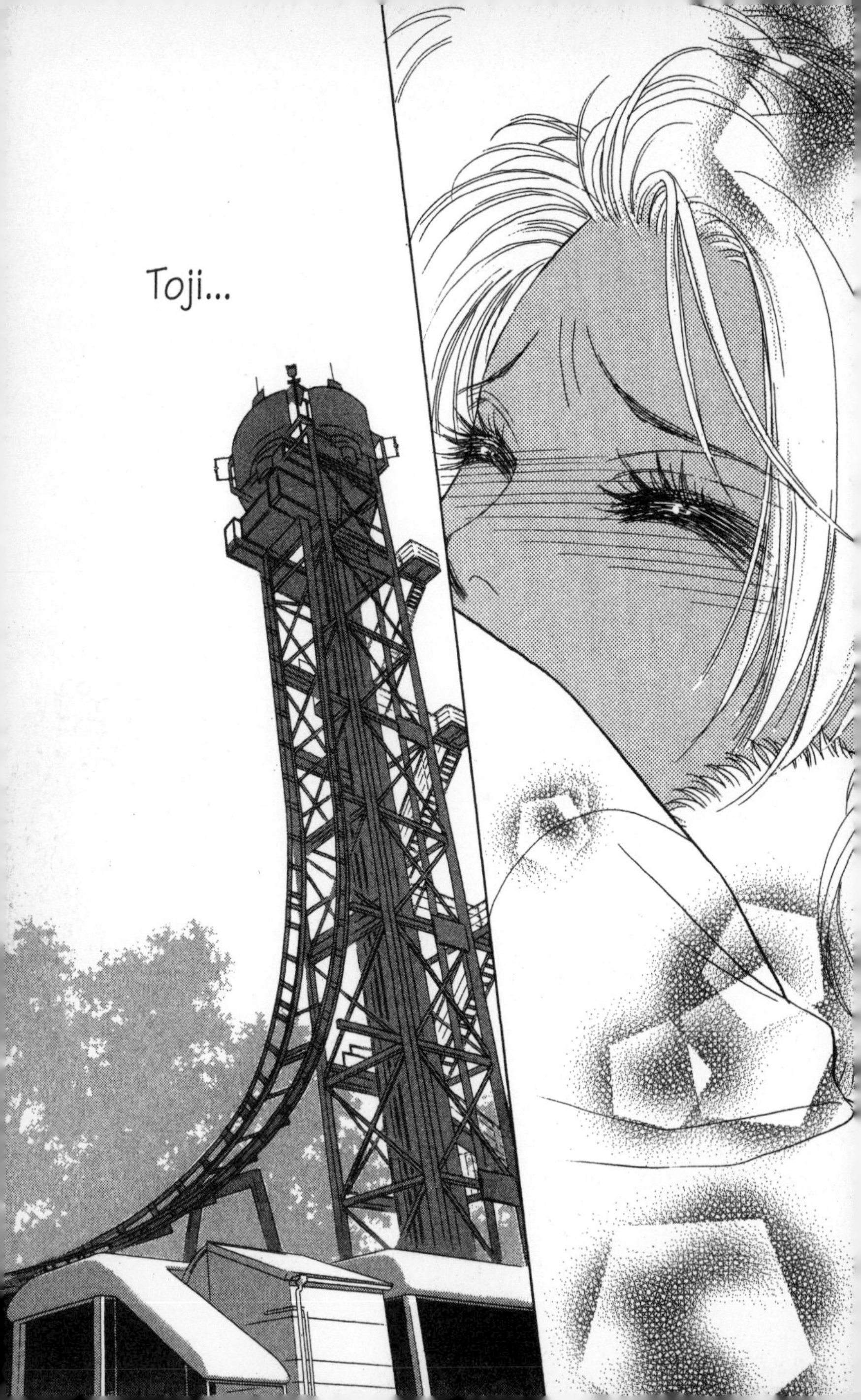
Toji...

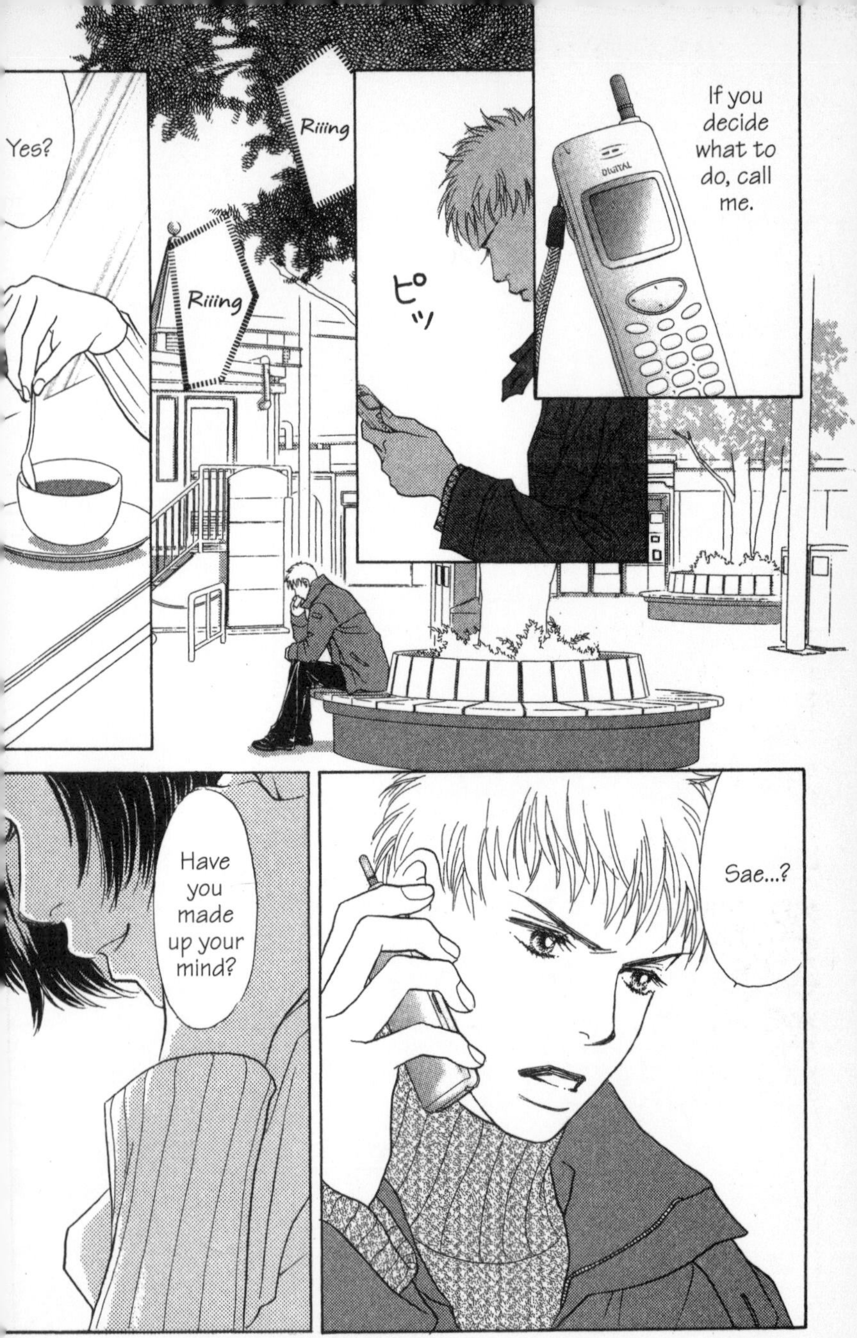
If you decide what to do, call me.
ピッ
Riiing
Riiing
Yes?
Sae...?
Have you made up your mind?

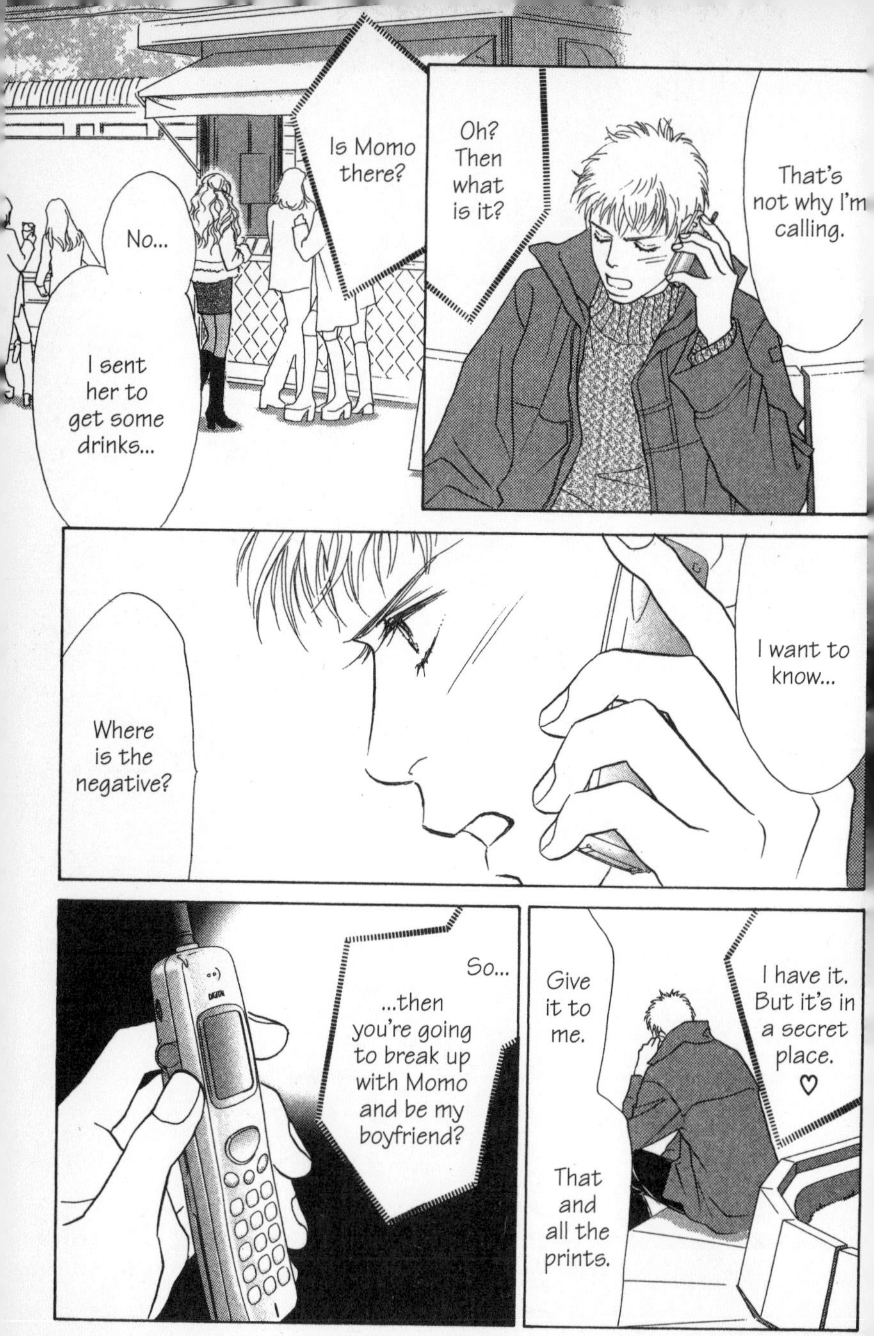
That's not why I'm calling.
Oh? Then what is it?
Is Momo there?
No...
I sent her to get some drinks...
I want to know...
Where is the negative?
I have it. But it's in a secret place. ♡
Give it to me.
That and all the prints.
So...
...then you're going to break up with Momo and be my boyfriend?

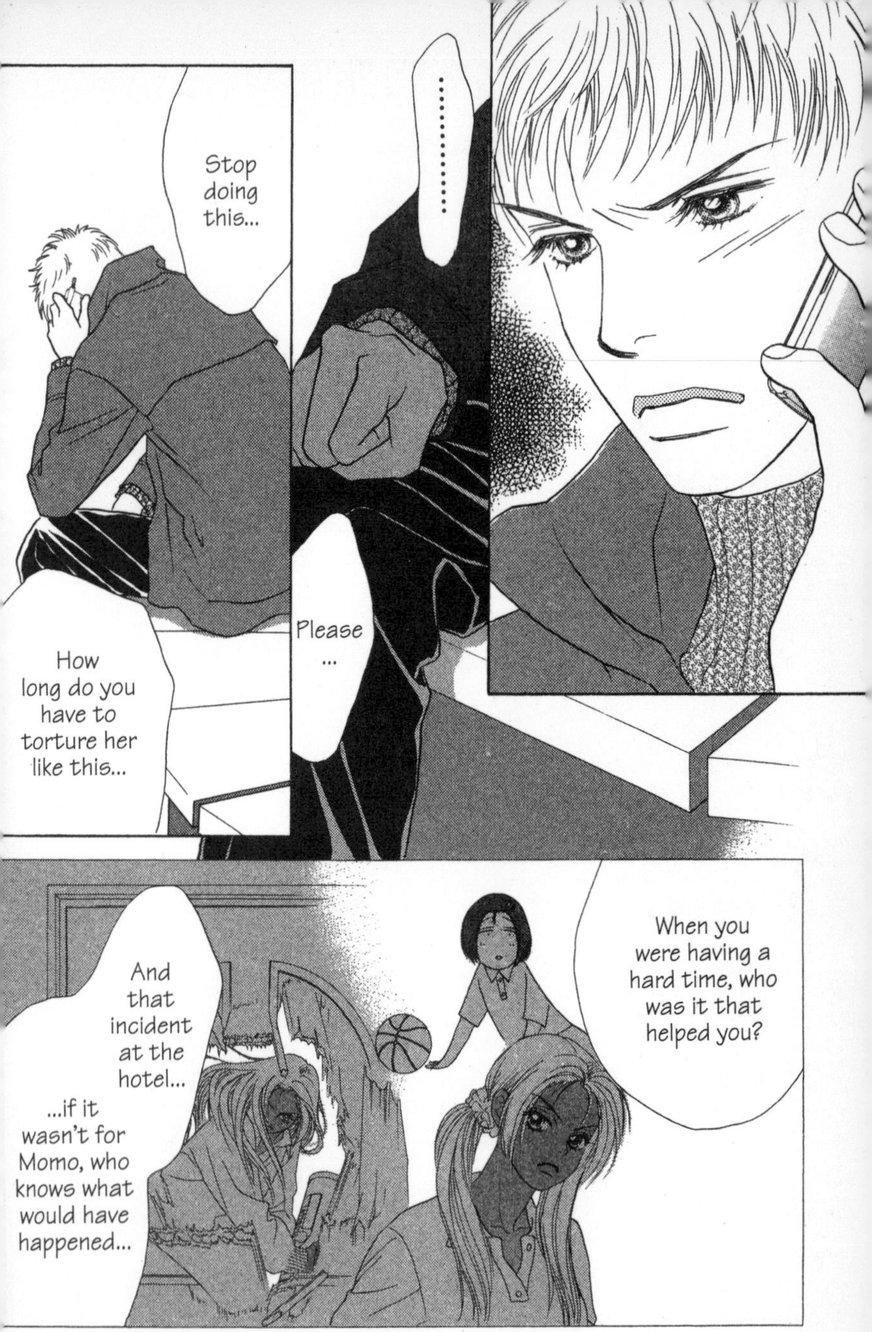
....
Please...
Stop doing this...
How long do you have to torture her like this...
When you were having a hard time, who was it that helped you?
And that incident at the hotel...
...if it wasn't for Momo, who knows what would have happened...

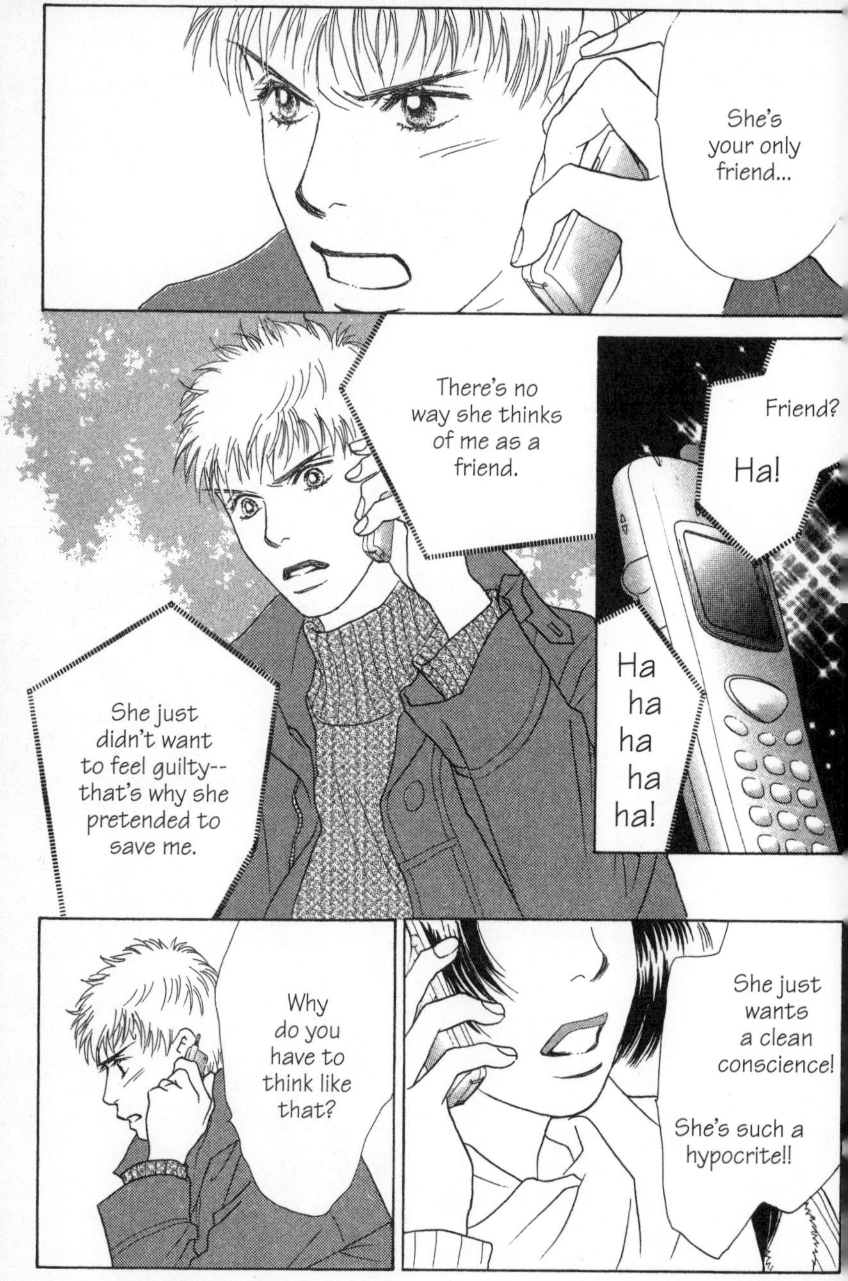

She's your only friend...
Friend?
Ha!
Ha ha ha ha ha!
There's no way she thinks of me as a friend.
She just didn't want to feel guilty--that's why she pretended to save me.
She just wants a clean conscience!
She's such a hypocrite!!
Why do you have to think like that?

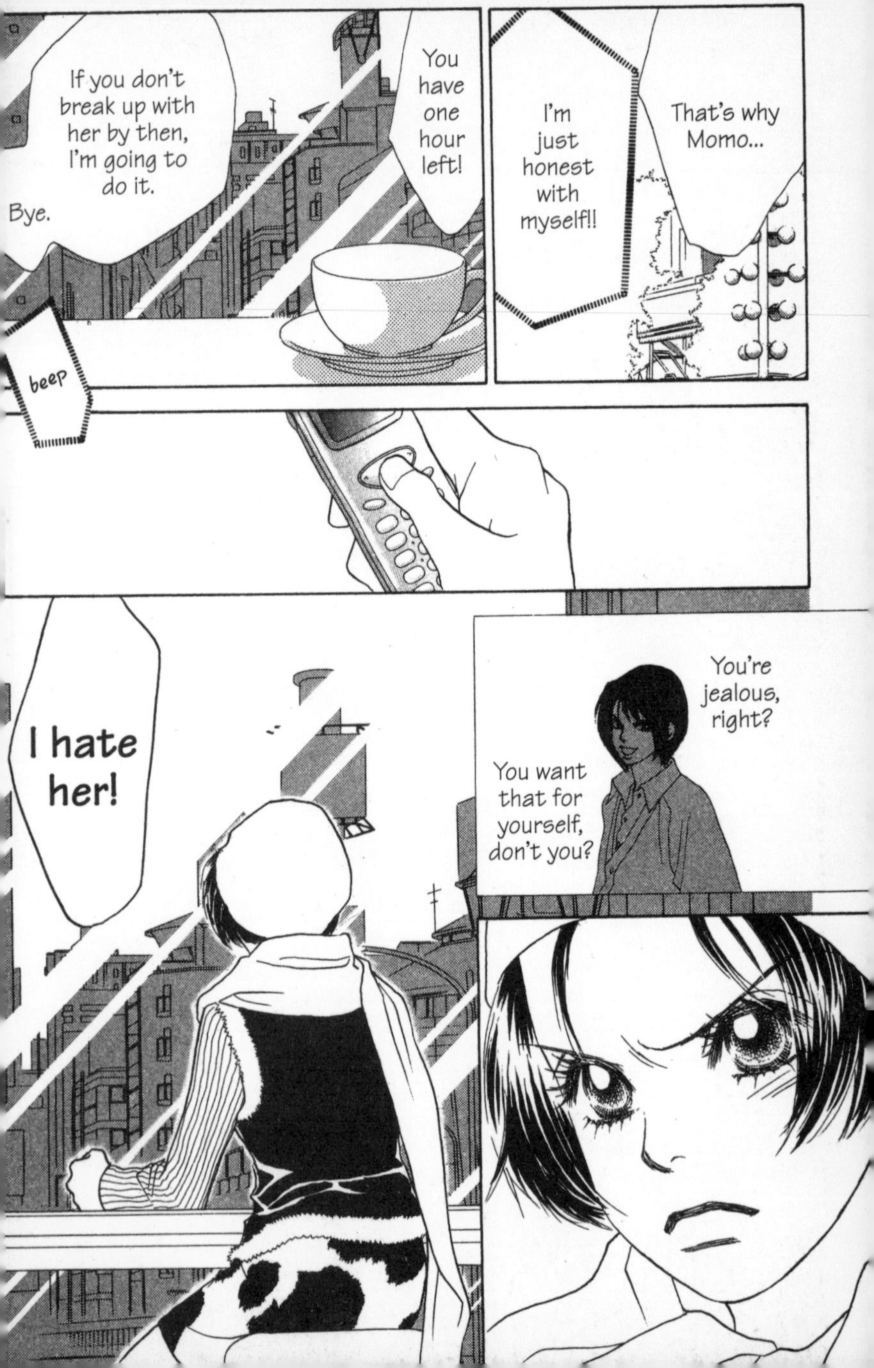
That's why Momo...
I'm just honest with myself!!
You have one hour left!
If you don't break up with her by then, I'm going to do it.
Bye.
beep
You're jealous, right?
You want that for yourself, don't you?
I hate her!

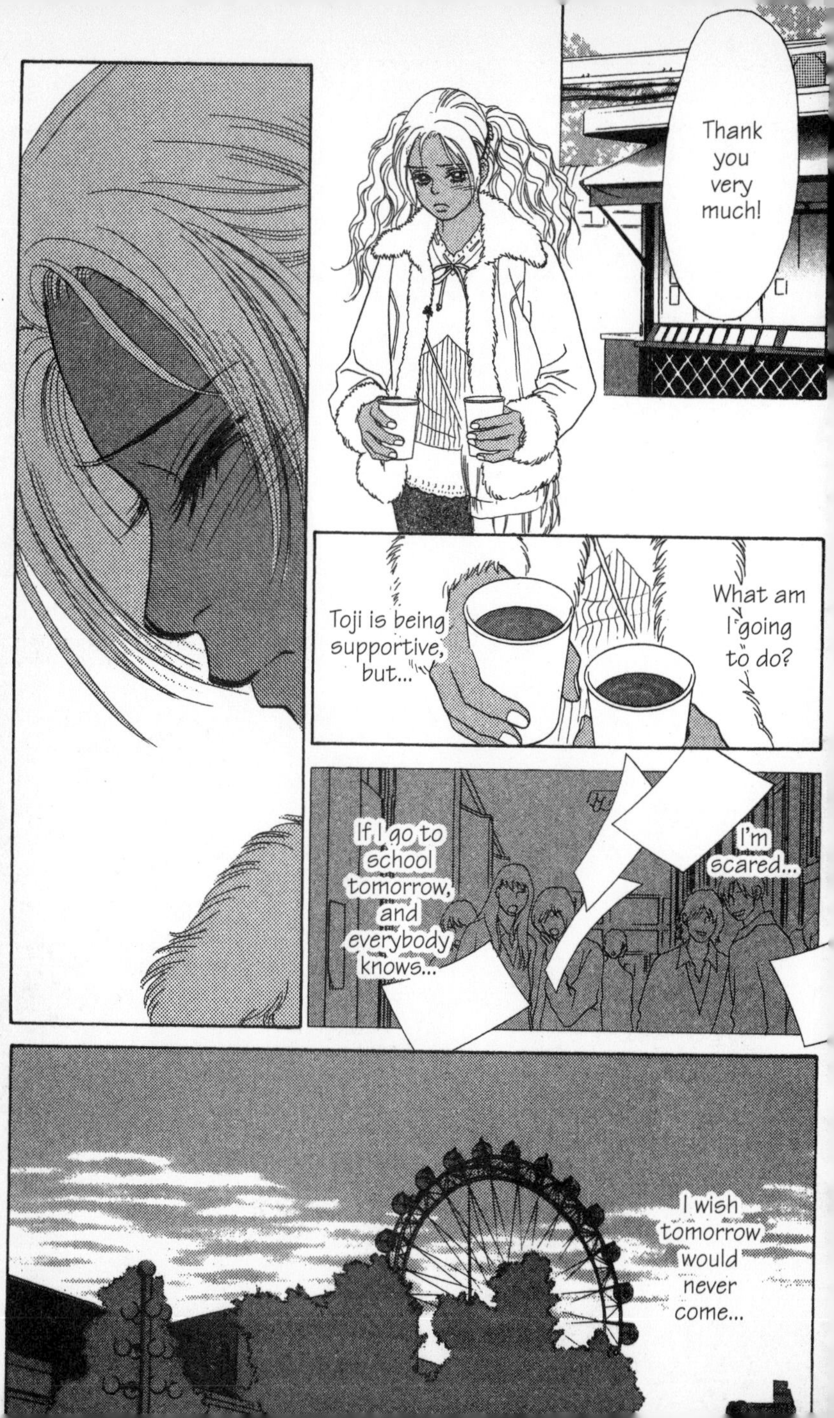
Thank you very much!
What am I going to do?
Toji is being supportive, but...
I'm scared...
If I go to school tomorrow, and everybody knows...
I wish tomorrow would never come...

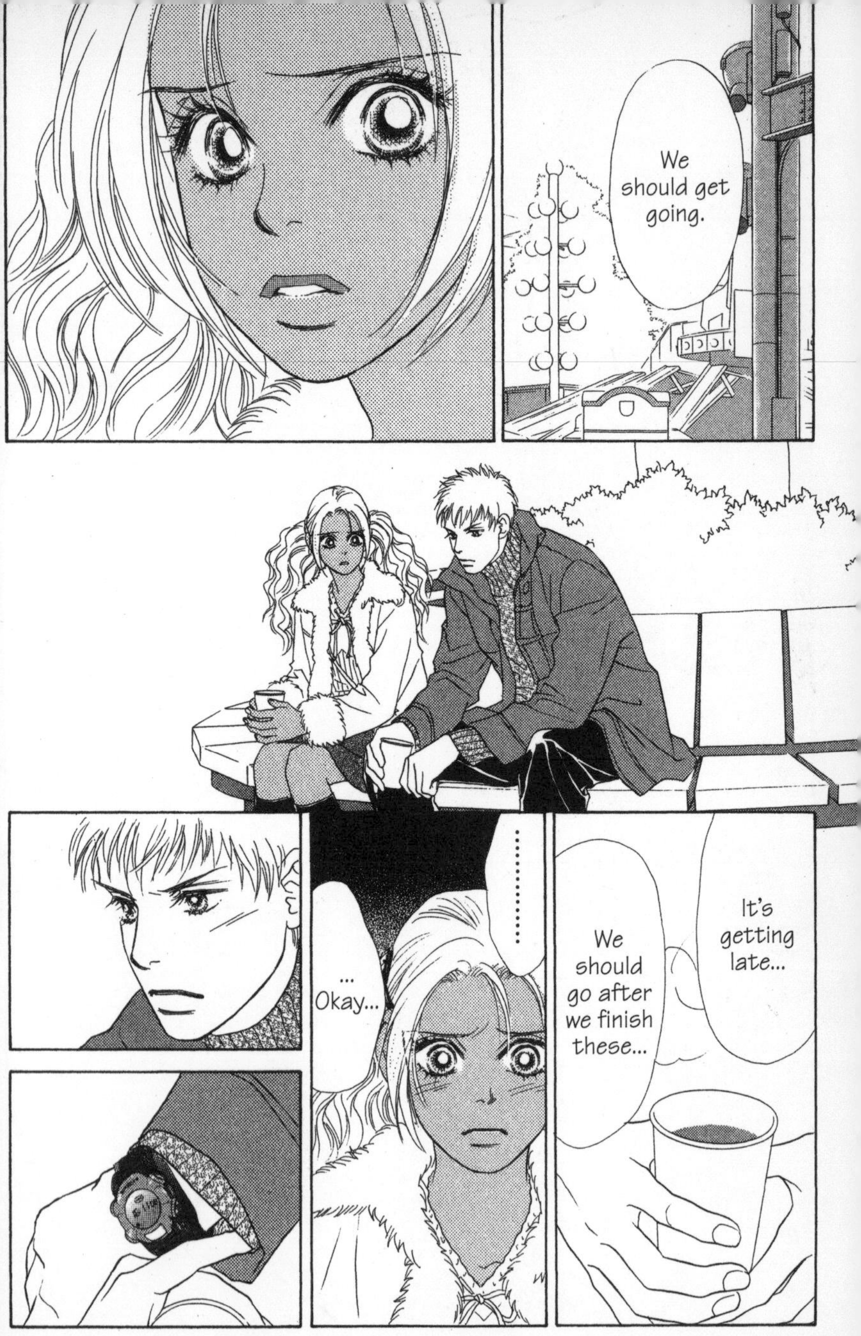
We should get going.
It's getting late...
We should go after we finish these...
......
... Okay...

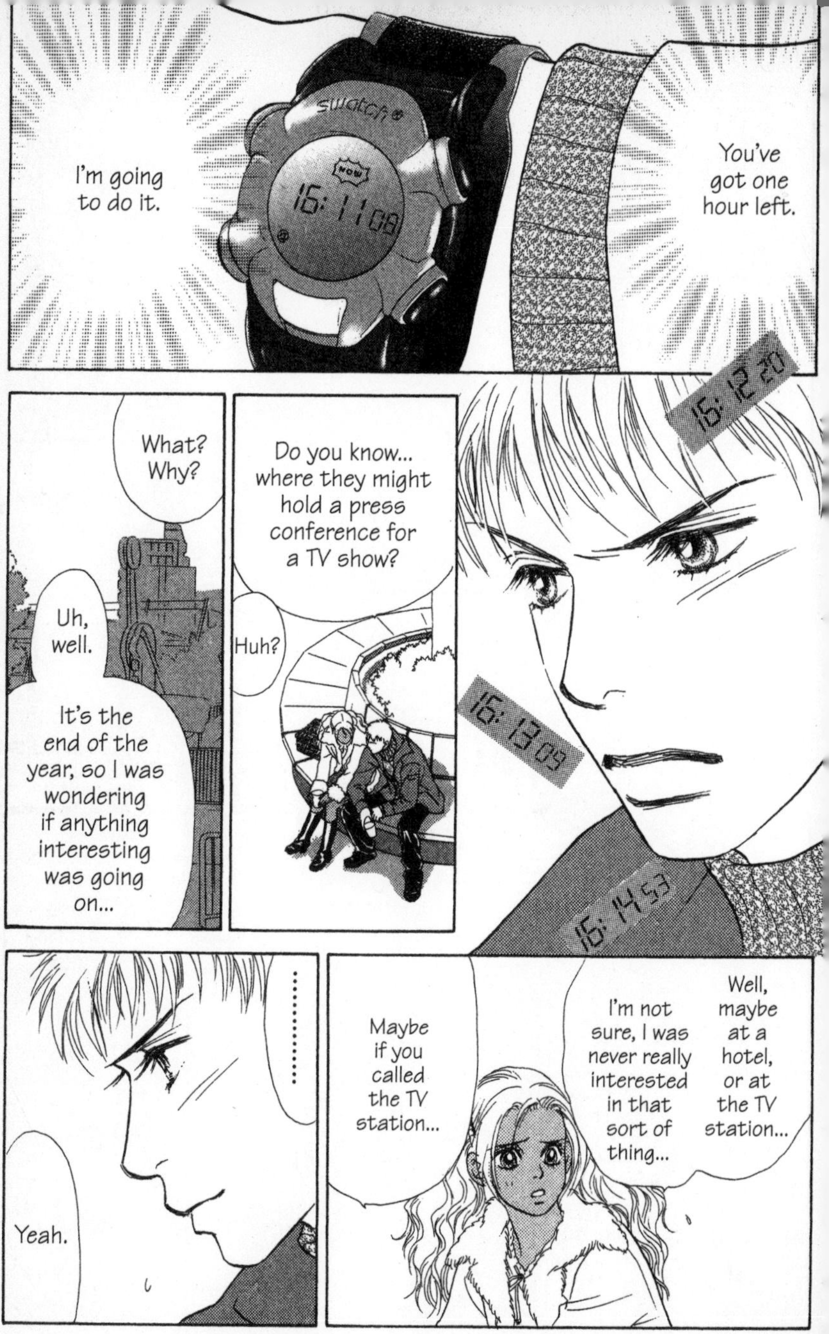
You've got one hour left.
swatch
NOW
16:11 08
I'm going to do it.
16:12 20
16:13 09
16:14 53
Do you know... where they might hold a press conference for a TV show?
Huh?
What? Why?
Uh, well.
It's the end of the year, so I was wondering if anything interesting was going on...
Well, maybe at a hotel, or at the TV station...
I'm not sure, I was never really interested in that sort of thing...
Maybe if you called the TV station...
....
Yeah.

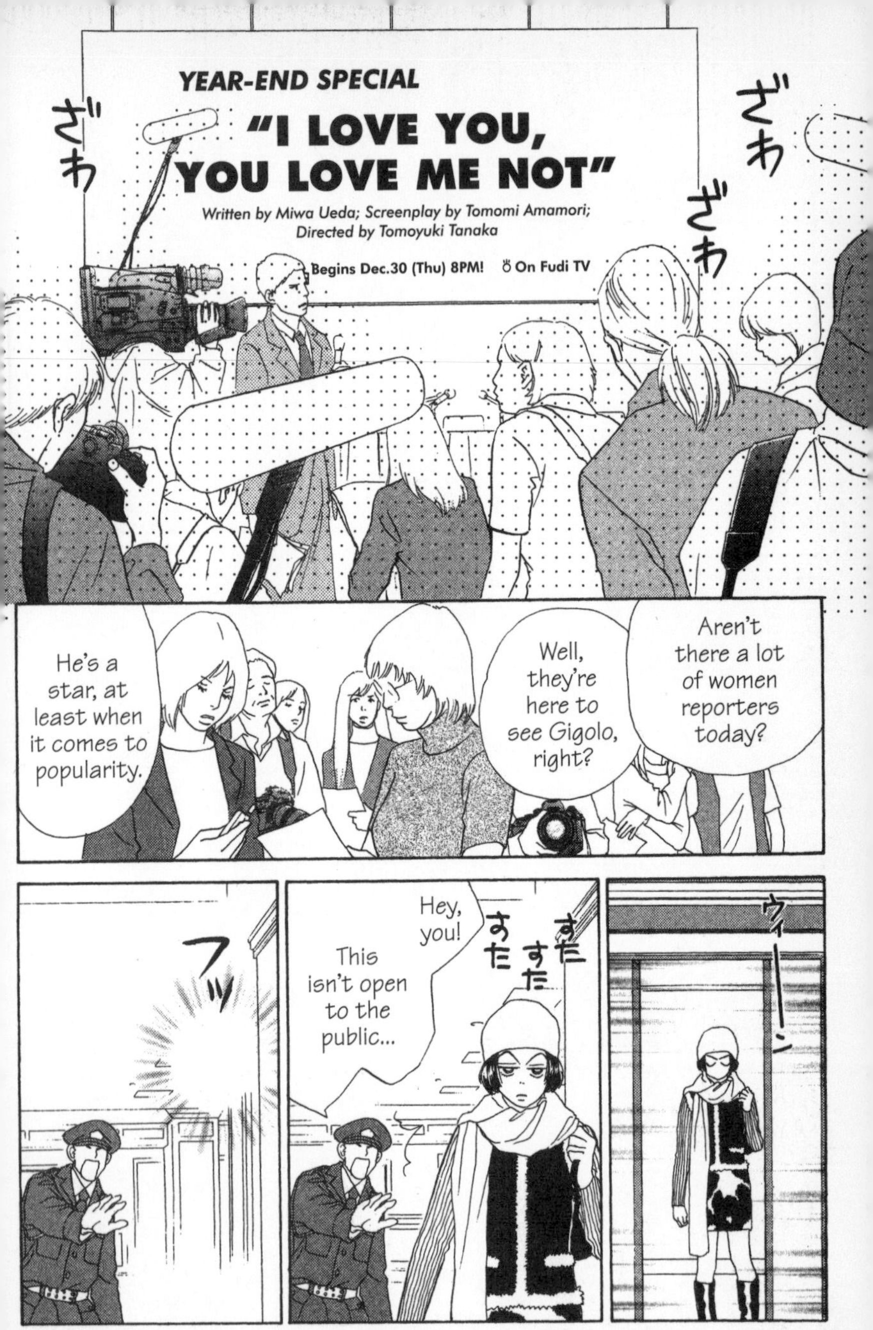

ざわ
ざわ
YEAR-END SPECIAL
"I LOVE YOU, YOU LOVE ME NOT"
Written by Miwa Ueda; Screenplay by Tomomi Amamori; Directed by Tomoyuki Tanaka
Begins Dec.30 (Thu) 8PM! On Fudi TV
ざわ
Aren't there a lot of women reporters today?
Well, they're here to see Gigolo, right?
He's a star, at least when it comes to popularity.
ウィーーン
すた すた すた
Hey, you!
This isn't open to the public...
フッ

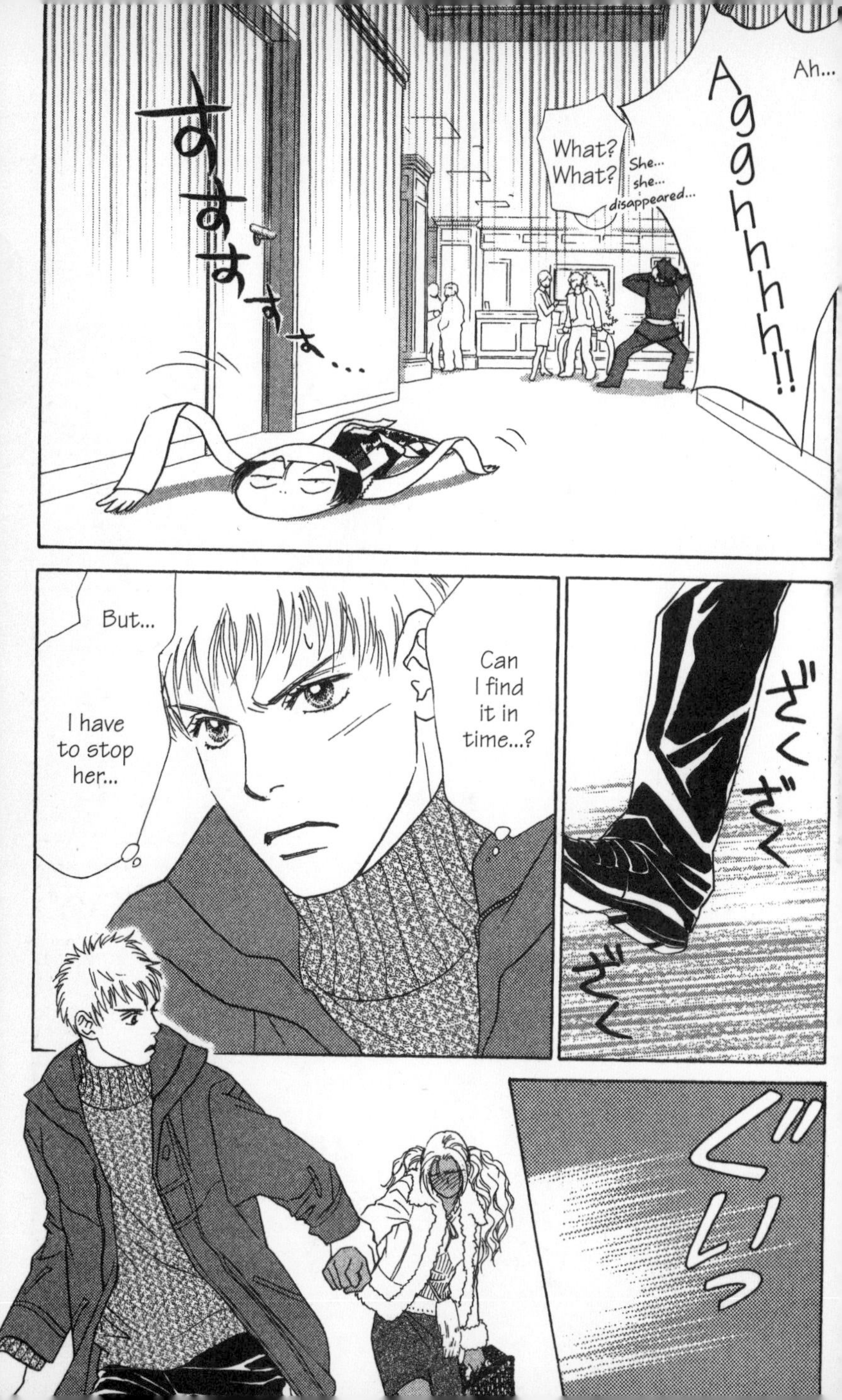
Ah...
Agghhhhh!!
She... she... disappeared...
What? What?
すすすす…
ざくざく
ざく
Can I find it in time...?
But...
I have to stop her...
ぐいーっ

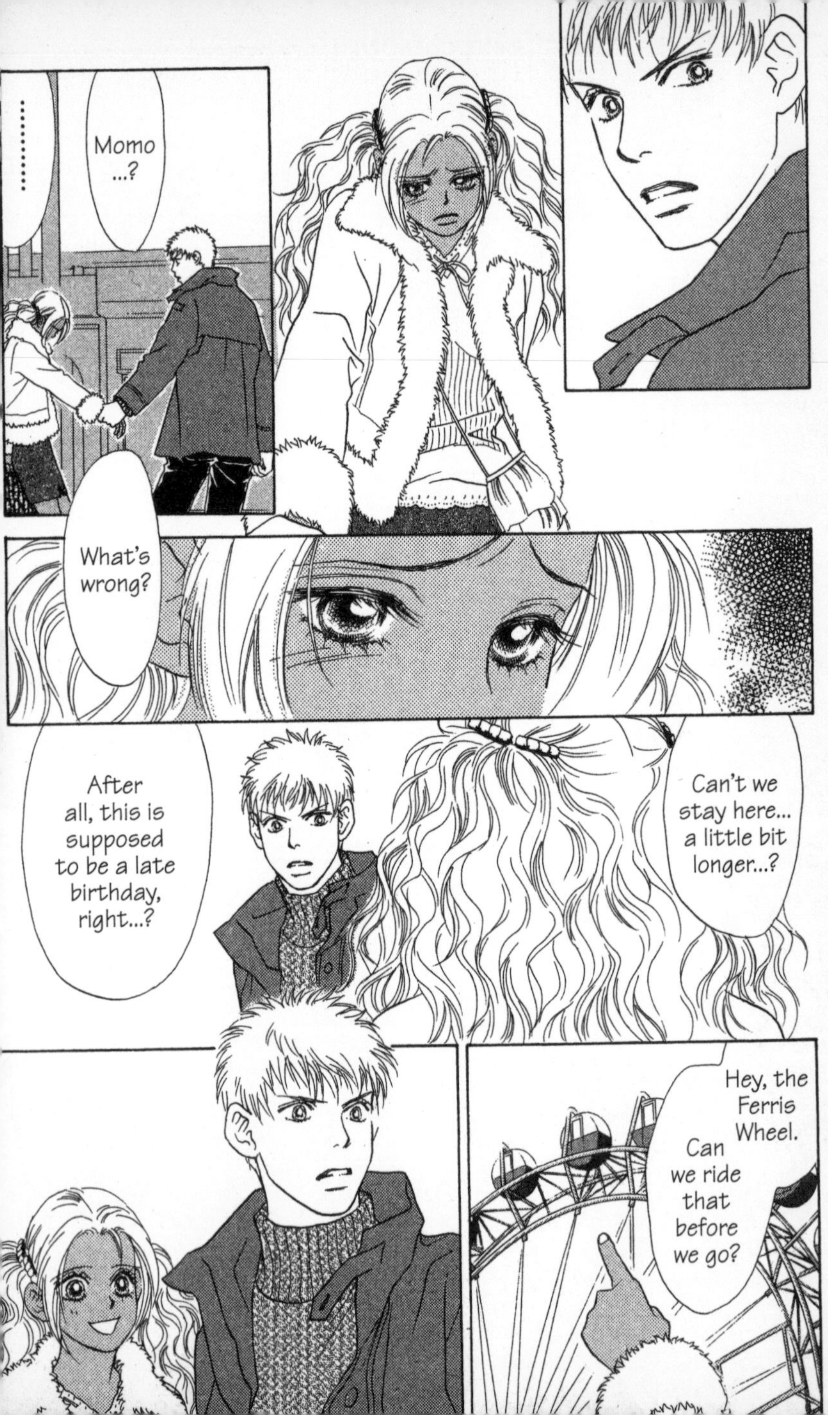
Momo ...?
......
What's wrong?
Can't we stay here... a little bit longer...?
After all, this is supposed to be a late birthday, right...?
Hey, the Ferris Wheel. Can we ride that before we go?

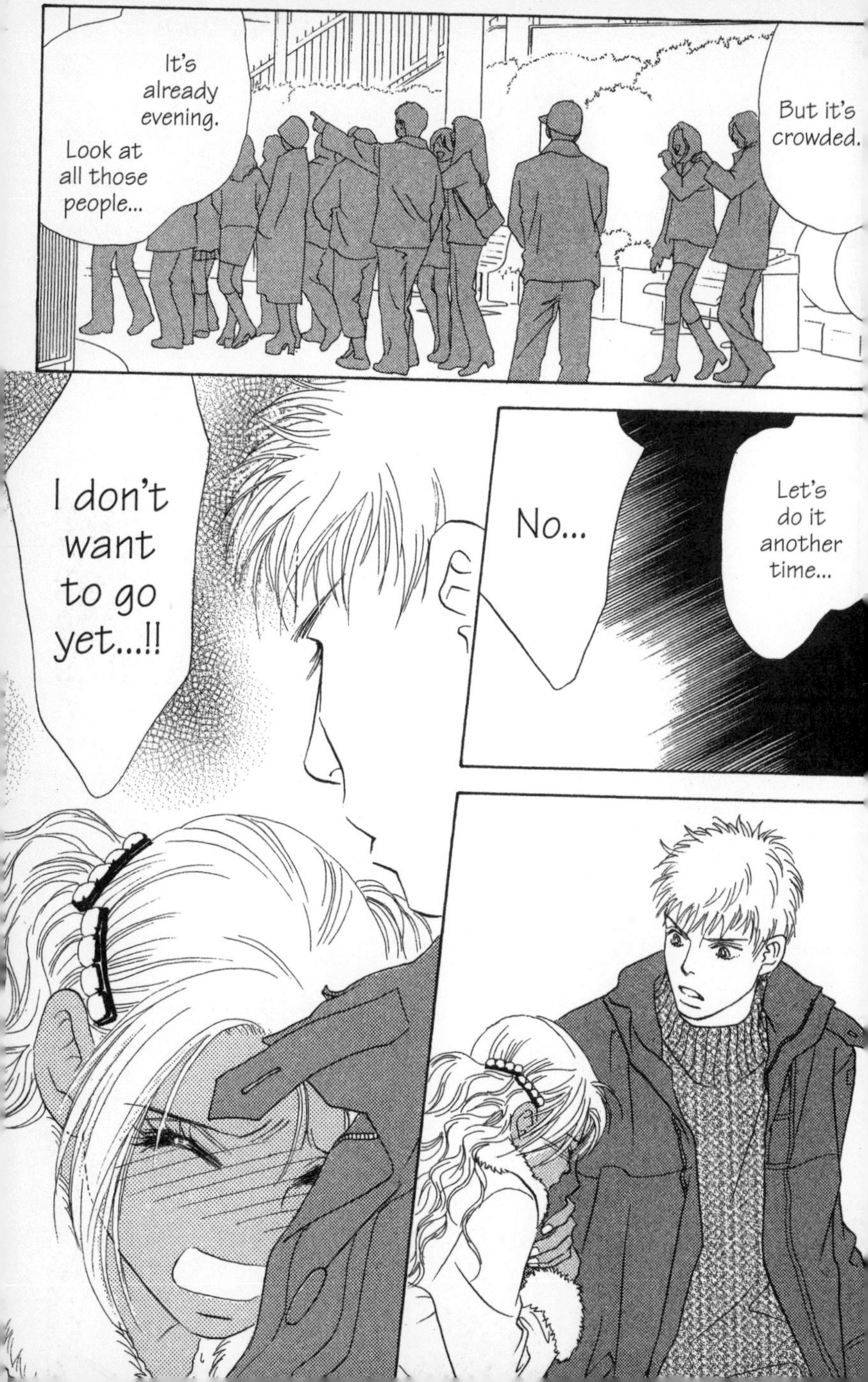
But it's crowded.
It's already evening.
Look at all those people...
Let's do it another time...
No...
I don't want to go yet...!!

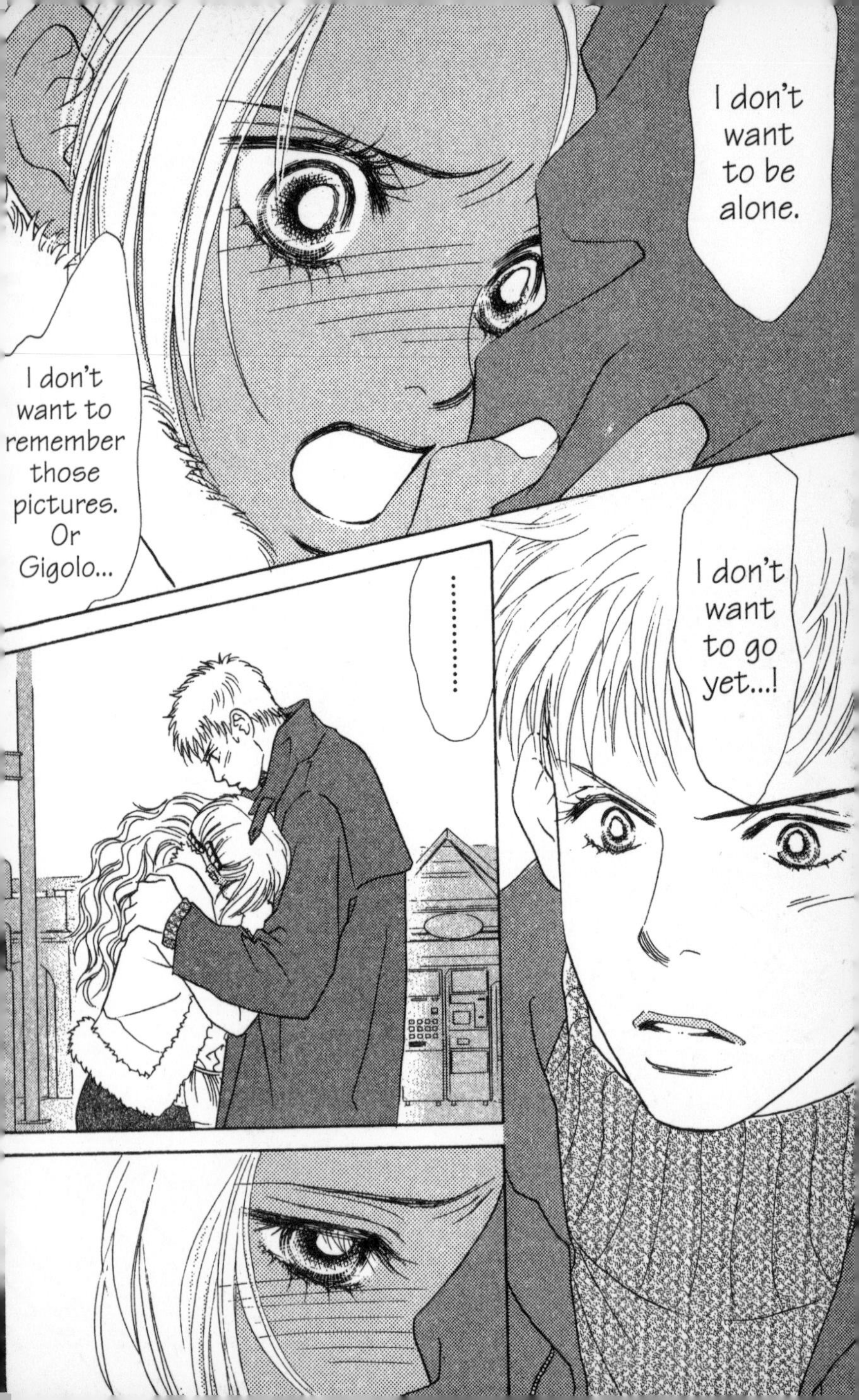
I don't want to be alone.
I don't want to remember those pictures. Or Gigolo...
I don't want to go yet...!
......

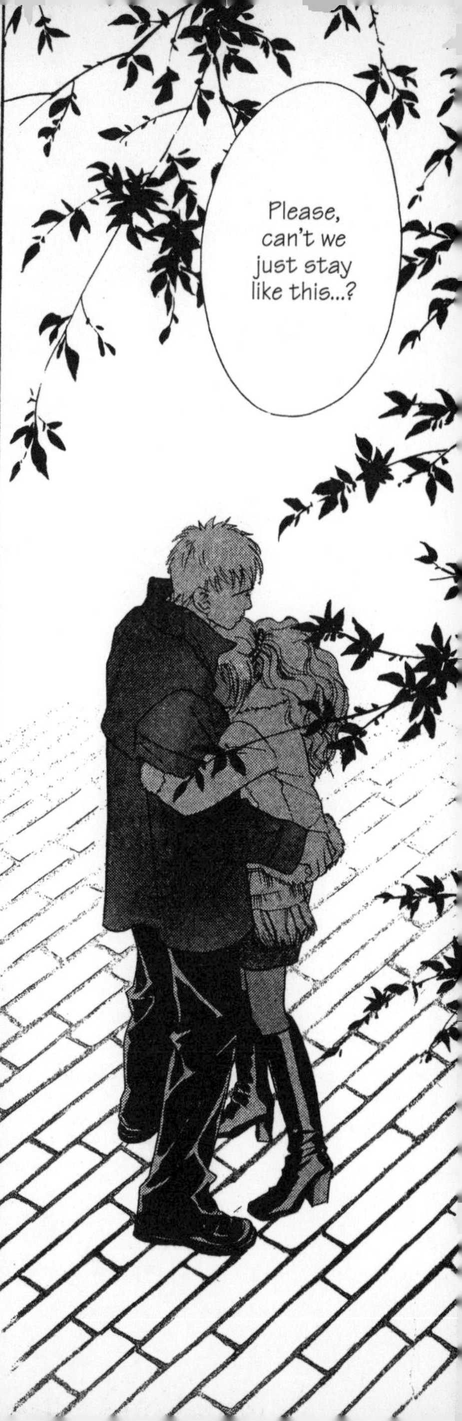
Please, can't we just stay like this...?

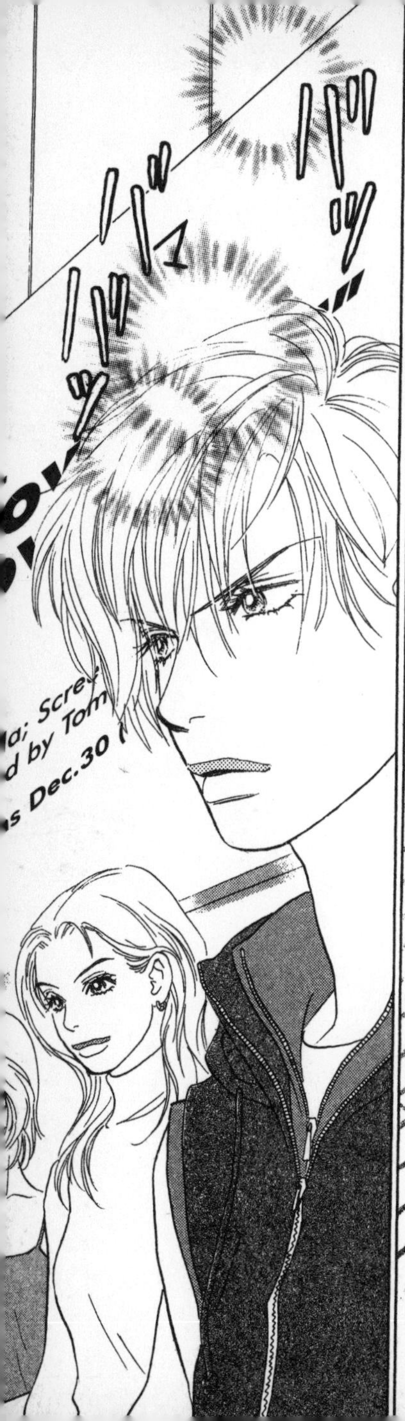
a; Scre
d by Tom
s Dec.30

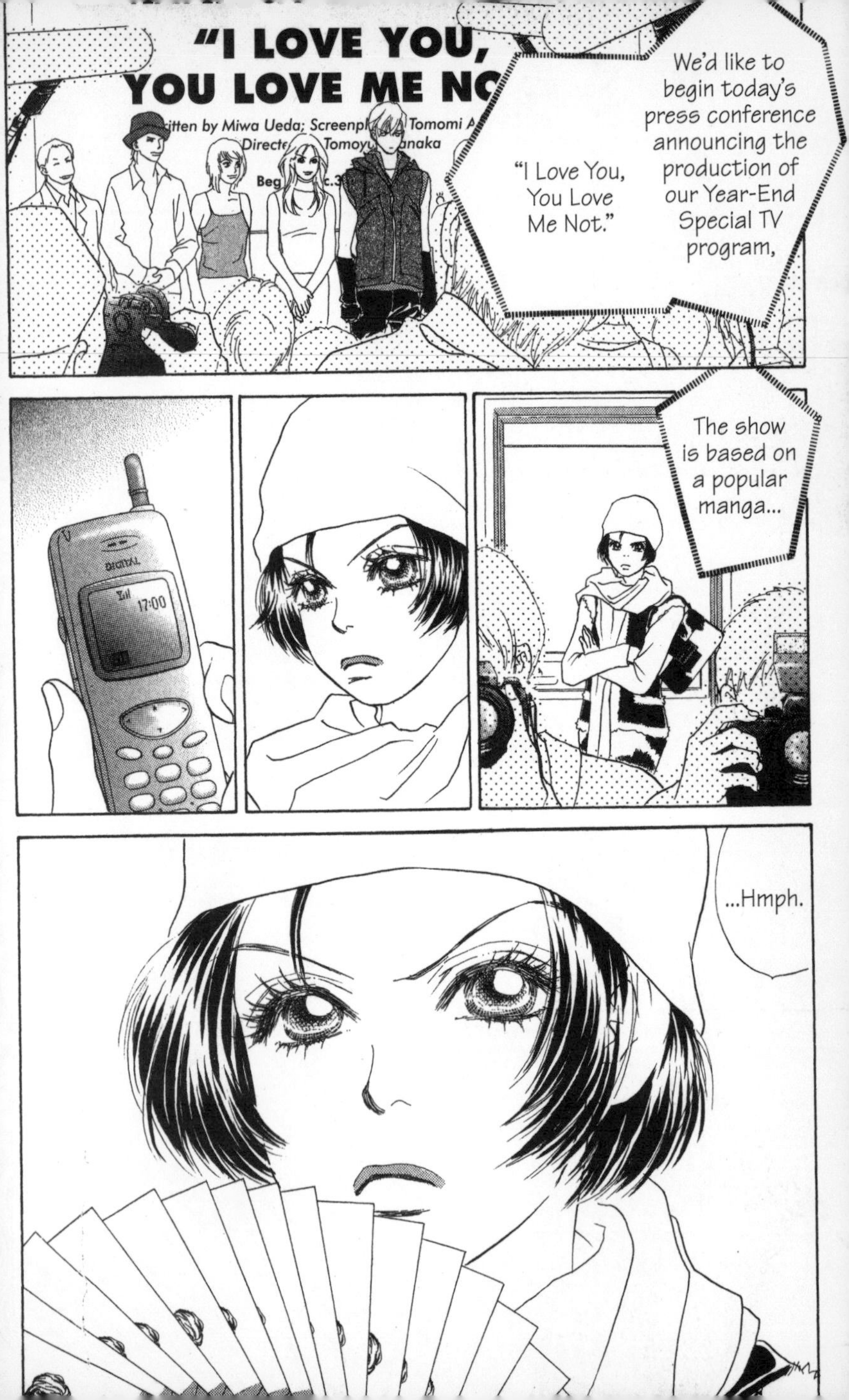
“I LOVE YOU,
YOU LOVE ME NO
ritten by Miwa Ueda; Screenp Tomomi A
Directe Tomoyu anaka
We’d like to begin today’s press conference announcing the production of our Year-End Special TV program,
“I Love You, You Love Me Not.”
The show is based on a popular manga...
DIGITAL
17:00
...Hmph.

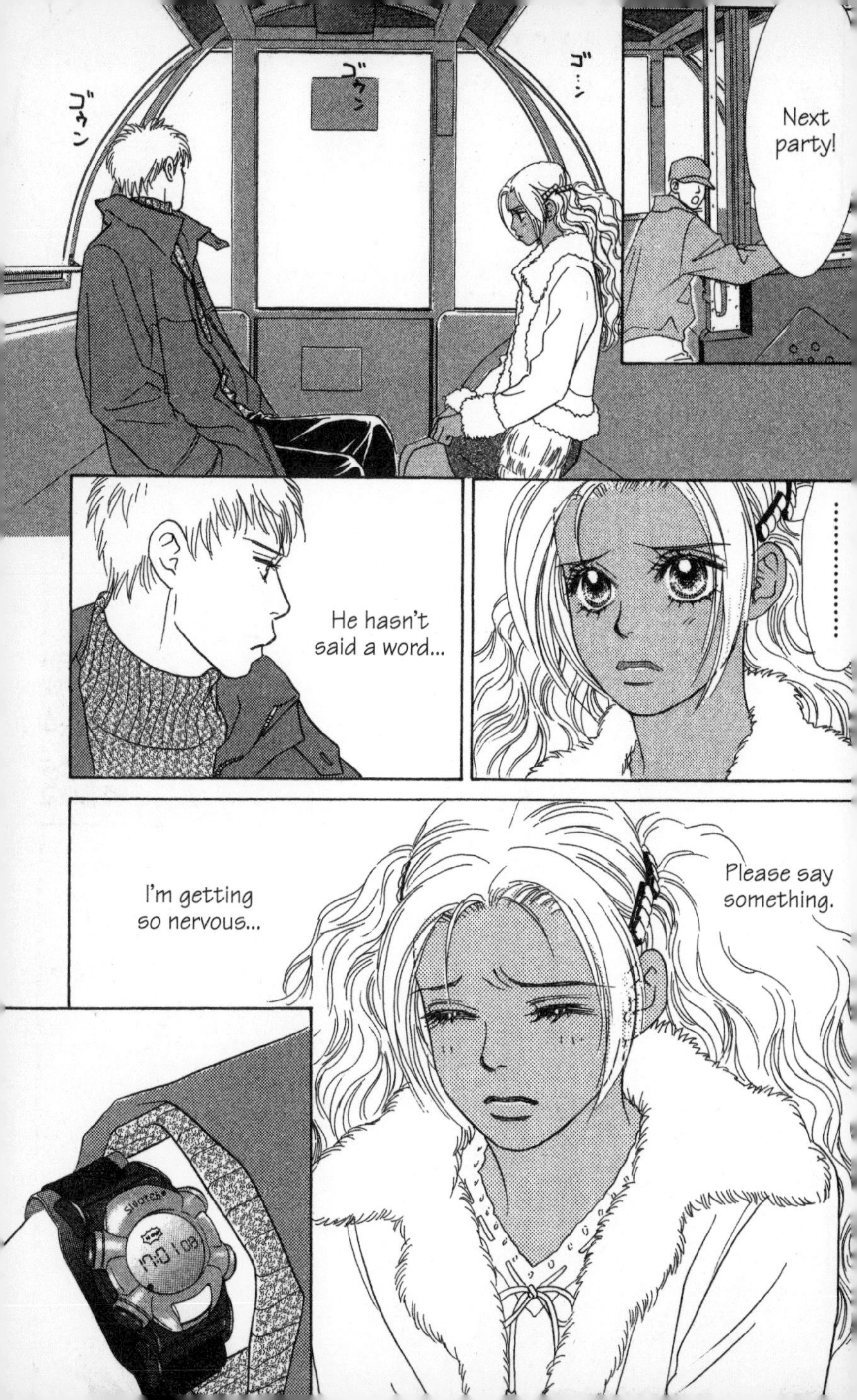
Next party!
ゴ…ン
ゴウン
ゴウン
……
He hasn't said a word...
Please say something.
I'm getting so nervous...

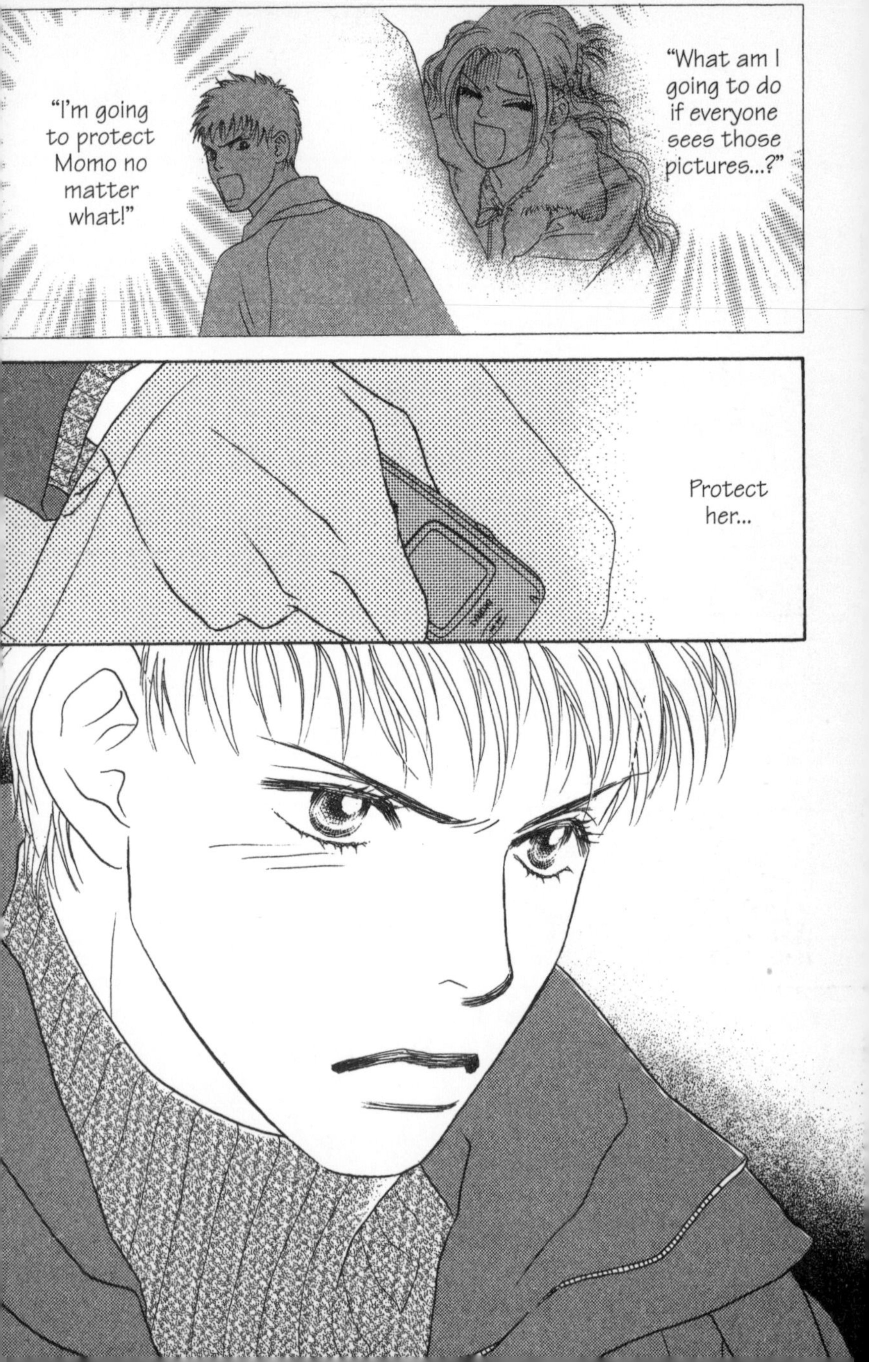
"What am I going to do if everyone sees those pictures...?"
"I'm going to protect Momo no matter what!"
Protect her...

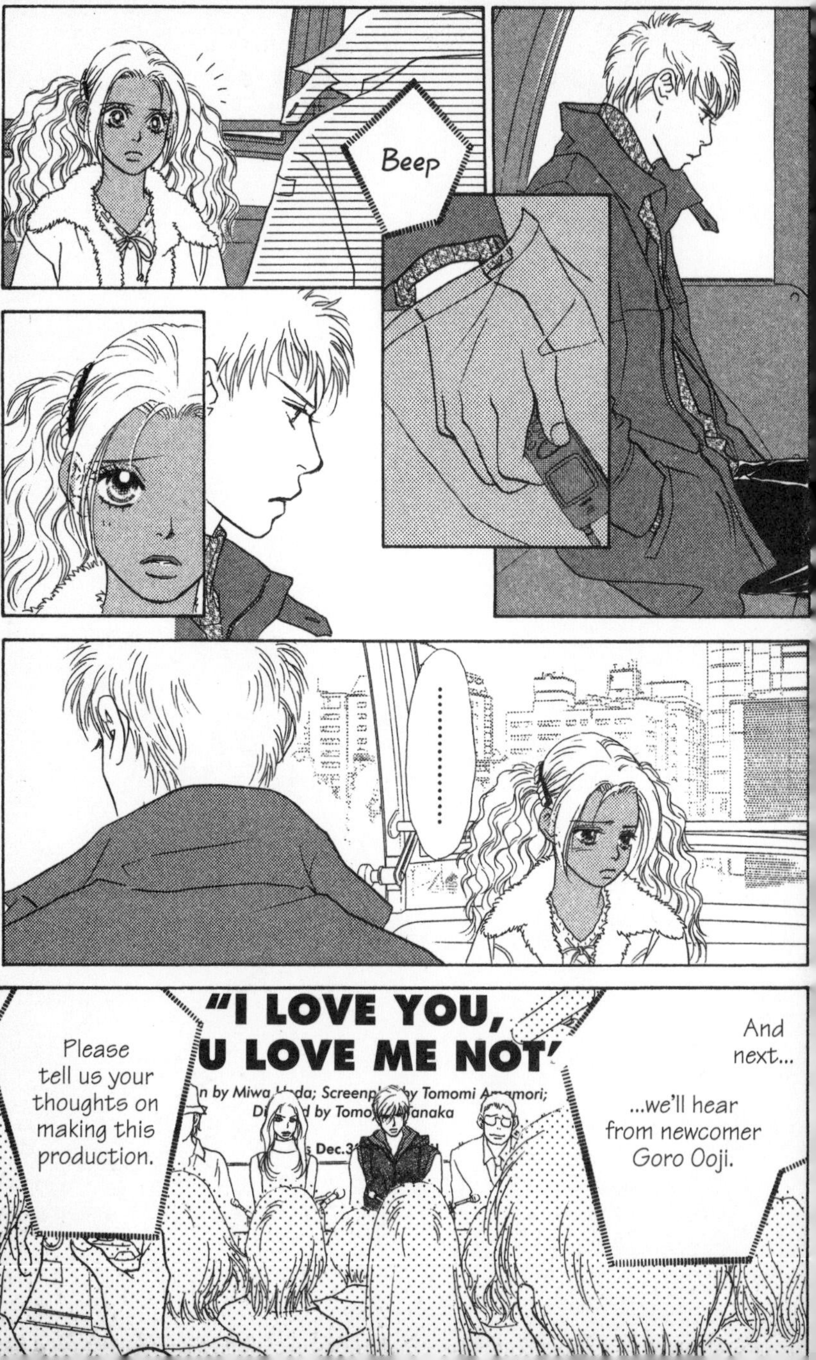
Beep
......
And next...
...we'll hear from newcomer Goro Ooji.
"I LOVE YOU,
U LOVE ME NOT'
Please tell us your thoughts on making this production.

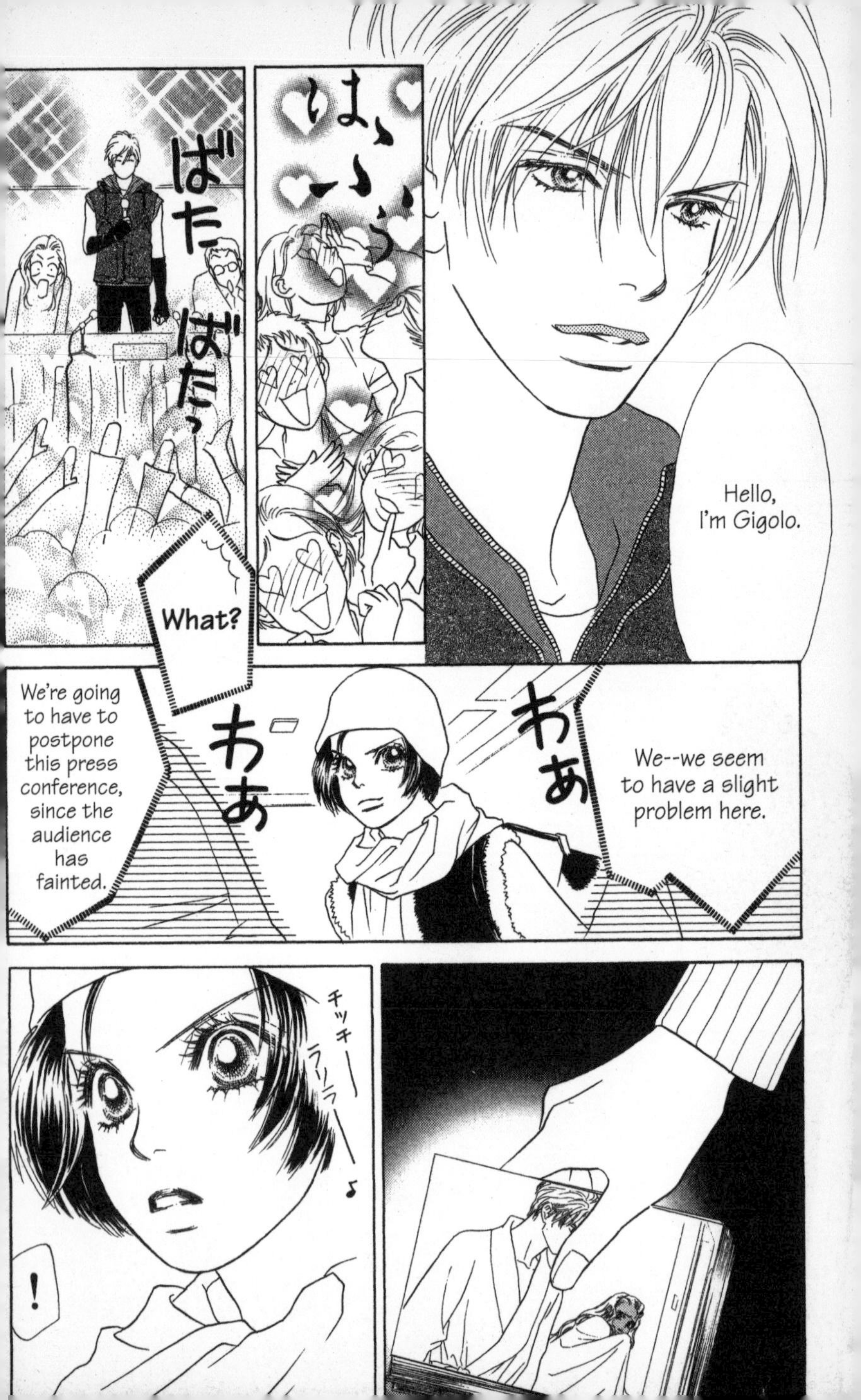
Hello, I'm Gigolo.
ばたばたっ
What?
We--we seem to have a slight problem here.
わぁ
わぁ
We're going to have to postpone this press conference, since the audience has fainted.
チッチー
!

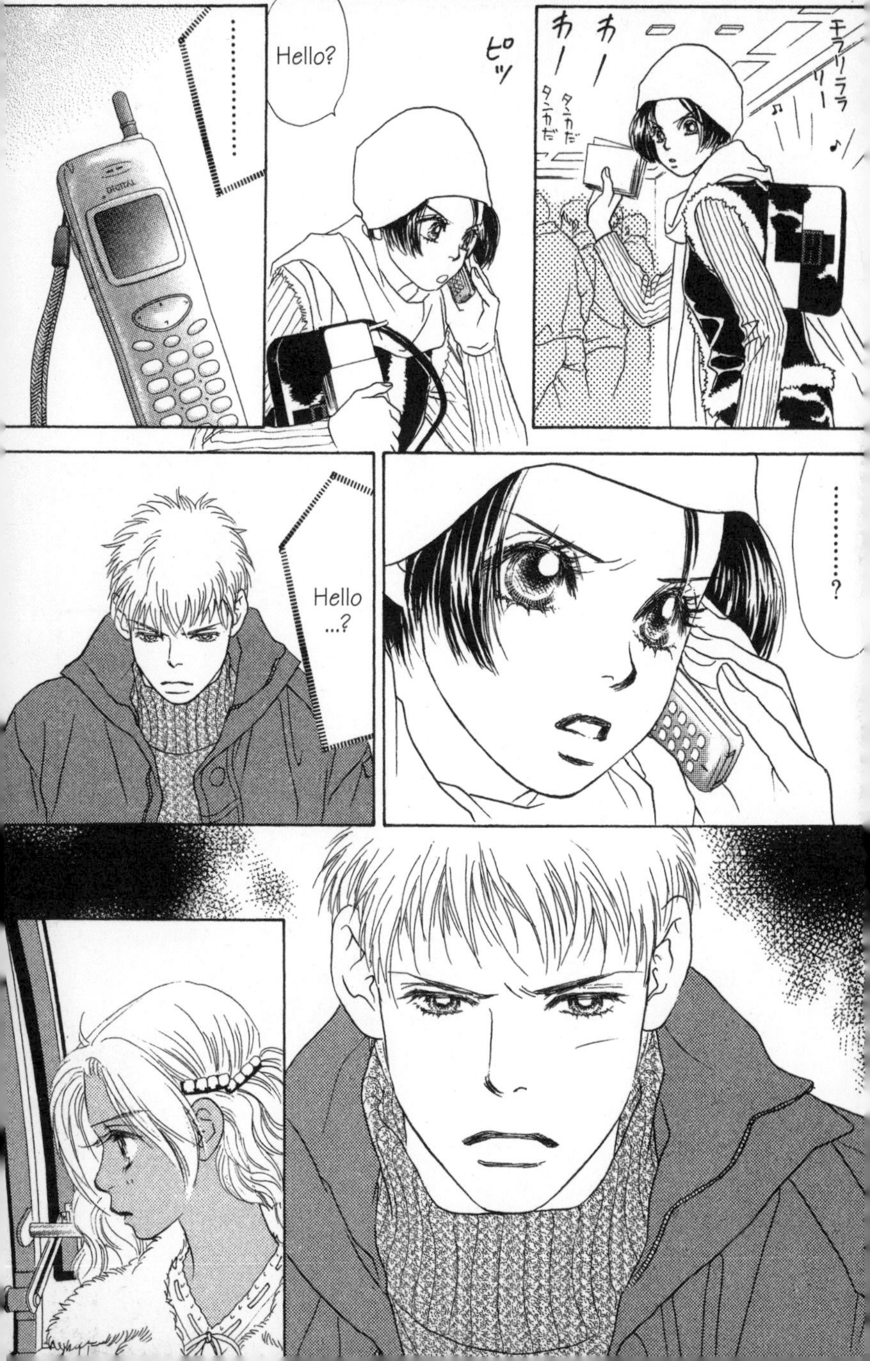
チラリララ
リー
♪
♪
ホー
ホー
タンカだ
タンカだ
ピッ
Hello?
……
……?
Hello
...?

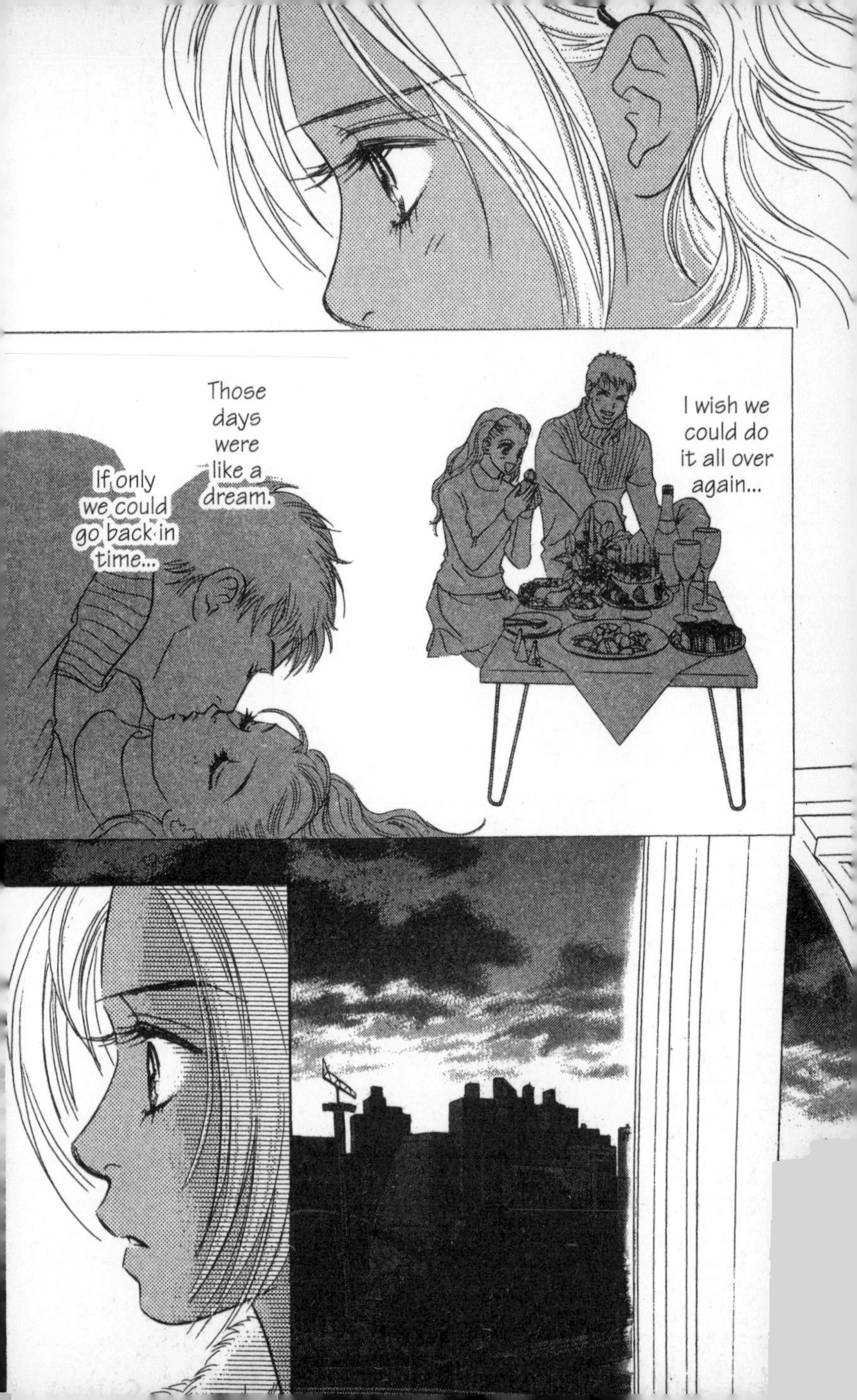
I wish we could do it all over again...
Those days were like a dream.
If only we could go back in time...

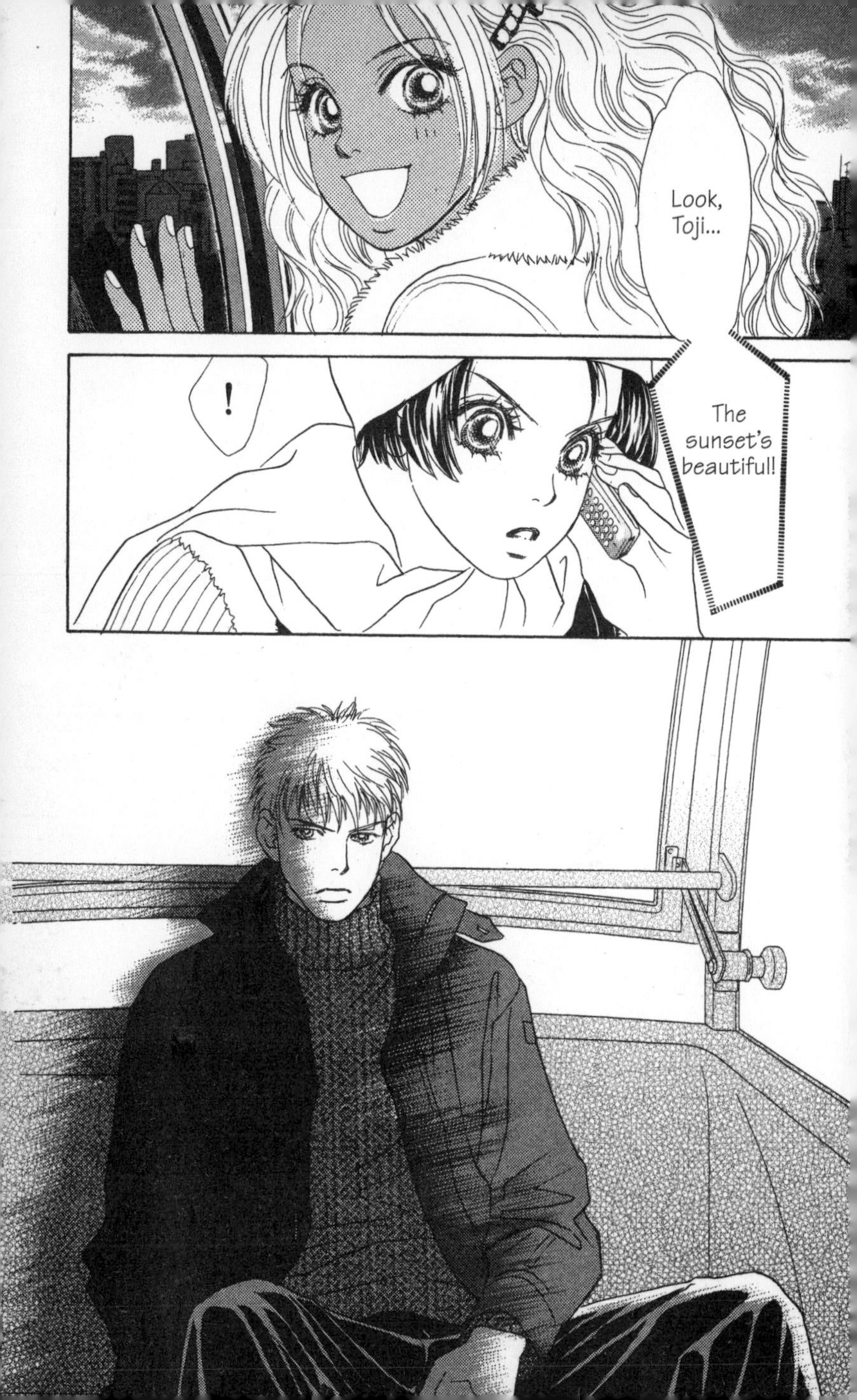
Look, Toji...
The sunset's beautiful!
!

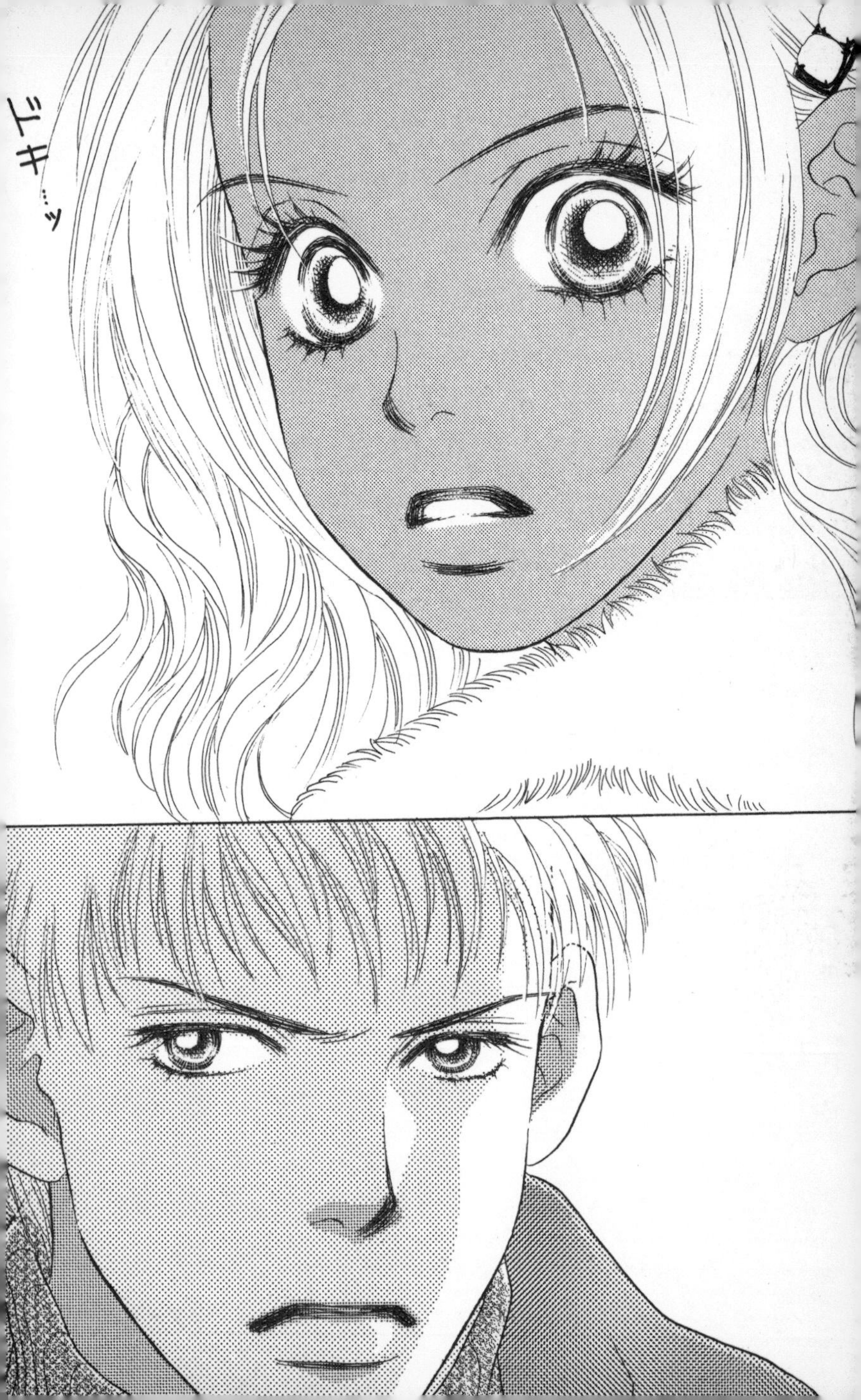
ドキ…ッ

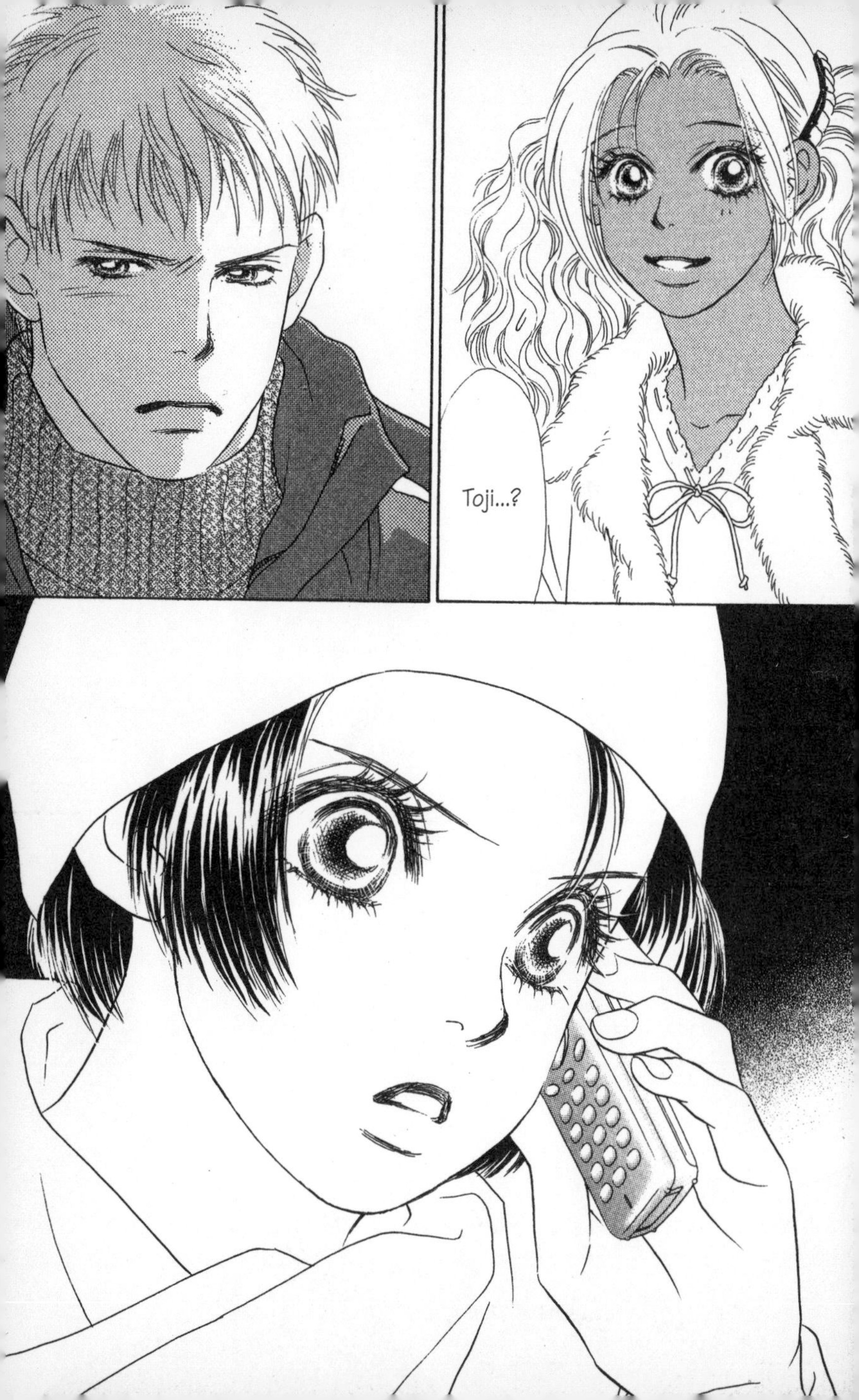
Toji...?

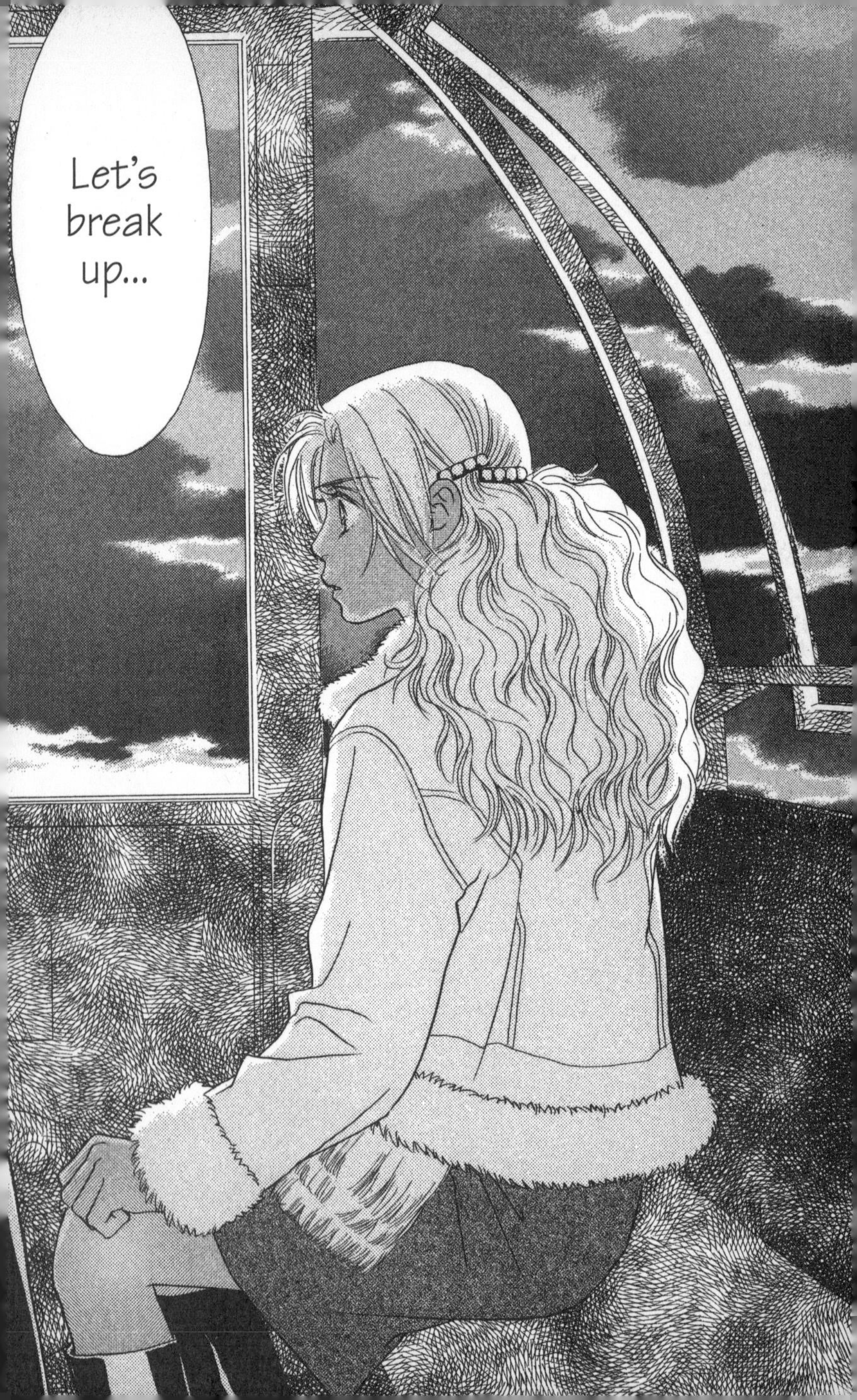
Let's break up...

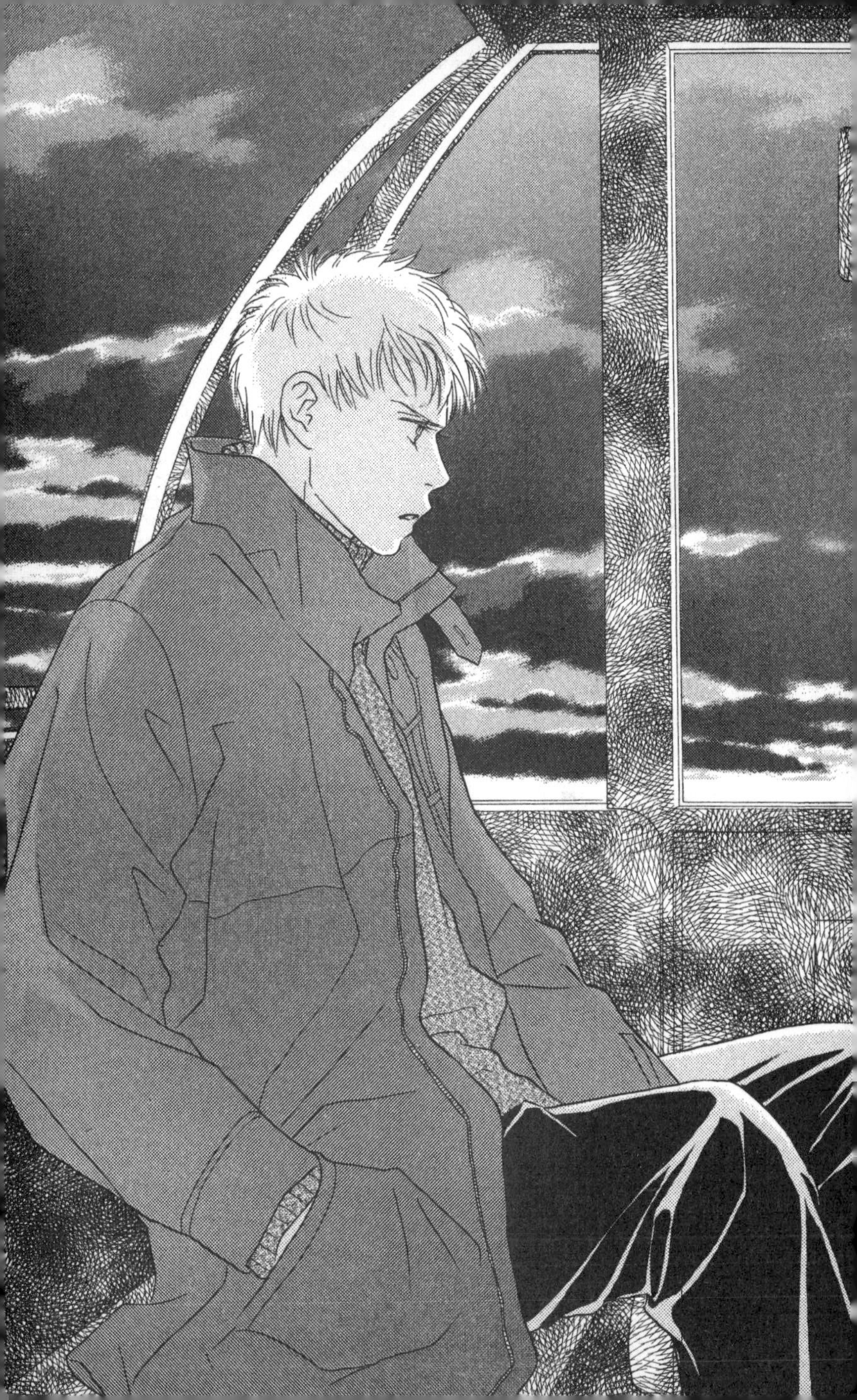

BONUS PAGE

What do boys think of girls who are unpopular with other girls?

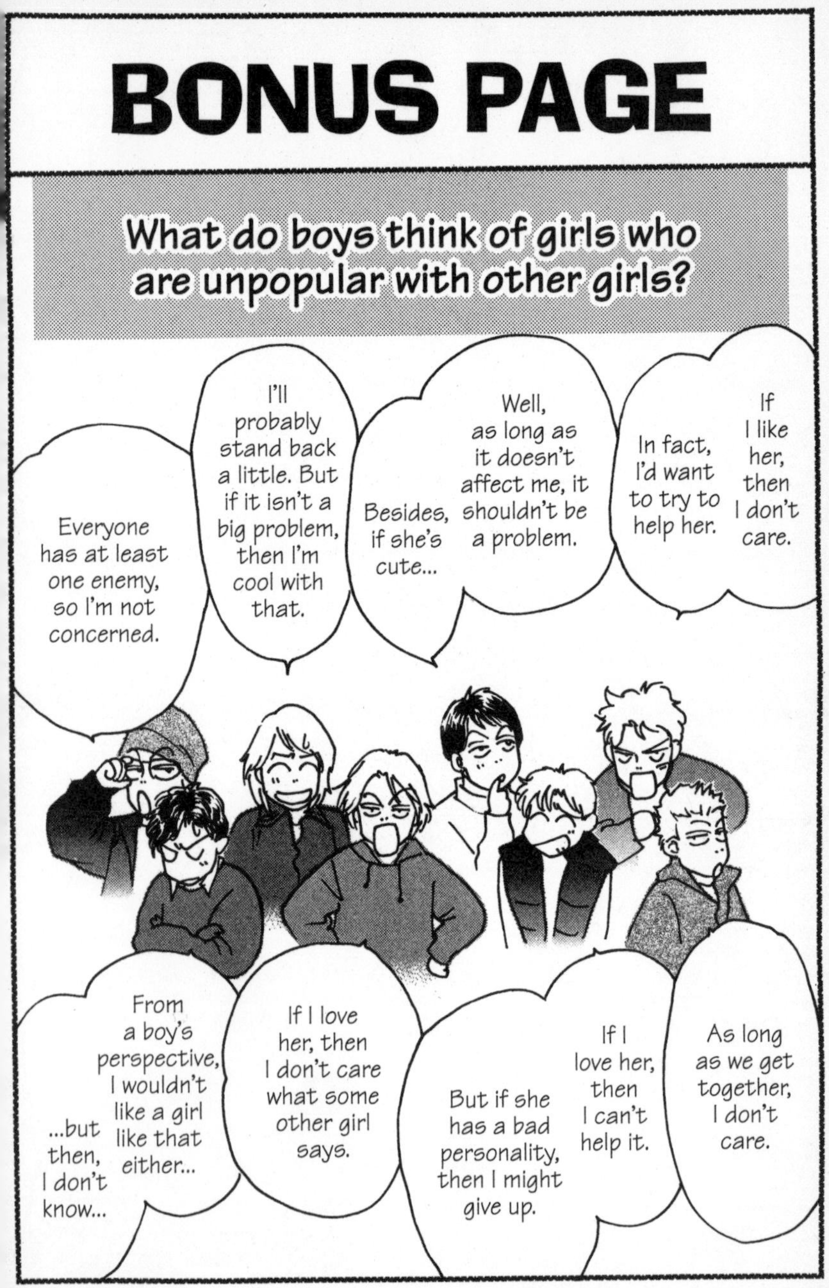
If I like her, then I don't care.
In fact, I'd want to try to help her.
Well, as long as it doesn't affect me, it shouldn't be a problem.
Besides, if she's cute...
I'll probably stand back a little. But if it isn't a big problem, then I'm cool with that.
Everyone has at least one enemy, so I'm not concerned.
As long as we get together, I don't care.
If I love her, then I can't help it.
But if she has a bad personality, then I might give up.
If I love her, then I don't care what some other girl says.
From a boy's perspective, I wouldn't like a girl like that either...
...but then, I don't know...

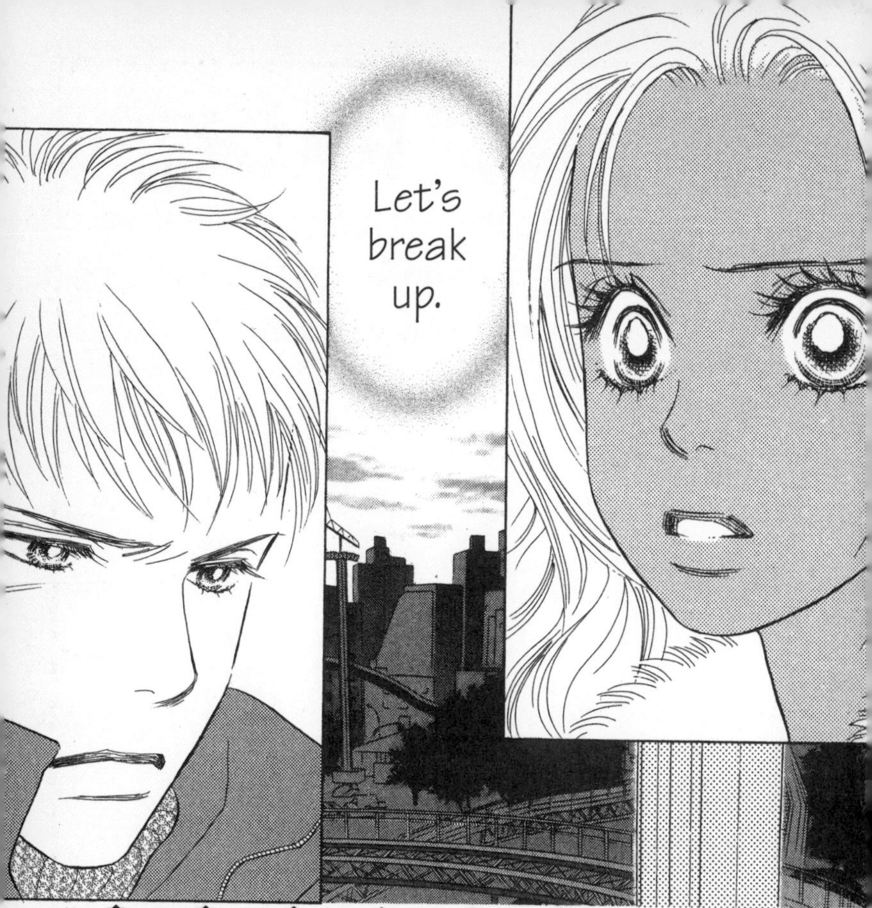
Let's break up.

PEACH CLUB

Let's hear from the boys!

Guys just end up believing whatever a cute girl says.

When a girl's as cute as Sae...

...you'd think she has a good personality too. Or at least, you want to believe that.

Sae doesn't look like the type to have a flip side.

You just want to protect a girl like that.

Guys just don't know the truth about girls.

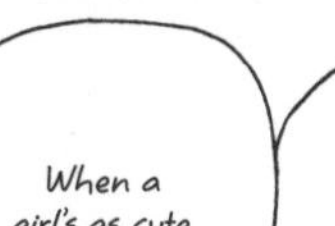

Before I began reading Peach Girl, I wasn't even aware such girls existed.

Author: Are you serious?

But I like Momo better. ♡

Even if you act cute, if you're in love with yourself you're going to be stuck up.

But if Sae's so bad, why would Momo be friends with her in the first place?

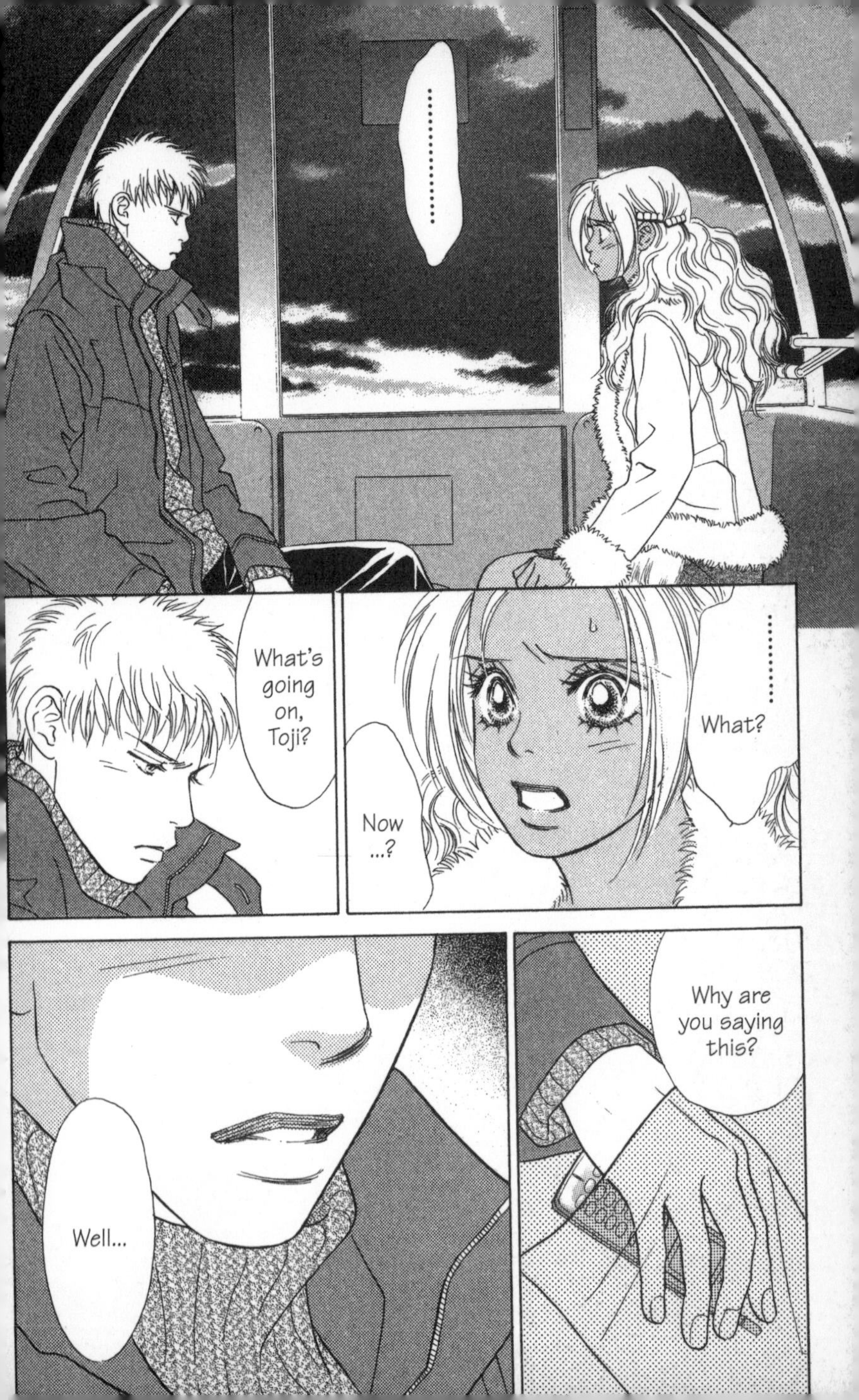
......
......
What?
Now ...?
What's going on, Toji?
Why are you saying this?
Well...

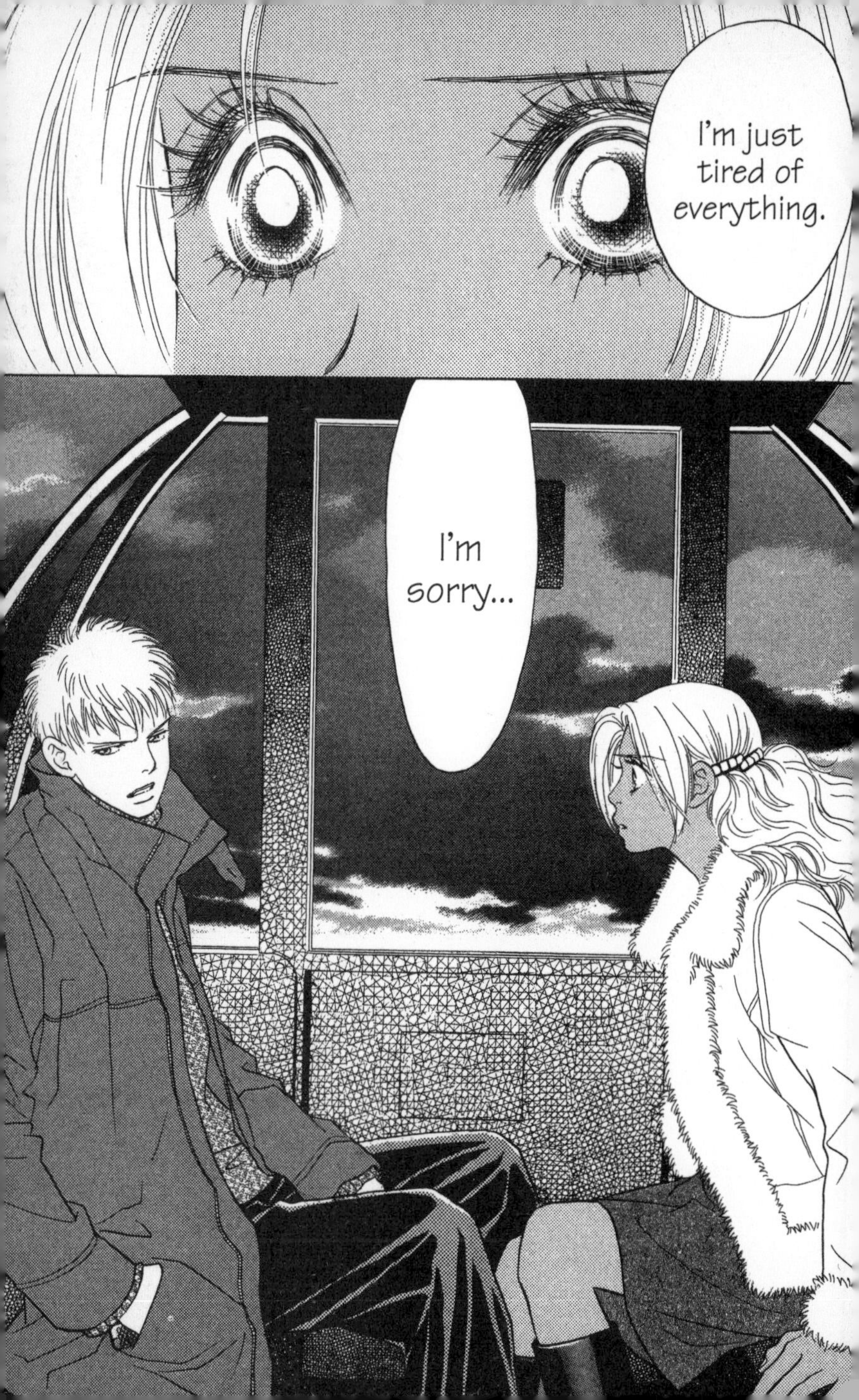
I'm just tired of everything.
I'm sorry...

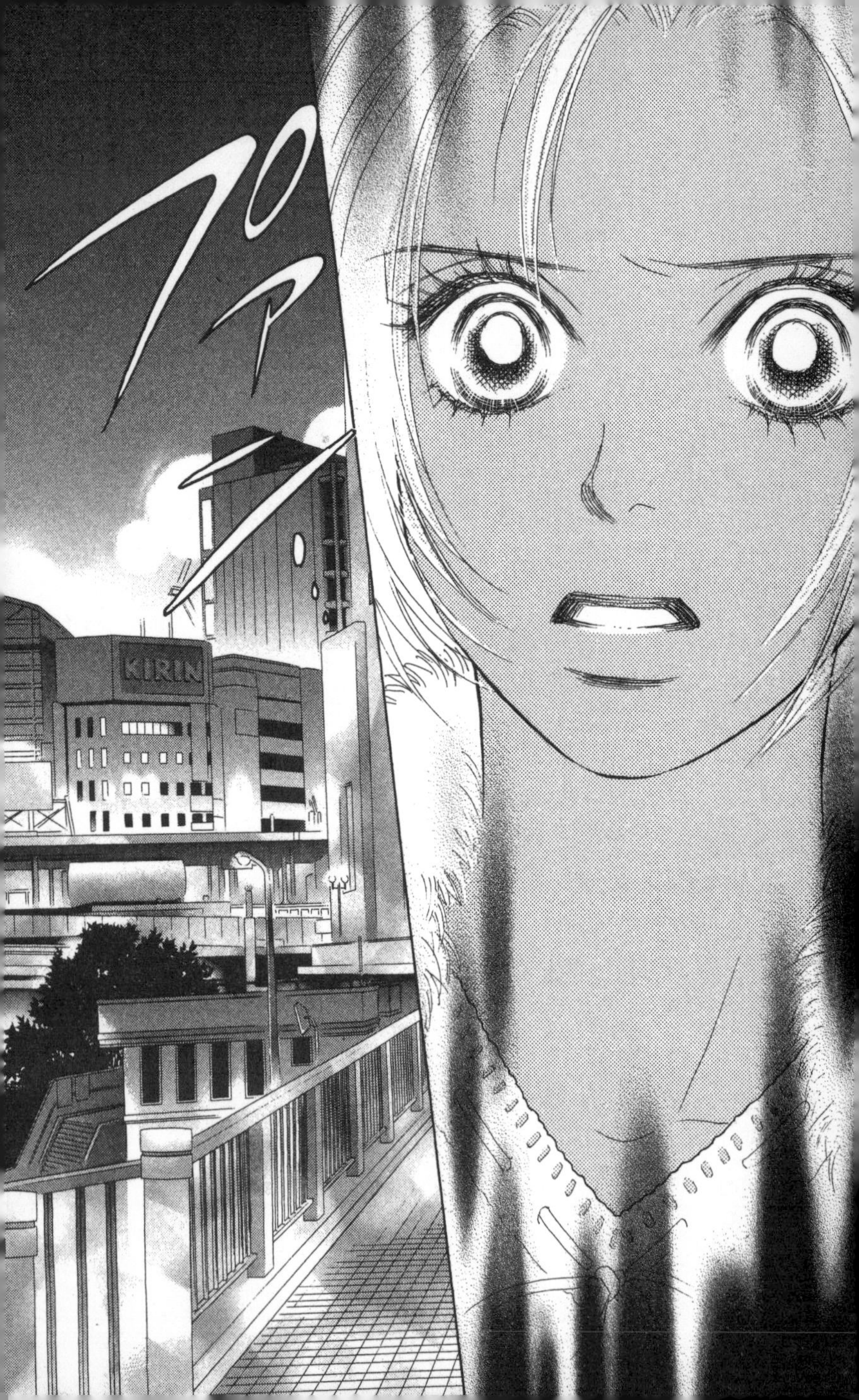
KIRIN

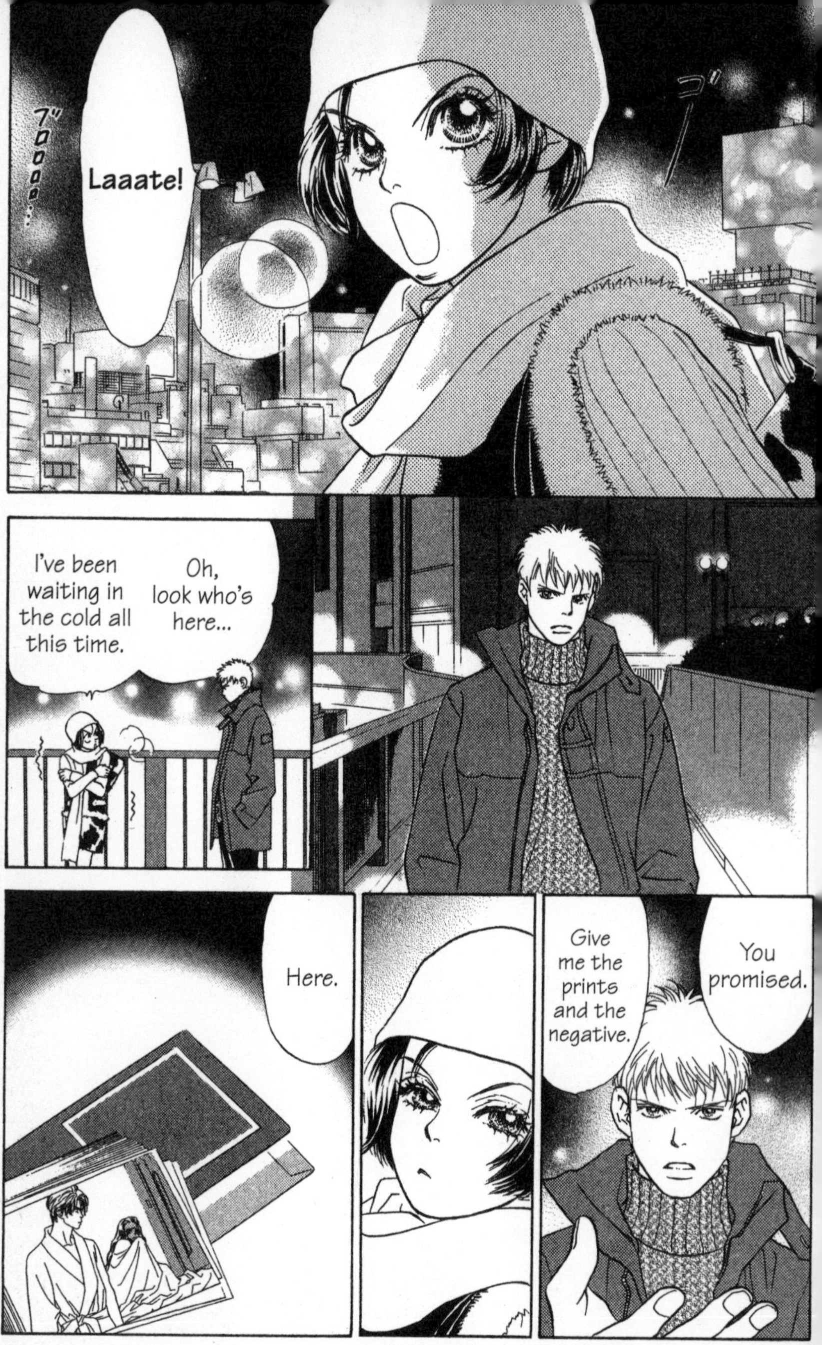
ゴ
Laaate!
ブロロロロ…
Oh, look who's here...
I've been waiting in the cold all this time.
You promised.
Give me the prints and the negative.
Here.

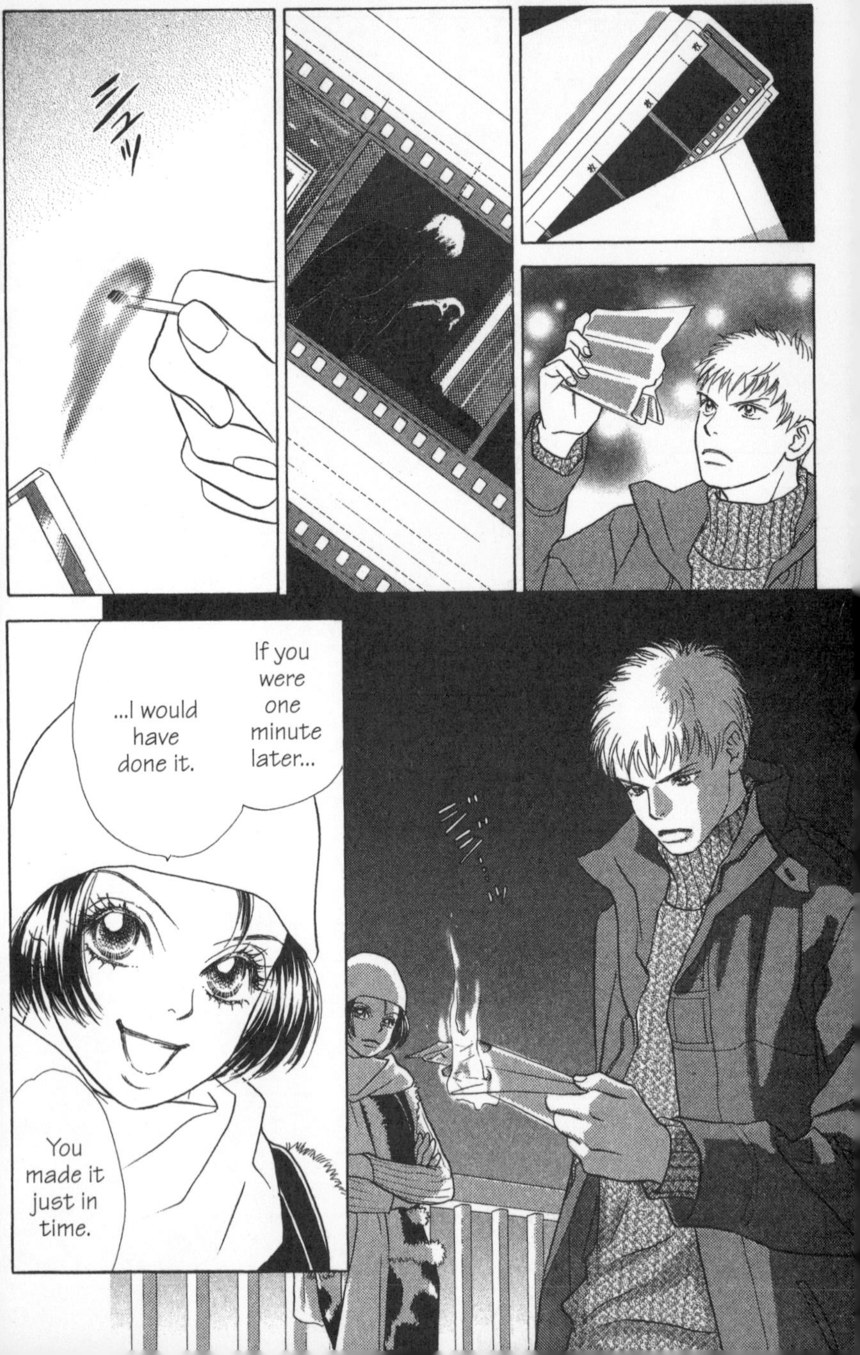
ジュッ
If you were one minute later...
...I would have done it.
You made it just in time.

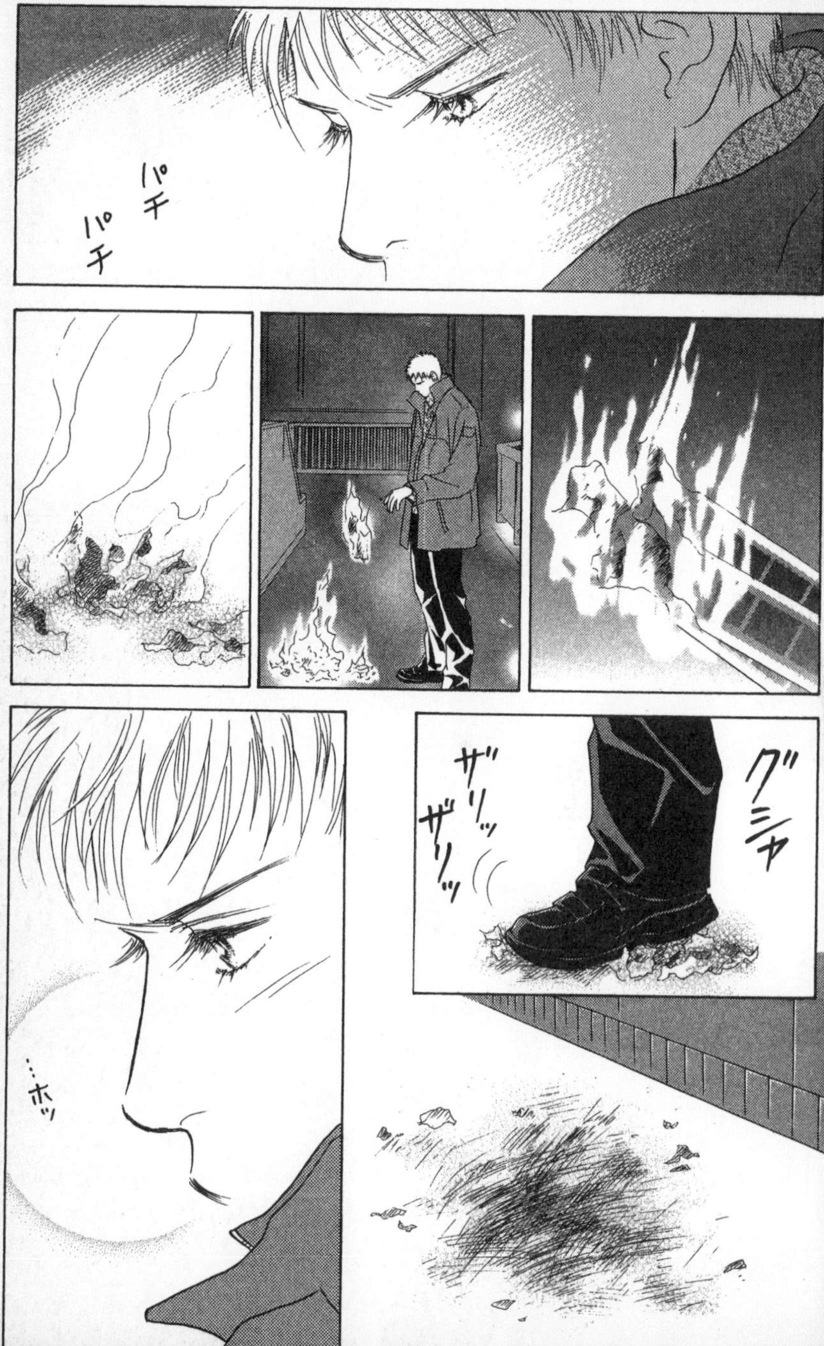
パチ
パチ
グシャ
ザリッ
ザリッ
…ホッ

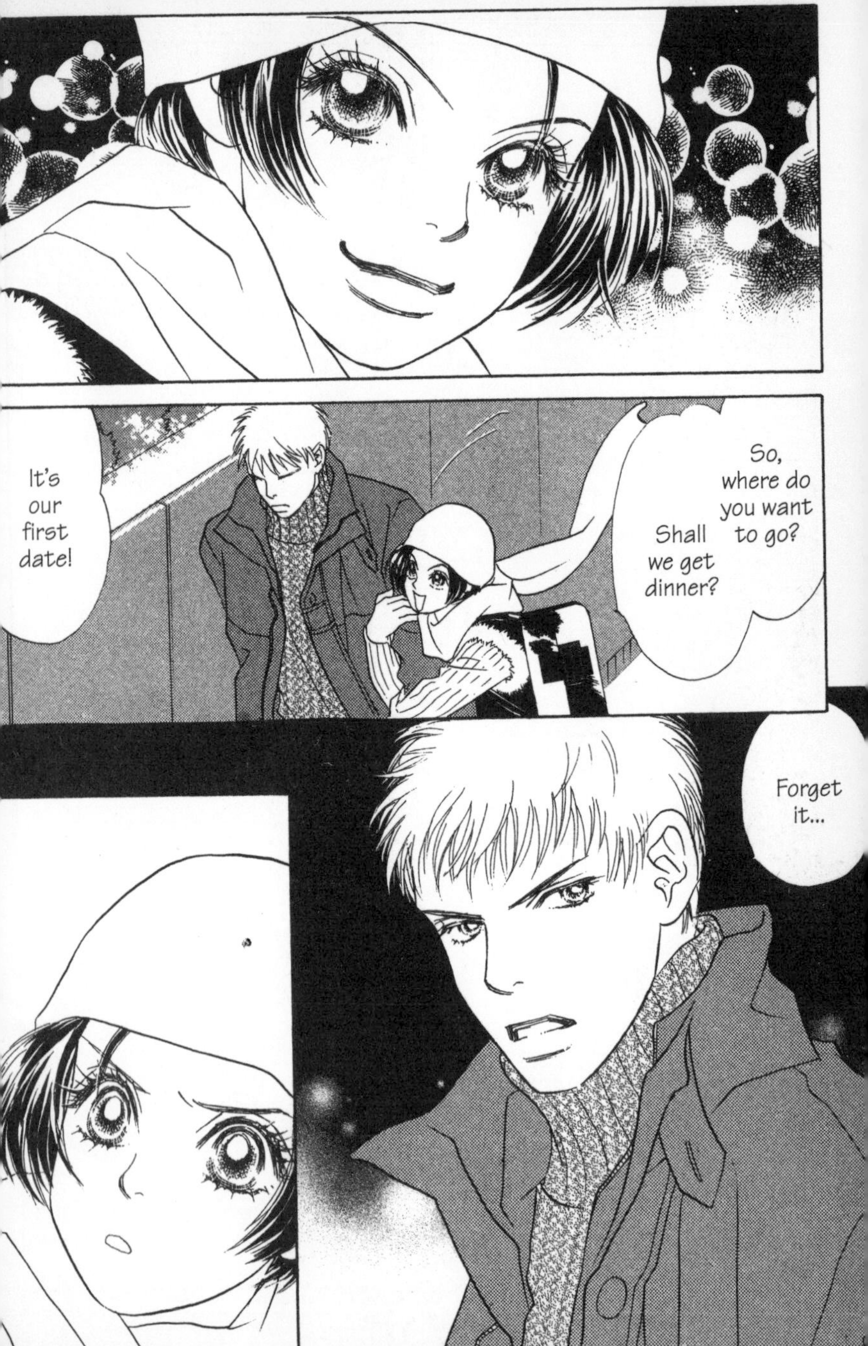
So, where do you want to go?
Shall we get dinner?
It's our first date!
Forget it...

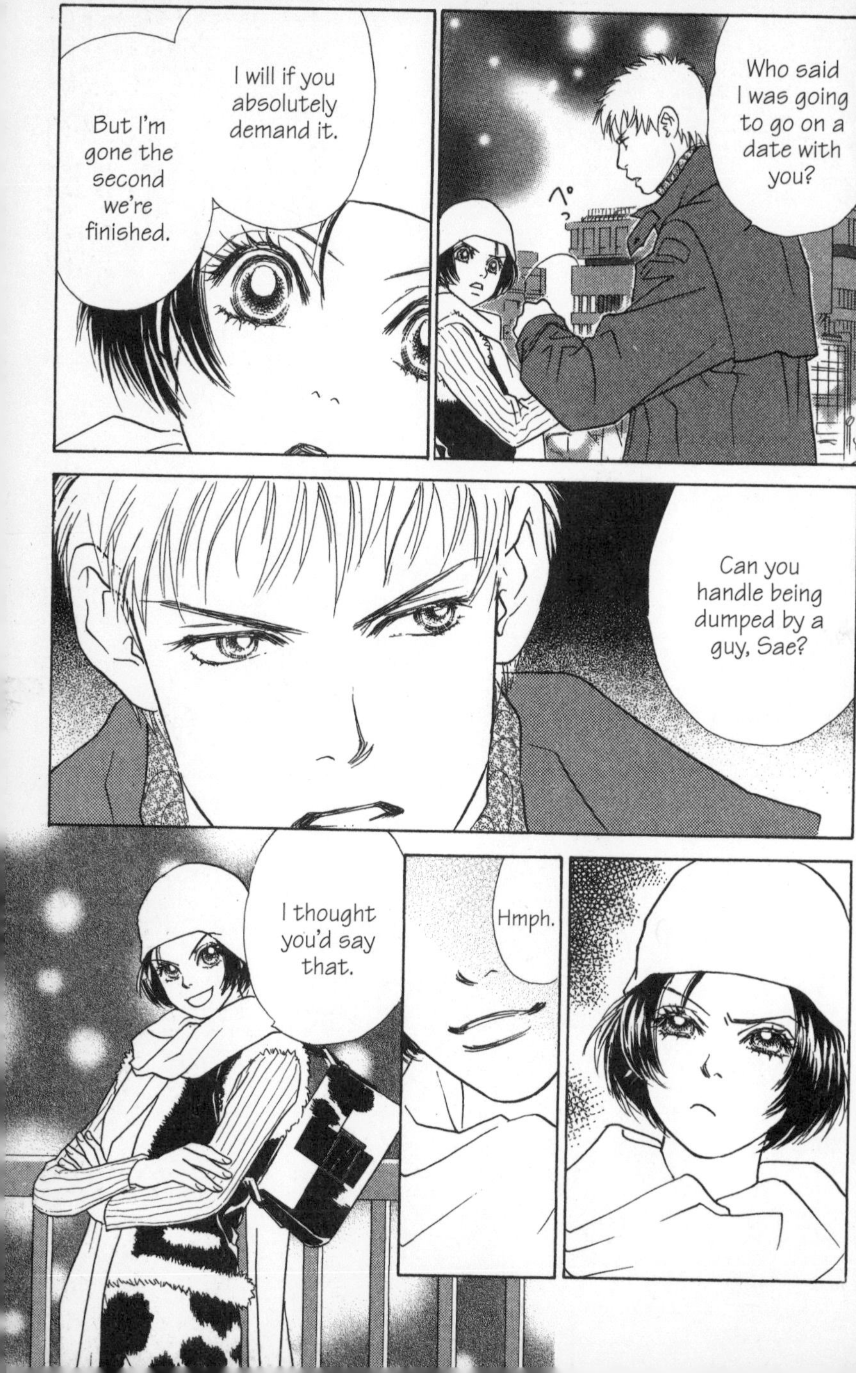
Who said I was going to go on a date with you?
I will if you absolutely demand it.
But I'm gone the second we're finished.
Can you handle being dumped by a guy, Sae?
Hmph.
I thought you'd say that.

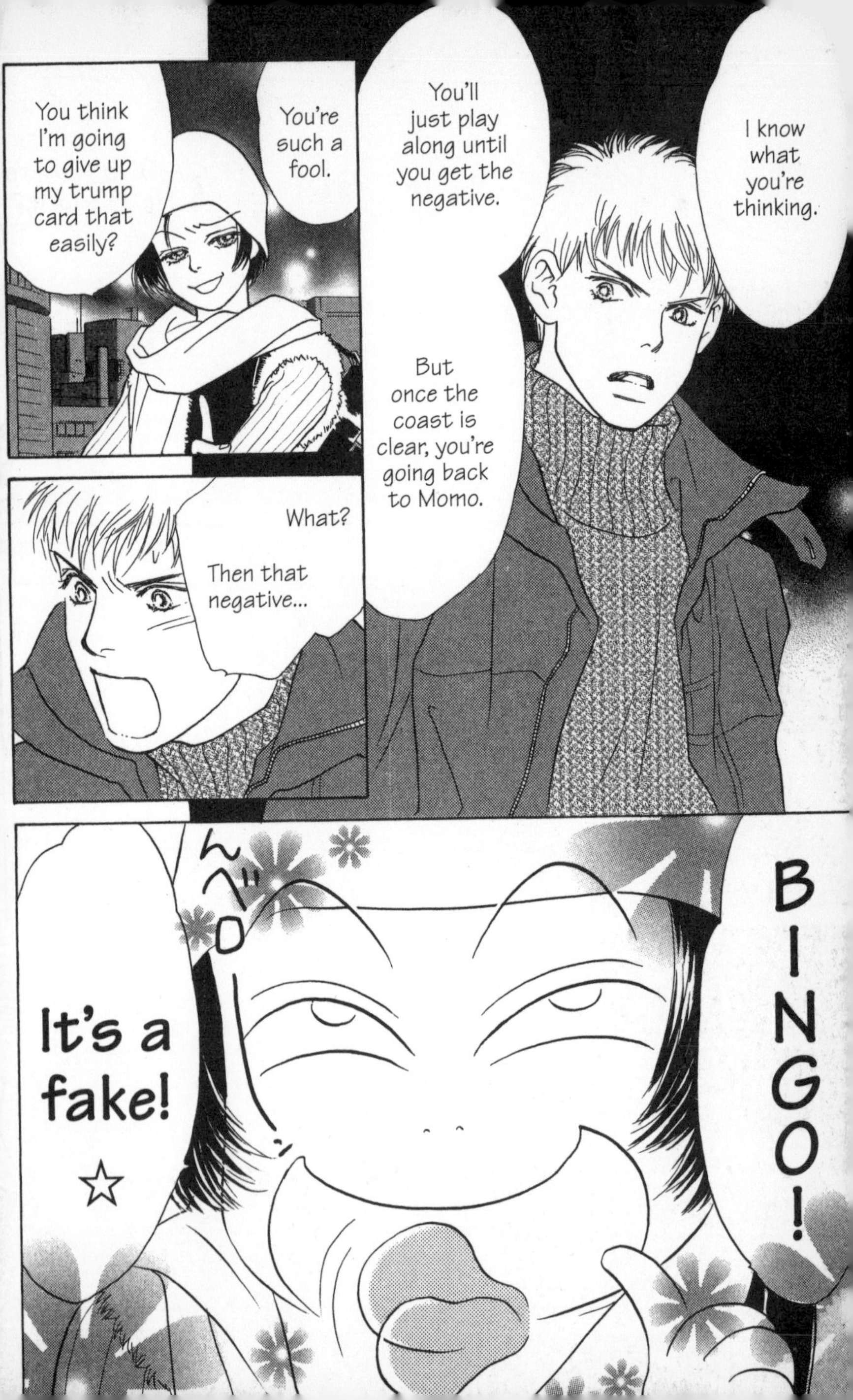

I know what you're thinking.
You'll just play along until you get the negative.
But once the coast is clear, you're going back to Momo.
You're such a fool.
You think I'm going to give up my trump card that easily?
What?
Then that negative...
BINGO!
んべ
It's a fake! ☆

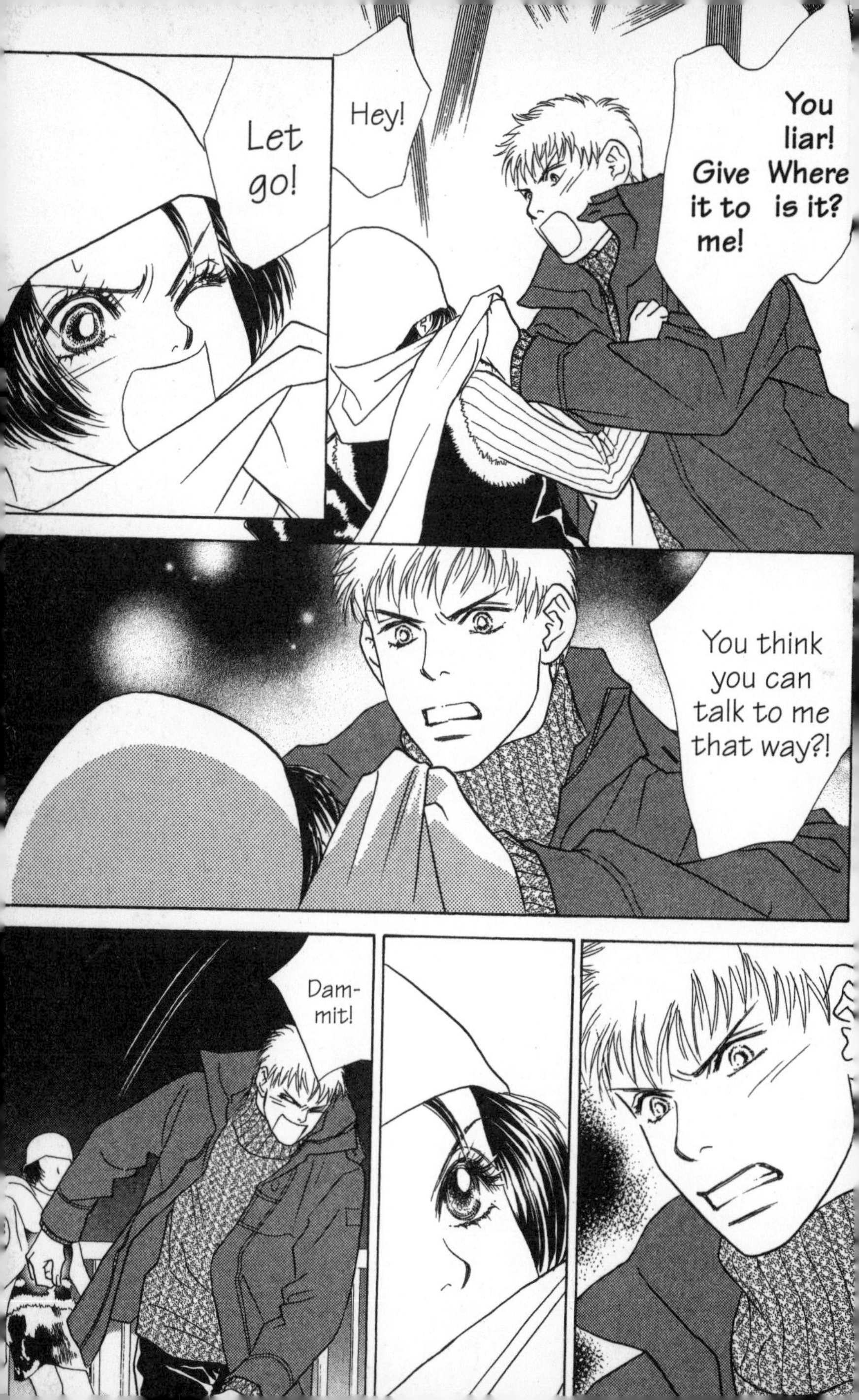
You liar! Where is it?
Give it to me!
Hey!
Let go!
You think you can talk to me that way?!
Dam-mit!

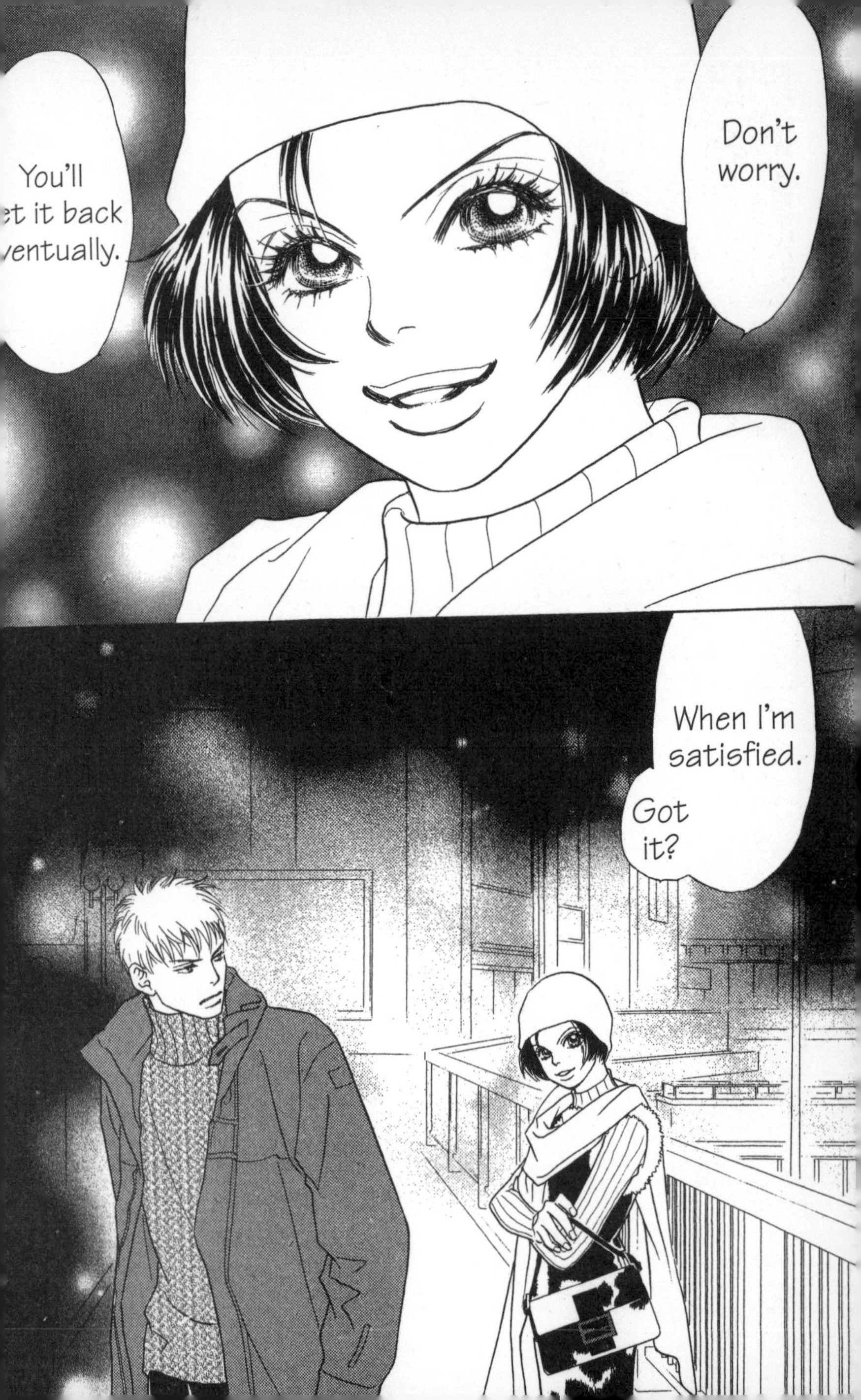
Don't worry.
You'll et it back ventually.
When I'm satisfied.
Got it?

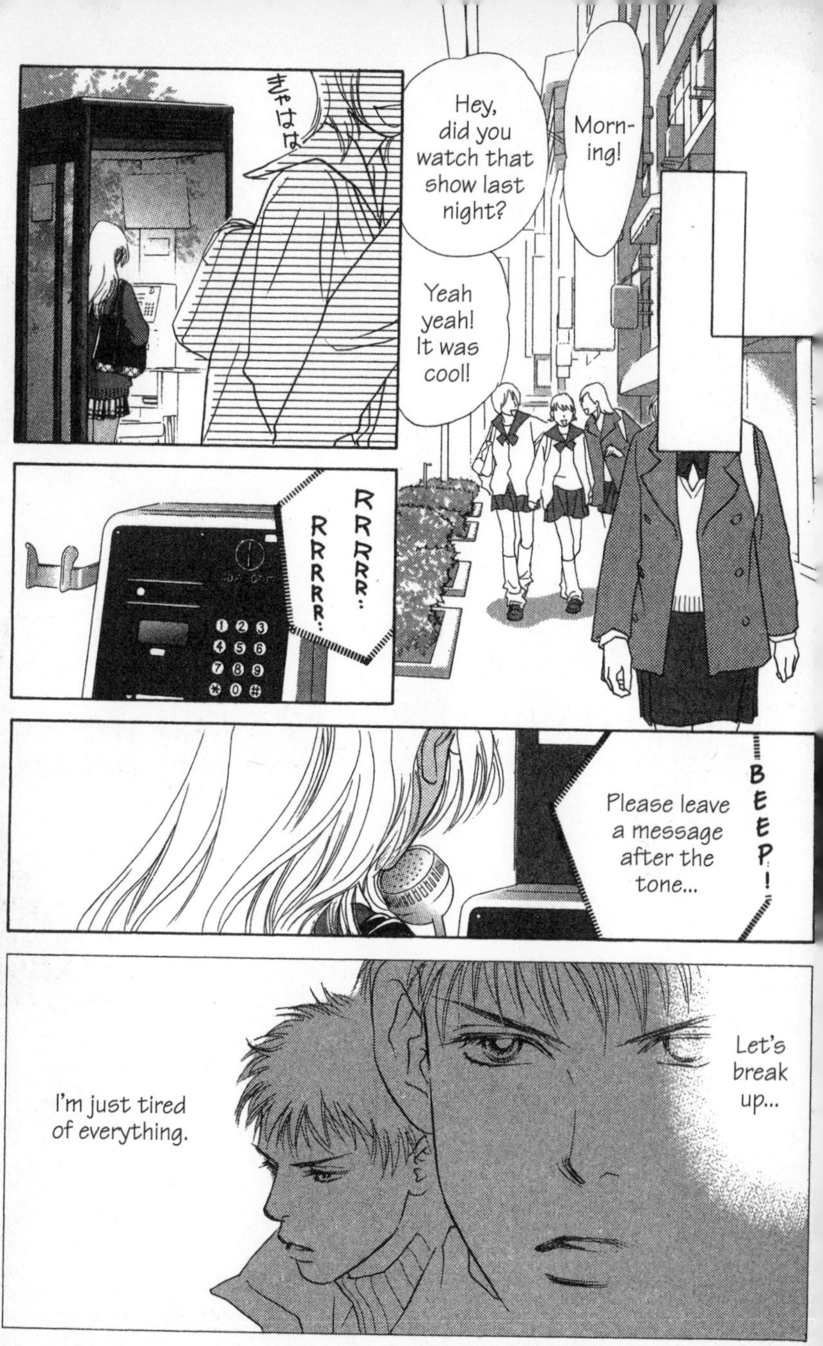
Morn-ing!
Hey, did you watch that show last night?
Yeah yeah! It was cool!
きゃはは
RRRRR..
RRRRR..
BEEP!
Please leave a message after the tone...
Let's break up...
I'm just tired of everything.

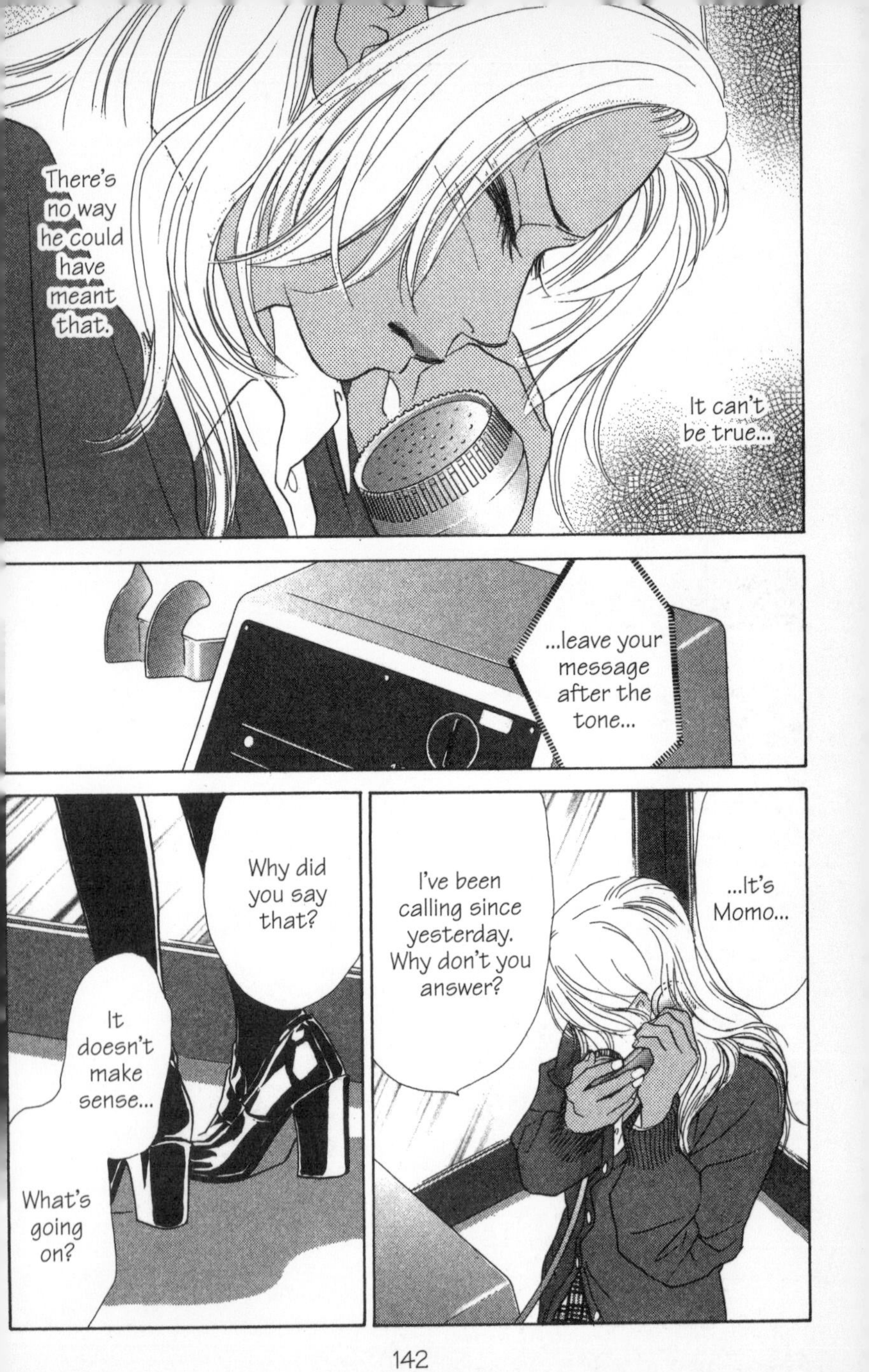
It can't be true...
There's no way he could have meant that.
...leave your message after the tone...
...It's Momo...
I've been calling since yesterday. Why don't you answer?
Why did you say that?
It doesn't make sense...
What's going on?

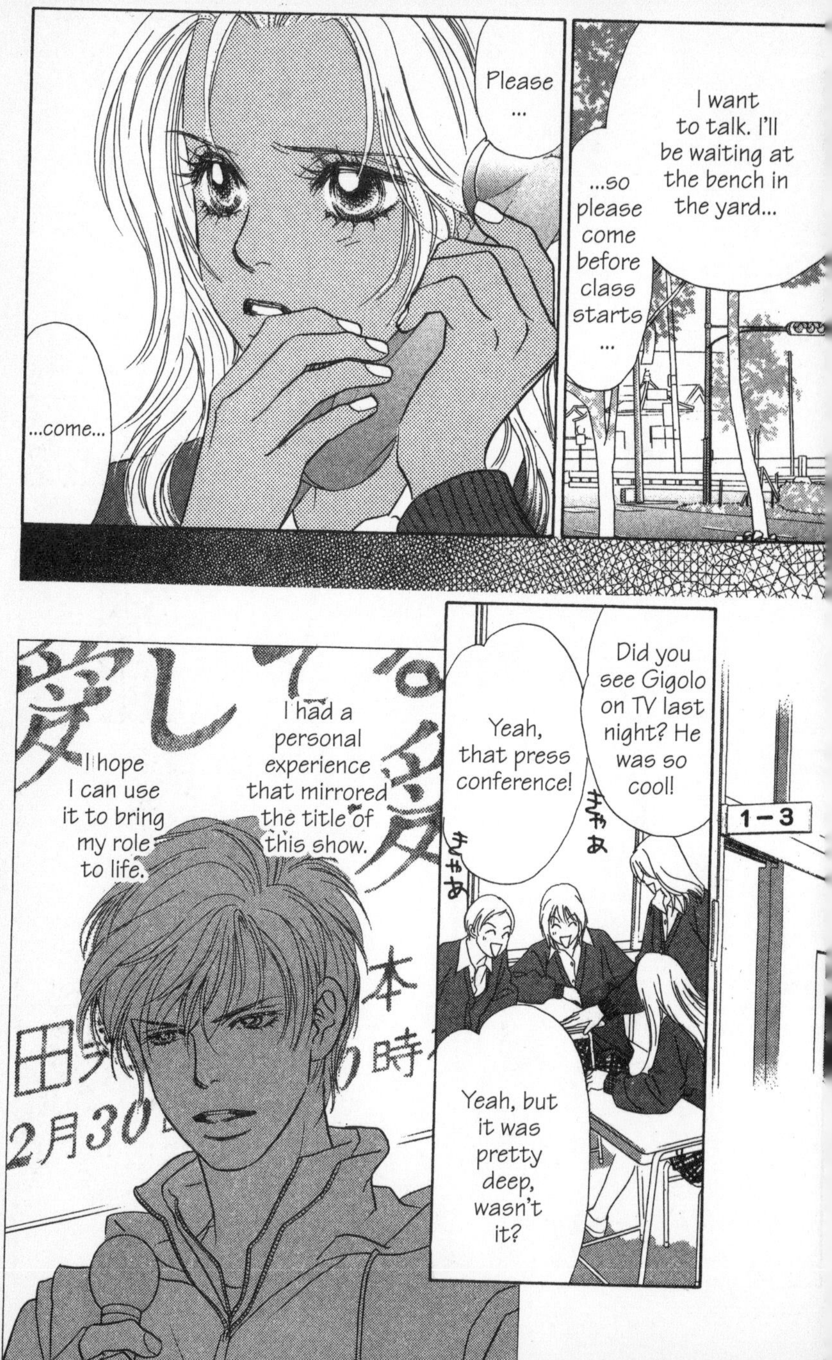
I want to talk. I'll be waiting at the bench in the yard...
...so please come before class starts...
Please...
...come...
1-3
Did you see Gigolo on TV last night? He was so cool!
Yeah, that press conference!
きゃあ
きゃあ
Yeah, but it was pretty deep, wasn't it?
I had a personal experience that mirrored the title of this show.
I hope I can use it to bring my role to life.

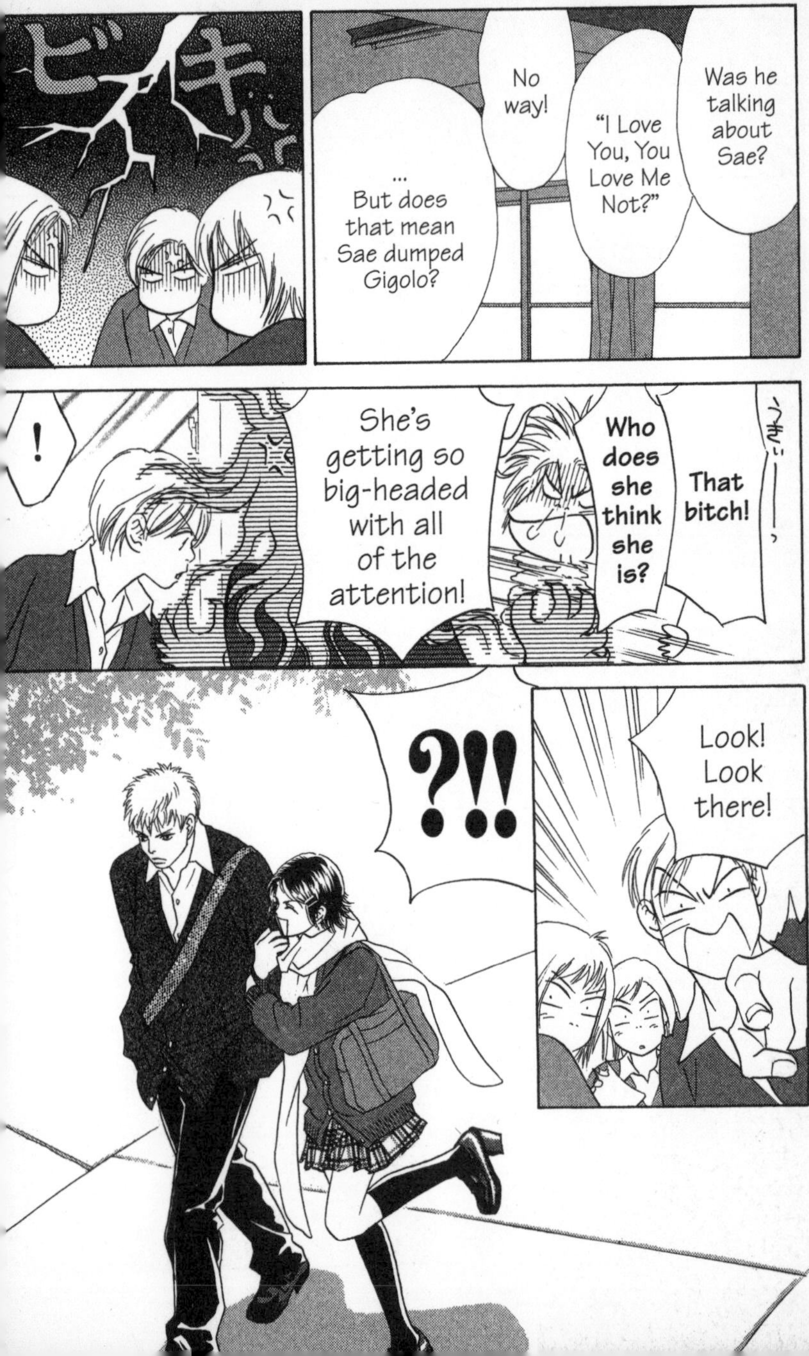

Was he talking about Sae?
"I Love You, You Love Me Not?"
No way!
... But does that mean Sae dumped Gigolo?
ビキ
うきぃーーっ
That bitch!
Who does she think she is?
She's getting so big-headed with all of the attention!
!
Look! Look there!
?!!

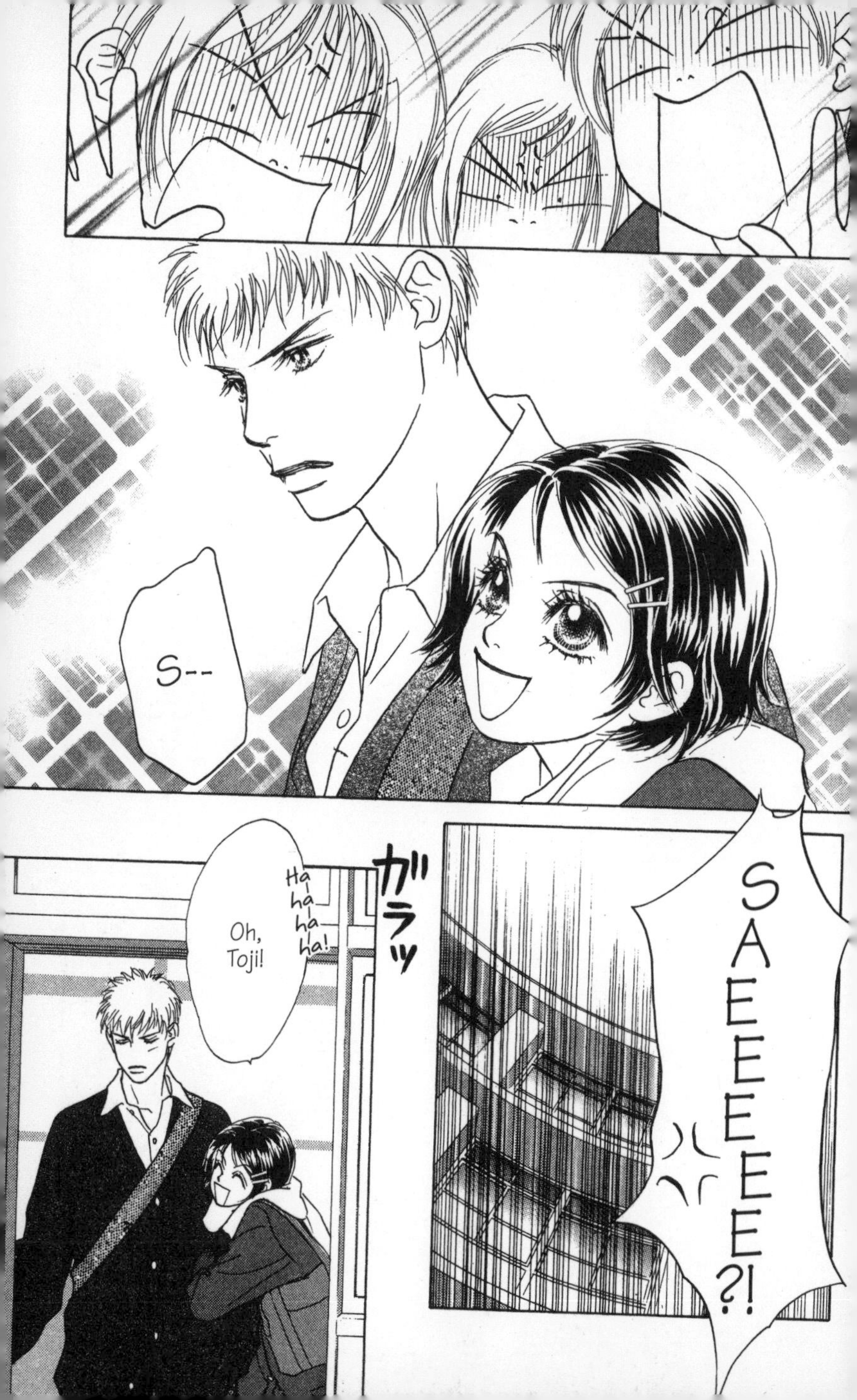

S--
SAEEEEEE?!
ガラッ
Ha ha ha ha!
Oh, Toji!

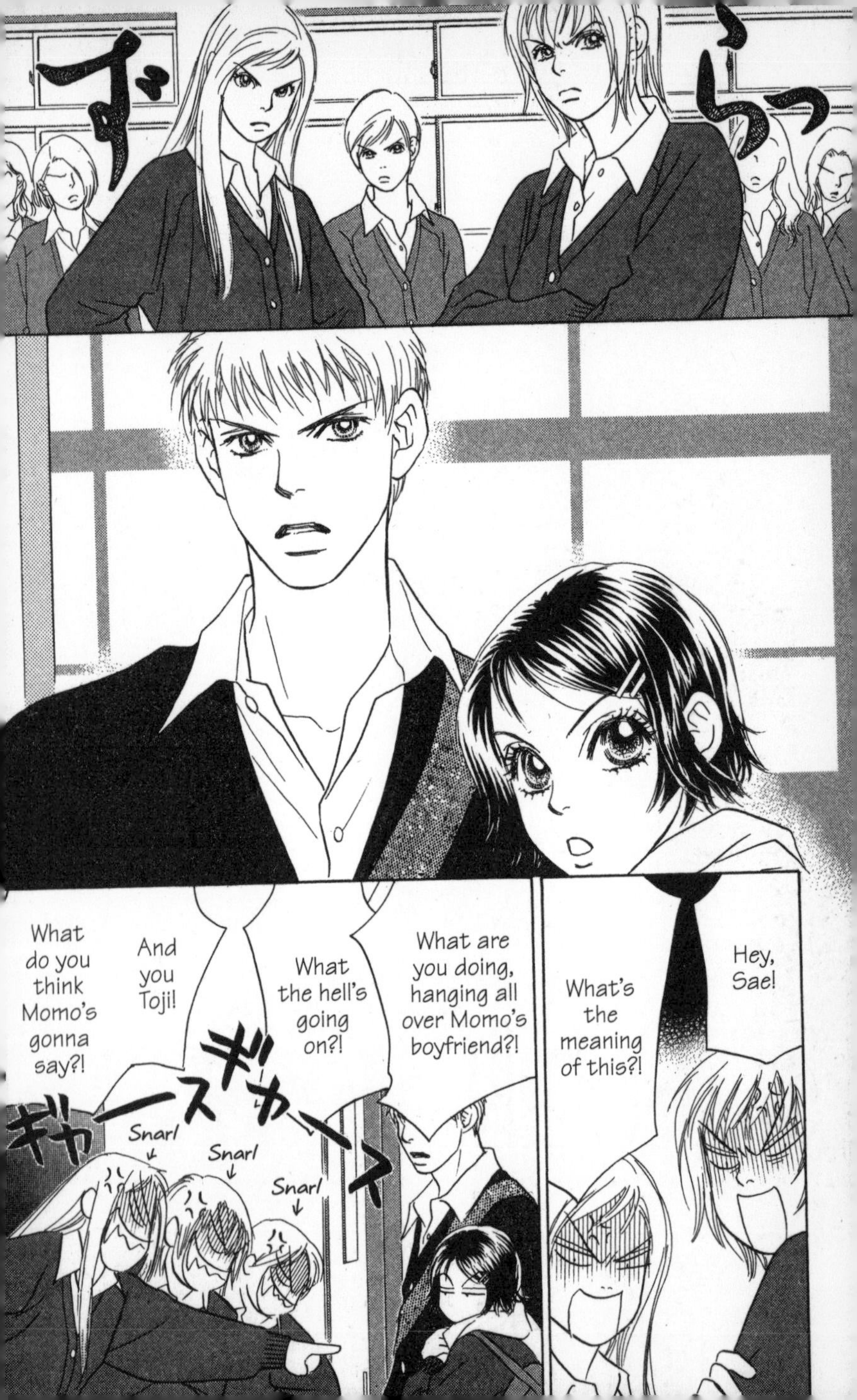
Hey, Sae!
What's the meaning of this?!
What are you doing, hanging all over Momo's boyfriend?!
What the hell's going on?!
And you Toji!
What do you think Momo's gonna say?!
Snarl
Snarl
Snarl

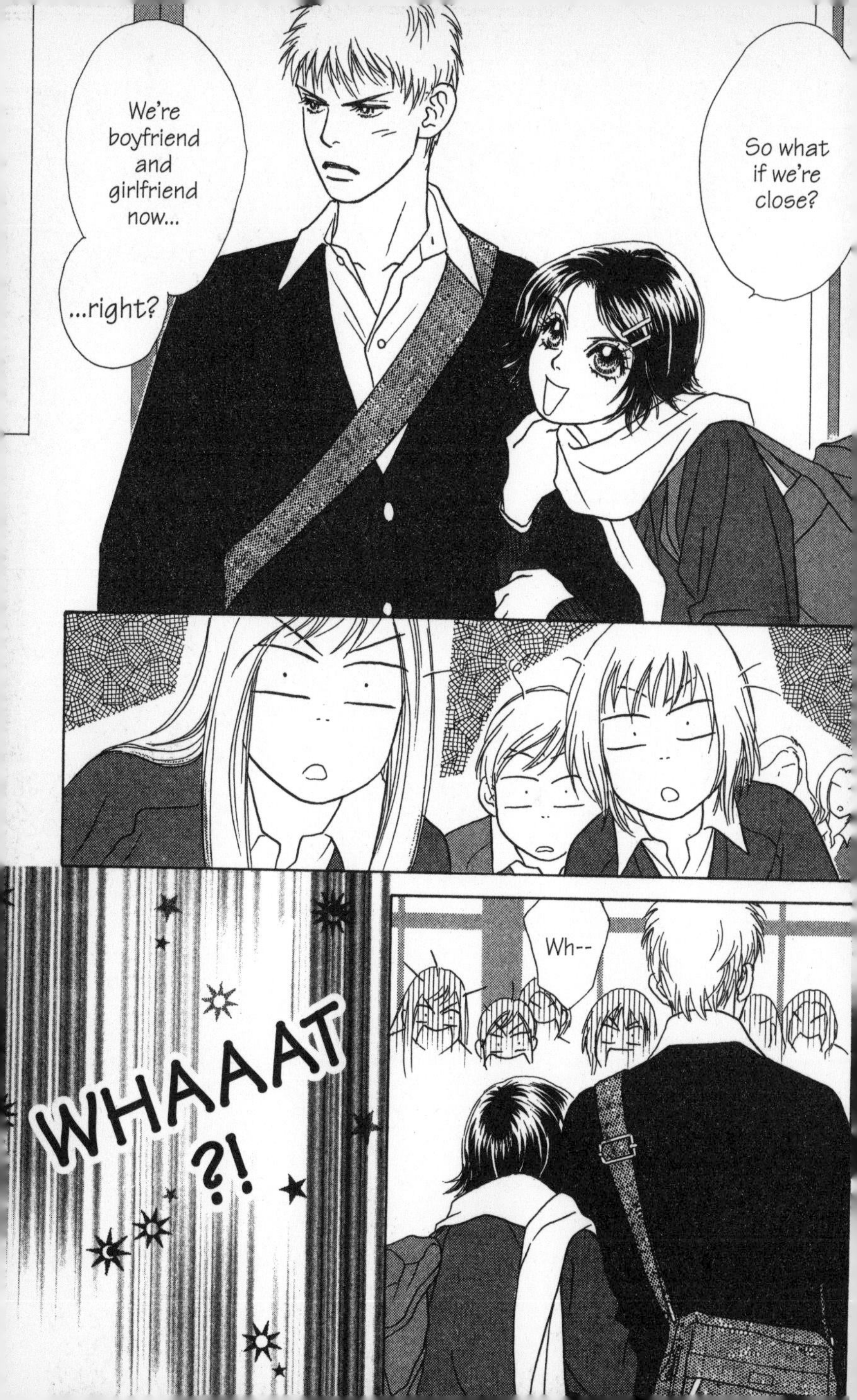
So what if we're close?
We're boyfriend and girlfriend now...
...right?
Wh--
WHAAAT ?!

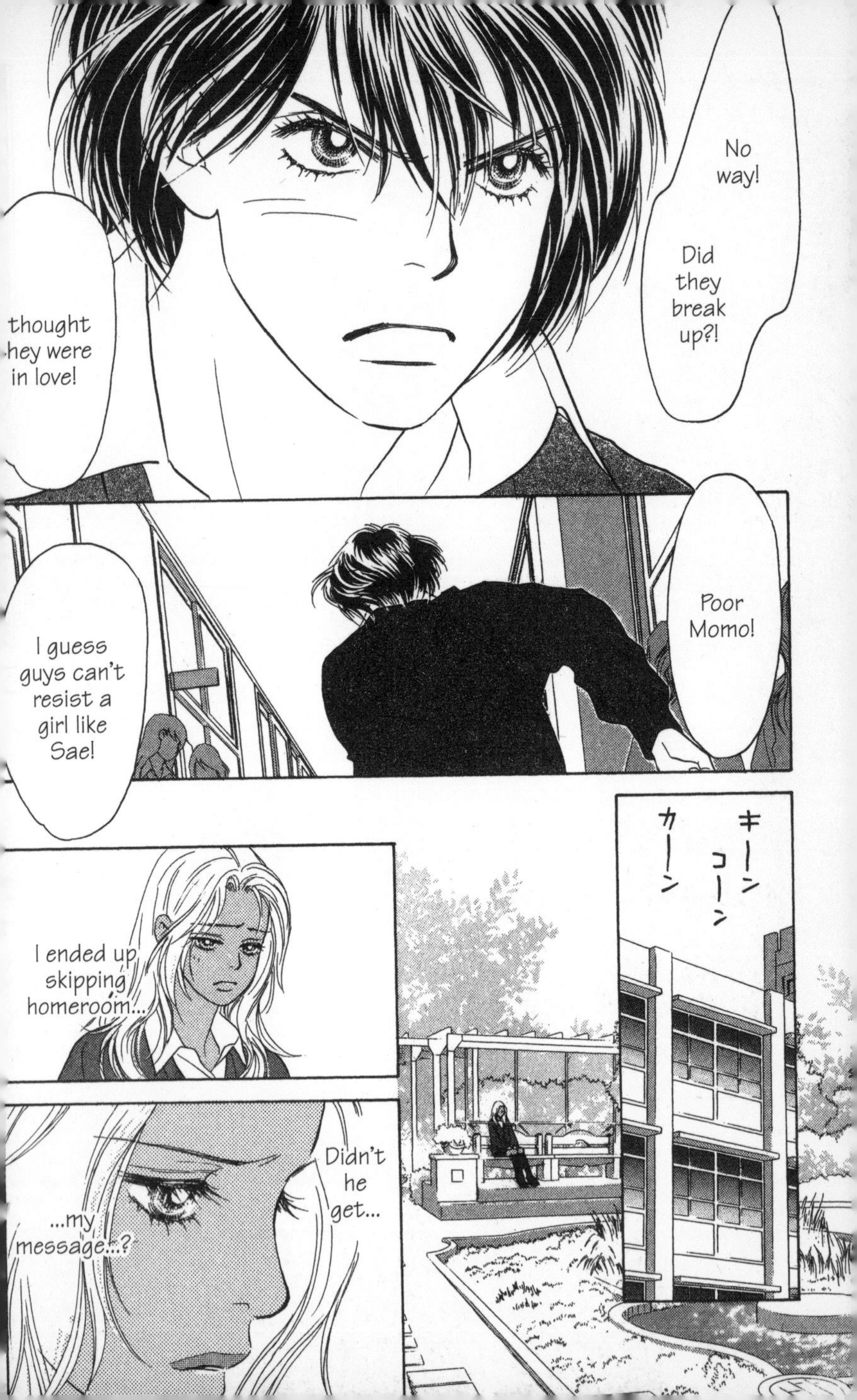
No way!
Did they break up?!
thought hey were in love!
Poor Momo!
I guess guys can't resist a girl like Sae!
キーン
コーン
カーン
I ended up skipping homeroom...
Didn't he get...
...my message...?

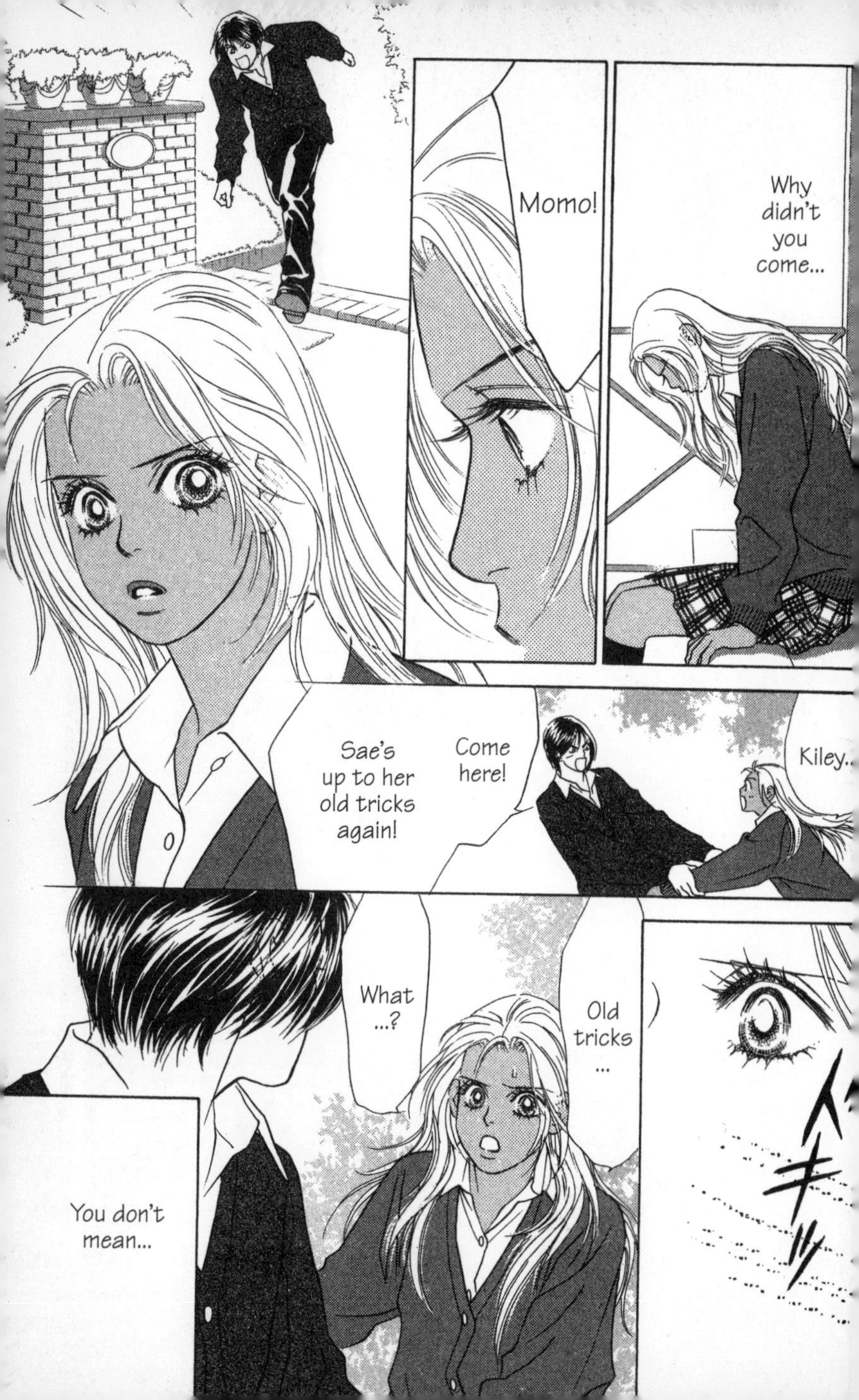
Why didn't you come...
Momo!
Kiley..
Come here!
Sae's up to her old tricks again!
Old tricks ...
What ...?
You don't mean...

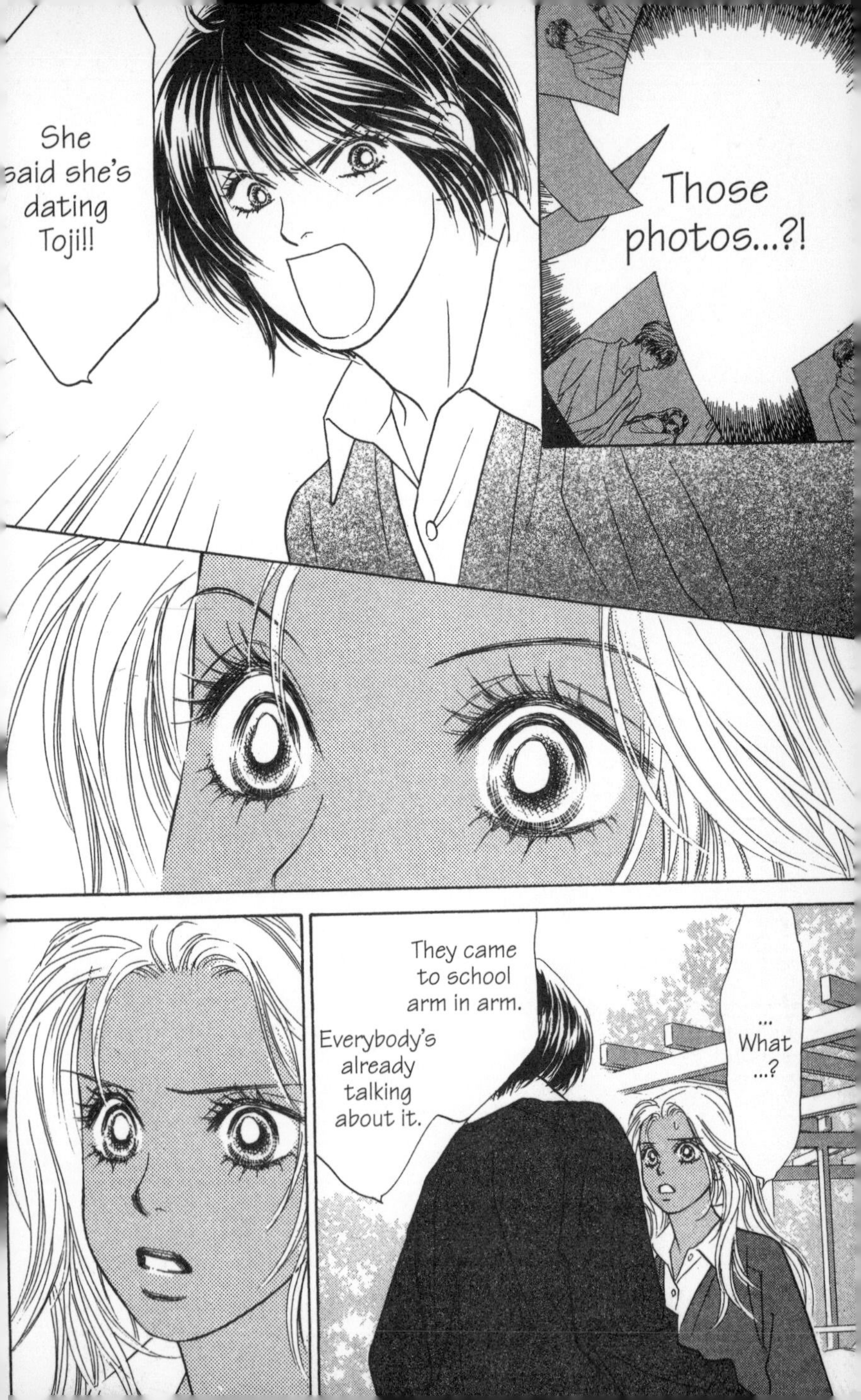
Those photos...?!
She said she's dating Toji!!
... What ...?
They came to school arm in arm.
Everybody's already talking about it.

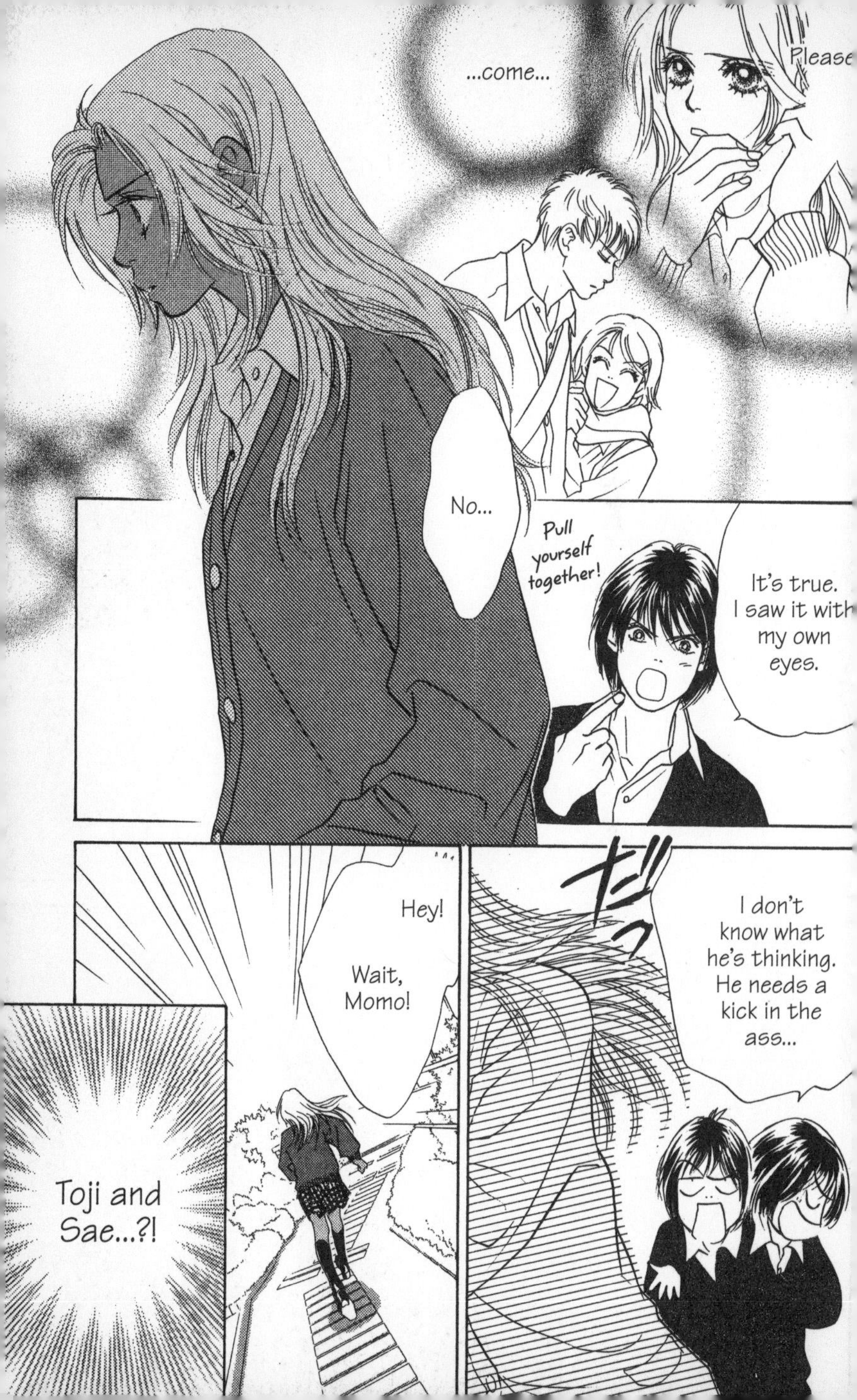
Please
...come...
It's true. I saw it with my own eyes.
Pull yourself together!
No...
I don't know what he's thinking. He needs a kick in the ass...
Hey!
Wait, Momo!
Toji and Sae...?!

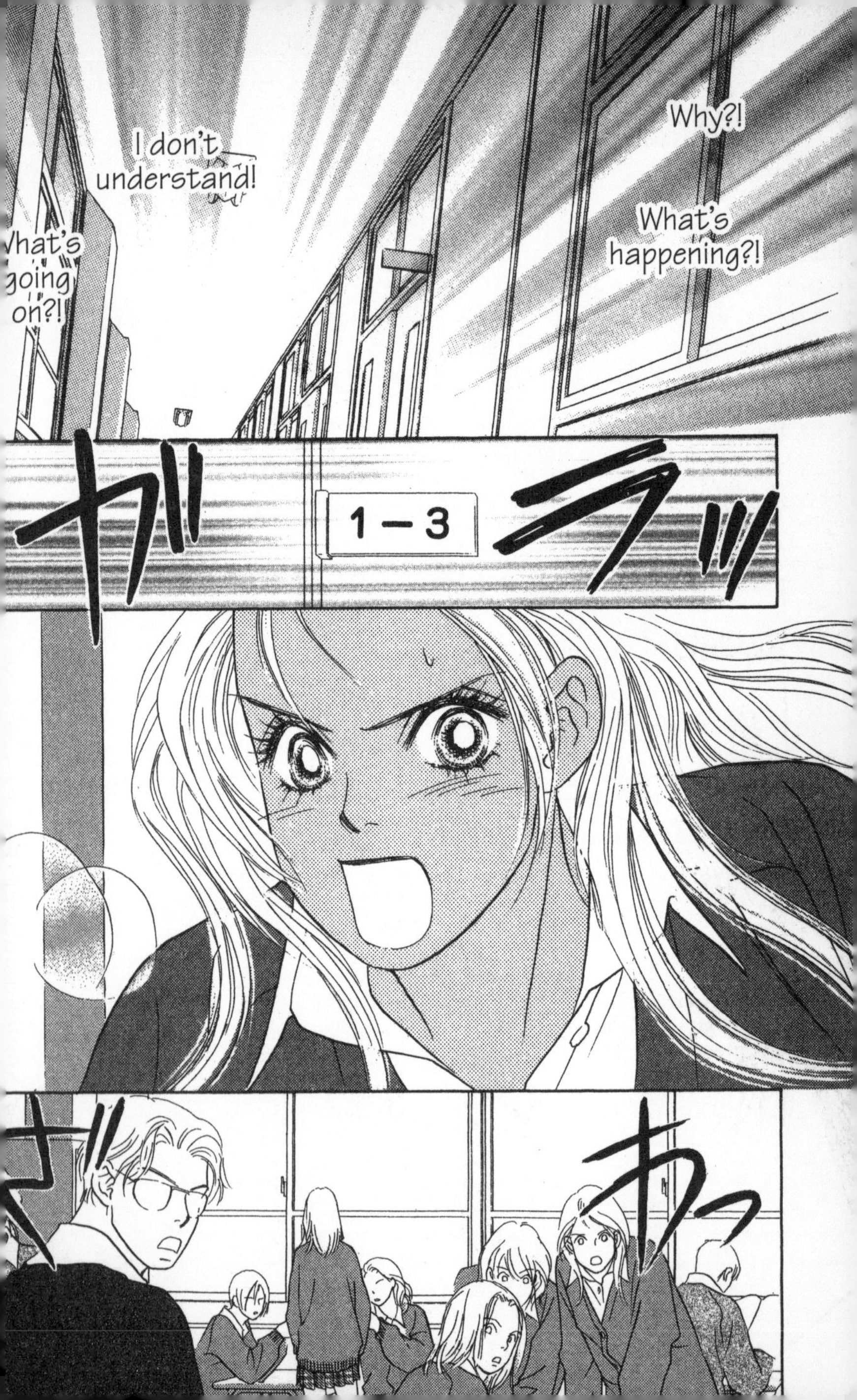
Why?!
What's happening?!
I don't understand!
What's going on?!
ガラッ
1—3
あっ
ざ

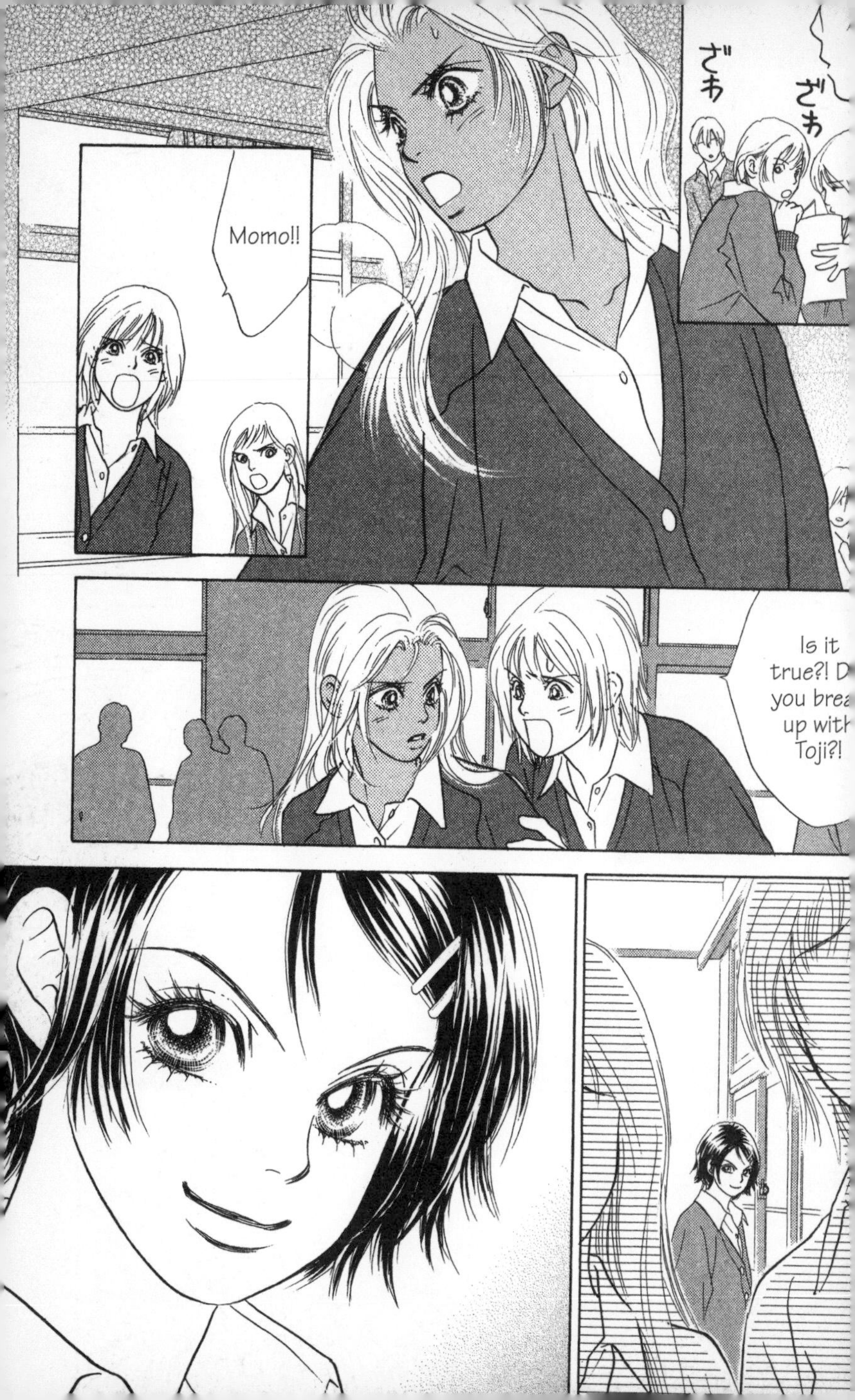
ざわ
ざわ
Momo!!
Is it true?! D
you brea
up with
Toji?!

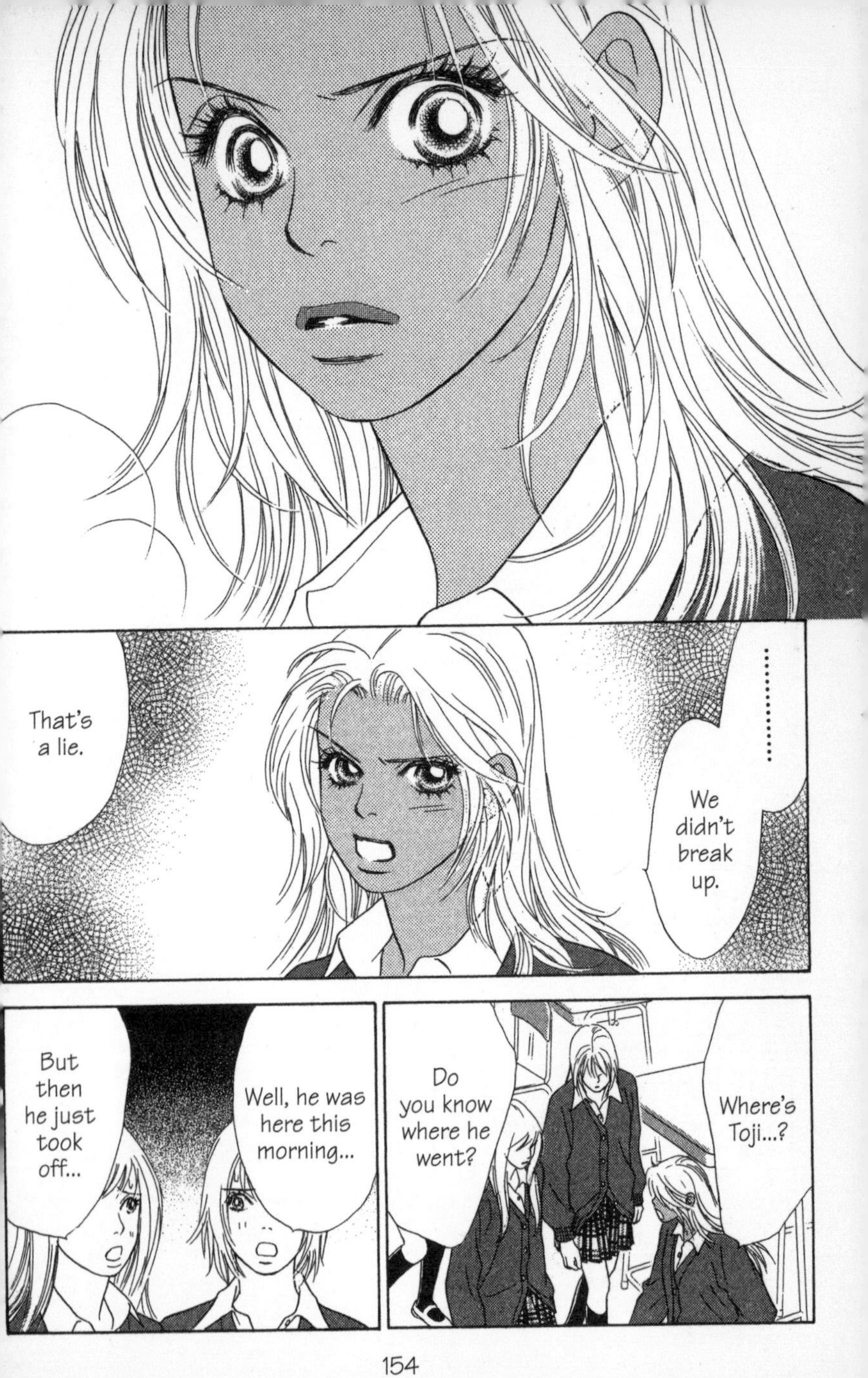
....
We didn't break up.
That's a lie.
Where's Toji...?
Do you know where he went?
Well, he was here this morning...
But then he just took off...

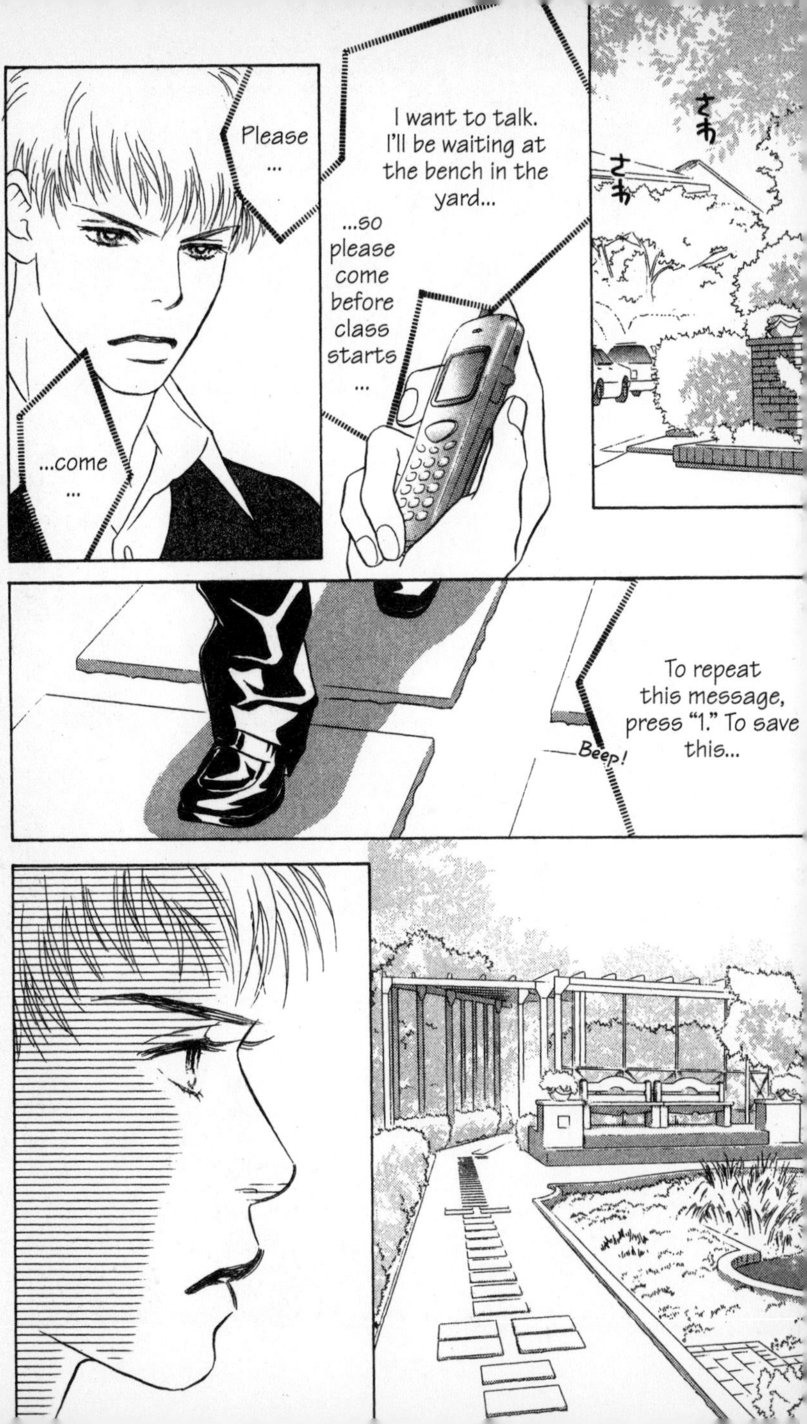
さわ
さわ
I want to talk. I'll be waiting at the bench in the yard...
...so please come before class starts ...
Please ...
...come ...
Beep!
To repeat this message, press "1." To save this...

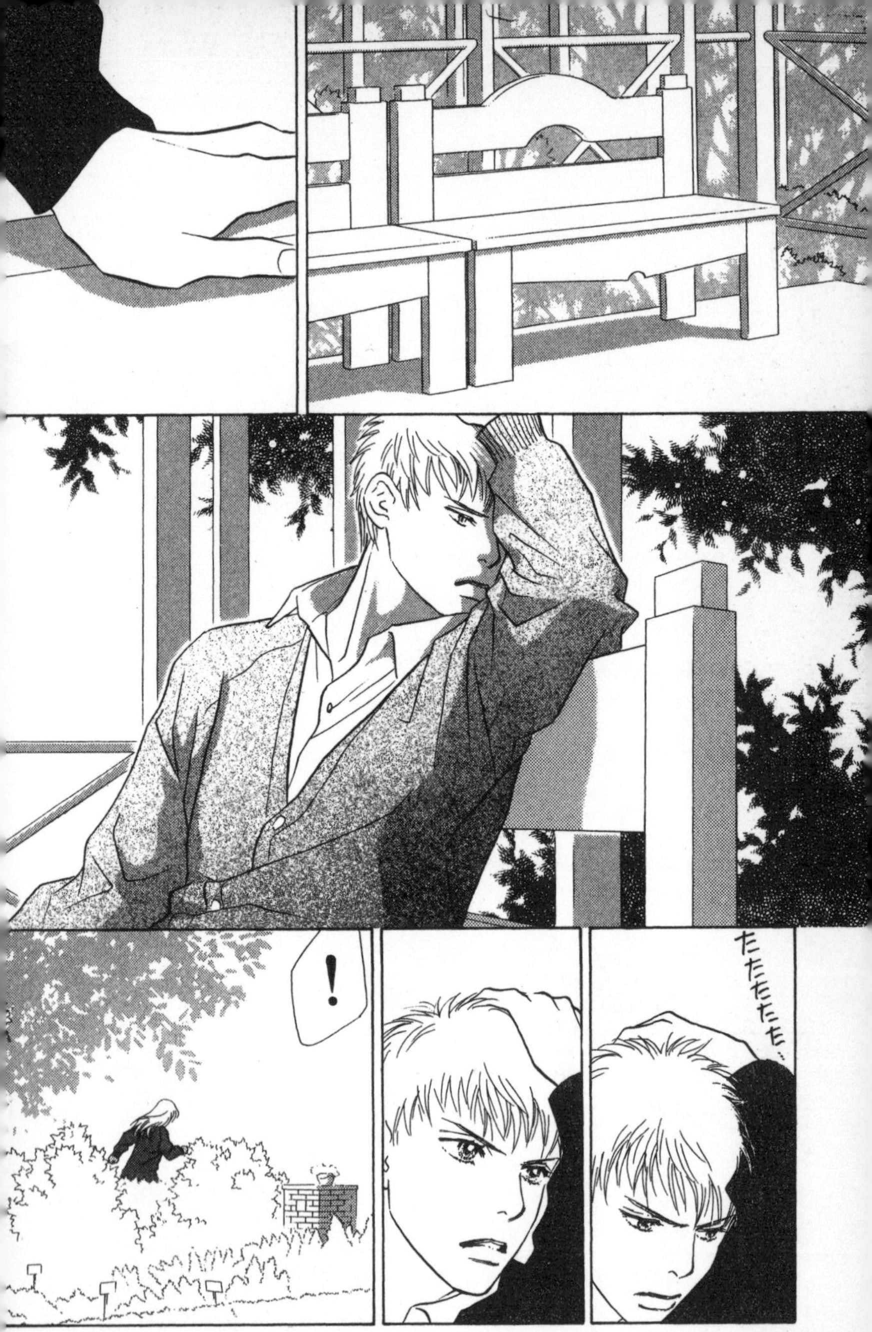
たたたたた…
!

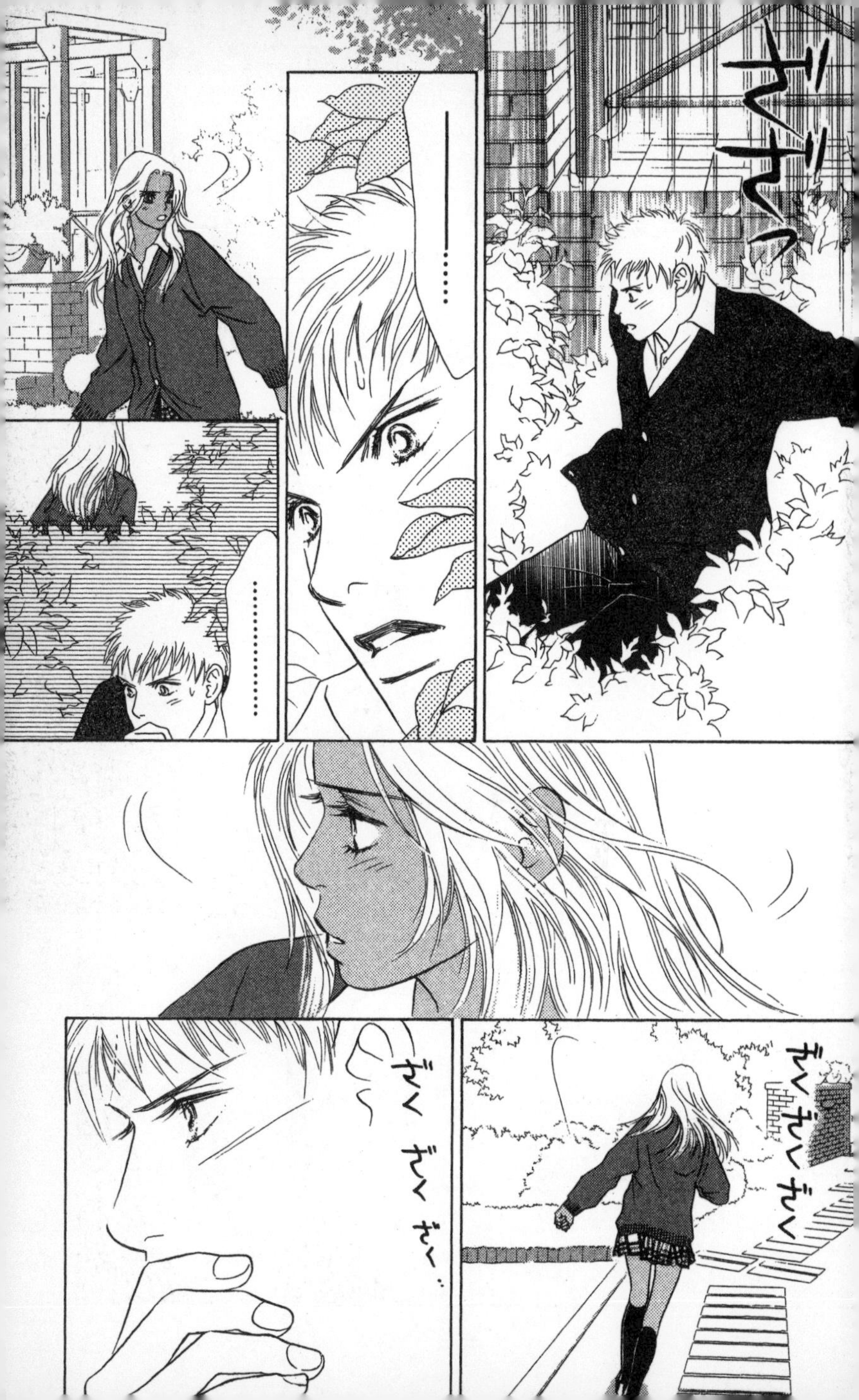
ざざっ
――――……
…………
ざく ざく ざく
ざく ざく ざく…

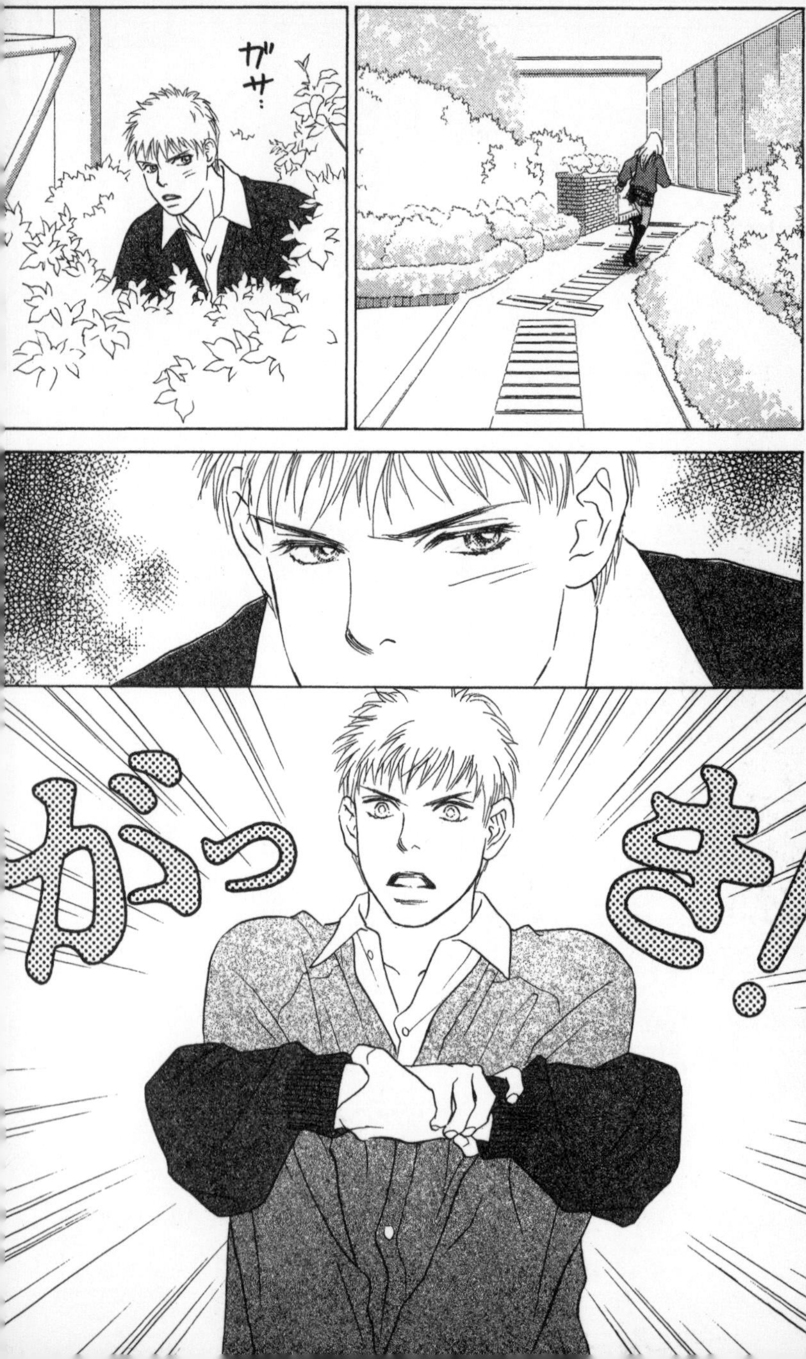
ガサ…
がっき!

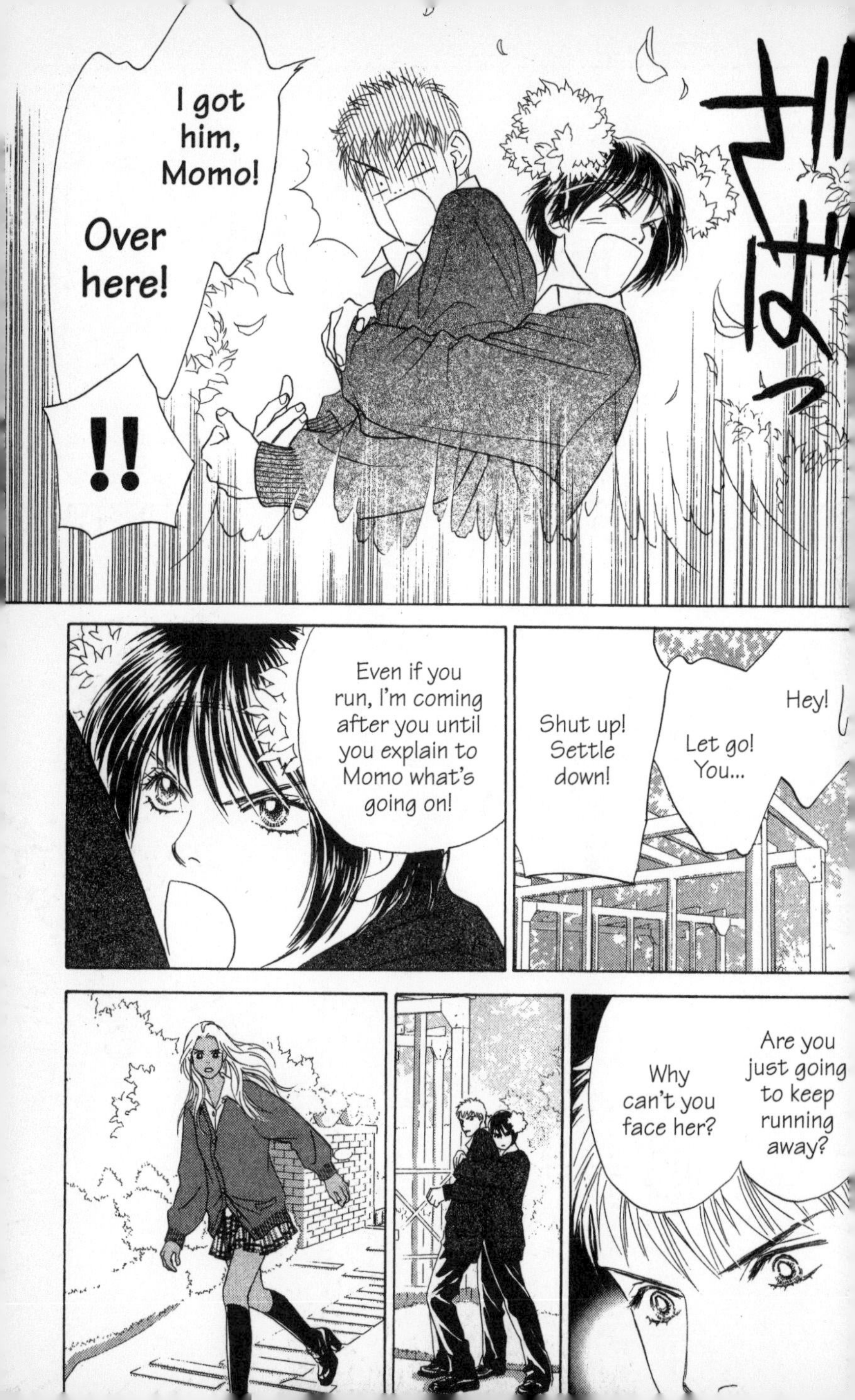
I got him, Momo!
Over here!
!!
Hey!
Let go! You...
Shut up! Settle down!
Even if you run, I'm coming after you until you explain to Momo what's going on!
Are you just going to keep running away?
Why can't you face her?

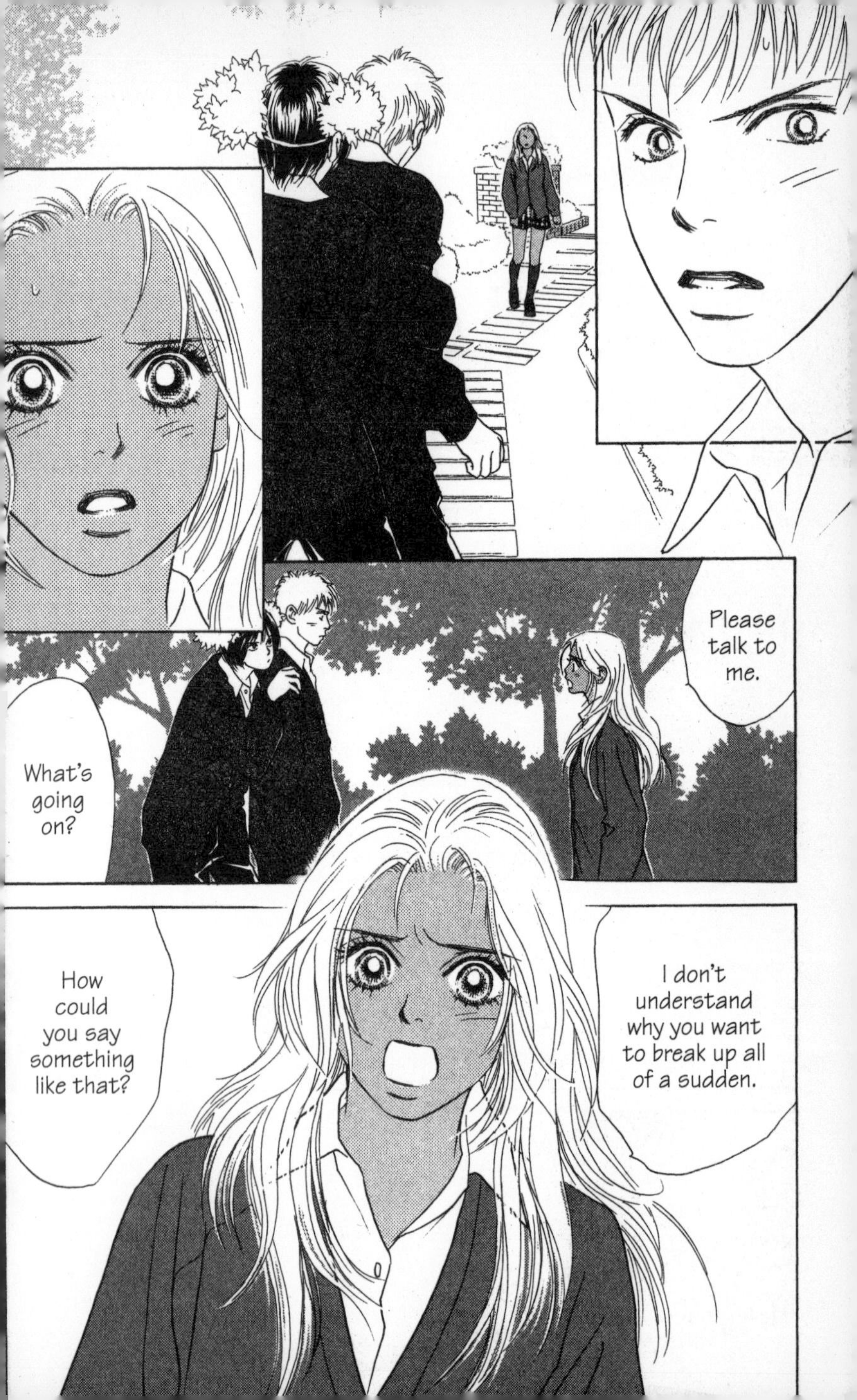
Please talk to me.
What's going on?
I don't understand why you want to break up all of a sudden.
How could you say something like that?

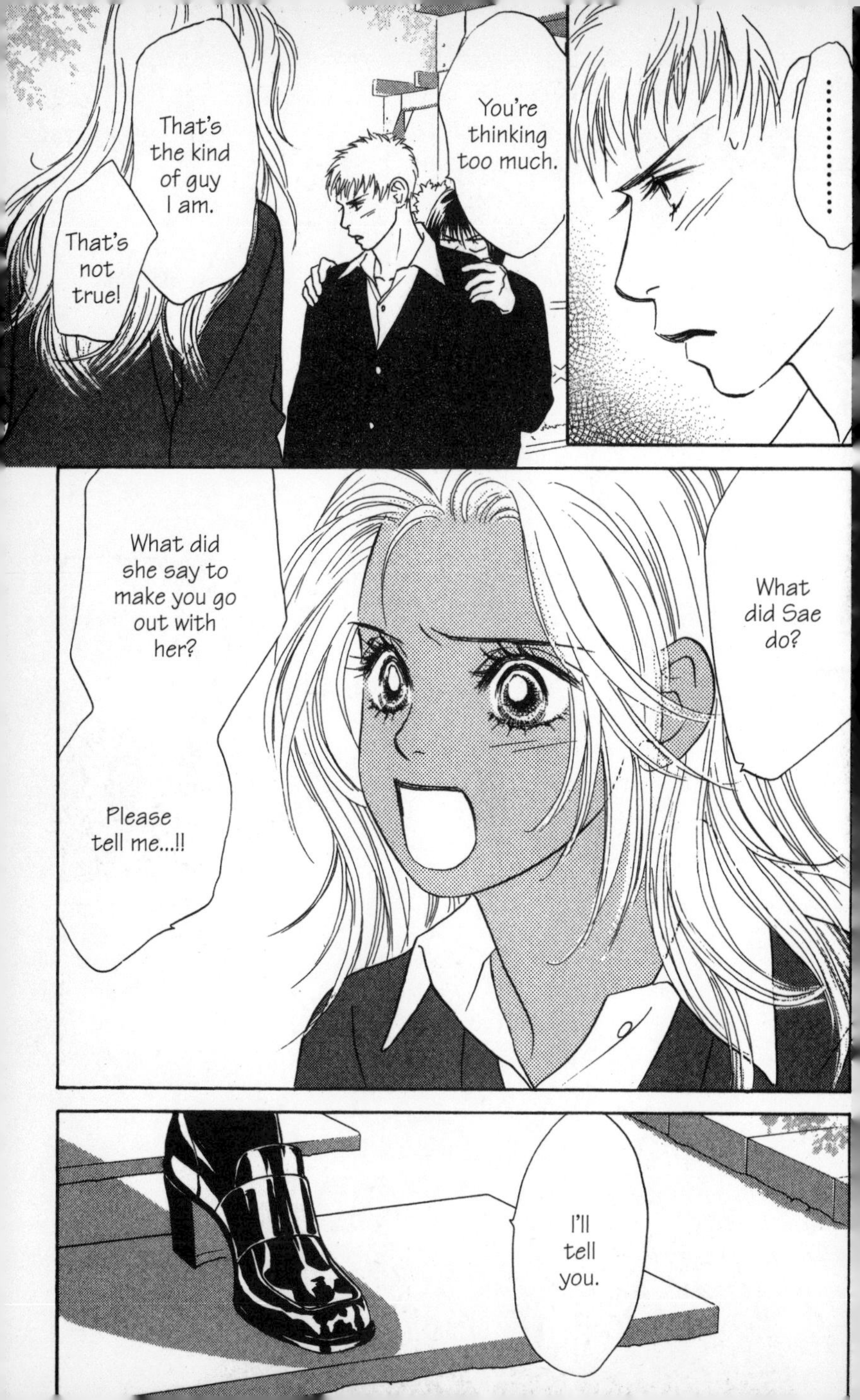
......
You're thinking too much.
That's the kind of guy I am.
That's not true!
What did Sae do?
What did she say to make you go out with her?
Please tell me...!!
I'll tell you.

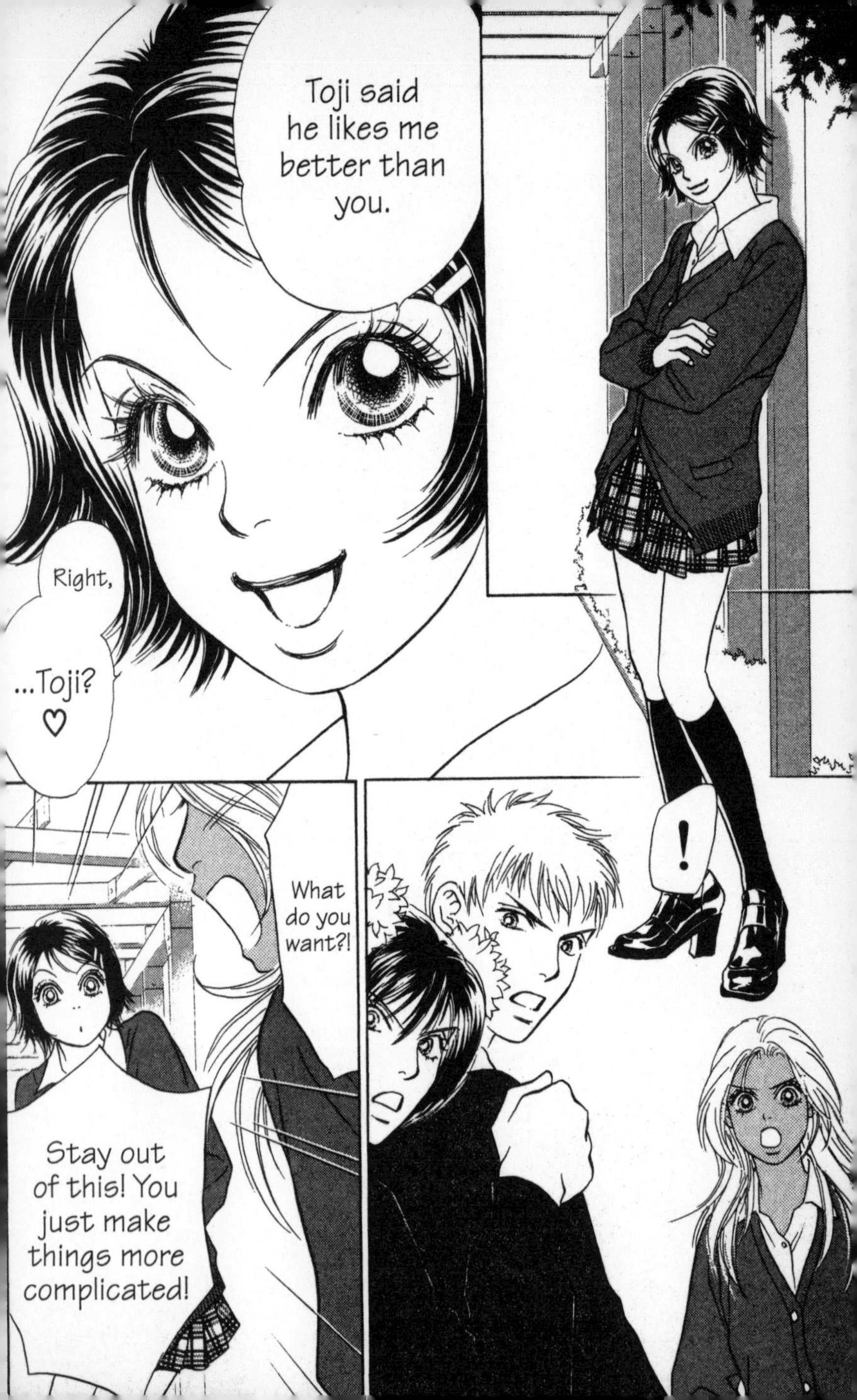
Toji said he likes me better than you.
Right, ...Toji? ♡
!
What do you want?!
Stay out of this! You just make things more complicated!

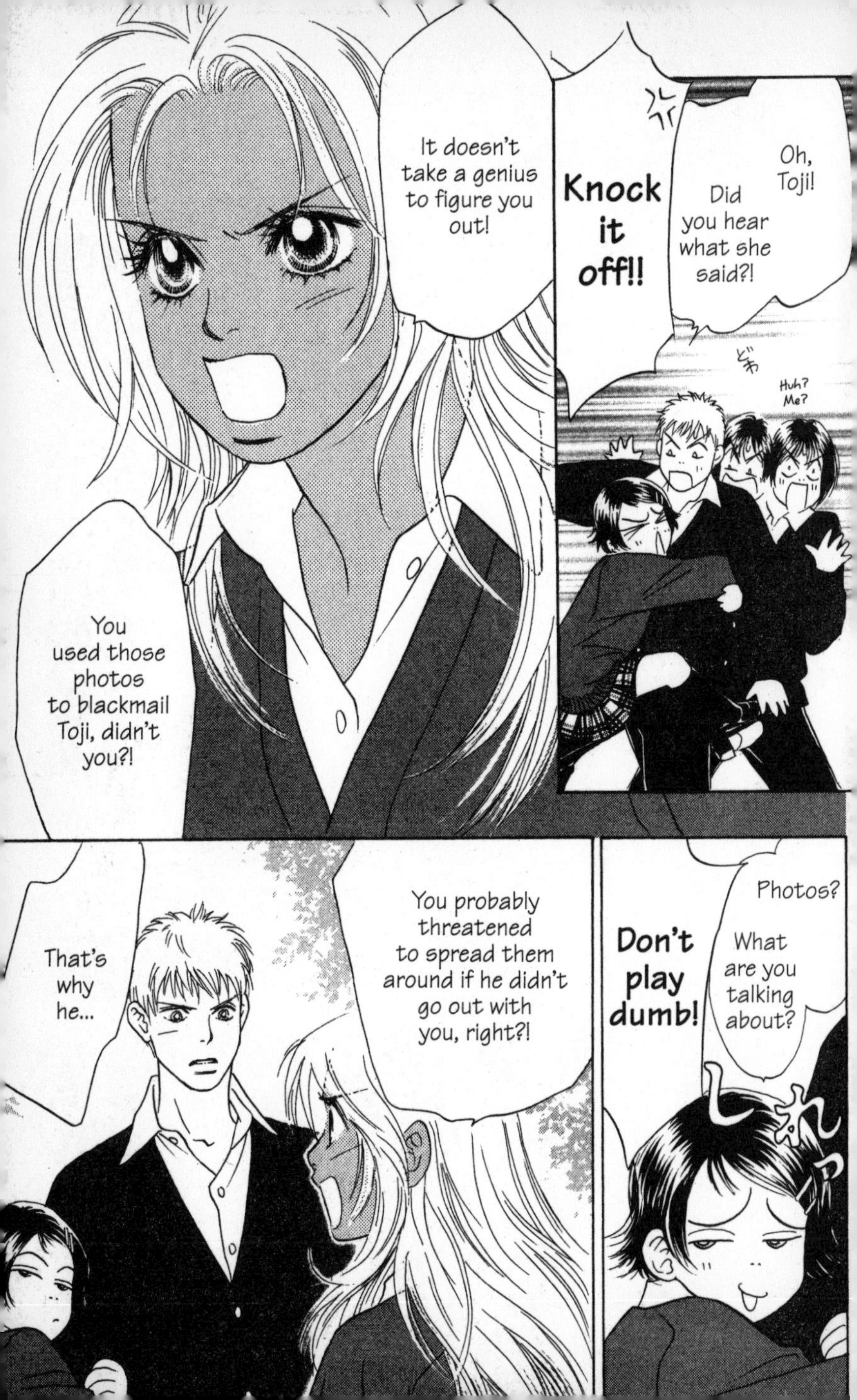
Oh, Toji! Did you hear what she said?!
Knock it off!!
Huh? Me?
It doesn't take a genius to figure you out!
You used those photos to blackmail Toji, didn't you?!
Photos? What are you talking about?
Don't play dumb!
しれ
You probably threatened to spread them around if he didn't go out with you, right?!
That's why he...

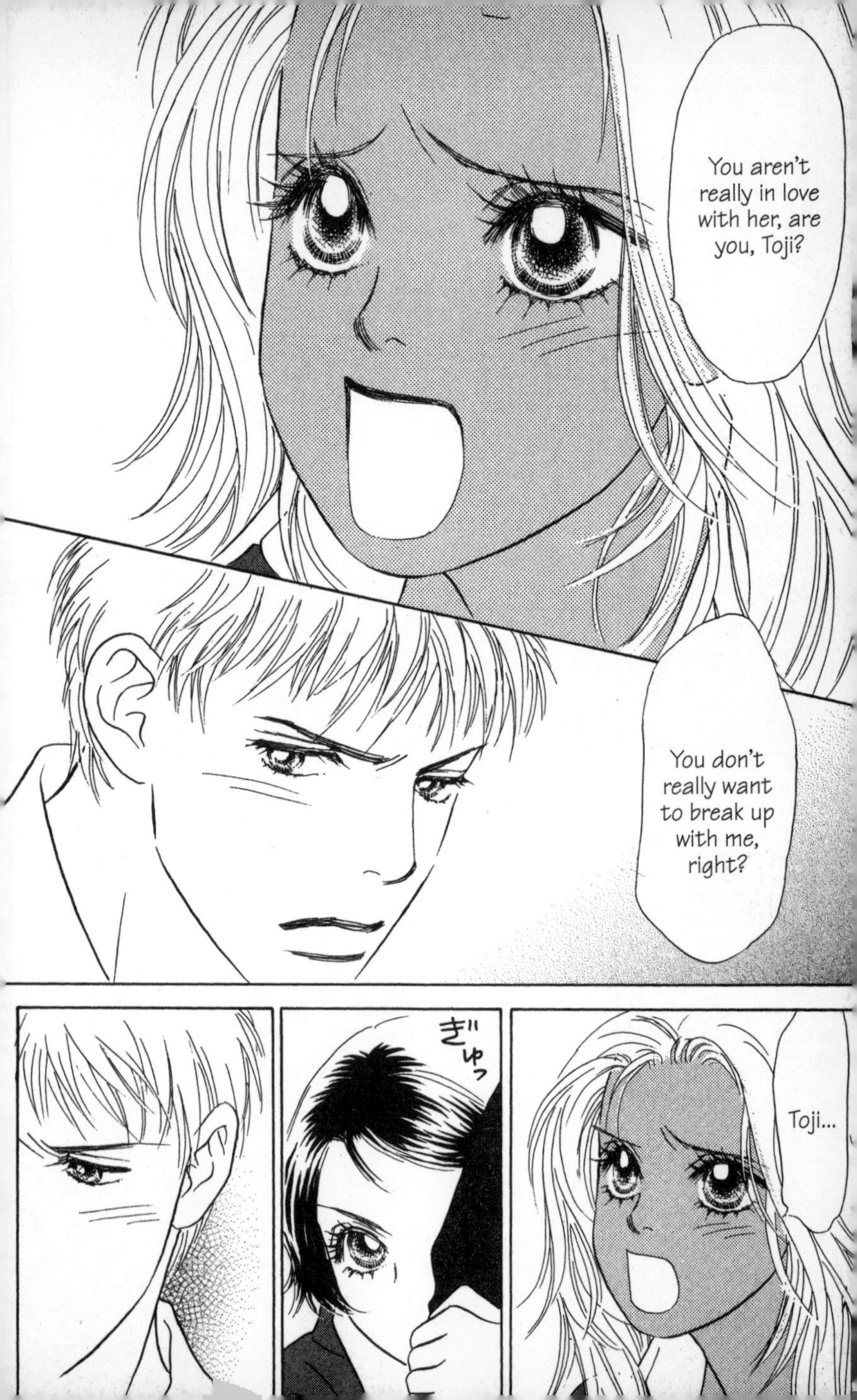
You aren't really in love with her, are you, Toji?
You don't really want to break up with me, right?
Toji...
ぎゅっ

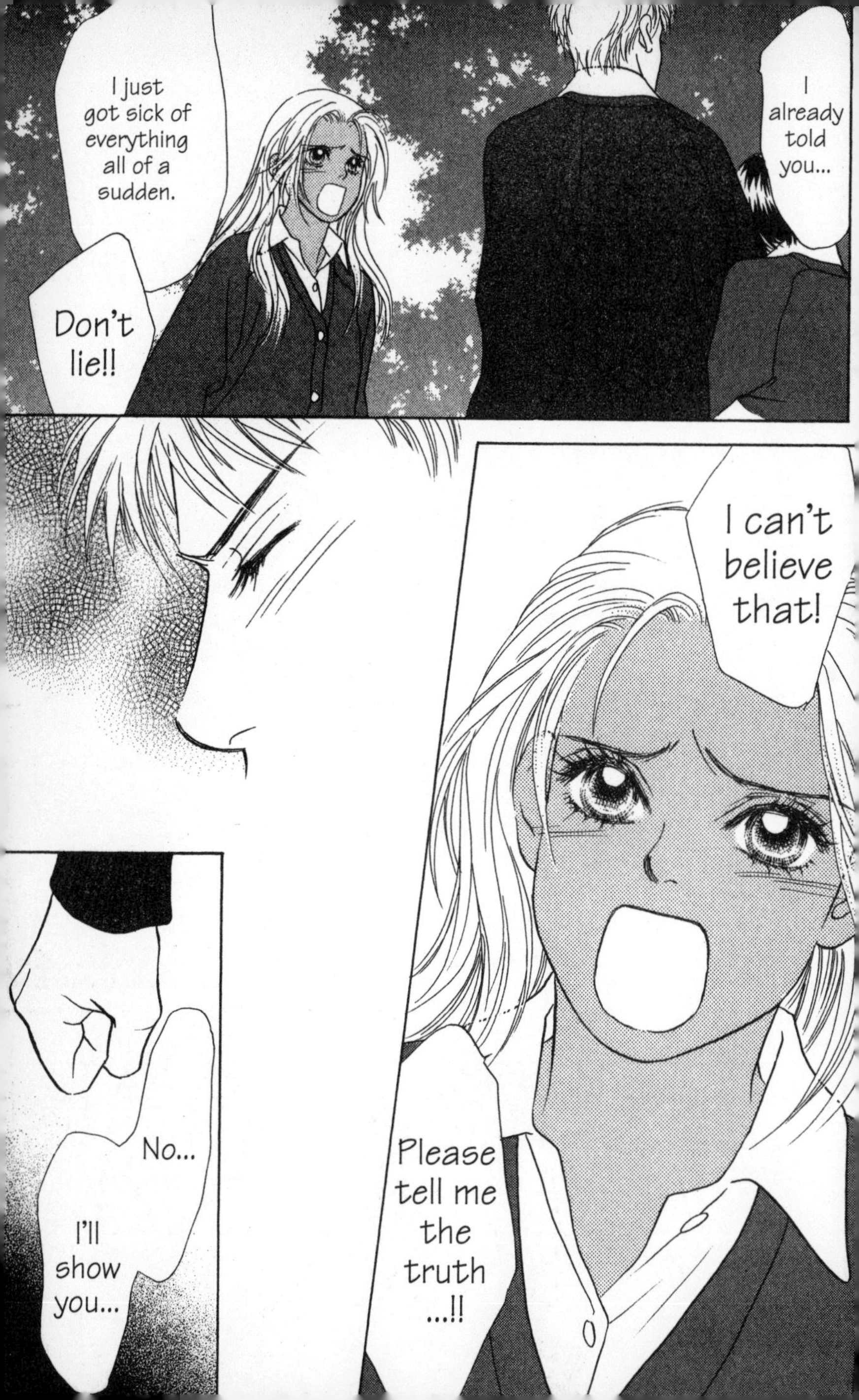
I already told you...
I just got sick of everything all of a sudden.
Don't lie!!
I can't believe that!
Please tell me the truth ...!!
No...
I'll show you...

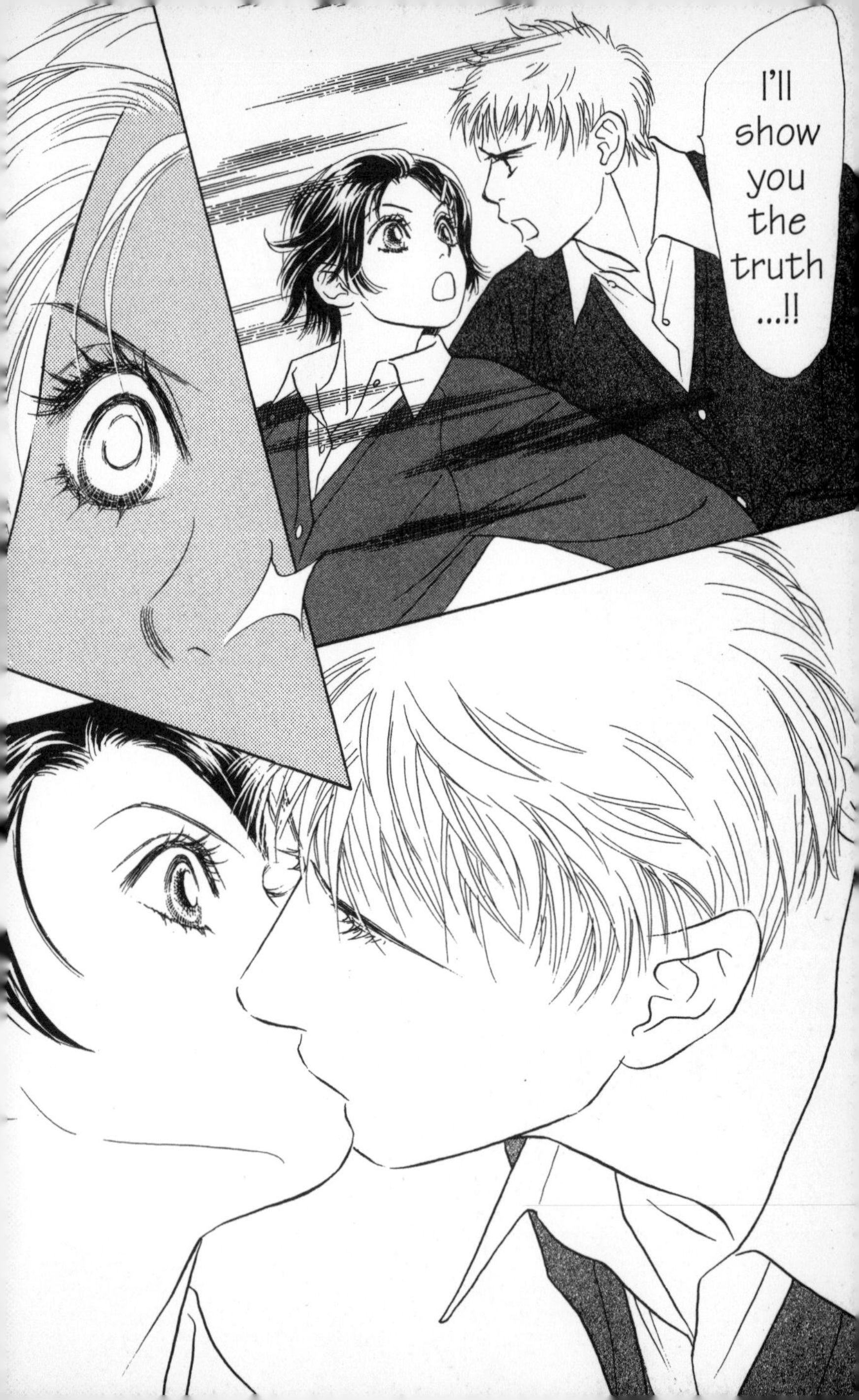
I'll show you the truth ...!!

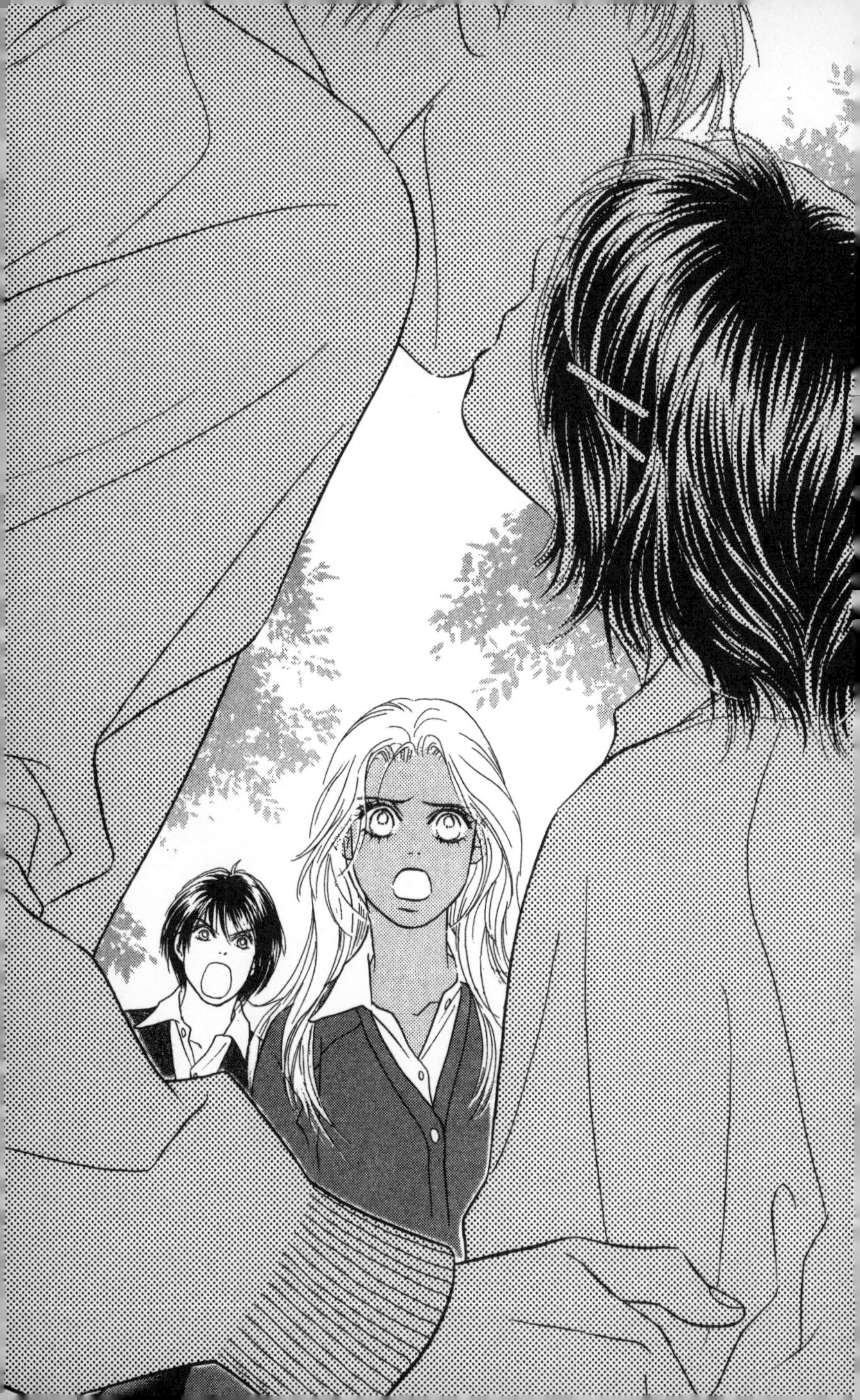

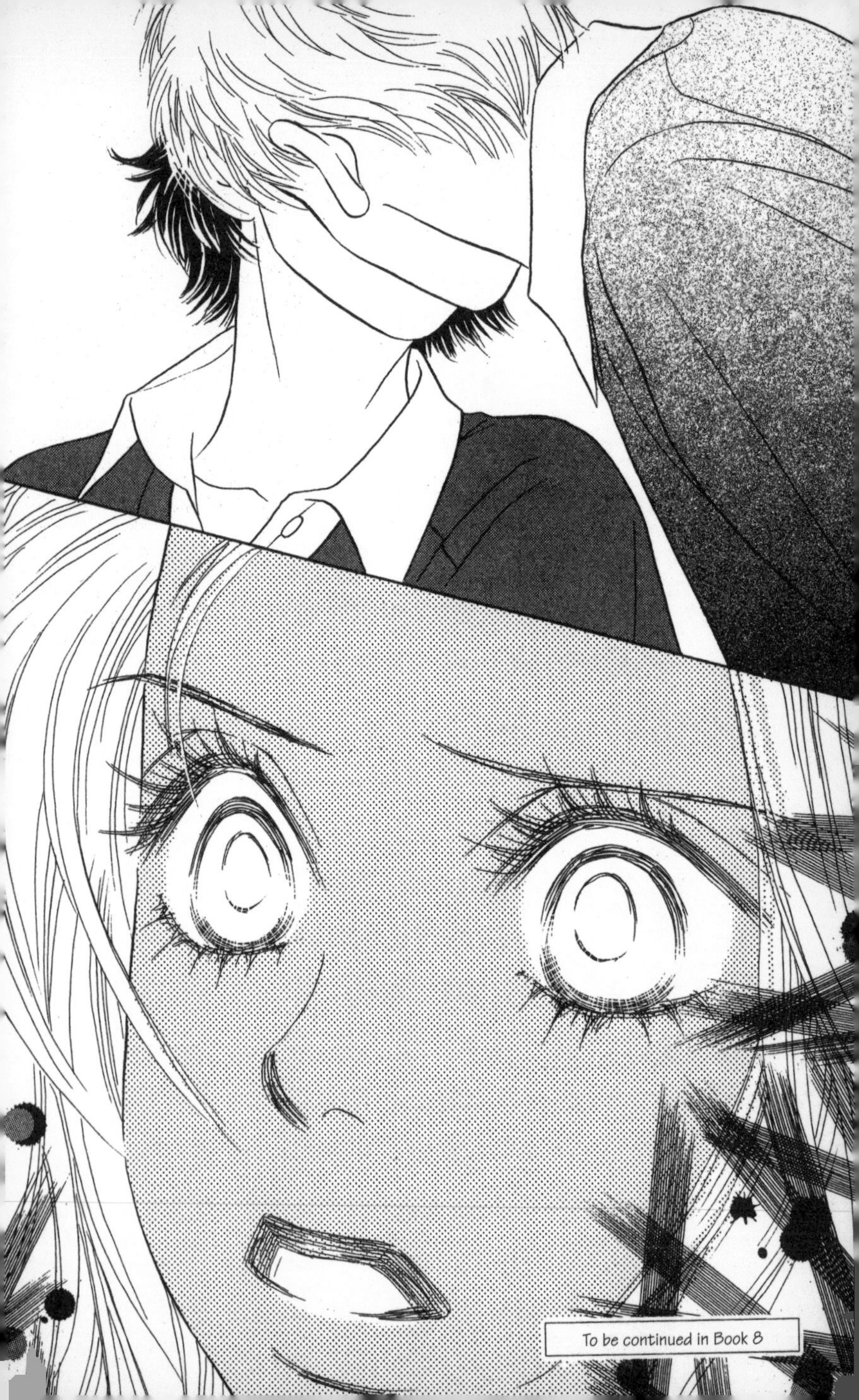
To be continued in Book 8

Staff

Aiko   Amemori

Tomomi   Kasue

Shiho   Murahira

Eri   Noda

Satsuki   Furukawa

Mariko   Kinugasa

Editor

Toshiyuki   Tanaka

2000 . 2 . 8

Miwa   Ueda

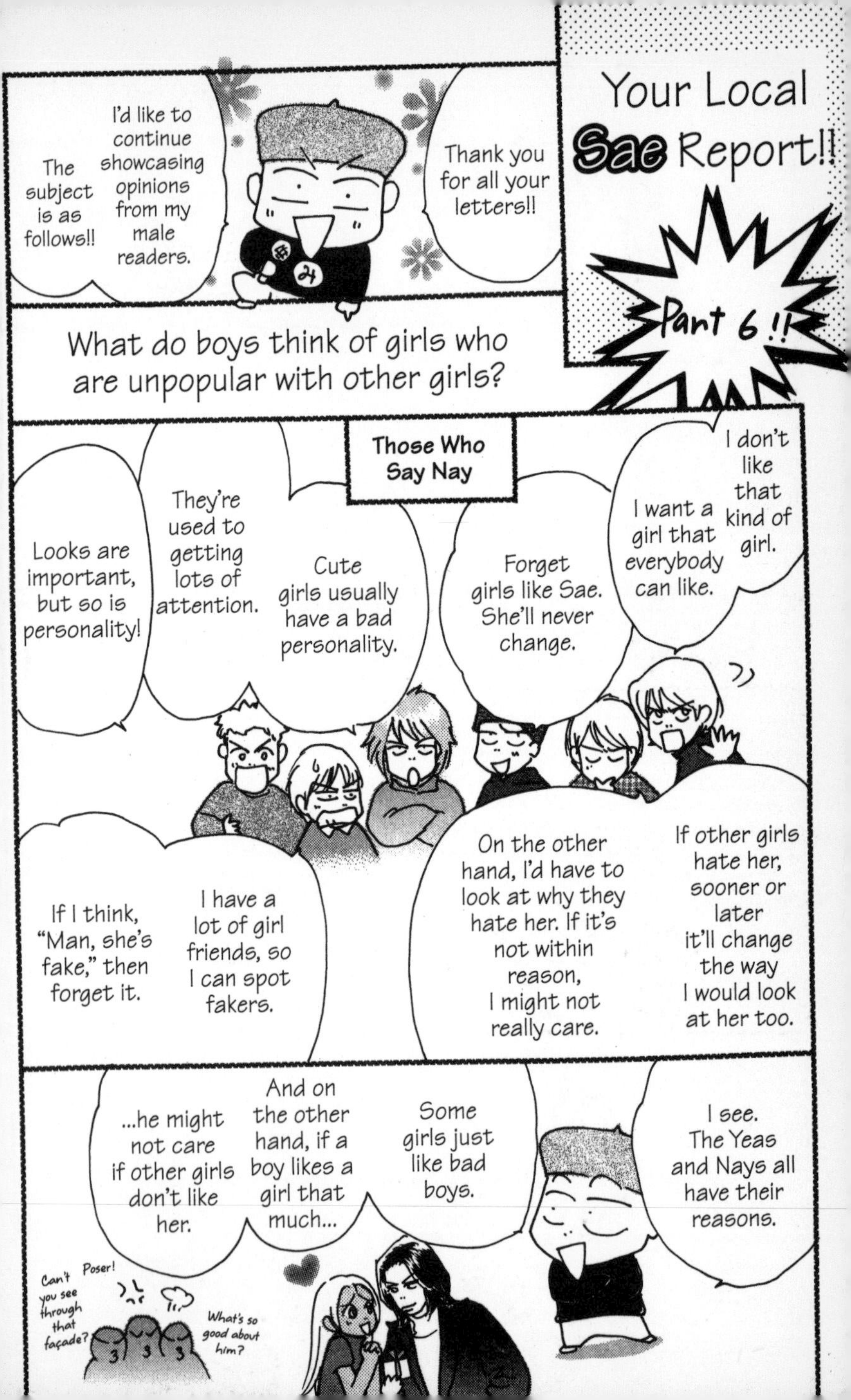
Your Local Sae Report!!
Part 6!!
Thank you for all your letters!!
I'd like to continue showcasing opinions from my male readers.
The subject is as follows!!
What do boys think of girls who are unpopular with other girls?
Those Who Say Nay
I don't like that kind of girl.
I want a girl that everybody can like.
Forget girls like Sae. She'll never change.
Cute girls usually have a bad personality.
They're used to getting lots of attention.
Looks are important, but so is personality!
If other girls hate her, sooner or later it'll change the way I would look at her too.
On the other hand, I'd have to look at why they hate her. If it's not within reason, I might not really care.
I have a lot of girl friends, so I can spot fakers.
If I think, "Man, she's fake," then forget it.
I see. The Yeas and Nays all have their reasons.
Some girls just like bad boys.
And on the other hand, if a boy likes a girl that much...
...he might not care if other girls don't like her.
Poser!
Can't you see through that façade?
What's so good about him?

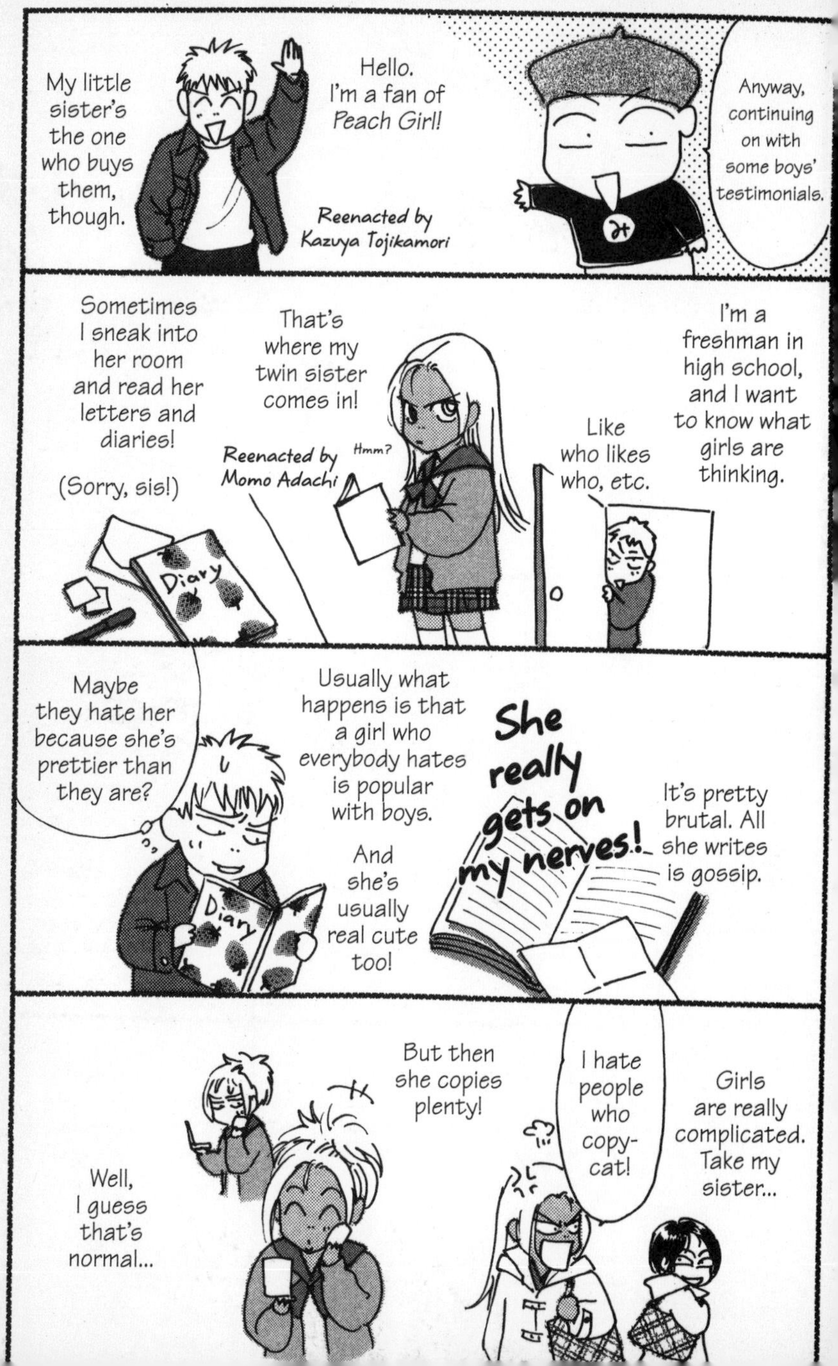

Anyway, continuing on with some boys' testimonials.
Hello. I'm a fan of *Peach Girl*!
Reenacted by Kazuya Tojikamori
My little sister's the one who buys them, though.
I'm a freshman in high school, and I want to know what girls are thinking.
Like who likes who, etc.
That's where my twin sister comes in!
Hmm?
Reenacted by Momo Adachi
Sometimes I sneak into her room and read her letters and diaries!
(Sorry, sis!)
Diary
It's pretty brutal. All she writes is gossip.
She really gets on my nerves!
Usually what happens is that a girl who everybody hates is popular with boys.
And she's usually real cute too!
Maybe they hate her because she's prettier than they are?
Diary
Girls are really complicated. Take my sister...
I hate people who copy-cat!
But then she copies plenty!
Well, I guess that's normal...

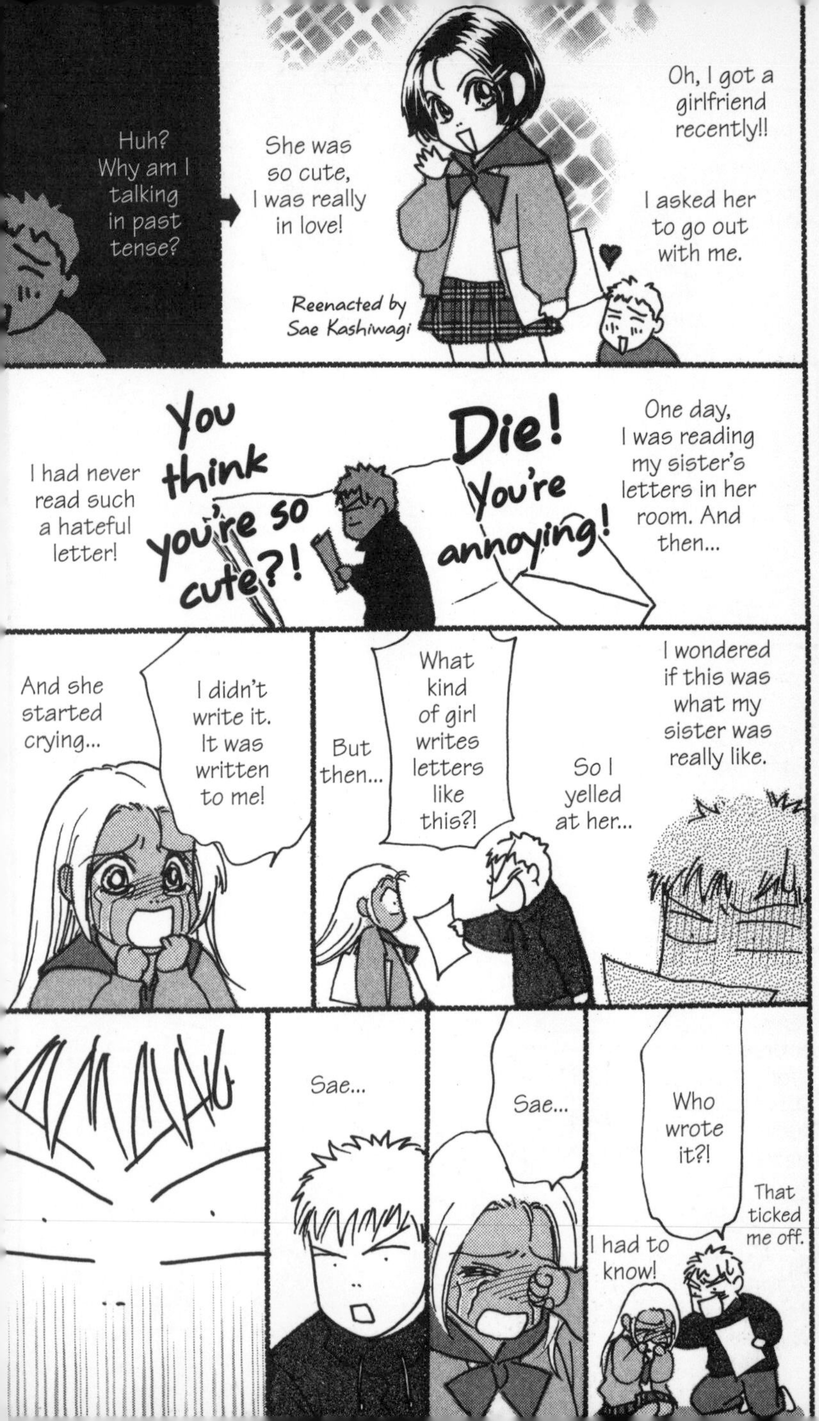
Oh, I got a girlfriend recently!!
I asked her to go out with me.
She was so cute, I was really in love!
Reenacted by Sae Kashiwagi
Huh? Why am I talking in past tense?
One day, I was reading my sister's letters in her room. And then...
Die! You're annoying!
You think you're so cute?!
I had never read such a hateful letter!
I wondered if this was what my sister was really like.
So I yelled at her...
What kind of girl writes letters like this?!
But then...
I didn't write it. It was written to me!
And she started crying...
Who wrote it?!
That ticked me off.
I had to know!
Sae...
Sae...

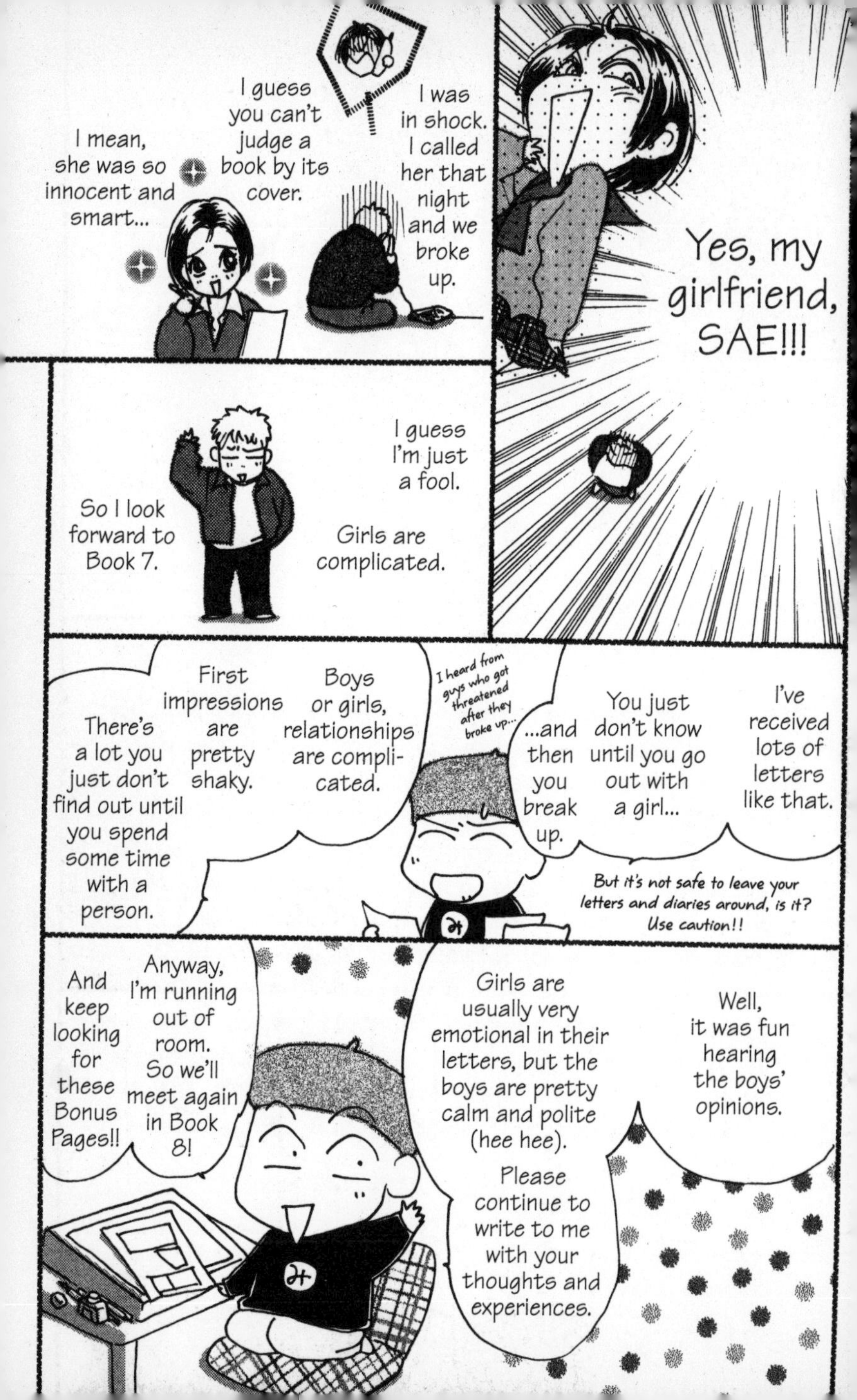
Yes, my girlfriend, SAE!!!
I was in shock. I called her that night and we broke up.
I guess you can't judge a book by its cover.
I mean, she was so innocent and smart...
I guess I'm just a fool.
Girls are complicated.
So I look forward to Book 7.
I've received lots of letters like that.
You just don't know until you go out with a girl...
...and then you break up.
I heard from guys who got threatened after they broke up...
Boys or girls, relationships are compli-cated.
First impressions are pretty shaky.
There's a lot you just don't find out until you spend some time with a person.
But it's not safe to leave your letters and diaries around, is it? Use caution!!
Well, it was fun hearing the boys' opinions.
Girls are usually very emotional in their letters, but the boys are pretty calm and polite (hee hee).
Please continue to write to me with your thoughts and experiences.
Anyway, I'm running out of room. So we'll meet again in Book 8!
And keep looking for these Bonus Pages!!

COMING SOON IN

Will Sae ever give up her shady ways?! When sly Sae blackmails Toji with incriminating pictures of Toji and Goro, he feels the only way he can protect Momo is to go along with Sae's scheme and distance himself from her. Momo can't believe that her red-hot romance has cooled so suddenly, and quickly falls into a deep depression. Kiley does his best to cheer her up, and Momo soon questions her fiery feelings for him. As the new school year begins, Momo and Kiley are assigned to the same homeroom—and so are Toji and Sae. Everything comes to a head at a school field trip in the mountains, when sneaky Sae can't resist pulling another dirty trick on Momo. When Kiley heroically saves the day, Momo can't help but wonder if he's her knight in shining armor...

Gina S.

Bronx, NY

Age 20

Peach Girl

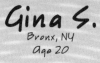

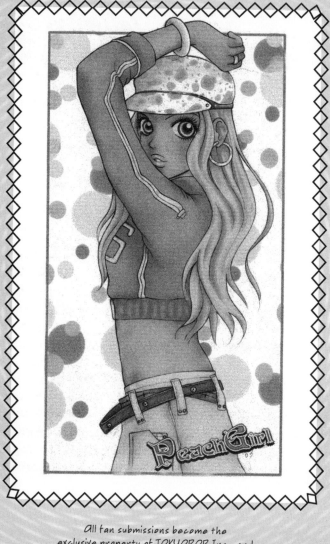

Jessica H.

Cary, NC

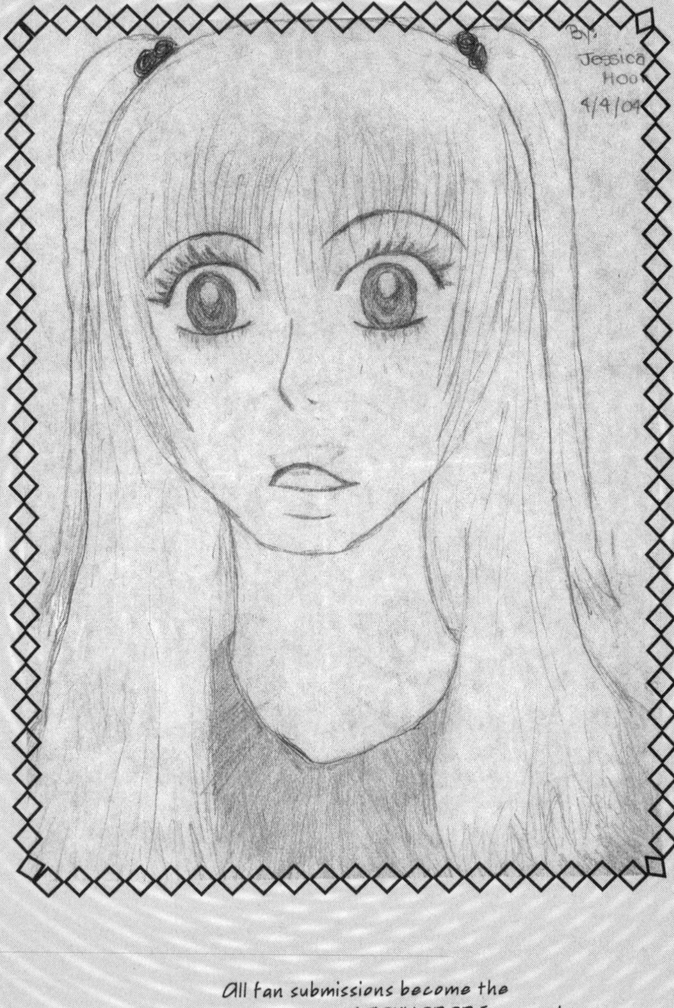
By:
Jessica
Hoo
4/4/04

Danielle T.

Cincinnati, OH

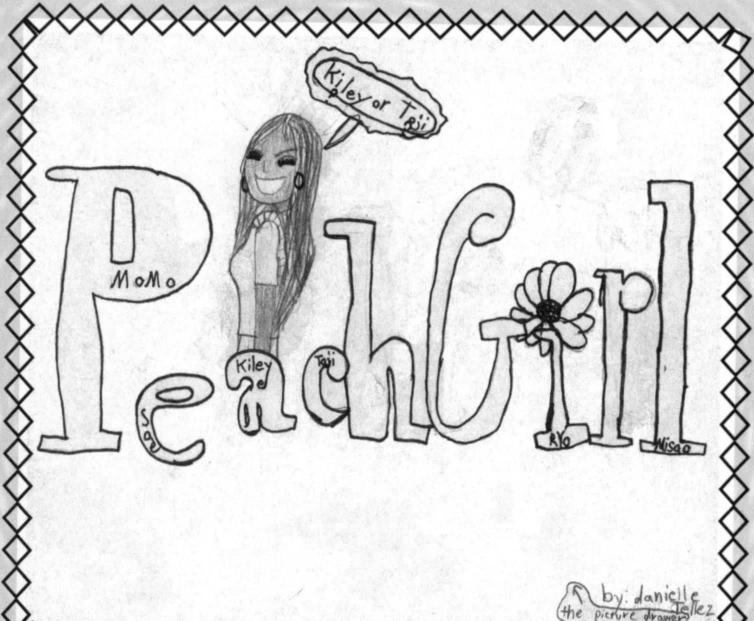
Kiley or Toji
Peach Girl
MoMo
Sae
Kiley
Toji
Ryo
Misao
by: danielle Tellez
the picture drawer
7/8/04

TOKYOPOP PRESENTS
MANGA 漫画
THE NEW SIZZLING HOT
FREE
MAGAZINE
ZELDA AND FRIEND FROM
WAR ON FLESH
© Justin Boring, Greg Hildebrandt and TOKYOPOP Inc.
SIGN UP FOR FREE WWW.TOKYOPOP.COM

TOKYOPOP SHOP

WWW.TOKYOPOP.COM/SHOP

HOT NEWS!

Check out the
TOKYOPOP SHOP!
The world's best
collection of manga in
English is now available
online in one place!

THE DREAMING

PITA-TEN
OFFICIAL FAN BOOK

WWW.TOKYOPOP.COM/SHOP

0 00000 00000 0

ARK ANGELS

- LOOK FOR SPECIAL OFFERS
- PRE-ORDER UPCOMING RELEASES
- COMPLETE YOUR COLLECTIONS

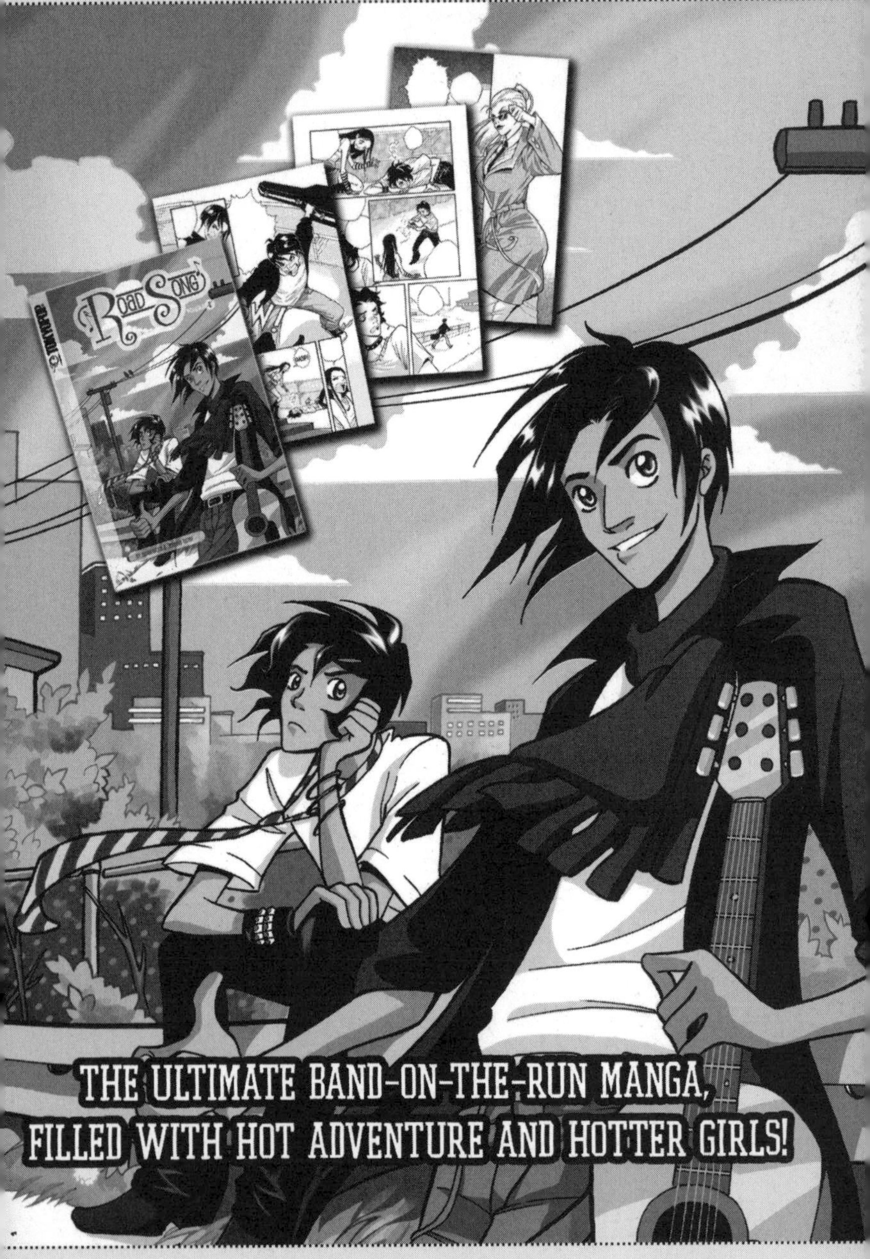
ROAD SONG
TOKYOPOP
THE ULTIMATE BAND-ON-THE-RUN MANGA,
FILLED WITH HOT ADVENTURE AND HOTTER GIRLS!

Music...mystery...and Murder!

ROADSONG

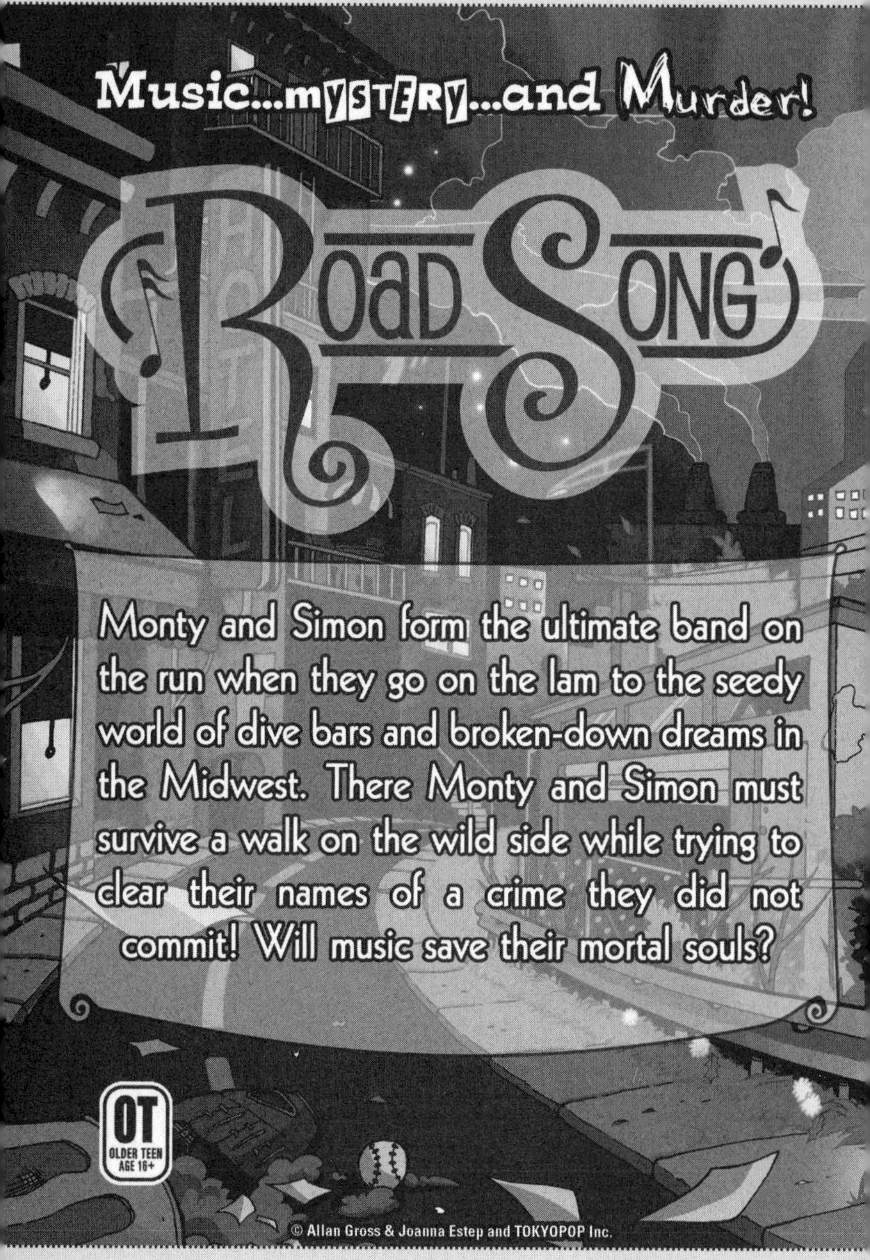

Monty and Simon form the ultimate band on the run when they go on the lam to the seedy world of dive bars and broken-down dreams in the Midwest. There Monty and Simon must survive a walk on the wild side while trying to clear their names of a crime they did not commit! Will music save their mortal souls?

OT
OLDER TEEN
AGE 16+

READ A CHAPTER OF THE MANGA ONLINE FOR FREE:

HONEY MUSTARD

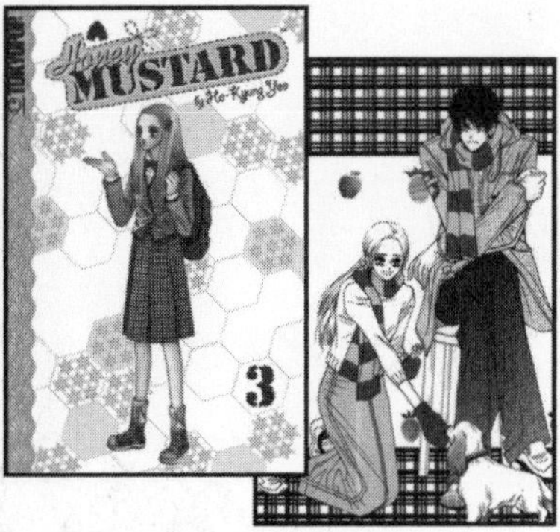
Honey MUSTARD
by Ho-Kyung Yeo
3
TOKYOPOP

BY HO-KYUNG YEO

I'm often asked about the title of *Honey Mustard.* What does a condiment have to do with romance and teen angst? One might ask the same thing about a basket of fruits, but I digress. Honey mustard is sweet with a good dose of bite, and I'd say that sums up this series pretty darn well, too. Ho-Kyung Yeo does a marvelous job of balancing the painful situations of adolescence with plenty of whacked-out humor to keep the mood from getting *too* heavy. It's a good, solid romantic comedy...and come to think of it, it'd go great with that sandwich.

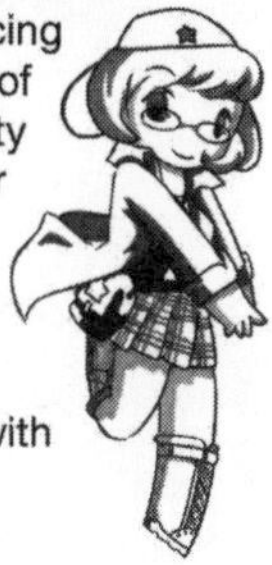

~Carol Fox, Editor

REBOUND

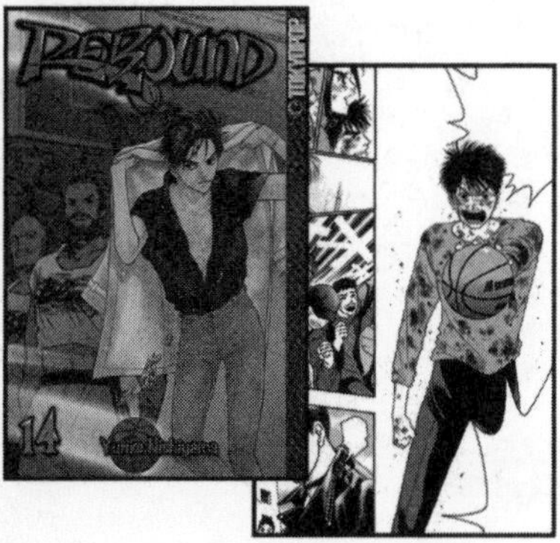
REBOUND
14
TOKYOPOP

BY YURIKO NISHIYAMA

At first glance, *Rebound* may seem like a simple sports manga. But on closer inspection, you'll find that the real drama takes place off the court. While the kids of the Johnan basketball team play and grow as a team, they learn valuable life lessons as well. By fusing the raw energy of basketball with the apple pie earnestness of an afterschool special, Yuriko Nishiyama has created a unique and heartfelt manga that appeals to all readers, male and female.

~Troy Lewter, Editor

© Minari Endoh/ICHIJINSHA

DAZZLE
BY MINARI ENDOH

When a young girl named Rahzel is sent off to see the world, she meets Alzeido, a mysterious loner on a mission to find his father's killer. The two don't exactly see eye-to-eye, until Alzeido opens his heart to Rahzel. On the long and winding road, the duo crosses paths with various characters...including one who wants to get a little too close to Rahzel!

An epic coming-of-age story from an accomplished manga artist!

© CHIHO SAITOU and IKUNI & Be-PaPas

THE WORLD EXISTS FOR ME
BY BE-PAPAS AND CHIHO SAITOU

Once upon a time, the source of the devil R's invincible powers was *The Book of S & M.* But one day, a young man stole the book without knowing what it was, cut it into strips and used it to create a girl doll named "S" and a boy doll named "M." With that act, the unimaginable power that the devil held from the book was unleashed upon the world!

From the creators of the manga classic *Revolutionary Girl Utena!*

© Keitaro Arima

TSUKUYOMI: MOON PHASE
BY KEITARO ARIMA

Cameraman Kouhei Midou is researching Schwarz Quelle Castle. When he steps inside the castle's great walls, he discovers a mysterious little girl, Hazuki, who's been trapped there for years. Utilizing her controlling charm, Hazuki tries to get Kouhei to set her free. But this sweet little girl isn't everything she appears to be...

The manga that launched the popular anime!

STOP!

This is the back of the book.
You wouldn't want to spoil a great ending!

This book is printed "manga-style," in the authentic Japanese right-to-left format. Since none of the artwork has been flipped or altered, readers get to experience the story just as the creator intended. You've been asking for it, so TOKYOPOP® delivered: authentic, hot-off-the-press, and far more fun!

DIRECTIONS

If this is your first time reading manga-style, here's a quick guide to help you understand how it works.

It's easy... just start in the top right panel and follow the numbers. Have fun, and look for more 100% authentic manga from TOKYOPOP®!

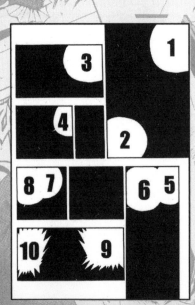